13.0
C
1975
VOL. III

THE ANNUAL
OF
PSYCHOANALYSIS

THE ANNUAL
OF
PSYCHOANALYSIS

A Publication of the Chicago Institute for Psychoanalysis

VOLUME III

International Universities Press, Inc.
New York

Library of Congress Catalog Card Number: 72-91376
ISBN: 0-8236-0363-6
Published annually and available in print:
   Vol. I, 1973; Vol. II, 1974.

Manufactured in the United States of America

CONTENTS

I

THEORETICAL STUDIES

II

CLINICAL STUDIES

III

PSYCHOANALYTIC EDUCATION

IV

PSYCHOANALYTIC HISTORY

V

A TRIBUTE

VI

PSYCHOANALYSIS AS SCIENCE

VII

APPLIED PSYCHOANALYSIS

I

THEORETICAL STUDIES

Perception, Consciousness, and Freud's "Project"

MICHAEL FRANZ BASCH, M.D. (*Chicago*)

In a recent paper (Basch, 1975), I examined the need for and the operation of psychological defenses mounted against anxiety-provoking environmental reality. The clinical evidence indicates that there is a transformation that must take place before a percept becomes conscious and it is here that defenses against potentially traumatic percepts are active. For example, hypnosis, hysterical blindness, and negative hallucination clearly show that it is not effective perception that is lost in these cases but rather that the path to subjective awareness of the anxiety-provoking percepts in question is blocked. That this sequence is not limited to pathological conditions or to artificial situations is shown by the universality of so-called subliminal perception, i.e., the brain's registration and transformation of percepts that have never reached conscious awareness.

Klein (1959) cites the impressive body of evidence validating the accuracy of subliminal stimulation experiments and discusses the difficulties this finding poses for the conceptualization of consciousness, attention, and defense in psychoanalysis. That the brain registers and utilizes stimuli from the external world which were never in subjective awareness contradicts a fundamental postulate of Freud's metapsychology, which equates perception with consciousness (*Pcpt.-Cs.*) and then makes that identity the basis for the test of reality (Freud, 1892-1899, p. 234; 1900, pp. 615-617 and 541, n. 1; 1917, pp. 231-233; see also McGuire, 1974, p. 38).

An earlier version of this paper was presented to the scientific meeting of the Chicago Psychoanalytic Society, November, 1968. Thanks is due the Center for Psychosocial Studies, Chicago, whose support made the revision of this essay for publication possible.

Although Klein (1966, 1970) called for the elimination of meta-psychology from psychoanalysis on the basis of this and other contradictions between metapsychology and empirical findings, I prefer to see in this situation a need for re-examination and revision of both the structure and content of psychoanalytic metapsychology (Basch, 1973). It is important to recall that Freud did not derive his metapsychology from his clinical experience, but, rather, brought a theory of mental operations to his clinical findings in an attempt to establish a complete psychology. The psychoanalytic method uncovers the hidden meaning of behavior, but not the nature of the underlying processes constituting that behavior. Freud's hypotheses regarding cognitive, affective, and perceptual processes were for the most part derived from the psychologies and neurologies of the day, his original contribution being the hypothesis that thoughts progressed from simple cognition of images to complete reasoning through the association of those sensory images with verbal memory traces. He first developed this concept in connection with neurological investigations of brain-damaged patients and reported it in his book *On Aphasia* (1891). The pathologic separation of perceptual capacity and descriptive ability in patients who had suffered cerebrovascular accidents led Freud to think that a reversal of the normal process of thought formation had occurred. From this disintegration he developed a concept of the basic operation underlying cognitive development that eventually guided him in his investigations of the neuroses.

Practically speaking, for Freud the neuroses were "functional aphasias," in which repression served to sever the association between percept and language as dramatically and effectively as the anatomical lesion had done in the organically ill patient. At first Freud believed that all that was necessary to reverse the damage of repression was to bring the disconnected percepts to consciousness, where, united once more, or for the first time, with verbal descriptions, they could be deprived of their noxious influence. Later, he recognized the limited effectiveness of the hypnotic-cathartic method, realizing that lasting curative effects could be obtained only if the hidden meanings expressed by nonverbal (unconscious) perceptions could be raised through interpretation to the verbal level and, thereby, to consciousness. The method of free association and the laws of the so-called primary process are Freud's revolutionary contributions through which the hidden language of the meaning of dreams, neurotic symptoms, errors of everyday life, and, indeed, of all conflicted human behavior can now be decoded. We now know that thinking does not take place in images — indeed, perception itself is not to be equated with imaging (Piaget & Inhelder, 1966) — and that Freud's observations can be explained in terms of the transformation of presentational to discursive symbols as the preoperative phase of cognition advances to the operational level (Basch, 1974). However, as has happened so often in science, a false hypothesis gave rise to valuable, valid, and lasting insights. Freud's discovery of the code that explains the deeper meaning of many of our activities was of inestimable value to psychology; however, his hope that he had thereby also discovered an explanation of thought processing proved to be false. Thus Freud's theory of cognition, as well as his derivative concepts about perception, affect, instinct, etc., fell short, and its contradictions have been noted by Klein and others. But to now suggest that revisions of psychoanalytic metapsychologic theory are made necessary by discoveries in other areas of psychology as well as in biology and neural sciences is not to question the clinical theories derived from the application of psychoanalytic methods.

Under the term *metapsychology*, Freud subsumed both the neurological hypotheses about the underlying brain processes that make thought possible (metaphorically expressed as the workings of a mental apparatus or mind) and the theories of perception, cognition, emotion, and volition that belong to the study of general psychology. In this essay, I shall have a more limited purview. The phenomenon of subliminal perception calls attention to the absence in psychoanalytic theory of an adequate systematic set of hypotheses dealing with the perception of external reality (sensory perception) and its vicissitudes. My objective here will be to trace the origins and significance of the System *Pcpt.-Cs.* in Freud's writings, in the hope that such clarification will make possible those theoretical revisions that will correlate psychoanalytic metapyschology with established findings in the area of perception.

In the "Project for a Scientific Psychology" (1895) Freud deals with the perception of external reality in a detailed and cohesive manner not found elsewhere in his writings. Since, as will be seen, the model of the mind constructed there also accurately foreshadows his later structural theory and accommodates it without difficulty, the "Project" may lay claim to being Freud's most comprehensive metapsychologic effort. Usually, however, it is not studied for its current scientific value, but only for its historical interest. That Freud did not publish this work and repudiated its significance when the manuscript was later rediscovered (Jones, 1953) need not deter us from appreciating its contribution. Because many of Freud's later formulations resemble those in the "Project," it is clear that he did not reject the ideas deduced there but, on the contrary, found that they were useful to him in the ordering of the ever increasing body of knowledge derived from clinical experience.

5

The rationale for overlooking the "Project" as a viable part of our present-day metapsychology usually rests on the argument that it represents an abortive attempt at a neuroanatomical explanation of psychology, which was later revised and expressed in psychological terms. A comparison of the "Project" with Freud's later theoretical papers shows, however, that it is in the "Project" and not in its later adaptations that one often finds the more comprehensive, better reasoned, and most accurate version of Freud's fundamental hypotheses.

Freud's use of neurologic terminology and his search for a correlation between psychology and the physical sciences make the "Project" no less a work of metapsychology. Breuer already addressed himself to this point in his introduction to the theoretical portion of the *Studies on Hysteria* (1893-1895) when he wrote:

Psychical processes will be dealt with in the language of psychology; and, indeed, it cannot possibly be otherwise. If instead of 'idea' we chose to speak of 'excitation of the cortex', the latter term would only have any meaning for us in so far as we recognized an old friend under that cloak and tacitly reinstated the 'idea'. For while ideas are constant objects of our experience and are familiar to us in all their shades of meaning, 'cortical excitations' are on the contrary rather in the nature of a postulate, objects which we hope to be able to identify in the future. The substitution of one term for another would seem to be no more than a pointless disguise. Accordingly, I may perhaps be forgiven if I make almost exclusive use of psychological terms [p. 185].

That Breuer found it necessary to make such an explanation is a reflection of the scientific orientation of his day. As Marx (1967) documents, not only Freud but all his contemporaries were really working with psychologic models, although they thought they were dealing with the neurologic apparatus because they expressed themselves in the language of the anatomical and physiologic disciplines in which they had been trained and to which they were committed.

The present study is not an attempt to give an overview of the meaning the "Project" has for psychoanalysis today. My intention is to clarify the basic model of mental life Freud developed there, since it is this model that most clearly illustrates the conceptualizations of perception, cognition, and affect he used to explain his clinical findings. The manner of interaction between the various mental agencies postulated by Freud in the original draft of the "Project" is unnecessarily complex and was simplified by a revision of his operational formulations in Letter 39 to Wilhelm Fliess, January 1, 1896 (1892-1899, p. 388). The present account takes this modification into consideration, since it is that version to which Freud implicitly adhered in his subsequent work. Whenever possible, the language of the "Project" has been correlated with current psychoanalytic terminology.

A Re-examination of the "Project"

Clinical observation convinced Freud that mental activity varied in intensity, a belief that he expressed in terms of quantity in motion. The fundamental purpose of the primitive mental apparatus was assumed to be the maintenance of the organism in a tension-free state of inertia by ridding it of excitation created by external stimulation. This was accomplished initially by flight and discharge through reflex movements. However, endogenous tensions generated by hunger, respiration, and sexuality, those internal needs later called instinctual drive derivatives, could not be discharged reflexively, but had to be eliminated through specific gratifying interaction with the external world. The existence of instinctual (endogenous) tension opposed a state of inertia, since a store of energy had to be available for necessary interaction with the environment. Therefore, the mental apparatus had to be structured so that it could mediate between conflicting tasks—eliminating any increase in the energic level due to external stimulation while still keeping itself apprised of situations favorable for instinctual gratification (1895, pp. 295-297). Freud postulated an ingenious model consisting of three inter-acting agencies that met both requirements and also accounted for the clinically observable aspects of mentation.

The mental agencies or systems were identified by letters of the Greek alphabet. The first agency described is the *System Psi*, which is directly influenced by the soma only and receives the instinctual (endogenous) stimuli. It will be seen that the System Psi corresponds to what would now be called the id-ego matrix. The elements, or "neurones" as Freud then called them, of which this system is composed offer resistance to the currents of intercellular quantity, the future "psychic energy," and are selectively and permanently altered by its passage. These cathectic modifications represent the mnemic traces and make memory possible.

A second agency, functionally separate from the first system, the *System Phi*, is said to be composed of completely permeable, nonresistant elements "which serve for perception" (p. 300); today we call this the perceptual system or the *System Pcpt*. This agency must always be uniformly receptive to fresh stimuli, which would not be possible if it were in any way permanently affected by the passage of excitation. Only

7

the hypothesis of two dissimilar agencies could account for the observable facts of both memory and sensory perception.

The sense organs are extensions of the System Phi (*Pcpt.*), serving both as stimulus barriers to excessive, and as transmitters of appropriate stimuli. Since in the external world there are only masses in motion, the stimuli impinging on the sense organs are quantitative in nature; sensory qualities, such as light and sound, are purely mental phenomena and exist in the environment only in the form of light waves and sound waves. Each sense organ is selective in its activity and is receptive only to a particular kind of matter in motion within a limited range of intensity. Because the activity of the external environment is on a much higher level of intensity than that of the internal one, even appropriate stimuli may not be transmitted directly from the sense organs to the mental apparatus but are modified, probably through a reduction in intensity, in their passage through the perceptual system (System Phi) (pp. 304-306).

Freud first hypothesized that these muted sensory stimuli impinged on the System Psi (id-ego matrix) directly and that an energy transfer took place which made possible and potentiated various forms of mentation. It should be noted that the mental apparatus as first designed in the "Project" had no place for consciousness in the process of receiving and registering sensory stimulation.

In this first model of mentation, consciousness performed no function, but, since it had to be accounted for in any complete psychology, it was treated as an epiphenomenon that accompanied the registration of sensory stimuli in the System Psi. It was postulated that the intensity of a stimulus that provided the energic input for perceptual registration also possessed a characteristic frequency or "period" which identified its qualitative characteristics. Freud hypothesized that the "period" of the percept invariably stimulated a third system, the *System Omega* (pp. 311-312, 360), which responded by generating awareness of the sensory qualities of the particular stimulus. This system corresponds to what Freud later called the System Consciousness, or *Cs.* (1900).

Having constructed a model of the mental apparatus, Freud proceeds in the remainder of the "Project" to examine the origin and vicissitudes of thought and affect. It would transcend the purpose of this essay to consider the detailed picture of mental functioning presented there or to examine the significant problems that emerged which led eventually to a fundamental modification of the operational concept outlined above. Suffice it to say that after the completion of the "Project," Freud, in Letter 39 to Fliess (1892-1899, p. 388), concluded that the System Omega (System Cs.) should be placed between the perceptual system (System

Phi) and the system in which memory traces are formed (System Psi). This implies that the registration of sensory stimuli no longer involves an energy input but only the characteristic frequency ("period") of every sensory stimulus that is transmitted to the System Omega (Cs), where sensory quality corresponding to the original quantity is aroused. That, in turn, stimulates the "interest" of the System Psi, which automatically sends a quota of mobile energy—which Freud equated with attention cathexis (1895, pp. 337, 362)—to the proper location for the registration of the particular quality aroused in the System Omega. Therefore, sensory quality is also no longer transferred from the environment to the System Psi; the latter only notes, so to speak, through attention cathexis (free Psi energy), the period of the stimulus that is activating the System Omega. The passage of attention cathexis through a resistant system creates a mnemic trace in the System Psi, recording permanently as a sensory percept the transient activity of the System Omega. In the System Psi the indication of quality lies in the location of the registration; in this one instance, Freud noted, the psychologic model actually corresponds to demonstrable brain anatomy, i.e., visual percepts register in the visual cortex, etc.

Freud's schematic conceptualization of three interacting agencies transforming quantity into quality and permanently registering indications of the latter met the requirements for a model of the mental apparatus that could receive information from the environment without being subjected to its higher energic intensity. To illustrate the operation of this construct, Freud used the example of the hunger drive in the newborn infant (pp. 317-319). The instinctual pressure of the nutritional need, an endogenous stimulus inherently without sensory quality arousing only a quantitative energic imbalance (unpleasure), mounts by summation in System Psi until a nonspecific general motor discharge, including a reflex cry, takes place. This cry brings the mother to feed the child, whose instinctual tension is discharged through appropriate gratification. That experience brings about three changes in the mental apparatus: some percept of the gratifying object is registered in the System Psi, a sensory percept is created by the infant's motor activity of sucking, and, thirdly, a neuronal facilitation is set up between these two sensory percepts and the endogenous stimulus (pp. 317-318).

Perceptual facilitation implies a lowering of neuronal resistance to the passage of quantity (psychic energy) so that future unpleasure, eventually identified as a hunger stimulus, will tend to activate the two sensory percepts that were involved in its previous gratification. Such an automatic cathexis of the facilitated complex with psychic energy

9

(quantity) results in motor discharge (sucking) and the hallucination of the former gratifying experience, and corresponds to what we now call primary-process discharge, but, since this does not effectively relieve the need for nourishment, instead of satiation there is mounting tension (unpleasure). Such experiences mobilize the inherited capacity of the infant to abstain from cathecting the hunger-gratification complex until evidence of the cathexis of a new registration of the desired object, i.e., a re-cognition, reaches the anticipatory precathected complex or "wish." Perceptual identity between image and object provides an indicator of reality. Only then is motor discharge permitted, since it will now result in genuine gratification and total discharge of instinctual pressure. The withholding of cathexis from facilitated pathways until reality testing is successful is called "binding." In the "Project" binding corresponds to what is now called "secondary-process activity," and the part of the System Psi that contains these bound elements is already called the "ego" (p. 323). As yet, Freud had not specified what the mechanisms might be that differentiate the hallucinatory recollection of a percept from a percept representing ongoing sensory stimulation from the environment, i.e., the differentiation that makes the test of reality possible — more will be said of that later.

Freud emphasized that all stimulation transmitted by the sense organs must undergo perceptual registration in the System Psi so that the cathexes of those stimuli being sought will have an opportunity to find their way to the facilitated complexes (wishes) (p. 361). Though it is true that the stimulus barrier of the sense organs initially screens out stimuli of inappropriate intensity, there is no selection of content per se by the sense organs. Which stimulus is useful for the operation of the mental apparatus and becomes hypercathected can only be determined after its registration through the medium of attention cathexis; were there to be any screening out of stimuli prior to their registration in the System Psi, the possibility that the anticipated stimulus might be lost would be too great. The sought-after stimulus enters into communication with and becomes part of the network set up between instinctual needs, previously registered sensory percepts, and perceptions of experiences of gratifying motor discharge. In keeping with the principle of inertia and the need to maintain the absolute level of quantity within the apparatus at the lowest possible level, there is no actual increase in the quantitative intensity through hypercathexis; instead, hypercathexis is equated with the extent of facilitation open to a particular percept. The many stimuli that are perceptually registered but not desired at the moment may or may not at some later time find their way to facilitated pathways and thus to hypercathexis (pp. 362-363).

10

Freud recognized that the hypothesis that every sensory stimulus must be registered meant that perceptions which had previously given rise to unpleasure would have to be registered when they reoccurred. Their recathexis would result in a high level of tension, and this posed a theoretical dilemma for, according to his theory, the brain adhered to the inertia principle and strove for minimal tension. He felt that the only possible solution to this dilemma would be a defense mechanism that rapidly decathected these dysphoric perceptions. However, since, in his schema, all sensory perceptions by their very nature were qualitatively endowed and therefore commanded attention cathexis automatically, the manner in which the proposed decathexis might come about before awareness of the percept occurred and aroused anxiety presented a problem in psychodynamics which Freud acknowledged he could not solve (pp. 370, 389). Though this question was not forgotten, he did not formally concern himself with it again until the clinical discovery of "disavowal" (1927) led him to believe that he had found the ego mechanism used in defense against anxiety-provoking external perceptions.[1] There was no difficulty, however, in conceptualizing the mechanism of defense against endogenous (instinctual) stimuli capable of arousing displeasure. The instinctual drive derivatives in and of themselves possessed no sensory quality, but could attract attention cathexis only through their association with residues of registered perceptions. Freud singled out especially, but not exclusively, the link between the drive elements and speech association, the latter being endowed with indicators of sensory quality because they were residues of the perceptions generated by the motor discharge involved in the complicated visual, tactile, and muscular mechanisms of the process of speech. When an instinctual drive threatened unpleasure, the ego, through its capacity to bind and divert psychic energy, prevented this necessary linkage from taking place and thus withheld attention cathexis from reaching the offending endogenous impulse. This defense mechanism of the ego directed against instinctual drives and their derivatives became known as repression.

Consciousness and Reality Testing

As was mentioned, Freud initially postulated the System Omega in the "Project" to account only for the subjective awareness of external sensory

[1] A detailed metapsychologic consideration of this topic would be too lengthy here and will be reserved for a future communication. Some discussion of this issue will be found in a previous paper (Basch, 1975).

percepts and internal stimuli in the pleasure-unpleasure series. He stressed that "awareness through consciousness" (p. 308), consists only of qualities (sensations) and that it is transient, changeable, and capable of ever new combinations of qualities. The elements that gave rise to consciousness had, therefore, to "behave like organs of perception" (p. 309) in their permeability, capacity for total restitution, and absence of memory.[2] The System Omega transforms the frequency or "period" of quantitative stimuli into sensory quality, but, Freud was careful to point out, the activity of the system is not the same as the phenomenon of subjective awareness. The latter is only the subjective accompaniment of the Omega activity, and nothing is known of how or why it comes about (p. 311).

Nevertheless, given the hypothesis that every sensory stimulus had to be registered and that consciousness of sensory quality accompanied such registration, it followed that perception and consciousness of perception were for practical purposes identical. Furthermore, consciousness always meant for Freud self-consciousness or subjective awareness of sensory qualities (1895, p. 307; 1912, pp. 260-263; 1923, pp. 13-18; 1933, pp. 69-72; 1940, pp. 144, 157, 159). With these formulations, Freud eliminated the distinction already made by Leibniz between perception and consciousness of perception (apperception), even though he may have been acquainted with it, if not from his own studies at least from Breuer's portion of the *Studies on Hysteria* (1893-1895, pp. 192-193). At first this error seems inexplicable, but it was probably an oversight in the interest of establishing a reality-testing mechanism.

Freud realized that he had to provide an indicator of reality that would serve to differentiate external perception from the memories of previously registered perceptions if the brain was to be able to carry out the reality testing postulated as already taking place in infancy. He apparently believed that the contrast experienced between the relative pallor of memory and the vividness of immediate sensation meant that memories did not possess sensory quality. He therefore concluded that the activity of the System Omega (*Cs.*) could function as an indicator of external reality (1895, p. 325). He suggested that all sensory perceptions invariably stimulated the System Omega (p. 360) through their "period," giving rise not only to consciousness (subjective awareness), but also to a

---

[2] This comparison may have led the editors of the *Standard Edition* to erroneously equate the System Omega with the "system of perceptual neurones" (1895, p. 294); however, the perceptual function was explicitly designated as residing in the System Phi (pp. 299-300), and the System Omega did not implicitly become a part of the perceptual system until the revisions of Letter 39 were made.

quantitative discharge which served to indicate to the System Psi that the registered perception represented environmental reality. Thought processes based on recall rather than on immediate perception took place through quantitative means (p. 335) and were without quality until they formed associations with residues of speech, which, being qualitatively endowed, could then stimulate the System Omega to discharge and indicate thought reality and incidentally arouse subjective awareness of the particular mental content (p. 365). Freud recognized some of the difficulties that this hypothesis created, but chose not to concern himself with them (pp. 372-376).[3]

One reason the "Project" is difficult to read and assimilate lies in the first attempt to describe the connections of the System Omega. Freud hypothesized originally that the Systems Phi and Omega were independently connected with the ego portion of the System Psi, and that the latter mediated communication between them. This led to many pages of complicated exposition which, as Freud realized, still did not resolve the confusions and inconsistencies generated by this arrangement. He solved this difficulty and provided a simpler explanation in Letter 39 (1892-1899), when he postulated that the Systems Phi and Omega invariably operate in concert, the flow of activity being from Phi to Omega and then to Psi, as has been described in the previous section of this paper. In today's terminology, the System Phi-Omega is the *System Pcpt.-Cs.*

[3] Here Freud "rediscovered" the formulation of thought processing first advanced by him in *On Aphasia* (1891) and tied it to the necessity for a test differentiating environmental events from remembered images, illusions, fantasies, etc. The feeling of vividness accompanying immediate sensory experience as opposed to the relative pallor of remembered images was the subjective criterion of reality (Breuer & Freud, 1893-1895), and the "qualitative" difference of these experiences was attributed to the effect that sensory stimuli had on the brain, an effect not shared by memories or ideas. We see here that Freud shared a philosophical prejudice of Aristotelian metaphysics, which suggests that extracranial events have a reality not shared by intracerebral activities. This necessitates all sorts of contrived arguments to explain how it is that dreams and hallucinations are not "real," even though they seem as vivid to the experiencing subject as any environmental stimulation. Most psychologies still labor, as does psychoanalysis, under the burden of defending this indefensible criterion of reality. Physical scientists have coined the term *objective* for those events that are capable of intersubjective sensory validation, as if this agreement had its roots in something other than the intracerebral, i.e., "subjective," state also shared by dreams, etc. The aims of this paper preclude a discussion of a psychology based on an alternative solution, namely, that all perceptual experiences are in the first instance alike and that the lack of sensory vividness of memories and ideas is the result of an inhibition (see, however, Basch, 1974). In such a schema, hallucinations, dreams, and the sensorily vivid images and memories of artistic persons are the result of failure or removal of inhibition and not the outcome of the reversal and regression of normal processes.

In any case, once Freud had persuaded himself that consciousness was a by-product of the indicator of reality, all sensory perception had to be conscious also. Even though this formulation (*Pcpt. = Cs.*) created difficulties at every turn, in the absence of any other conceptualization of reality testing this equation had to be maintained.

Although the model of the mind set forth in Letter 39 provided the basis for all of Freud's subsequent descriptions of the mental apparatus, he did not take into account that this correction altered the significance that the System Omega (*Cs.*) now had for mental functioning. Initially conceived only to explain the origin of the phenomenon of subjective awareness and then assigned the function of reality testing *after* perceptual registration, Omega now became a part of the perceptual system (System Phi) and was instrumental in the registration of all stimuli, whether of external or internal origin, by arousing attention cathexis through the transmutation of all mental quantity into quality. Since registered perceptions of stimuli are the building blocks fundamental to all mentation, and since now only quality was involved in their registration, the hypothesis that it was the quantitative input involved in perception that made thought possible was no longer tenable. By the same token, the descriptions in the "Project" of the manner in which subjective awareness arose and the method of reality testing should also have received reconsideration. Nevertheless, Freud continued to link the phenomenon of subjective awareness (consciousness) with the System Omega, as shown by its transformation into the *System Cs.* This implies, as Freud recognized (1923, p. 19), that all sensory perception entails subjective awareness, an assumption refuted by the phenomenon of subliminal perception; logically, furthermore, it implies that there can be no unconscious thought, since thought processes now involve sensory quality.

From the vantage point of modern technology, one might say that the "Project" as amended by Letter 39 provided a computer-like model of the mind in which the System Omega serves to transform the signals it receives into the "computer language" of quality, thereby producing messages capable of being utilized by the system. Inasmuch as subjective awareness involves perception, there is no doubt that the activity of the System Omega (*Cs.*) must be involved in the process in some manner, but the two should no longer be equated. Although all percepts in subjective awareness must also be endowed with sensory quality, the converse is not true, for there are psychic processes that possess "quality" without being in subjective awareness. The latter fall into two categories, the so-called preconscious psychic processes, which are qualitatively endowed but only potentially in subjective awareness, and the contents of the so-called unconscious ego, which possess quality, since, as Freud pointed out (1923, p. 18; 1915, pp. 192-193; 1933, p. 75), though they function according to the laws of the preconscious, they are nevertheless unable under ordinary circumstances to rise to subjective awareness.

The revision of the perceptual system in Letter 39 afforded Freud the possibility of establishing a metapsychology that dealt adequately with sensory perception because, implicitly, the element of subjective awareness was no longer an integral part of the perceptual process.

This opportunity was lost again with the formulation of the so-called topographic theory, in which Freud labeled mental contents representing instinctual drives "unconscious," "preconscious," and "conscious" when he clearly meant "inadmissible to subjective awareness," "potentially in subjective awareness," and "in subjective awareness," respectively. The formal distinction between perception and apperception remains lost to Freud, and the topographic theory recreated the problem of the original formulation in the "Project." Furthermore, he mistakenly regarded these phenomenological categories as being fundamental functional divisions of mental content. In this way Freud elevated a phenomenon, i.e., being conscious, to the level of a system, indeed to the highest order of thought and, thereby, to the standard against which all thinking was measured — this in spite of the fact that he knew all mental processes were unconscious in the first instance and that no thought activity, no matter how complex, needed consciousness for its fulfillment.

In order to be consistent with his own underlying theoretical formulations, he should at least have considered external perceptions as well as endogenous stimuli in his construct. The fundamental division should have been between mental content essentially endowed with the quality of sensation (i.e., all registered perceptions, whether actually in, potentially in, or defensively excluded from subjective awareness) and content essentially without sensory quality (i.e., instinctual impulses), whose fate depended on whether or not it became secondarily linked with perceptual residues, regardless of whether or not these were in subjective awareness. The inevitable confusion generated by the topographic theory eventually did lead to such a move, and in *The Ego and the Id* (1923) the topographic divisions were limited to their descriptive sense and no longer represented psychic agencies or systems. Therefore, in essence, the division of the mind that existed in Letter 39: an area in which the primary process — the id — dominated and one in which the secondary process — the ego — reigned was restored.

The contention that perception and subjective awareness were the functions of the same system and, for practical purposes, identical, remained unaltered, however, and led to the unsatisfactory solution of subsuming under the terms *consciousness* or *conscious* an attribute of mental content, a subsystem of structure, and a sense organ. Although these three usages are metapsychologically incompatible, this posed no

15

immediate problem so long as Freud's emphasis was on the struggle between forbidden instinctual impulses and a hypothetically "normal" or adequately functioning ego. The therapeutic problem was one of enabling the repressed material to acquire qualitative links through the patient's perceptions of the analyst in the transference and then, through interpretation, bringing these percepts to subjective awareness. But, when the ego itself became an object of psychoanalytic examination, the vicissitudes of sensory perception had to be dealt with actively, for, as Freud (1933) said, "The relation to the external world has become the decisive factor for the ego...." (p. 75; see also Freud, 1923, p. 40). Now the language of the "topographic theory" adapted to and integrated with the structural theory led to serious problems. When Freud said that sensory percepts were "conscious" from their inception (1923, p. 19), he could only have meant that they were by their very nature endowed with sensory quality and capable of attracting attention cathexis by again stimulating the activity of the *System Cs.*, but, since qualitative endowment had also been equated with subjective awareness, the misconception arose that all percepts are first in subjective awareness. Freud would have been more accurate had he said, in the language of the "topographic theory," that sensory percepts are "preconscious," (i.e., potentially capable of becoming conscious) from the very first.

Subliminal Perception

Subliminal perception, that is, sensory perception outside subjective awareness, does not create problems for the operational theory of the mental apparatus delineated in the "Project" as modified by Letter 39; on the contrary, it can be predicted from and is readily explained by that construct. Since subjective awareness is not an essential accompaniment of the activity of the System Omega (*Cs.*), the various functions of the mental agencies, including perception, can and do take place in its absence. If subjective awareness does arise, it is only incidental to the basic operation of the mental apparatus; this, of course, does not diminish its importance for mental life; it only means that its presence or absence is peripheral to an understanding of the process of perception.

Interestingly, recent experiments (Shevrin, 1968) tend to corroborate the validity of Freud's operational hypotheses in the "Project"; Shevrin not only reconfirms the registration of subliminal stimulation through the use of the tachistoscope, but also demonstrates that these stimuli are invested with attention cathexis, since the particular segment of the electroencephalographic recording that corresponds to "attention" is lengthened while the subject is exposed to subliminal stimulation. Furthermore, though not subjectively aware of the content of such a stimulus, the subject's attention is increased if the subliminal stimulus is inherently more interesting, that is, if it is of a more sexual nature. This increased facilitation corroborates the finding that percepts outside subjective awareness are being utilized by mental processes.

Because subjective awareness is incidental to perception, the term *subliminal perception* is a tautology. The unresolved problem for metapsychology is that of "liminality"; that is, the manner in which a percept attains the state of subjective awareness remains unknown.

Conclusion

Just as Freud continued to revise his metapsychologic speculations, so should we today continue the struggle toward formulating a comprehensive and viable explanatory theory for our clinical findings. Unfortunately, much time is expended in defending clearly inadequate and inaccurate metapsychologic concepts, perhaps out of a concern that acknowledgement of their failure would vitiate the clinical method of psychoanalysis and its results. In this paper I have tried to show, by tracing the development of a particular metapsychologic concept, i.e., *Pcpt.-Cs.*, that this construct is not a "psychoanalytic" one in the sense of having been directly inferred from Freud's clinical work as a psychoanalyst and that its only reason for existence is its potential utility in explaining clinical findings in the area of perception. Insofar as the formulation fails to achieve this and, furthermore, directly contradicts independent evidence gathered by other valid methods of investigation, it deserves to be replaced.

The origin and significance of the equation between perception and consciousness was traced to prepare the way for a formulation of a reality-testing mechanism consonant with the findings of perceptual physiology and psychology.

An incidental, but not insignificant, by-product of that investigation was at least a partial demonstration that the "Project for a Scientific Psychology," far from being only a historical curiosity in the annals of psychoanalysis, is Freud's most detailed and extensive exposition of metapsychology. Eventually, the explanatory psychology of the "Project" found its way bit by bit into Freud's later metapsychologic writings, albeit without the clarity of reasoning and cogency of argument that character-ize the original. Today, when the need for corrective revisions is accepted by many, it is possible to trace the origins of our problems with meta-psychology to certain assumptions Freud made in the "Project" regard-ing perception, memory, and thought, which, while in keeping with the state of knowledge of his day, we now know to be false. Armed with new insights in these areas, we can move forward in constructing a theory of mentation that will serve our clinical constructs while forging the link between psychoanalysis and other sciences. Freud's painstaking and brilliant creation of a hypothetico-deductive theory of mentation in 1895 should encourage us in furthering that quest and may well serve as a model of epistemologic elegance for its eventual twentieth-century counterpart.

REFERENCES

Basch, M. F. (1973), Psychoanalysis and theory formation. *This Annual,* 1:39-52. New York: Quadrangle/NYT.
_____ (1974), Toward a theory which encompasses depression: A revision of existing causal hypotheses in psychoanalysis. In: *Depression and the Human Existence,* ed. E. J. Anthony and T. Benedek. Boston: Little Brown (In press).
_____ (1975), Interference with perceptual transformation in the service of defense. *This Annual,* 2:87-97. New York: International Universities Press.
Breuer, J., & Freud, S. (1893-1895), Studies on hysteria. *Standard Edition,* 2. London: Hogarth Press, 1955.
Freud, S. (1891), *On Aphasia.* Trans. E. Stengel. New York: International Universities Press, 1953.
_____ (1892-1899), Extracts from the Fliess papers. *Standard Edition,* 1:175-280. London: Hogarth Press, 1966.
_____ (1895), Project for a scientific psychology. *Standard Edition,* 1:281-397. London: Hogarth Press, 1966.
_____ (1900), The interpretation of dreams. *Standard Edition,* 4 & 5. London: Hogarth Press, 1953.
_____ (1912), A note on the unconscious in psychoanalysis. *Standard Edition,* 12:255-266. London: Hogarth Press, 1958.
_____ (1915), The unconscious. *Standard Edition,* 14:159-215. London: Hogarth Press, 1957.
_____ (1917), A metapsychological supplement to the theory of dreams. *Standard Edition,* 14:217-235. London: Hogarth Press, 1957.
_____ (1923), The ego and the id. *Standard Edition,* 19:3-66. London: Hogarth Press, 1961.
_____ (1927), Fetishism. *Standard Edition,* 21:149-157. London: Hogarth Press, 1961.
_____ (1933), New introductory lectures on psycho-analysis. *Standard Edition,* 22:3-182. London: Hogarth Press, 1964.
_____ (1940), An outline of psycho-analysis. *Standard Edition,* 23:141-207. London: Hogarth Press, 1964.
Jones, E. (1953), *The Life and Work of Sigmund Freud.* Vol. 1. New York: Basic Books.

Klein, G. S. (1959), Consciousness in psychoanalytic theory. Some implications for current research in perception. *J. Amer. Psychoanal. Assn.,* 7:5-34.

_____ (1966), Two theories or one?: Perspectives to change in psychoanalytic theory. Presented at Conference of Psychoanalysts of the Southwest, Galveston, Texas, March, 1966.

_____ (1970), Freud's two theories of sexuality. Presented at the scientific meeting of the Chicago Psychoanalytic Society, March 24, 1970.

Marx, O. M. (1967), Freud and aphasia: An historical analysis. *Amer. J. Psychiat.,* 124:6, 815-825.

McGuire, W., ed. (1974), *The Freud/Jung Letters.* Princeton, N.J.: Princeton University Press.

Piaget, J., & Inhelder, B. (1966), *The Psychology of the Child.* New York: Basic Books, 1969.

Shevrin, H. (1968), Visual evoked response correlates of unconscious mental processes. *Science,* 161:295-298.

May, 1974

19

In Defense of Libido Theory

MARVIN HYMAN, PH.D. (*Southfield, Mich.*)

I know you believe you understand what you think I said, but I am not sure you realize that what you heard is not what I meant. — *Anonymous*

The concept of psychic energy, and particularly of libido as a form of psychic energy, is a central one in psychoanalytic theory. From this central concept, the main hypotheses and formulations that make up the theory have been derived: repression, sublimation, psychosexual development, the structural hypothesis, ego psychology, and the theory of dreams. The various elaborations and extensions of the concept of libido are too numerous to mention here, nor would their enumeration be consistent with the purposes of this presentation, but certainly, beside the metapsychological formulations of Freud's (1900, 1905, 1915a, 1915b, 1915c), two contributions of Sterba's do deserve mention. In his text on libido theory, Sterba (1968) provides both an elementary statement of the theory and, at the same time, an example of the coherence that psychoanalytic theoretical presentations ought to, but frequently do not, have. In that same text, we also find a remarkable observation that provides, as will be elaborated below, the basis for the continued utilization of the energy concept in psychoanalytic theory. Sterba's (1930) paper on sublimation illustrates beautifully the descriptive uses to which libido theory can be put and the value of the concept as a theoretical tool.

My purpose in citing Sterba's works at this point is to provide examples to which the reader can refer in assessing the manner in which psychoanalytic theory has utilized the concepts of psychic energy and libido.

This paper was originally written in honor of Dr. Richard Sterba, on the occasion of his 75th birthday.

21

These examples will provide a basis for comparison between the concepts as they have been traditionally used in psychoanalytic theory and the points of view that are offered in the substantial critical literature that has grown up during the past decade. This literature questions sharply the concepts of psychic energy, libido, instinct and drive, and the structural hypothesis. It is my contention that such a comparison is a vital necessity at this time, in light of the calls for a total reformulation of psychoanalytic theory and the abandonment of many, if not all, of the concepts currently used by our discipline.

Critiques of Libido Theory

Although I shall not attempt here to review exhaustively the criticisms of libido theory that have been offered, it is important to categorize them in order to appreciate the issues involved. For more detailed presentations of the critiques, the reader is referred to Holt (1962, 1965, 1967a, 1967b, 1972), Modell (1963), Peterfreund (1971), and Rubinstein (1965, 1967). The following paragraphs summarize the accusations that have been made.

MECHANISM

This criticism holds that libido theory in particular and metapsychology in general assume a mechanistic view of man. In this view, libido theory is the conceptual heir of Freud's attempt to neurologize psychology. As such, the theory is seen as describing and explaining man as a kind of hydraulic system that operates according to laws analogous to the laws of hydrodynamics. Such a mechanistic system implies a reductionistic point of view as well, since the machine that man is supposed to be must be explained by a regression to the principles of a "more basic" science, i.e., physics.

VITALISM

Of interest is that, for its critics, libido theory is vitalistic at the same time that it is mechanistic. The point would seem to be, if we set aside the philosophical contradiction, that the material that flows through the hydraulic system is an entelechy, an *élan vital,* a life force, the nature of which is not and cannot be known to the physical sciences. The basis for this criticism is the use, in psychoanalytic writing, of metaphoric terms as part of the description of the libido concept and its implications, e.g., the "mobility of cathexes."

ANTHROPOMORPHISM

Also based on the vocabulary of psychoanalytic writing is the criticism that libido is endowed by psychoanalysts with human characteristics. Libido has been said to "advance," to "retreat," to "demand," etc., with the implication, according to the critics, that the concept becomes a doer, as a person is a doer. Closely related to this notion is the criticism that psychoanalytic theorists have reified the concept of libido. It is claimed that libido, as used by such theorists, starts out as a concept and gradually becomes a "thing" which has a host of properties and functions.

CONCEPTUAL AND LANGUAGE CONFUSION

In psychoanalytic writing statements sometimes appear that use simultaneously the language of clinical experience and observation, the language of theory and conceptualization, and the language of another science or discipline. The result is a presentation with confused levels of ideas and meanings. The thrust of this criticism, moreover, reflects the view that psychoanalytic theory is confused not only in its vocabulary and language, but in its concepts as well.

DUALISM

Related to some of the foregoing criticisms is the contention that psychoanalytic theory is conceptually a metaphysical dualism. The attempt to describe and explain phenomena on a psychological basis alone is seen as evidence that the theory presumes separate mind and body entities, which, although they may interact, are nonetheless distinct and different from each other. We are all aware that a dualistic solution to the mind-body problem is currently out of fashion.

SCIENTIFIC ISOLATION

As a dualism that attends only to the mind, to the exclusion of the body, libido theory, according to its critics, is totally isolated from the main body of natural science, particularly biology, neurology, and neurophysiology. Not only are its findings at odds with those of physical science, but future rapprochement is also impossible as long as psychoanalysis formulates its concepts in terms that are not translatable, now or in the future, into those of neurophysiology. The critics hold that a dualistic position denies that a statement about the mind is also a statement about the brain, with the consequence that the theoretical model of psychoanalysis is devoid of existential meaning.

MENTALISM

If libido theory is viewed as a purely psychological theory, then it faces the dilemma of explaining behavior and experience in nonexistential terms, without reference to other organismic events and, ultimately, without reference to the brain. Since the critics take the view that the brain must be implicated in behavior, the mentalistic view of nonexistential entities must therefore be fallacious.

THE IMMATURITY OF PSYCHOANALYTIC THEORY

It is currently fashionable, as it seems to have been for many years, to protest that psychoanalysis is a young science that must, therefore, be permitted and forgiven the gaucheries of youth. In this light, the metaphors of the theory are excused as primitive attempts at explanation, which, after sufficient maturation, will give way to more sophisticated and less anachronistic theoretical principles that correspond to those of the older sciences.

Because the seeming deficiencies of psychoanalytic theory (particularly the failure of the model to make a place for neurophysiological findings) are so overwhelming to its critics, we are offered such alternatives as the following:

The solution — a radical one — is to rebuild the psychoanalytic model completely as an explicitly anatomical-physiological one, perhaps starting with Freud's *Project*. . . . A great deal of work would be involved, and the end product would inevitably look distressingly unfamiliar to most psychoanalysts. Yet I believe that this will have to be the ultimate solution, and that we had better get started working at it [Holt, 1967a, p. 491].

An Assessment of the Critiques

Since it is not the primary aim of this presentation to refute the above criticisms of psychoanalytic theory in general and libido theory in particular, I shall call attention only to selected aspects of these arguments. My intention is to point out that the validity of libido theory is not a closed issue, even when evaluated by the criteria of the philosophy of science.

When studied further, the criticism that psychoanalytic theory presupposes a mechanistic view of man seems to reduce to the criticism, not that man is conceptualized as a machine, but, rather, that he is conceptualized as the *wrong* machine. Because current findings of neurophysiology do not conform to a hydraulic model, the model must be changed to one that does suit the findings, e.g., a computer model or some other mechanism of information processing. It is difficult to see how the argument that libido theory is mechanistic can be maintained in the face of what seems to be an equally mechanistic point of view. The point that the "right" machine would function more in accord with known neurophysiological findings and conceptions does not justify the argument.

In like fashion, critics who argue that psychoanalysis is reductionistic go on to fault it because its concepts do not conform to those of a more "basic" discipline—neurophysiology. In effect, there seem to be two criticisms: (1) that psychoanalysis is reductionistic, and (2) that it is not. If we address ourselves to the first criticism, we should first note that Freud several times explicitly disavowed any relationship between metapsychology and neurophysiology (in which he had been so interested earlier in his career). The fact that Freud at times used language that seemed to negate his disavowal does not warrant the conclusion that he was indeed doing so. Freud said what he was trying to do, and the fact that he may have done it imperfectly and inconsistently does not justify the inference that he was trying to do something else. Such an inference would have merit only if it were drawn as a conclusion about Freud's unconscious motives. It may be that Freud intended unconsciously to negate his disavowal of a reductionistic position, but the merits of a scientific endeavor could not possibly be judged on the basis of such a possibility. It would indeed be questionable science if the merits of the theory of relativity were to be judged on the basis of the unconscious motivations that led Einstein to develop the theory.

Addressing ourselves to the argument that libido theory is not reductionistic and should be considered flawed because its concepts do not conform to those of neurophysiology, we may ask: why stop there? Even if the assumption that neurophysiology is "basic" to psychoanalysis is granted, the question remains: why not reduce neurophysiology to biochemistry, and biochemistry to physics, and physics to...? As Eacker (1972) points out, "this type of explanation leads to a finite regression with one science left unexplained—unless, of course, it is self-explanatory; no one is likely to admit that of physics" (p. 559).

Apart from asking whether there is a justifiable reason to reduce the concepts of libido theory to a more basic science, we must also ask whether it is possible to accomplish such a reduction. Hempel (1966) points out that "the reduction of psychological laws would require suitable connecting principles containing psychological terms as well as biological or physico-chemical ones" (p. 107). At the present time, there

25

is no evidence that such connecting principles have been developed between the laws of psychic reality and the laws of physical reality. Indeed, it is difficult at this time to conceive even of a protoneurophysiological model of psychoanalysis (Rubinstein, 1965), i.e., of psychoanalytic theory as, in part, a metaphorical expression of neurophysiological theory. Attempts to accomplish the development of such a protoneurophysiological model have used for their basic data either armchair formulations or the findings of experiments in psychology as opposed to metapsychology. Schafer (1967) offers this cogent observation:

I think it is correct to say that there are two legitimate (in the sense of being consistently psychoanalytic) endeavors open to those concerned with the scientific aspects of psychoanalysis. The first is to continue gathering clinical data and studying them as to their descriptive and causal textures. The second is to refine existing concepts and propositions or replace them with better ones; in other words, to engage in a process of theoretical clarification, selection and coordination. In this second respect, although not every concept or proposition must be close to the clinical phenomena to which it ultimately refers, it should at least be referable to those phenomena through a series of lower order concepts and propositions. But in any case, the ultimate referents, the essential raw data of psychoanalytic formulations, can only be gathered within the clinical psychoanalytic situation. Notwithstanding that other types of data, such as are gathered from observations of infants or individuals in groups or laboratories, may suggest new questions, hypotheses and concepts, or may point to special difficulties or inconsistencies in accepted formulations, nonanalytic data cannot be taken at face value. It is never self-evident. If nothing else, psychoanalysis has demonstrated that manifest phenomena, and especially the adult's immediately available conscious and preconscious experience and his overt actions, do not reveal the fullness, complexity, and strangeness of psychic life [p. 516].

Schafer goes on to point out that it is in exactly this respect that students of psychoanalytic theory have sometimes fostered nonanalytic, implicitly repressive attitudes. Certainly, the comments just quoted permit the conclusion that, at this time, metapsychological data do not lend themselves to the development of connecting principles that would permit the building of protoneurophysiological models. Such models can be developed if the connecting principles stem from essentially nonanalytic observations. Peterfreund (1971) illustrates this issue in his attempt to develop such a model on the basis of information theory. The nature of the observations on which metapsychological theories are based will be discussed further below.

To the extent that connecting principles do not exist between the "laws of the mind" and the "laws of the body," and to the extent that we desire to seek conceptualizations of mental data and events, we must assume a hypothetical dualism or an idealistic monism. Both amount to the same thing: either we focus only on mind and ignore body or we assert that all we can know is mind. The issue at this time is not to make an ultimate determination about the nature of man, but rather to develop a strategy of conceptualizing the events we are currently able to observe. Perhaps it would throw more light and less heat on the matter if we were to set aside the mind-body problem and approach the issue as a matter of choice between the two metaphysical positions of realism and phenomenalism. Eacker (1972) defines them as follows: Realism is the "view that a real, objective world exists, with real objects and phenomena in it, and that it would continue to exist whether there were anyone around to observe it or not; that is, it exists independently of any observer" (p. 555). After distinguishing between phenomenalism and phenomenology, Eacker goes on to define the former: "what exists is whatever it is that occurs when the senses experience, that is, [phenomenalism is] sense experience" (p. 555).

In discussing the choice between the realistic and phenomenalistic (or mentalistic) positions, Eacker (1972) offers this observation:

It is somewhat instructive to consider these two positions with respect to the activities of scientists, behavioral or otherwise, who might hold either of them in apparent opposition. As scientists they would both be empiricists, that is, subscribe to the observational basis of knowledge in science.... The chief difference between them would seem to be what they did with their observations. The realist would tend to "put aside his heuristic devices and proclaim the truth as to the nature" of the universe. He would argue from his observations, that is, his sense experience, to a realm of objects or behavioral events which, if known, could be known at all only through sense experience; he would "go beyond his data." By contrast, the phenomenalist would tend to stop at the point where observation occurred and perhaps emphasize the fact that his knowledge claims, and those of others, were limited to, or by, sense experience.

Since realism has been the traditional and predominant metaphysical position in science, and since phenomenalism appears equally defensible though perhaps less appealing to common sense, the metaphysical problem for psychologists is which one of them to adopt. Realism has been tried; phenomenalism might well lead to greater theoretical and experimental insights than have so far been obtained, particularly in those sciences concerned with what are called observed events, or behavior, as opposed to observed objects [p. 556].

Muddling the issue still further is the fact that language and vocabulary are the means whereby concepts, models, and theories are communicated. To the extent that psychoanalytic theorists write about libido as though it were simultaneously physical energy, a psychic concept, and a description of clinical events, the criticisms are valid. Similarly, if concepts are reified in the mind of the theorist, i.e., if he no longer sees his metaphors as analogues, but as existential events, then confusion must follow.

On the other hand, it appears that the critics of libido theory tend to focus on the confused language forms that are sometimes chosen for the presentation of the theory. Certainly, it would be helpful if concepts were presented in consistent language that did not imply reification; but it would be equally helpful if critics would focus on the conceptualizations intended rather than on the form of their presentation. This tolerance is particularly needed in the case of concepts that deal with data that are, by their very nature, irrational. The clinical observables of psychoanalysis are the products of unconscious fantasy. Although psychoanalysis has dealt with such observables for only a comparatively short time, it is not true that the concepts developed to describe, order, and explain them are unsophisticated or inherently unscientific. The difficulty lies in the fact that language is sometimes an inefficient tool for presenting concepts.

The Data of Psychoanalytic Research

Most psychoanalysts are bewildered when they are presented with alternatives to current psychoanalytic theory. This bewilderment is not the result of scientific or conceptual naïvete, but rather the reaction that might be expected when one is confronted with a theoretical schema that, on the face of it, has nothing to do with the data to be explained. For example, on reading Peterfreund's (1971) suggested alternative to psychoanalytic theory, which is based on information and systems theory, one is tempted to ask, "What has this to do with psychoanalysis?" One notes further that such an alternative might be a good way to conceptualize the *behavior* that is studied in psychology, but it in no way adds to a greater understanding of *fantasy* and fantasy formation. And in psychoanalysis, "fantasy is where it's at," as they say. Sterba (1968) writes in respect to this point:

> The primeval and primitive understanding of the dynamic process in our surrounding physical world is brought about by anthropomorphic projection. Primitive man, or the young child, in his first attempts to grasp what occurs in the physical world, considers the physical processes in the surroundings to be set in motion by forces equivalent to the dynamic processes of which he becomes aware in himself. In this early animistic world concept, nothing occurs that is not equal to the processes which he himself sets in motion or feels are set in motion in himself. The first dynamic world picture is a motivational one created through projection of the primitive's, or the child's intrapsychic awareness of the motivational pressures within himself. Thus the concept of physical energy was in the

beginning of human world-conception a projection of the psychic dynamic processes which were proprioceived. Physical energy is therefore an anthropomorphic concept. As science progressed, the necessity of making the concept of physical energy a useful one demanded that it be stripped of its anthropomorphic features. However, there can be no question but that it is legitimate to use the concept in its original primitive form in attempting to understand the dynamic occurrences in the mind. Nowhere is an anthropomorphic concept applied with more justification than in its place of origin, in "anthropos," i.e., with man. But it is inappropriate to demand that the properties which with the progress of science had to be attributed to physical energy in order to make the concept useful for the explanation of the phenomena of the physical world should be equally applied to "psychic energy." Psychic energy is a concept that corresponds to our immediate awareness of the dynamic processes within our mind. The expressions of everyday language which we use when we relate to psychic dynamic occurrences betray the underlying concept of psychic energy. "To feel driven by an irresistible power," "to exhaust one's energy fighting it," "to feel new strength" and many other expressions demonstrate this. Therefore we find it justified to continue to work with the conceptual tool "mental energy," ever ready to replace it if somebody offers a better one. Until then, we will consider "Libido" the term for "Sexual Energy" [p. viii].[1]

The raw data of psychoanalysis are fantasy: Fantasies emanate from a realm of experience entirely different from the one in which we think we live and about which we think science teaches us. This is the world of psychic reality (Freud, 1895; Krystal, 1973), where none of the laws of physical reality hold, as such. It is the world of unconscious experience, and it makes its appearance through those behavioral manifestations that are, in respect to the physical world, incomprehensible. Reports of dreams, slips of the tongue, free associations, reports of symptomatology — these are the behavioral manifestations from which we infer the existence of a psychic reality for the individual whose psychic processes we study. Psychic reality is an experiential reality; physical reality is an existential reality.

When there is confusion about the nature of the data to which one is addressing oneself, it follows that there will be confusion about the manner in which one orders and conceptualizes that data. Peterfreund (1971) provides a good example when he asks, in regard to psychoanalytic theory:

...can a specific statement be made within the present conceptual frame of reference to correspond to each and every clinically observable phenomenon? And if such statements cannot be made at present, does current psychoanalytic theory offer us any hope whatever that it will someday be able to make such statements? Here, I believe, is exactly the point where the failure of the theory is most complete.

For example, here are a few typical clinical observables:
1. A patient may be sexually anesthetic.

[1] Quoted with the permission of the publisher, Robert Brunner, Inc.

2. A male patient may be unaware of having ejaculated.

3. A male patient may be aware of having had an ejaculation, but may have no orgastic sensation [p. 64].

There can be no question that these are clinical observables; but what manner of clinical observables are they? These are not the data of psychoanalysis; these are the data of either neurology or psychology. To make the distinction clear, the following propositions have to be taken into account:

a. The data of physical science are the structure and function of physical entities.

b. The data of psychology are behaviors.

c. The data of psychoanalysis are fantasies (inferred from verbalizations and other behaviors).

In the light of these propositions, we would have to conclude that the clinical observables quoted above would have to be presented in quite a different form if they were to be considered as the data of psychoanalysis. To illustrate, we can cast the list quoted from Peterfreund into the following form:

1'. A patient *reports* that he may be sexually anesthetic.

2'. A male patient *claims* that he may be unaware of having ejaculated.

3'. A male patient *laments* that he may be aware of having had an ejaculation, but may have no orgastic sensation.

The clinical observables here are the report, the claim, the lament, and what can be inferred from them, regardless of their existential reality. One could go on with other illustrations, but the one that I have offered is sufficient indication of the issues involved. The neurologist, hearing such complaints from the patient, takes them as statements of fact, statements of physical reality relating to the structure and function of the body. The psychologist hears such statements as descriptions of behavior that has occurred. The psychoanalyst makes no assumptions that what the patient reports is real, i.e., is an event in physical reality. Nor does he assume that what the patient reports is not real. The question of the reality of the clinically observable event is simply not relevant. Rather, the psychoanalyst asks what psychic reality can be inferred from the patient's reporting of whatever it is that he reports. Sexual arousal, for example, is not an event in time or space; nor does it have to do with matter. It is an experiential event in a psychic reality having to do with the fantasies of experience.

In any discussion of the data of psychoanalysis, attention has to be paid to the manner in which the data is collected. In the world of physical reality, including the world of behavior, the objectivity of the observer of the clinical phenomena is assumed. He is an instrument that contributes nothing to the phenomena being observed. In psychoanalysis, on the other hand, the instrument by which the clinical phenomena are observed is the experience of the observer. In other words, what we know of the patient is a function of the psychic reality of the analyst. When the analyst as an observational instrument distorts the observation to an unacceptable degree, we call the phenomenon "countertransference"; when the distortion is minimal, we call it "empathy." Whatever the name, we have to recognize that we know the psychic reality of the patient only through the psychic reality of the analyst.

The laws of psychic reality do not conform to the laws of physical reality. The world of psychic reality is like the world "through the looking glass." It is, as Sterba (1968) indicated, a world of anthropomorphism, animism, and magic. It is the world of the child, where, as Piaget (1937) has shown, conclusions about the nature of the world and the objects in it are not based on logic. It is a world where, because "bigger is better," the child takes the nickel instead of the dime when both are offered to him. It is the world of the unconscious, where ideas are linked solely in accordance with the rule of contiguous association. It is a world that is timeless and where the past exists in every present moment.

Psychic Reality and Psychic Energy

Within the world of psychic reality, psychoanalysis (as a phenomenalistic science) has developed the concept of psychic energy — a formulation that is explicitly different from physical energy. It is a concept designed to describe and explain certain experiential phenomena of fantasy.

Freud used the term *psychic energy* as a synonym for two other terms in his metapsychological writings: *libido* and *interest* (e.g., Freud, 1915b, p. 152). In this discussion, I would like to emphasize the last term because, in my view, it adds clarification to the status of psychic energy as an experiential concept. It also helps us to understand why Freud chose the adjective *economic* to describe this aspect of his metapsychology.

In the language of experience, individuals have a finite quantity of interest to invest. They can invest their interest in themselves (narcissistic cathexis) and/or in others (object cathexis). They can shift their investments (displacement), and/or they can combine them (condensation). They can withdraw their investments of interest (repression proper), and/or they can use one investment against another (after-pressure).

The analogy could be continued indefinitely. But it will be sufficient to note Modell's report (Panel, 1963) of Waelder's statement that this analogy is highly useful in psychoanalytic conceptions: "in economics, for example, prices are a kind of measurement for the evaluations which people put on things. It is a relative measurement, and, in the last analysis, it is a list of priority. Waelder continued, 'I submit that psychic measurement in the economic sense, namely, a list of priorities existing for a person, is possible' " (p. 614).

Libido theory, like economic theory, deals with the distribution of "interest," of experienced psychic resources, and with a sense of innervation and depletion — an experience of the investment of oneself. Is this view, however, merely descriptive, a metaphor that provides no explanation of the phenomena it describes? I submit that it is more than an analogy; that evidence can be adduced with respect to its merits as a contribution to knowledge.

The Scientific Utility of Libido Theory

UTILITY FOR THE FORMATION OF GENERALIZATIONS

One of the laws of psychoanalytic theory is that the experiential past lives in the experiential present. For the naïve realist, the past is the past and the present is the present, and, in a given instance, one has nothing to do with the other. For the psychoanalytic phenomenalist, however, significant quotas of libido are invested throughout life and in myriad ways. Libido theory specifies the general nature of those investments and their vicissitudes, particularly in its formulation of the development of childhood sexuality. From the formulation, it is possible to elucidate those correlations between past and present psychic experiences in the psychic reality of a given individual. Such correlations provide explanations for current psychic manifestations, and even figure in an understanding of their causation. Certainly, this is no mean scientific feat.

To take another example: The psychoanalytic theory of dreams is a landmark breakthrough in the understanding of this universal experiential phenomenon. Notwithstanding recent neurophysiological work on dreams, only psychoanalytic theory can account for their specific content. The details of the manner in which the psychic apparatus deals with the excitations experienced by the dreamer to produce a specific dream do not seem susceptible to even a protoneurophysiological explanation.

As a final example, we might note how the theory of sublimation as a vicissitude of instinctual drive permits an explanation of those peculiarly human experiences that are usually expressed in the conceptualization and explanation of the artist. Sterba's (1930) contribution to the theory of sublimation provides hypotheses regarding such phenomena as tenderness, artistic experiences, the desire to do good and the aggressive forms it sometimes takes, and the performance and activity of the scientific research worker. Such explanations are fundamental to the data of psychoanalysis.

My purpose in this paper is to defend libido theory; not to make a contribution to it. I have presented the above examples, not because they add to understanding, but because they illustrate the widespread utility of the theory. In addition, the examples demonstrate that postdictive and, to a lesser degree, predictive statements can be made about events in psychic reality, statements that suport the continued utilization of libido theory as part of psychoanalytic theory and as an explanatory tool in knowing the world of psychic reality.

THE CLINICAL UTILITY OF LIBIDO THEORY

Peterfreund (1971), in his critique of the concept of psychic energy, attempts to demonstrate that clinical work in the psychoanalytic mode is possible without the utilization of such anachronistic concepts as libido. In his clinical case presentations, he describes the case of a young woman (pp. 296-302) who, during a particular therapeutic hour, reported moving experiences of extreme frustration that initially defied interpretation. Finally, Peterfreund reported, he had been able to think of his patient's mother and, from that thought, had gone on to a hypothesis of how the patient must have experienced her feeding during childhood. When he shared this reconstruction with his patient, the response was confirmation, pleasure, and relief from the distress the patient was experiencing. Although my summary does little justice to Peterfreund's description of a beautiful piece of clinical work on his part, it will serve to illustrate how useful the very theory he wishes to discard was to him and is to all analysts.

Peterfreund accounts for the clinical events he describes in the following way: "... every good piece of analytic work in the classical sense may implicitly and automatically carry with it a corrective emotional experience — new information making change and restructuring possible" (pp. 300-301). Implicit in this formulation is the necessity for the patient to suddenly discover that the analyst, and others in her life, was not her mother, or, at least, did not act like her mother. Yet, we can be

33

sure that if the analyst had told this to his patient she would have retorted that she knew that very well—although, of course, she acted as if she did not.

As an alternative to Peterfreund's explanation, let us consider this vignette in terms of the issues that have been raised in this paper. In the first place, the analyst was not dealing with events that he knew had taken place in the patient's life. Nor did the patient. They were both dealing with fantasy, the fantasy that events, as the analyst reconstructed them and as the patient perceived them unconsciously, actually took place. Whether or not they did is as irrelevant as whether or not Freud's hysterical patients actually were seduced sexually. In other words, both patient and analyst were dealing with events in psychic reality and were applying to those events their understanding of the laws that govern psychic reality.

Second, I submit that the analyst, in thinking about the patient's mother and about the patient's feeding experiences, was using his knowledge of libido theory to generalize from the theory to the patient. If the patient had not made a significant libidinal investment in her mother and in the experience of being fed, the issue would never have arisen in the treatment. Further, does not the report of intense frustration of desires to make contact bring the oral stage of psychosexual development to the mind of every analyst as he attempts to formulate the explanatory hypotheses for the report? It would seem clear from the case report that the theory of libidinal investment at early stages of childhood development was at work in Peterfreund's considerations of the case, much as he might not have been aware of it.

Finally, he used his empathic experience of the patient's reported experiential state to bring forth from himself an intuitive understanding of the psychic events that were making their appearance in the treatment. Truly, here was sublimated libido at work.

Although it is still a matter of "paying one's money and taking one's choice" between an understanding of clinical events in terms of psychoanalytic concepts and an understanding in terms of protoneurophysiological information theory, I would like to offer the observation that the latter theory seems to have far less explanatory power in respect to the experiential phenomena of the clinical situation discussed above.

THE RELATIONSHIP BETWEEN PSYCHOANALYSIS AND THE PHYSICAL SCIENCES

Freud (1915a) stated: "If we now apply ourselves to considering mental life from a *biological* point of view, an 'instinct' appears to us as a concept on the frontier between the mental and somatic, as the psychical representative of the stimuli originating from within the organism and reaching the mind, as a measure of the demand made upon the mind for work in consequence of its connection with the body" (p. 121-122).

This statement has been taken to mean that Freud intended libido to be understood ultimately as a form of physical energy. Those who take the statement in this way then go on to demonstrate how Freud failed to achieve such understanding. From this, they draw the conclusion that the concept ought to be abandoned.

I would like to suggest that there is an alternative interpretation that can be given to Freud's statement. I submit that he is indicating that he has discovered a psychic world that exists, so to speak, within a physical body. Within this psychic world, bodily events are subjected to the same subjective interpretations that all phenomena are subjected to in the formation of fantasy. It is these subjective interpretations that are the work of the mind that is demanded "in consequence of its connection with the body." Part of that work, at times, includes influencing the body to act as though it were a part of the psychical world rather than the physical one.

With his statement, Freud is saying further that the task of biology and the other physical sciences ought to be expanded in the direction of developing principles that govern the relationship between the psychic world and the physical one.

If this alternative interpretation has merit, then it would seem that it is not psychoanalysis that should be developing protoneurophysiological models; rather, it is neurophysiology that should be developing protopsychoanalytic ones.

REFERENCES

Eacker, J. (1972), On some elementary philosophical problems of psychology. *Amer. Psychologist,* 27:553-565.

Freud, S. (1895), Project for a scientific psychology. *Standard Edition,* 1:283-397. London: Hogarth Press, 1966.

_____ (1900), The interpretation of dreams. *Standard Edition,* Vols. 4 & 5. London: Hogarth Press, 1953.

_____ (1905), Three essays on the theory of sexuality. *Standard Edition,* 7:130-243. London: Hogarth Press, 1953.

_____ (1915a), Instincts and their vicissitudes. *Standard Edition,* 14:117-140. London: Hogarth Press, 1957.

_____ (1915b), Repression. *Standard Edition,* 14:146-158. London: Hogarth Press, 1957.

_____ (1915c), The unconscious. *Standard Edition,* 14:166-215. London: Hogarth Press, 1957.

Hempel, C. (1966), *Philosophy of Natural Science.* Englewood Cliffs, N.J.: Prentice-Hall.

Holt, R. (1962), A critical examination of Freud's concept of bound vs. free cathexis. *J. Amer. Psychoanal. Assn.*, 10:475-525.

—————— (1965), A review of some of Freud's biological assumptions and their influence on his theories. *Psychoanalysis and Current Biological Thought,* ed. N. S. Greenfield & W. C. Lewis. Madison: University of Wisconsin Press, pp. 93-124.

—————— (1967a), Ego autonomy re-evaluated. *Internat. J. Psychiat.,* 3:481-503.

—————— (1967b), Beyond vitalism and mechanism: Freud's concept of psychic energy. *Science and Psychoanalysis,* 11:1-41, ed. J. Masserman. New York: Grune & Stratton.

—————— (1972), Freud's mechanistic and humanistic images of man. In: *Psychoanalysis and Contemporary Science,* 1:3-24, ed. R. Holt & E. Peterfreund. New York: Macmillan.

Krystal, H. (1973), Psychic Reality. Paper presented at the meeting of the Michigan Psychoanalytic Society, Southfield, Michigan.

Panel (1963), The concept of psychic energy, A. H. Modell, reporter. *J. Amer. Psychoanal. Assn.*, 11:605-618.

Peterfreund, E. (1971), *Information, Systems, and Psychoanalysis* [*Psychol. Issues,* Monog. 25/26]. New York: International Universities Press.

Piaget, J. (1937), *The Construction of Reality in the Child.* New York: Basic Books, 1954.

Rubinstein, B. (1965), Psychoanalytic theory and the mind-body problem. In: *Psychoanalysis and Current Biological Thought,* ed. N. S. Greenfield & W. C. Lewis. Madison: University of Wisconsin Press, pp. 35-56.

—————— (1967), Explanation and mere description: A metascientific examination of certain aspects of the psychoanalytic theory of motivation. In: *Motives and Thought,* ed. R. Holt. New York: International Universities Press, pp. 20-77.

Schafer, R. (1967), Ego autonomy and the return of repression. *Internat. J. Psychiat.,* 3:515-518.

Sterba, R. (1930), Zur Problematik der Sublimierungslehre. *Internat. Z. Psychoan.,* 16.

—————— (1968), *Introduction to the Psychoanalytic Theory of the Libido,* 3rd ed. New York: Robert Brunner.

March, 1974

A Conceptual Analysis of Empathy

FAY HORTON SAWYIER, PH.D. (*Chicago*)

Empathy is a polymorphous concept. It is used as a capacity word, a disposition word, and an activity word, but the category of capacity has a general logical priority. All the branches of the concept of empathy depend on whether or not we can feel (perceive) the feelings (emotions) of other people. It is this perceptual core of the various usages of the concept that I explore in what follows.

In the opening sections, I examine some of the ordinary descriptions of and objections to this concept. Next, I isolate and try to support those properties associated with the thesis that empathy is a feeling, a "-pathy." Following that, I develop the further implications associated with the prefix "em-", leading up to some admittedly speculative attempts to explain how a capacity analyzed in this way is possible. And, in conclusion, I suggest several human tasks that are facilitated by the capacity for empathic perception. For, in empathy, one comes truly to feel with another individual, and access to this individual and to his idiosyncratic temporal ordering is exactly what empathic "observation" can order and detached registration cannot.

Many students of behavior mention a kind of awareness that is not identifiable with sense perception. In anthropology and sociology and history, one finds advocates of the need to understand from the inside — for example, members of the *Verstehen* school. In order to understand what something *means* to a person or a culture, one is admonished to get inside the skin of the members of this alien culture. Since important areas of human activity are meaning-bound, and, moreover, since these meanings can never be gained by detached outsiders, one is urged to somehow get inside and feel these meanings for oneself. Consequently the social scientist will discover the key to the meaning if he can rightly and genuinely feel some elements from the alien culture. Once he has

37

hold of a part of himself, as it were, within the feelings of a cohesive alien group, he can use his own network of feelings to learn his way around their maze. Such an act, in turn, requires that the social scientist truly allow closeness, that he not utilize any of the available array of distancing techniques.[1]

The term empathy has also been used by aestheticians and by psychotherapists. And I believe that it is implicit as well in certain areas of what we think of as the moral point of view. Nor are recent studies in animal behavior wholly remote from this concept; in order to understand the key to another species, we must enter in: the observer often must almost become a mountain gorilla, a seal, an ape, etc. Lastly, common to all these disciplines is a clearly sustained sense of the difference between, for example, *thinking* what it would be like if you were a hunted rabbit and suddenly getting from some bodily posture or motions—a frantic over-the-shoulder glance?—the *feel* from the animal, there and then.[2]

So far, a rough approach to the concept of empathy seems to be unproblematic, and the position it plays in the behavioral sciences appears to be central. Yet powerful criticism of this concept has been made by scientists, positivistically minded philosophers,[3] and some behaviorists. Roughly, they either deny that there is any such capacity or activity as empathy, or they say that, were it to exist, it would be untestable and therefore empirically meaningless. Let me try to summarize their objections.

1. Since our understanding of an external world arises out of sensations, and since the person understood in presumptive empathy is external, it follows either that the inner structure of empathic dynamics also rests on sensation or else that it is a confused name for a nonexistent process.

2. The common tendency to reify attitudes, activities, and needs is only a kind of shorthand, and the "things" so constructed must not be construed as real. The language of empathy is full of such reifications and encourages us to lose sight of the actual entities out of which these abstractions have been built.

---

[1] Obviously, there will be times when a group simply will not permit an outsider to catch its emotional key. It is important to take from this discussion of cultural empathy the underlying assumption that cultures are not encapsulated behind impenetrable walls.

[2] Indeed, is it not this very "feel" from which hunters and surgeons must wall themselves off? One thinks of the rabbit hunt in Lampedusa's (1960) novel *The Leopard*.

[3] Inner states (at least those of others) are inferred and therefore hypothetical. They need, as Wittgenstein (1953) remarked, outer criteria. Frequently, and perhaps always when the inner state *is* "factored" into its observable constituents, the inwardness is redundant—a ghost, as Ryle (1949) commented, whose function is to save the day for mentalists.

3. No science and no responsible truth-claim can be a purely private matter. But feelings have always been construed to be the central example of what we mean by the "purely private" (the invisible, for instance). Consequently, either feelings are in truth not private or else empathic understanding is a misnomer for there is no question of true or false at stake and no meaning to right or wrong.

The attitude of hard science toward the empathic and *Verstehen* schools, then, is that they are silly and unscientific and will soon, like the concepts of the ether and of the soul, fade away. I would add that the more thoughtful hard scientists probably believe that these "empathizers" are yielding to the ancient temptation to endow man with some special and nonnatural qualities; that they are, as Freud might have put it, reacting to the scientific shocks to our species' narcissism.

From what has been asserted about feelings, it is probable that before we can advance much further into the articulation of the concept of empathy we must get a clearer idea of the concept of feeling, of "-pathy." The results reached in this section will tend to show that emotions are not only "real" and "objective," but can, like reasoning and sense perception, responsibly be said to be tools for understanding. Whitehead (1929) argued that our notion of sense perception or sensation is already itself a sophisticated, high abstraction, and that the primordial datum is one of feeling; it is emotion-laden. For him, the primacy of feelings was a philosophical as well as a biological fact. Freud (1915), although working in another medium, is saying something similar when he puts the metaphor of the infant's dawning differentiation of inside and outside in terms of (a) pain/pleasure and (b) those pains that are escapable by some bodily motion, as against those that travel along with one, indeed, even into sleep. Supporting evidence for this primitive unity or conglomerate can be seen in certain aesthetic phenomena. We experience something like synesthesia with respect to some colors, sounds, shapes; that is, they, too, are emotional, and not merely sensations. (Doubtless a good phenomenologist could do an extensive job in this area, for example, with the interplay of touch and feeling.) My first point, then, is that although we learn to categorize certain feelings as out-there sensations and certain others as in-here emotions, the radical dichotomy between them is artificial.

Secondly, feelings are had, not made, at least with respect to the moments of their occurrence. This is an important point, because when we fill in the concept of empathy, part of what we imply is that the empathizer has himself had some things happen to him right then; it is not just that he has thought hard, or tried to figure something out.

39

Thinking itself cannot be utterly distinct from feeling either, of course, but Kant and Freud were probably right in proposing that thinking is more active than passive and that, although we can in some degree *decide* to think about *a, b,* or *c,* we cannot, by thinking, quite taste apricots.

However, having established that feelings happen to us and are in some sense event-like, we now leave the temporal for the spatial dimension, and raise the problem of where feelings take place or exist; i.e., we confront hard-line realist objections. The natural response to such an odd inquiry is something like "inside" or "nowhere" or "most inwardly and privately." What, then, would it mean to say that an emotion, a fear, for example, is visible? Surely I can conceal my fear from you. Often, in curious ways, I conceal my fear even from myself. Yes, but an entity that can be concealed is necessarily an entity whose ordinary position is open and visible. Obviously, if my fear were *in principle* private and invisible, then there would never arise a language of concealing it. Consequently, in the first instance, emotions are public and observable entities. But what can that mean? How can my fear be something that *you* can see?

The idea that emotions, like thoughts, constitute a separate realm of reality—the "mental" or the "psychic"—to which the feeler or the thinker alone has access, is enmeshed in a highly complicated antique mythology into which I do not plan to enter. Instead of trying to undermine such dualism, I suggest that there is, at least originally, no real gap through which one can drive a wedge between the inward feeling of an emotion and the outward expression of it. The specific ways in which emotions are expressed vary somewhat from culture to culture and are taught (or "shaped") from mother to infant, for the most part. Furthermore, whatever neurophysiology may be involved, I suspect that the James-Lange theory of emotions (which is in large measure picked up later by Sartre) was helpful at least in its focus on the primary unity of feeling and showing. But to say this is to repeat that the inner, nonphysical feeling and the expression of it in words or gestures or quakes and quavers are not finally two distinct events.

This does not settle all problems—even those of observation, let alone of empathy. First of all, in order to understand or to see that what I am visibly showing is, say, jealousy, you must have a working concept of jealousy. You must not only be a co-member of my emotional language community (those for whom jealousy appears in such and such characteristic behaviors), but you must put these behaviors together, interpret, and integrate them correctly. Take even a simple case: I scream "in pain" and you have no problem with deafness, etc. How is it that you hear it as a "scream of pain"? In particular, if you had (a) never felt pain and (b) never had the fleeting self-awareness required to associate your own pain and your screams, would you hear my pain? I think not, at least not as pain. As Aristotle said, the principle of the unification of a number of superficially unrelated signs would be missing unless you had yourself been hurt. One might want to object that a sophisticated machine could give a read-out of fear, jealousy, etc., quite well, even though, as we assume *a priori*, it cannot itself have "felt" them. To say this is really to support the importance of the unification thesis, for the principles of grouping assigned to the machine are assigned (ultimately) by creatures who do know the language of feeling. For the rest, one might argue with some plausibility that a machine could be a better observer inasmuch as it is incapable of switching off.

But we remain rather remote from empathy, as I started to describe it in earlier sections of this paper. So far, in this discussion of "-pathy," we found that emotions are not primordially "ghostly" invisible entities and also that the read-out of the language of feelings can be made only by a receiver that has at some point experienced at least the gross constancies involved. But this seems rather like a weatherman who reads off the signs of a tornado. To be sure, he must know what "tornado" means in order to put together its signs, but it does not at all follow that tornados matter to him. By contrast, it does seem to be the case that a potentiality for arousing the feelings of the empathizer is essential to the empathic process. Here it is appropriate to recall the anthropological allusions with which this paper opened, for I want to bring back the idea that aroused feelings can themselves serve as observational modes. You remember we suggested that to understand alien cultures one must, ultimately, *feel* with at least some fragment of them and then let that wisp of co-feeling constitute a guide to the alien network. So do we now consider it implicit in the concept of your empathy with me *not only* that my feelings matter to you, that you are not emotionally detached from me or from them, but also that a part of your very "noticing" of my feelings is not exclusively a sensory attention to cues and expressions of my emotion, *but* that this noticing is itself emotional. You have a kind of resonant access to my feelings through your own feelings. Contrary to the orthodox philosophical and scientific positon, therefore, emotions become a third partner, along with reason and sense perception, in the enterprise of understanding.

It is steadying to drop back once again to the dictionary, to the roots of this compound noun, which was a term invented by Theodore Lipps in 1903. Lipps suggested that when we "see sadness" in a painting or "hear

41

joy" in music, it is because we have projected a certain subliminal, sensory-muscular accompaniment of emotion onto the object and have then, as it were, seen the feeling there. I feel my feelings inside of something external to me. I feel inside of an outside. I have commented briefly on the senses in which emotions are public[4] objects (externalizable), and I shall now consider what is implied by the little phrases "in another" and "external to me."

Someone has counted to two. It is logically necessary that the sense of this/not-this or of two countably distinct entities be in the mind of anyone who conceives the term empathy. We can repeat what is essentially the same point in less austere language by recalling Freud's (1914) descriptions of what was confusingly named "primary narcissism": when there is no distinction between a baby's self and what happens to him and the people and sounds about him; when he is a glorious universal blob, all things are everywhere and all are "in" him. But that empathy is a species of protomerging and is clearly not what is signified by feeling your feelings in me. Still, we recognize that infants, preverbal children, some retarded persons, and many animals — also, it has been suggested, many so-called primitive peoples — have a sensitive and powerful ability to feel what is around them, to know (without awareness or understanding that they know) how the people they are with feel from moment to moment. Within the limits of this paper, no explanation for this asserted fact will be developed, partly because I shall try to avoid discussing the concept of regression, which would probably have to be introduced at about this point. Instead, I suggest that the young child may feel something sad in the air — or may sense, as we sometimes put it, the feeling tone of an occasion, without always recognizing *whose* feelings these are. Indeed the child will often experience them as his own.

Simply by logical analysis, several psychogenetic factors may be extracted by considering the difference between the overwhelmed child and the empathic adult. First of all, since the label "empathic" is not, like "air-breathing," of universal and continual application to human animals, it follows that some interference has arisen since infancy. Many investigators have called attention to a so-called stimulus-barrier, but generally their reference is to the torrential input of sensory stimuli. If it makes sense to claim that the feelings of people (and probably of other animals) around us are themselves a kind of input, that I am subject to them, as it were, then it may make good sense to extend the concept of

---

[4] Analysts (and others) claim to *know* what someone else is feeling, but this claim can make sense only if the emotions of others are perceptible, if they admit intersubjective access. Consequently, it was a necessary step to show the publicity of feelings.

stimulus-barrier to include emotional inputs. If the adult once had an ability that has become ordinarily inaccessible (lost) through the erection of a kind of wall, then what was walled off, and why? To reply that it is others' feelings that are safely quarantined does not satisfy the "why?" part of the question. Only if others' feelings commonly and immediately roused uncomfortable resonances in me would there be any need to wall them off.

We have teased two meanings out of "em-": that there must be two entities involved and that the one who is empathizing must be aware of his separation from the other in order to make emotional as well as cognitive sense of anything like sharing or feeling with. Now, in effect, we want to explore whether we can say anything more restrictive about the kinds of beings with whom we can empathize or the kinds of creatures that are themselves capable of empathy. The latter is an easier question to deal with. Since the concept of empathy implies that an empathizer *feels* something and, according to my argument, that he notices or is perceptually aware of something, it follows that he must be a sentient creature with consciousness of at least some of his feelings. According to our present understanding of machines and with reference to the present generation of computers, this rules out mechanical members of the E-set.

But what about the former issue? Is there a limitation on the range of creatures whose feelings I can feel, especially if I try to do so? Consider a hunted rabbit. In order that I have something akin to empathy with this rabbit, I must have had some notion or experience of what it feels like to be hunted, to be significantly weaker than my pursuers, what it feels like to have my life depend on swiftness, to be desperate for air, etc. Or again, since we know, for we feel it bodily, what it is like to fall, for example, there is no intrinsic problem in putting ourselves in the position (experiential place) of some animal or person falling. This is the necessary shared integration referred to in the earlier discussion of screams of pain. The question naturally arises of whether or not a roughly similar background or culture is essential for person-to-person empathy. For my part, I accept Terence's comment that "I am a man, and nothing human is alien to me." My guess is that there are no emotions of other human beings that are not in principle matchable by every human being, and therefore none that are not in principle accessible. The words *in principle* or *can empathize with* indicate that empathy does not have to occur smoothly, or involuntarily—it includes the effects of art and of *trying*. It is hard to conceive of any human being whose feelings I can in no way feel, no matter what I do or how hard I try. Some presenting states may take a very long time to understand, just as the insides of some cultures may take an exceedingly long time to reach and "internalize." But if John cannot in fact be brought to feel in himself a shadow of Jane's feelings, even though a skilled artist or guide to the imagination has worked and urged and beguiled, then I believe it is safe to assume that John is determined not to feel (or re-feel) such things. Often this rejection of feeling is based on something comparatively obvious, such as the realization that to let oneself feel the feelings of a woman or of an addict or of a "savage" is tacitly to acknowledge his or her humanity; many people are not prepared to do this. Often, the cause of the rejection is purely individual and not generic or racial, etc. And sometimes, of course, the cues, signals, and guides *for* empathy are weak and brief, or the observer is tired, or has his mind on something else. To side with Terence, however, is in effect to deny that any personal or cultural barriers are logically or naturally impregnable and to claim that there are no persons into whose inners we cannot move at least some distance,[5] although feeling one's way "in" — especially when the destination is seemingly alien — may be a slow, stepwise voyage guided by sensitive feedback sensors[6] and carried along by our own feelings.

As a working principle, it is usually held that whenever an organ or a capacity is considered we should ask what use it is, what function it serves. First of all, I want to go back to a comment I made earlier in this paper while reflecting on the prefix "em-"; I said that "contrary to the orthodox scientific position, emotions become a third partner, along with reason and sense perception, in the enterprise of understanding." But of what special use or function might feelings and emotions be in this enterprise? And how can we make sense of someone using his emotions as a method of discovery?

The thesis emerging from the earlier sections is that one can use one's own feelings to gain comprehension of the feelings of someone else. This

---

[5] This claim is opposed to a position developed by some contemporary anthropologists to the effect that a person chiefly is his culture, that the idea of any other meaningful denotation for the concept "basically human" is a special type of pre-Darwinian fantasy. Commonly coupled with this cultural relativism is the axiom that cultures themselves are almost as radically distinct as two different species. The operational metaphor that defines *species* as a biological category involving no cross-breeding is, I suggest, exported inappropriately and perhaps unconsciously into anthropology. My position denies this; in particular, I believe that all human experience (to date at least) is importantly alike, in that every person travels the same route through helpless dependence, language learning, socializing, sexuality, illness, and, usually, grief and pain. Moreover, no human animal occupies a thing-world, but lives primarily in a symbolic or meaning-world in which the particular meanings themselves are often culturally determined.

[6] The best working metaphor here is "following" your partner in dancing, for even the relaxed attentiveness of the follower recalls the loose alertness involved in empathic perception and reminds us of "evenly hovering attention."

proposition implies objectivity, i.e., in the sense that an empirical claim cannot be inaccessible to intersubjective inquiry. It follows that the claim-form "I know your feelings," if empirical, must not only be about quasi-public objects, as I argued earlier, but must be open to confirmation. I must, in principle, be able to err in this claim, and I might be obliged to show that I am right. Furthermore, empathy considered as a heuristic device or tool is still a capacity, and a capacity of any sort (for instance the capacity to hold water) is known or is shown by performance; for capacities are potentialities, the true assertion of which depends upon at least occasional actualizing of them. Similarly, since we have shown empathy to be constituted by feelings, and since feelings in general have been shown to be things-expressed not just things-had or -registered, it follows that empathy, too, must be shown or expressed in order to exist. Therefore, it follows that empathy is not only a feeling of the feelings of another, coupled with a consciousness that such is the case, it also involves a response to those feelings of the other. These responses constitute in turn a partial test[7] for the truth of a claim that one is empathic with another particular person.

Returning, then, to the basic thesis that "one can use one's own feelings to gain understanding of the emotions of another," we derive a further proposition. These feelings of the other person are either inaccessible, or else very much less accessible, through any means other than empathy. Therefore, the general empathy thesis not only lays claim to some empirical objectivity, but also to having some special value. How can this be? For one thing, what could I learn by using my feelings that I might be unable otherwise to glean?

First of all, we may recall that emotions are not abstractions or generalities; they occur in particular, temporal, situational contexts. They are individuated by the time and place and speed and intensity by which they are experienced. Our own voyages in and out of the depths and the heights involve a tremendous number of such relational tags; in the Freudian sublanguage, these tags are characterized as "associations." It is precisely this logic of particulars that reinforces the necessity of the "associations to" a dream or to some other event. It is, as it were, *my* event only when I express those contextual feelings in which the event is embedded for me.

Secondly, and more speculatively, there may be a task specifically associated with the enterprise of being a human being that is facilitated

---

[7]Details of these tests can be found in the psychoanalytic literature. Here I have tried to show only that the idea of a test is intrinsically sound.

by empathy. Consider two people, *A* and *B*, and ask, "what's the good of *B*'s knowing *A*'s feelings? Doesn't *A* already know them?" Now, one reply is that *A* might *not* know; he might be a baby or he might be out of touch with himself and his emotions. But the more illuminating case is the second, the one in which *A* *does* more or less know his own feelings. What, then, is gained by *B*'s knowing them too?

First of all, the possibility of comparison and thus of judgment is created. Emotions can be inappropriate as to intensity, source, direction, etc., and two "hearts," so to speak, are also better than one. Second, we recall my earlier claim that feelings are initially showings or expressings and, as such, are unfinished until seen and understood. Also, as Paul Ricoeur has suggested (1970), specifically human desires and emotions are concerned not with things so much as with the reactive emotions of others. These suggestions, and undoubtedly many others, may converge on one of the ways in which human beings qua human beings are genuinely linked together.

Let us grant that *if* someone could get his own feelings in lockstep with someone else's, then the various extraordinary achievements of shared individuation would be possible. That is, we have described tasks that are not capable of being performed by detached observers but which might be performed by in-tune associates. Yet we do not know *how* two people can become attuned or what the dynamics are. The "now I get it!" of people-perception is usually a kind of inner click; can we make any sense at all of this "inner click"? How can we characterize such fitting together?

Let us focus again on the fleeting rabbit or, better, on Swann standing lopsided on the curb before the Verdurins' party. Note the prevalence of kinesthetic verbs. When we are asked to think about lopsidedness or falling or reaching, we do not ordinarily take flight into abstract and detached description, but allow, and indeed encourage, our bodies to re-feel, to reactivate these kinesthetic states. We stretch a little or we are just a little off balance. This is a kind of physiological imagination and involves, I am convinced, the actual use of nerves and muscles on a microscopic scale. I suspect that some analogous operation may be at work when we feel-with or feel-into another's emotional position — that when *B* feels with or empathizes with *A*, then something like *B*'s "muscle" patterns are reactivated. In feeling your grief, for example, I do not (only) feel compassion and feel sorry for you, nor do I recognize that you are grieved only by your outward signs and by my knowledge of recent events in your life; I feel a shadow of your grief inside of me. I *discover* your grief. By being, usually passively, stimulated to re-experience some grief-muscles of my own, I feel what it is like to be you right now. And here I deliberately use the odd expression "muscles," for, as I have argued in another paper (1964), re-evocation and recall involve a reshaping of a learned past orientation of cerebral nerves and muscles. Somewhat in the way that we make micromuscular adaptations in imagining how it is to be leaning very, very far outward (otherwise we would not, in my view, really be imagining it), so perhaps do we make a microneuromuscular adaptation in imagining what it is like to be in pain or to be the rabbit in flight. In this way, then, the dynamics of empathy may be like that of recollecting particulars from our own pasts, of rediscovering a self. Accordingly, it would be the free use of one's own (previously) felt emotions that characterizes the dynamic description of empathy. By permitting oneself, in effect, the reuse of matching muscles, one lets loose a wave of matched and individuated feelings.

In this last section I have tried to sketch a possible empirical denotation for some of the ordinary language discussions of empathy. We often hear not only that it is timid and morally wrong to distance oneself from another's feelings, but also that only if we relax a bit and trust our own feelings can we indeed come to feel with and understand others. I have tried to suggest that feelings are potentially accessible, that particular and individuated sequences and contexts of emotion (i.e., the real other person instead of the abstraction) are accessible only if we can somehow lock in or tune in our own feeling patterns, and, finally, that this trick may sometimes be comprehended neurophysiologically in a way similar to that by which we reactivate our own past selves.

I have only hinted at the ethical aspects of this task, although I wish now in closing to acknowledge them. To withhold such emotional recognition of other people, even when we are with them, is one factor contributing to the creation of invisible men and to the loss of humanity.

REFERENCES

Freud, S. (1914), On narcissism: An introduction. *Standard Edition*, 14:67-102. London: Hogarth Press, 1957.
_____ (1915), Instincts and their vicissitudes. *Standard Edition*, 14:109-140. London: Hogarth Press, 1957.
Lampedusa, G. di (1960), *The Leopard*. New York: Pantheon.
Lipps, T. (1903), *Psychological Studies*. Baltimore: Williams & Wilkins, 1926.
Ricoeur, P. (1970), *Freud and Philosophy*, trans. D. Savage. New Haven: Yale University Press.
Ryle, G. (1949), *The Concept of Mind*. New York: Barnes & Noble.
Sawyier, F. H. (1964), Remembering particulars. Ph.D. dissertation. University of Chicago.
Whitehead, A. (1929), *Process and Reality*. New York: Macmillan.
Wittgenstein, L. (1953), *Philosophical Investigations*. New York: Macmillan.

September, 1974

Problems of Metascience and Methodology in Clinical Psychoanalytic Research

H. THOMÄ, M.D., and H. KÄCHELE, M.D. (*Ulm, Germany*)

A voluminous literature about the ranking of psychoanalysis among the sciences has sprung up in recent years. The planning and carrying out of our research projects necessitated the clarification of our own ideas about the scientific status of psychoanalysis by discussing essential controversies. Here we want to take up primarily those points of view that influence methods of clinical research. The integration of psychoanalysis with the nomothetical or ideographic sciences, with natural, social, behavioral sciences, or the arts, must be considered an unimportant academic question, unless this coordination results in relevant consequences for research and practice.

There are many reasons for the fact that psychoanalysis has become a focal point for discussion. We would like to specify some of these. Psychoanalysis shares its theoretical problems with all the other sciences that examine human behavior and its psychological and social motivations in the field of human relations. It was Freud who discovered the role of the participant-observer and its far-reaching influence on the observational situation. Since it goes beyond "understanding" in its description of phenomena and in its proposed theories of "explanation" about the

Dr. Thomä is head of the Department of Psychotherapy and Chairman of the Psychosocial Center of Ulm University. Preparation of this paper was aided by the Deutsche Forschungsgemeinschaft (German Research Foundation). This paper was originally published in *Psyche,* XXVII (1973), 205-236, 309-355. The translation, by Hilda Spiegel, is printed with permission of the editor, Dr. A. Mitscherlich.

observations it has obtained, psychoanalysis is situated in a border region of scientific theory.[1]

This anomolous position might account for the fact that there is hardly a modern philosophical movement that has not been concerned with psychoanalysis and its methodology of research. The exponents of "unity of science," those of the logical-empirical theory of analytical science, as well as the followers of the dialectic and hermeneutic movements in philosophy and sociology, all find psychoanalysis to be interesting matter for discussion. It is remarkable that psychoanalysis will not fit into the hermeneutic claim of universality, nor will it be forced into the Procrustean bed of the uniform scientific method of "unity of science." It is not surprising that the exponents of "unity of science" cast doubts on psychoanalytic explanations, because these can only be proven in an interpretive context, while on the other hand psychoanalysis as an "explanatory" theory is not hermeneutic enough. It would be appropriate to react to the critical courting of psychoanalysis with a question in the manner of Gretchen of Goethe's *Faust*: Why should one believe in a unity of science of one or the other kind?

We do not, however, intend to psychoanalyze the claims of the unity-of-science movement in order to have the last word in all matters of scientific truth. Rather, we will endeavor to turn the many valiant efforts and disputes about psychoanalysis to its own advantage. The application of scientific criteria (in the sense of the positivistic theory of science) like replicability, objectification, and validation poses special problems which have been discussed for a long time within psychoanalysis. The discussion of these problems encompasses a field between two extremes, which, in their distribution and valuation, can be seen to belong either to the Anglo-American or to the French-German sphere. While, often too flippantly, we dismiss as positivism the effort to see psychoanalysis as an empirical and verifiable science, the group of behavioristic social scientists rejects "understanding" as a constituting element of the dialogue. If, in psychoanalysis, "understanding" is attained by way of explanation, as stated by Radnitzky (1973, p. xxv), there is the danger that its model will be distorted by exaggerated emphasis on one aspect to the detriment of the other. These diverse attitudes have considerable practical consequences for research and treatment in psychoanalysis because it is a behavioral science with highly theoretical implications. The history of

---

[1] In this translation the terms "understanding" and "explanation" are set in quotation marks when it is important to indicate their terminological rather than their colloquial character. See also Eissler (1968) and Hartmann (1927, 1958).

psychoanalysis itself, up to the most recent arguments among psycho-analysts, shows how vulnerable and unsure it is with regard to "under-standing" itself as a science.

I. Hermeneutics and Psychoanalysis

We will critically illuminate those aspects of hermeneutics that are important for the interpretative technique of psychoanalysis. In this we will proceed along the lines of Apel (1955, 1967, 1971), Gadamer (1965, 1971a, 1971b), Habermas (1967, 1971a, 1971b), and Radnitzky (1973). Our theme will be limited to the relation between the hermeneutic and the psychoanalytic *technology of interpretation*; this limitation will determine our selection and our critical attitude toward its literature. We have arrived at our conclusions by including arguments from philosophy and the theory of science that have also entered into the dispute on the metascientific basis of sociology.[2] They prove useful for the resolution of certain methodological problems in psychoanalysis.

Within this fixed framework, we will content ourselves with examining from a historical point of view those aspects of hermeneutics that are close to the interpretative technique of psychoanalysis in its psychology of "understanding." In order to facilitate communication, we would first like to give a definition in accord with Radnitzky's explanation. The term "hermeneutics"[3] dates from the seventeenth century. It was formed from *hermeneutike techne* and meant a procedure to interpret texts ("the teaching of the art of text interpretation"). In the Greek *technai logikai* (*artes sermonicales*), hermeneutics was in close relation to grammar, rhetoric, and dialectic. Hermeneutics is the science of interpretation according to which interpretation is based on a previous comprehension of the complete meaning of what is to be interpreted and proceeds to the exploration of presumed situational contexts. It is thus a circular theory.

---

[2] This debate is called "Der Positivismusstreit in der deutschen Soziologie" (Adorno et al., 1969). It originated during an International Sociological Congress in Tübingen, 1952. Among others, Adorno and Popper were the prominent proponents.

[3] *Hermeneuo* = I denote my thoughts by words, I interpret, I explain, I expound, I translate. We assume that there was an etymological relation between hermeneutics and Hermes because Hermes, the god of commerce, messenger of the gods, had the duty of an interpreter: he had to translate their messages. Prof. K. Gaiser of Tübingen University, whose help in this and other matters we gratefully acknowledge, has given us the philological opinion that the coupling of Hermes and hermeneutics is based on popular etymology, i.e., on the fortuitous resemblance of these words. *Hermeneuo* actually derives from a root with a meaning identical to "speaking."

Thus it indicates an indissoluble interplay between an "understanding" of the whole and an "understanding" of a part, or between a (subjective) pre-comprehension and an (objective) comprehension of the object. This circle implies a correction based on the feedback between the preliminary "understanding" of the whole text and the interpretation of its parts. The development of hermeneutics was essentially influenced by the exegesis of the Bible, to which the theological background of our present discussion should be ascribed. The theological debate over the theory of hermeneutics is documented in (among others) the principle of Schleiermacher: initially one does not usually arrive at an "understanding," but rather at a misunderstanding, so the problem of "understanding" becomes a theme of epistemology (the theory of knowledge), namely, that we have to already know — that is, we have to have a previous comprehension — in order to investigate something. The clearest expression of the hermeneutic procedure can be found in the arts, in the philology of text interpretations. There, the basic question is: what meaning, what significance did and does this text have?

The step from the interpretation of old texts to the question of their present meaning adds a historical dimension to hermeneutics. Instead of practicing a precritical, normative, and dogmatic transfer and passing-on of tradition, the art of hermeneutics nowadays claims to promote the mediation of traditions within a critical "understanding" of self and history.

Hermeneutics has thus become the instrument of the arts. Albert (1972, p. 15) affirms that it is a technology of interpretation having at its base unspoken assumptions about the regularity and legitimacy of insights in art. Only Heidegger and his followers raised hermeneutics to a "universal outlook with its own peculiar ontological claims" (Albert, 1971, p. 106), which has significantly influenced the humanities.

From philological, theological, and historical hermeneutics, a line leads to "understanding" psychology. The common denominator that connects the psychology of "understanding" with the arts is the claim of putting oneself into somebody else's place, of empathy with a text or with the situation of the other. The sharing of the experiences of another person is one of the prerequisites that makes psychoanalytic treatment possible. Introspection and empathy are essential characteristics of the technical rules of "free association" and of "evenly hovering attention," which supplement each other.

The sentence, "Each understanding is already an identification of the self and of the object, a reconciliation with the one who would be separate, were he outside of this understanding; what I don't understand remains different and alien to me," when translated into contemporary language, could have been written by a psychoanalyst who concerns himself with the nature of empathy (compare, for example, Greenson, 1960, Kohut, 1959). The quoted sentence is from Hegel, as quoted by Apel (1955, p. 170). Kohut (1959, p. 464) affirms that Freud utilized introspection and empathy as scientific instruments for systematic observation and discovery.

The relation between general hermeneutics and psychoanalytic situations works two ways. The analyst starts to understand the patient's (up to now) incomprehensible behavior by retracing its development. Historically genetic "understanding" is thus accomplished, the "understanding" of psychological or psychopathological phenomena in the greater context of a life history. Consequently, the problem of the relation of the part to the whole and vice versa, as well as its interpretation, has to be solved. According to Gadamer (1965), the interpretation starts "where the sense of a text is not immediately comprehensible. One has to interpret wherever one does not trust the immediate appearance of things. The psychologist interprets, not by evaluating life histories in their intended meaning, but by asking about what happened in the unconscious. The historian interprets the data of tradition in the same way, in order to grasp their true meaning, which is expressed and at the same time hidden by them" (p. 319).

In this statement, Gadamer seems to visualize a psychoanalyst; his description highlights depth-psychological questioning. It was precisely the incomprehensible, the seeming senselessness of psychopathological phenomena, that would yield to understanding when it was traced back to its unconscious roots in childhood. The problem Gadamer presents is more than an unimportant little detail: it is the problem of disguised and encoded writing, one of the most difficult ones within hermeneutics. Here, hermeneutical philology seems to arrive at a frontier similar to the one the psychology of "understanding" could not transcend. It is a fact of scientific history that neither static nor genetic "understanding" — in Jaspers' sense — has made essential contributions to the psychogenesis of neurotic or psychotic symptoms, or to their psychotherapy. We have to inquire, therefore, by what means the psychoanalytic method has achieved a larger degree of "understanding." Is the method of psychoanalysis a special, at times partially complemented, hermeneutical, interpretive science? Were old, traditional rules of interpreting only adapted by a special technique in order to conform to the conditions of pathopsychology, or to the psychotherapeutic relation of physician and patient? Do we have to look for the difference that first created the new technical means of interpretive understanding in practice, or is the novelty a new theoretical, explanatory paradigm, as the historian of science, Kuhn (1962), put it? No doubt, by accepting the unconscious, these new technical means, especially the ones concerned with treatment, have added another significant dimension, the dimension of depth, to the philological and historical rules of interpretation. One could therefore call the interpretive technique of psychoanalysis "depth hermeneutics," as do Habermas and Lorenzer (1970). According to Habermas (1971a), psychoanalytic interpretation is concerned with those symbolic connections through which a subject deludes himself. *Depth hermeneutics*, which Habermas contrasts with the philological hermeneutics of Dilthey (1900), is concerned with texts, which show the *self-delusions* of the author. Besides the obvious content (and its connected indirect but intended comments), the texts document a latent part of the orientation of their author that is not available to him, from which he is alienated, but that is nevertheless his own. Depth hermeneutics appears in this context as a process that marks the lifting of alienation, but Habermas states that the real task of hermeneutics, which does not limit itself to philological procedures, consists of combining the analysis of language with the psychological investigation of causal connections.

As we will show later, the subject and method of psychoanalysis, and especially its empirical steps of confirmation, are essentially very different from philological-theological or language-analyzing hermeneutics, so that the concept of "depth hermeneutics" suggests too close a relationship between them. Surely, Freud had taken an understanding attitude: "He had talked to patients, he believed what they told him, instead of using objective methods. But what did he do? He developed methods, while looking at phenomena, that suited these phenomena, and these methods proved to be teachable: this means that a scientific method was created here which would never have originated if the phenomenon had not first been observed by a person endowed equally with the wonderful gift of apprehending phenomena, on the one hand, and understanding them, on the other, with a very critical and very methodical intellect" (von Weizsäcker, 1971, p. 301).

II. The Limits of the Hermeneutical Point of View

The digression into hermeneutics served to put the interpretive technique of psychoanalysis into a larger scientific and historical context. We have disregarded the fact that the psychoanalytic situation implies very special rules of interpretive technique. This accounts for the fact that its interpretive art is very different from all hermeneutical movements and schools. Philological and historical hermeneutics do describe the relationship of interpreter and text as a sort of dialogue, a kind of talk. It is evident, however, that the text, unlike the patient who interacts with the physician, can neither talk nor take an active position pro or con.

This difference becomes equally clear when one considers the methodological difficulties of psychoanalytic biography. In this field, the problem is that a solution of the biographical riddles, as Helene Deutsch (1928) called them, must be found "not by the psychoanalytic method, which can only be used directly and on the living person, but by being armed with analytic knowledge of the processes of mental life" (p. 85). In his introduction to *Neurose und Genialität*, Cremerius (1971) also shows the basic shortcomings of hermeneutical occupation with texts. "The process of interpreting the material, the cornerstone of technique, lacks the cooperation between physician and patient, which, in this context, means deliberation by the patient of the interpretive attempts of the physician. Without it, the psychoanalytic process would be protected neither from speculation and error, nor from arbitrariness and indoctrination" (p. 18).

The basic difference between a textual interpretation and a psychoanalytic situation could be defined by the fact that between physician and patient there exists not only an imaginary interaction like the one in the hermeneutic circle, but also a mutual and real interchange of a very unique kind. From this arises the claim, we believe, that psychoanalysis not only gives plausible interpretations, but also develops an explanatory theory from which one could derive recommendations for actions that have the power to change behavior. As a result, the perception of the psychically alien, the "understanding," becomes integrated into a new function. No consequences for the text arise from its interpretation, be it right or wrong; the interpreter remains to the end bound to his separate world. But for the patient, who has to be understood, the consequences of a correct or incorrect interpretation of the psychically alien are far-reaching. Ricoeur (1970) has underlined the psychological "understanding" aspect of hermeneutics from the point of view of philosophy. In his work, the difference between interpretation of texts and psychoanalytic technique runs the danger of being wiped out. Lorenzer (1970), like Ricoeur, also tries to put reliable insight into the psychically alien on a hermeneutical and psychologically "understanding" basis. His thesis incorporates a fruitful revision of the psychoanalytic theory of symbols and an attempt to reinterpret psychoanalytic work as work about

55

language which tries to comprehend the origins of symptoms and the deformation of language as "excommunication" of private contents from consciousness.[4] We cannot develop these themes of "language destruction and reconstruction" any further in this discussion.

Such attempts to attach the psychoanalytic method unilaterally to *szenisches Verstehen*[5] and to hermeneutics are doomed to fail. It is by chance that psychoanalysis has always been used against the claim of universality by the philosophical advocates of hermeneutics (Gadamer). The "radicalization of the hermeneutical point of view" by Lorenzer (1970, p. 7) leads us to the limits of hermeneutics, where its principal weaknesses become visible. A discussion of Lorenzer's ideas will afford a special opportunity to further analyze the relation between interpretive practice and explanatory theories in psychoanalysis.

In the following discourse, we assume that the psychoanalyst fulfills certain basic conditions and that the process of comprehension is achieved by empathy with the psychically alien. The importance of imagination in the process of insight can hardly be overestimated. As Paula Heimann (1969) states, "We can imagine what and how somebody else feels and thinks; how he experiences anxiety, hope, desperation, vengeance, hate, love, and murderous impulses; what kind of imaginations, fantasies, wish-dreams and impressions, physical pains, etc., he has and how he fills these with psychic content" (p. 9). The psychoanalyst, however, would not only want to understand the thoughts and feelings of the other with the help of his ego functions, which Paula Heimann believes to be the most essential parts of a soberly defined concept of empathy. Rather, he finds himself seeking for insights that are reliable. He is confronted here with a crucial problem of research into the processes of psychoanalysis. How to arrive at a *reliable* knowledge of the psychically alien is, in our opinion and that of Lorenzer, a question of life and death for psychoanalysis as a scientific discipline.

Our preliminary answer to this question is that the psychoanalytic process has to be carried by empathic understanding because it would not otherwise occur. The question of the reliability of the understanding brings us to the problem of validation or falsification in the framework of explanatory theories. There is the question of how it will be decided whether psychic and psychopathological phenomena and their genetic significance have been rightly or wrongly "understood." Is it the "understanding" itself that assumes the decisive validating or falsifying function?

[4] Compare Stierlin's (1972) extensive review.
[5] "Scenic understanding" = a kind of intuitive perception of the whole gestalt by way of the findings of the situations that are conserved in the unconscious in their original gestalt.

We know that, according to its principal proponents (cf. Jaspers, 1948), the psychology of *Verstehen*, though it has not developed a method of systematic observation similar to that of psychoanalysis and does not lay down any general or specific theories of psychogenesis, has to give proof through objective data: "Not by subjective or intersubjective evidence do we ascertain a 'comprehensible context,' but through objective data" (p. 251). In contrast to Jaspers, Lorenzer (1970) believes that, by enlarging static to scenic understanding, the experiencing of evidence can be introduced as a decisive scientific test of reliability. Unlike most other psychoanalysts, by omitting explanatory theories from the treatment situation, he reduces the test of reliability almost completely to the intuitive experience of evidence.

According to Lorenzer, scenic understanding and this assurance occupy a special place in the psychoanalytic apprehension of the psychically alien, along with logical understanding and empathy. Indeed, in the course of a discussion about the process of psychoanalytic conceptualization, one really arrives at matters that cannot be resolved by any logical or psychological understanding of the psychology of consciousness. Scenic understanding embodies a large number of intrapsychic processes in both the analyst and patient, as well as the interpersonal processes of transference and countertransference. In so-called scenic understanding, unconscious processes are involved and are described according to the principles of established models of interaction (Lorenzer, 1970, p. 109). The analyst makes sure of his understanding according to the same psychic mode that occurs in logical and psychological understanding under the name of experiencing of evidence. The experiencing of evidence in scenic understanding is attached to the models of interaction. These models of interaction make it possible to recognize the most varied events as the expression of one and the same scenic arrangement.

These concepts need closer scrutiny, inasmuch as Lorenzer makes them the guide to his treatment process, and even uses them to ascertain the reliability of the recognition of the psychically alien. Since he denies the assumption that explanatory steps are integral parts in the formation of analytic understanding, he is the most exemplary and weighty exponent of putting psychoanalytic knowledge on a basis of pure "understanding" psychology. Lorenzer is convinced that his thesis — that psychoanalytic practice consists in a pure and self-contained process of "understanding" without explanatory steps — will be proven absolutely right by a discussion of the conceptual innovation of scenic understanding. This concept can undoubtedly incorporate elements of psychoanalytic insight into the mental life of others.

57

Scenic understanding finds its conclusive certainty as follows: "It proceeds in analogy with logical comprehension and empathy; it is guaranteed to the analyst through the experiencing of certainty" (Lorenzer, 1970, p. 114). "Experiences of evidence correspond to the perception of good *Gestalten*." It is through the points of view of gestalt psychology, which Devereux (1951), Schmidl (1955), and even earlier, Bernfeld (1934) had evoked in order to explain the successful closure of interpretations, that Lorenzer tries to prove the reliability of experiences of evidence. Indeed, there are some experiences that end up in a persuasive, possibly common "Aha" experience (a "covariant of action") (Bühler, 1927, p. 87). Did the "Aha" experience end all doubt because an insight had become a meaningfully significant gestalt? But precisely what is such a gestalt that will lead up to reliable evidence in the dialogue? Freud's analogy (1896, p. 205), in which he compared the interpretive construction of an infantile "scene" with fitting the pieces of a "child's picture puzzle" together, could perhaps be inserted into some theory of gestalt psychology.[6] For Freud, the crucial step of the scientific procedure in psychoanalysis does not rest upon the subjective evidence, though it might be accompanied, for example, with convincing reconstruction of a traumatic scene, but rather it is that of "therapeutic proof," an observable change of behavior. The additional understanding of the "scene" — in 1896 this consisted of sexual traumas in childhood — could not by any means be justified as correct from within itself, but had to prove itself through the hypothetically required resolution of the symptoms, and through "objectifying of the trauma." Lorenzer's (1970) abstention from securing more supportive evidence has serious consequences for the requirement of reliability. Sometimes he has doubts about the reliability of scenic understanding (pp. 150, 163); the question thus arises: when scenic understanding tries to pinpoint the original incident through all the falsifications of meaning, on what is it based?

Scenic understanding relates to psychoanalytic-drive — or rather motivational — theory, even if Lorenzer (1970) rejects the concept of motivation for psychoanalysis. He sees it as an alien element within psychoanalysis, especially on account of its relationship to behavior. He even fears that the concept of motivation excludes the particular essential task of psychoanalysis (p. 27).[7] We don't have to further substantiate here

---

[6] Kurt Lewin's (1937) gestalt theory is especially close to psychoanalytic theory. It seems very dubious to us that experiences of evidence could gain more reliability through gestalt psychological descriptions (see Bernfeld, 1934).

[7] Lorenzer cannot help but speak of "the unconscious determinants of behavior" (p. 165) and so abolishes his own argument against the use of motivational and behavioral concepts.

that these theses cannot be sustained. Recently, Loewald (1971, p. 71) further developed the psychoanalytic theory of drives into a theory of motivation, proposing the thesis that personal motivation is the basic assumption of psychoanalysis (p. 99). We believe that, in scenic understanding, motivations and their unconscious antecedents are created figuratively through the imagination. It is through his imagination that the psychoanalyst—as Paula Heimann described it—puts himself into the scenes the patient calls forth. However, since Freud's discovery of certain contents of psychic reality, we know that the scenes did not really happen at all in the way the patients remember best. Lorenzer seems to have this problem in mind when he speaks of falsification of meaning. In this context, what is meant by the thesis that the psychoanalyst should approach the original event through scenic understanding? We first have to assume the validity of the theory of trauma in its original and uncut form ("an original event"). Out of this arise, among others, several questions for empirical research: if one defines original events, which mean traumas, according to exterior characteristics, then one should endeavor to objectify these events after one has found them (Freud, 1896; Bonaparte, 1945). If, on the other hand, one considers the inner, the psychic side, in shaping and displacing highly affective events or experiences, then the scenic understanding of these events ought to be proven by a newly created edition of these events in the treatment situation, revealed also by close scrutiny of written records of treatment, until finally the full scene would be reconstructed through "try-out" interaction and language games in the psychoanalytic situation. However, the search for the original events, in the sense of the old trauma theory, or of later psychoanalytic theories is not an end in itself. Rather, psychoanalytic theories advance the hypothesis that a change in behavior should occur after the release of repression and the working through of an incestuous wish, and an imaginary castration threat in the transference neurosis. There is a definite "if-then" hypothesis implied, and therefore psychoanalytic theories can be clinically validated or falsified. The proverb *tertium non datur* is valid for a successful analysis. Here lies the possibility of validation through empirical studies of process, which will prove to be a stronger assurance against errors than gestalt-psychological, weakly supported "experiences of evidence." The latter have a more heuristic function, making possible the formation of hypotheses rather than the corroboration of them. Dilthey (1894) ascribed the formation of hypotheses to "descriptive" as well as to "explanatory" psychology, if only in the various stages of the process of cognition. "Descriptive psychology ends with hypotheses, while explanatory psychology starts with them" (p. 1342). How far descriptive psychological or psycho-pathological-phenomenological comprehension is already governed by hypotheses, and whether theoretical preconceptions have not always and predominantly directed the description and influenced the selection of the phenomena to be described, are questions that have no importance here.[8] Along the lines of Dilthey, Kuiper (1965) would also like to incorporate hypotheses into a decisive stage 'of the psychoanalytic process of cognition and in this way assure its examination.

The problem then shifts to the question whether psychoanalysis is an "explanatory" or, rather, an "understanding" psychology (Eissler, 1968, p. 187). Because of its methodological consequences, we will here discuss the kind of relationship that exists between *understanding* and *explanation* when they intermingle in psychoanalysis. Kuiper (1964) also regards his critical-historical works, and those in the philosophy of science about "understanding" psychology and psychoanalysis, as a contribution toward a methodological consideration of psychoanalysis. He writes: "Without first accounting to oneself which form of psychology to use, one uses all sorts of methods, explanations, and modes of thought indiscriminately. Empathic insight is employed alternatively with constructs that contain models; psychologically empathic connections are not sufficiently differentiated from speculation about the theory of drives: one proves hypotheses in one area with arguments that are taken from the other" (p. 32).

Kuiper believes it especially dangerous if "experiences of evidence" are regarded as decisive (p. 19). Psychological connections are not proven by a feeling of certainty, as is so often stated. Some have wanted to reserve empirical proof for basic correlations—e.g., organic brain disease and dementia—and they have thought that the experiencing of evidence would be sufficient for other psychological connections (in a narrow sense). This is, of course, false. The fact that we deem a connection to be evident does not at all mean that this connection is also valid for the patient whose attitude, or rather whose experience, we try to fathom.

---

[8] Freud (1915a) gives a remarkable example of his scientific thinking in which he describes the interplay between ideas and empirical trial and error:

The true beginning of scientific activity consists rather in describing phenomena and then in proceeding to group, classify and correlate them. Even at the stage of description it is not possible to avoid applying certain abstract ideas to the material in hand, ideas derived from somewhere or other but certainly not from the new observations alone. Such ideas—which will later become the basic concepts of the science—are still more indispensable as the material is further worked over. They must at first necessarily possess some degree of indefiniteness; there can be no question of any clear delimitation of their content. So long as they remain in this condition, we come to an understanding about their meaning by making repeated references to the material of observation from which they appear to have been derived, but upon which, in fact, they have been imposed [p. 117].

Material proof has to be given for a satisfactory explanation; in any case, our opinion has to be supported by empirical inquiry. If we regard the "experiences of evidence" as sufficient reason to accept a connection, then "understanding" psychology becomes a source of error. The "intuitively 'understood connection' stays hypothetical until proven in a definite case" (p. 19). Kohut (1959), another author who has focused particularly on the special importance of introspection, affirms that the insights gained through empathy need many safeguards. We believe that, for the same reason, Eissler emphatically defines psychoanalysis as an explanatory theory, because questions of validation of hypotheses as well as general scientific dialogue would cease with the acceptance of subjective certainty, just as all decisions would be attributed to individual and subjective infallibility. Though Eissler defines psychoanalysis as *psychologia explanans* and not as *psychologia comprendens,* a position opposite to Kuiper's strong affirmation of understanding, we find the two authors in agreement on most of the methodological points. Both ask for objectifying proof, which has to go beyond the descriptive understanding of feelings or certainty. Eissler seems to think of this kind of understanding in saying that it could become the antagonist of scientific explanations. So long as understanding psychological statements claim that the proof of hypotheses is already rendered by exact descriptions, further scientific investigations would indeed be superfluous because the process of cognition would be ended. In our view, Eissler ranks psychoanalysis as a *psychologia explanans.* Like Kuiper, he asserts the provisional quality of descriptive understanding statements and affirms the necessity of proving hypotheses. As a result of the possibility of falsification of psychoanalytic theories. Eissler predicts their reconstruction, which also means a partial refutation. That is why Eissler, like Rapaport, ascribes to various parts of psychoanalytic theory a longer or shorter life expectancy.[9]

In our opinion, it is now clear why, in the history of psychotherapy and psychoanalysis, the question whether psychoanalysis belongs to the explanatory or to the "understanding" psychologies recurs over and over again. For Freud and important theoreticians after him, like Heinz Hartmann, David Rapaport, and many others, the claim that psychoanalysis is an explanatory theory implied a "mental science" (Hartmann, 1927, p. 13), requiring, first of all, strict proof of its hypotheses, proof along the lines of "natural science." As a result of the fact that the

---

[9] That Eissler (1971), on the other hand, tries to revive the generally discarded death drive, fits in well with his prognosis, because the ontological assumptions hidden in the hypothesis of the death drive are explained in their psychological significance. Briefly, Eissler is concerned with the psychological-existential meaning of death and not with its reduction to a drive.

natural sciences and their contemporary norms were to be the principal models for proof, the methodological originality of the empirical, specifically psychoanalytic line of argument was neglected. On the other hand, the radicalizing of the hermeneutical point of view has not enlarged the empirical basis of psychoanalysis at all; to the contrary, it has narrowed it extremely. Abstention from proving hypotheses has been replaced by the autarchy of an intuition that confirms itself by *evidence*. According to Albert, the theological past of hermeneutics is obvious here, as much as it is with Heidegger. It is indisputable, according to authors of such different backgrounds as Abel (1953), Albert (1968, 1971, 1972), Jaspers (1948), Kuiper (1964, 1965), Stegmüller (1969), Weber (1951), that understanding has a heuristic or helpful effect on treatment. But scenic understanding also requires additional proof; hence Lorenzer cannot support his extreme thesis.

How Lorenzer himself views the failure of his hermeneutic radicalism, and at which point of his argument he lets the explanatory theories of psychoanalysis enter into the concept of scenic intuition, is typical. His argument, reduced to its bare essentials (1970, p. 12), is that there is one place inviolate from all errors of theoretical language: psychoanalytic practice (p. 198). Here scenic understanding would be rounded off with a self-contained, flawless, ideal operation, if the inevitable scotomata of psychoanalysts would not disturb their intuition. It is assumed, then, that there is one absolutely certain place for recognizing the psychically alien: psychoanalytic practice — if only the blind spots of psychoanalysts would not cloud their scenic understanding. The psychoanalyst, completely liberated from his scotomata, would know with absolute assurance — and therein lie the consequences of the theory of cognition of this psychologistic utopia — which experiences of evidence are true. Since in ordinary practice the ideal operation of the closed understanding circle is never achieved, the experience of certainty will prove more or less right. That way it would be left completely to subjective judgment whether an understanding curve has come to a convincingly right or wrong closure.

According to Lorenzer, the psychoanalyst tries to fill the gaps in his understanding by bringing in explanatory theory as compensation. This helps him find the thread of understanding again. No doubt, theory can serve as a help in orientation, whenever it functions from the beginning — not, we believe, at the end or as a compensation. The theoretical crutch could only help to point to the right way of perceiving the psychically alien if it no longer had to be examined as to its empirical proof. According to Lorenzer, it seems to be sufficient that the explanatory theories of psychoanalysis can smooth over blind spots and close interrupted understanding curves. In this way, the validity of theory is either presumed or is left to be proven by continued subjective scenic understanding. However, in order to make psychoanalytic practice the crucial place where the proof of its explanatory theories is to be rendered — we would not know where else they could be fully tested — one cannot rely on one single and, as we have seen, uncertain criterion. The radicalization of the hermeneutical point of view and the absolute refusal to objectify anything connected with it can serve neither as a practical nor as a scientific guide.

III. On the Relationship Between the Interpretive Practice of Psychoanalysis and its Explanatory Theories

The closing remarks of the preceding paragraph have a rather large implication: we said that explanatory theories could find their decisive scientific proof nowhere but in psychoanalytic practice. If the psychoanalytic method is not employed and the process takes place outside of the treatment situation, only those parts of a theory can be tested that do not need a special interpersonal relation as a basis of experience and whose statements are not immediately related to therapeutic practice.[10] So, when we speak about explanatory theory here, we mean clinical explanatory theory.

When clinical theories are concretely proven by a given dyad (patient-psychoanalyst), special problems result because method and theory have an especially close connection in psychoanalysis. From here on, we will base our argument on the assumption that there is a close connection between practice and theory; we believe that the psychoanalytic art of interpretation needs theories as a guide. Paraphrasing Popper (1959, p. 423), we would say: interpretations of facts are always made in the light of theories. That the light of psychoanalytic theories can only illuminate very insufficiently each given case, especially at the outset of a treatment, is attributable not to the weaknesses of the theories, but to the inevitable lack of information. However, hypothetical assumptions, by which the interpretive action is directed, come into play at once. But there are

---

[10] Rapaport (1960) believes that experimental proof of psychoanalytic theory for the most part is dubious because "the overwhelming majority of experiments designed to test psychoanalysis propositions display a blatant lack of interest in the meaning, within the theory of psychoanalysis, of the propositions tested. Thus most of them certainly did not measure what they purported to; as for the rest, it is unclear whether they did or not" (p. 113).

other, even contradictory opinions: MacIntyre (1958) claims that psycho-analysis as psychotherapy is relatively autonomous in relation to psycho-analytic theory. He adds for emphasis: "Freud's method of treatment is not altogether dependent — and this may be an understatement — on his theoretical speculation" (p. 86).

When one looks at the reasons given for the relative or even absolute autonomy of the technique, one finds a *mixtum compositum,* which is made up of presumably practical experiences and of judgments about the state of the theory. We will first present some condensed arguments for the first category — the practical.

Thesis No. 1: There are successes in psychotherapy by physicians whose theoretical knowledge is minimal, not to say zero.

Thesis No. 2: In the course of a treatment, psychoanalysts often grope their way in the dark. In spite of insufficient, and in some situations even completely absent, theoretical orientation, they do the right thing intuitively, as is often said.

Both theses seem to be applicable. But the question arises: what are they advocating? Their arguments are not, as we will show, in favor of the autonomy of practice. Such observations, which are not by any means systematically researched, show that actions that are unconsciously influenced by theory also exist. In every interpersonal relationship the right word can appear at the right time without the necessity of any further theoretical derivations or deliberations. Psychotherapeutic inter-actions are no exception. To put this in psychoanalytic terms, as much can "happen preconsciously" in these interactions as in the psychothera-peutic learning process itself. Practical knowledge can be gained during training, just because psychotherapy is concerned with imparting not theoretical knowledge but immediate experience, whereby it might appear as if theory were abandoned. It is said, for instance, that no theoretical knowledge of neurosis or psychopathology is imparted by the training course in Balint groups. Were this true, it would support the thesis of autonomy of practice because the undebatable therapeutic success of doctors instructed in Balint groups would by definition have been independent of theory. But the appearance is deceptive. Anybody who has participated in Balint groups for a while and, especially, anybody who has seen Balint himself in workshops, knows that theoreti-cal psychoanalytic models were created there in such an effective manner that they were transformed into "prescriptions for action" (see Uexküll, 1963). The most important element in the process of learning in the Balint groups is the fact that one's own action and its continuous correc-tion are the focal point. A continuous effort toward trial and error is maintained in this manner, although its relation to theory is covered up. We would like to remark in passing that it is a rather poor process of learning when theories are only covertly transmitted to students, as if they are being implanted into the "preconscious" in the hope that they can be called forth to action at the right moment. The "preconscious" is neither the proper place of proof, nor has it the proper criteria for showing what constitutes error is the trials and where proof lies.

The untenable thesis of the relative or absolute autonomy of practice from theory contains the old theme of the role of intuition in technique. However, proof of theories by psychoanalytic methods does not require a previous clarification of the question of how the psychoanalyst arrives at interpretations in the course of his practical technique, whether they came about rationally or intuitively. The deciding factor is that the treating psychoanalyst or competent colleagues can agree, on the basis of consensus (see Seitz, 1966; Meyer, 1967), whether or not theoretical guidelines are apparent in the interpretations given.[11]

Theory-testing research into process is further complicated by the combination of general and special variables. We make this distinction to be able to separate the typical variables of the psychoanalytic process from nonspecific factors. Research in psychotherapy demonstrates that the mere expression of empathy and interest for the patient can be helpful and beneficial by itself. An understanding attitude toward the patient, as is demanded by the basic rule of psychoanalysis, can itself have a favorable effect, as we know from the investigations of the Rogerian school (Truax & Mitchell, 1971).

Empathy, "evenly suspended attention," and other typical patterns of ideal behavior, which the psychoanalyst should be able to adopt, are highly susceptible to disturbances. Countertransferences are unavoidable. An insurmountable countertransference can exert an unfavorable influence on the process of treatment, so that success or failure would not be attributable to theory in that particular case. It is completely conceivable that the psychoanalyst in such a case can explain the psychopathology of the patient very well and can give interpretations with correct content. The idea seems to be justified that therapeutic success or failure cannot be cited in the service of validation or falsification of a theory. In the psychoanalytic situation, the light of the "theory" is deflected by the occurrence of subjective influences and by favorable or unfavorable therapeutic and patient variables—not to speak of external factors,

---

[11] "Scientific objectivity can be described as the inter-subjectivity of scientific method" (Popper, 1944, Vol. II, p. 217).

which also can impede treatment. Therefore, it seems justifiable to think that successes or failures cannot be used for validation or falsification of theory. This frequently voiced opinion is partly right and partly wrong. Psychoanalytic theories can only be proven in their subjective form, which they take on in each dyad. Here, "understanding" in the commonly understood sense of the word comes to the fore. Without empathy, the situation would be so transformed, that it would be a completely unsuitable setting for testing psychoanalytic hypotheses (see Rosenkötter, 1969). These reflections show that in psychoanalytic research concerning treatment processes, those situational variables have to be encompassed which codetermine the course of the treatment in a nonspecific way. In order to give validity to the psychoanalytic data gained, scientific research has to be directed especially at the processes of interaction, for instance, phenomena of countertransference, which Perrez (1971, p. 226) has recently pointed out. If, because of countertransference, the psychoanalyst deviates too widely from the typically ideal behavior pattern that the basic rule prescribes, then the ground of psychoanalytic technique has been abandoned and neither falsification nor validation of psychoanalytic theory can be derived from this study of the process.

The struggle to observe the basic rule (A. Freud, 1936), which marks one side of the psychoanalytic interaction, is not lost as long as the interaction is continued. This means that the minimal conditions are fulfilled, i.e., the patient comes, and the psychoanalyst is there for him. The highlights of the struggle show in particular that the psychoanalytic situation serves essentially to clarify the disturbances of communication. Radnitzky's (1973) stylized, pure dialogue, which proceeds by understanding alone, does not exist in practice. Radnitzky, along the lines of Apel (1967), speaks about quasi-naturalistic phases in psychoanalytic treatment, which should start at the limits of understanding. Radnitzky believes that when the dialogue is interrupted, explanatory operations set in, which enlarge the understanding of the self and of the other. This artificial dismemberment seems to have contributed to the idea that explanatory operations, which prove hypotheses, find a satisfactory conclusion and corroboration only through understanding and resumption of an interrupted dialogue. Actually, the dialogue is disturbed from the first moment on, since the psychoanalytic situation is asymmetrically designed, in order to make the hidden distortions of communication clearly visible.

Psychoanalytic theory as a scientific system is, of course, already operative for the psychoanalyst at the outset of a dialogue with a patient.

It offers a special terminology for causal connections and affords a comprehension of the modes of behavior that cannot be grapsed without explanatory schemata.

We will now explore the question of the special means psychoanalytic theory employs. No doubt, the light of the theory shines where interpretations are given in the psychoanalytic situation. It is in the art of interpretation that psychoanalytic hypotheses become instrumental. We want to add a few qualifying remarks to these statements, to avoid misunderstanding. We do not mean to say that theoretical explanations are given in the process of interpretation. In spite of the great variations in individual techniques in psychoanalysis, there is general agreement that theoretical explanations are not effective in therapeutics. Theory itself offers explanations for this fact, but we cannot take these up here.

It would certainly be simpler to prove the scientific reliability of theory if the derivation of interpretations could be easily recognized, i.e., if they were pure hypotheses. Thomä and Houben (1967) have discussed the theoretical and practical difficulties in the employment of interpretations as a means of validating psychoanalytic theories. Our efforts and reflections since then have shown that the problem is even more complex than we had originally thought. It is the instrumental character of interpretations that complicates their functions in proving theory: "We intervene by interpretation in an existing setup with the intention of bringing about certain changes" (p. 681). Due to the instrumental character of interpretation, Farrell (1964) denies their hypothetical basis. He tried to substantiate his argument by referring to Freud's (1909b) statements that psychoanalysis is not an impartial scientific investigation, but a therapeutic measure. Its essence is not to prove anything, but merely to alter something (p. 104). Actually, for a real change in the patient, there is no better proof for the theory than empirical findings; thus, Freud's words imply a true clinical as well as a scientific aim. Consequently, Farrell has to abolish his extreme point of view: he eventually concedes that an interpretation "retains hypothesis-stating, and hence declaration, features. But these are apt to be overlaid by, and lost in, the complicated instrumental context in which this sort of statement functions. Consequently, even though such a statement has declaratory features, it may be difficult on many occasions to discover from its context just what its truth criteria are" (p. 321). Indeed, it is most difficult, especially because it is not enough to test an interpretation within a session (see Wisdom, 1967)—each series of interpretive repetitions in the psychoanalytic process must be evaluated (p. 681).

It does not mitigate against the central role of theory in scientific proof that interpretations as communications always contain more than their — at best — discernible guideline. Interpretations as verbal communications also have unspecified content, which might in a given case outweigh the special psychoanalytic point of reference. Therefore, empirical investigations show that many statements cannot be considered interpretations in a narrower sense. In order to demonstrate the kind of conditions that have to be met in order to derive theoretical proof from interpretations, let us say proof should be shown that prognosticated changes in a patient occur by interpretations referring to the hypothesis of fear of castration, but not by using interpretations referring to the hypothesis of separation anxiety. This way, falsification or validation would be possible only in individual cases. The proof would be limited by the special conditions of trial and error relative to the examination of two alternative hypotheses during a protracted phase of treatment. These limitations result from the structure of psychoanalytic theory, which we will discuss later. We are also omitting here the problem of circularity. This problem exists because proof has to be established of just those theories from which hypotheses are to be derived with the help of interpretations, which in turn contain these hypotheses. We shall discuss the problem of circularity and the question of suggestion in section VI. Here we want to remark that the proof has to be oriented to a standard of the prognosticated change in the patient. In this procedure, the role of resistance has to be considered in advance and not retrospectively. (It does not have to be predicted, but it must be defined. Similarly, in other fields of medicine, one expects no change in a patient if he sabotages therapy.)

For this kind of theoretical proof, it does not matter how the interpretations originate in the mind of the psychoanalyst. Along the lines of Levi's (1963) work, Loch (1965) presented a schema that emphasizes the rational root, the theory-related planning of interpretations, while fully considering the emotional relation to the patient. Lorenzer, who wants to reduce his arguments to a common denominator, affirms in opposition to this that intuition is the origin of interpretations. Cautioned by the controversy between Reik and Reich, one is well advised to take into consideration as valid factors the personal bias of the psychoanalyst. Nothing needs to be added to the work of Kris (1951), who clarified the long-standing controversial issues of "intuition and rational planning" in psychoanalytic psychotherapy. Moreover, neither planned nor intuitive interpretations can take a preponderant place in the studies of process and interaction. Both have to prove themselves through given prognoses and by their effects, which can be objectified. To this end, we presume that certain phases of treatment and their predominantly interpretive working through can be recognized by the analyst himself, and/or consensual validation of other experts. If psychoanalyses are recorded, the psychoanalyst who interprets intuitively can afterward recognize the presumably theoretical and practical points that relate to his intuitive perception. We do not want to hide our own personal bias and would like to express our skepticism about intuition that thinks it can work on objective data and continuous validation without reinsurance. Even retrospective explanation (after the analysis as a whole and after each session), in many instances remains hypothetical and is subject in the further course of analysis to "trial and error." We believe that Freud had the same idea when he cautioned analysts not to draw scientific inferences about a case before the treatment is ended. Freud even advised against interim reports so as not to limit either therapeutic or scientific openness—either "evenly suspended attention" or interest in theoretical proof. Freud seemed to fear that provisional theoretical explanations of the origin of symptoms could, once they are formulated, assume a status they cannot merit: "The distinction between the two attitudes would be meaningless, if we already possessed all the knowledge (*or at least the essential knowledge*) about the psychology of the unconscious and about the structure of the neuroses that we can obtain from psycho-analytic work. At present we are still far from that goal and we ought not to cut ourselves off from the possibility of testing what we have already learnt and of extending our knowledge further" (Freud, 1912, pp. 114-115, italics ours).

All this is about the provisional nature of theoretical assumptions and about creating the best conditions for their proof. Besides the danger that premature theoretical explanations of neuroses, psychoses, and psychosomatic syndromes can amount to fixed prejudices, there exists another, equally unfavorable to therapy and science. This is a technique that overlooks its hypothetical nucleus and thereby the necessity of continuous practical and scientific validation. Technical interpretations in the course of treatment, because of their (latent) hypothetical component, are just as provisional as are theories. Practice reflects the imperfection of theory. At best, it can have the same reliability as theory; otherwise practice would be better than theory. We see in Freud's "Methodology" (Meissner, 1971) that the advice to postpone explanatory synthesis until the end of treatment cannot be taken literally. Even during his education the future psychoanalyst learns something else. Interim reports that present unsystematic clinical proof of theory are currently given in the technical seminars of psychoanalytic institutes. Supervision also has as its aim to try alternative strategies of interpretation according to the behavior of the patient. It is the changes in the technique of interpretation, whether they have been intuitively or rationally arrived at, that, in the course of a treatment or in relation to various symptoms, afford the possibility of giving the clinical theoretical proof that Freud demanded. One should strive to focus on a systematic approach analogous to the aims of brief psychoanalytically oriented therapy (see Malan, 1963). The awareness of the danger Freud described furthers clinical flexibility. Moreover, the repetitions of the transference neuroses will also help to prevent random interpretation and promote the use of a flexible system that can adjust to changes in the patient.

Keeping in mind the previously discussed limiting factors pertaining to interpretations containing a possible hypothetical nucleus, we now take up the question of which kind of theories can be proven clinically.

Empirical inquiry of this type has to confront the problem of falsification. When and why does a psychoanalyst give up one "strategy of interpretation" (Loewenstein, 1951), in favor of another? Are the underlying theoretical explanations already refuted in this case only, or in general? The behavioral and the social sciences have special problems of proving and refuting, which arise from their subject matter and which psychoanalysis confronts in an exemplary way: The combination of method and theory and the mediation by a subject have made it a paradigm for other disciplines (Kuhn, 1962). All this has made psychoanalysis the butt of criticism by theoreticians of science. MacIntyre (1958, pp. 82-83) describes the difference between an experimentalist and a clinician as follows: The experimentalist would like to conduct experiments in which his hypotheses would be falsified and in which situations would arise that would show false hypothesis to be unserviceable. Since he is looking for flaws in his hypothesis, it constitutes a victory for him when he discovers a situation in which his hypothesis breaks down. In contrast to the experimentalist, the clinician's only interest is to promote healing, but it is not true that the clinician is only interested in matters that further the healing process. To the contrary, he is also very much occupied by the question of which factors stand in the way of healing. Thus, the psychoanalyst looks for alternative hypotheses in a given case, even if these cannot be isolated in a way that would permit strict experimental disposition and proof, independent of the subject. MacIntyre then raises the question of what kind of refutation would be valid for psychoanalysts and what would move them basically to change theoretical conceptions. He answers along the lines of Glover (1947) that nothing would move psychoanalysts to change their conceptualizations. But a closer look at Glover's statements shows the reason for MacIntyre's error:

"The basic ideas of psychoanalytic theory could and should be employed as a discipline to survey all theoretical reconstructions of mental development and all etiological theories, which cannot be verified immediately by clinical psychoanalysis.... It is often said, that Freud was ready to change his formulations, if this was necessary for empirical reasons. This is true for some parts of his clinical theory, but in my estimation not for his basic ideas" (p. 1).

It is illuminating that MacIntyre has left out a large part of the original. In the missing part Glover gives some examples of basic ideas: the mobility and quantity of energy of drives and memory traces. Glover is of the opinion that the dynamic, economic, and topographic, namely the metapsychological points of view, can be reduced to three basic ideas. These are the ideas that, according to Glover, cannot be immediately proven empirically by the clinical method and, unlike clinical theory, have not been changed. It is not true, however, that the basic ideas, the metapsychological points of view, have never experienced any changes (see Rapaport & Gill, 1959). Even if these ideas had proved to be rather resistant empirically, one would, first of all, have to explain the reason for it. It is a fact that the psychoanalytic method can only indirectly examine the metapsychological points of view empirically. These are in no way the basis of psychoanalytic practice or clinical theory, but are, rather, their "speculative superstructure" (Freud, 1925, p. 32). Freud (1915b, p. 77; 1933, p. 211) characterizes metapsychology throughout his whole work in this way, but the "witch" keeps on exercising a singular fascination on his whole thought. We believe we can attribute this to the fact that Freud never gave up the idea that the day would come when the psychological and psychopathological observations of psychoanalysis could be traced back to universal laws. Speculations about mental economy in particular show that Freud never completely abandoned "his audacious thought" of the 1895 "Project for a Scientific Psychology," "of fusing the theory of the neuroses and normal psychology with the physiology of the brain" (Kris, 1950, p. 33). Freud's expectations that one day all scientific theories, including the ones of psychoanalysis, could be reduced to microphysical theories can also be seen in the fact that his formulation of specific economic metapsychological assumptions is couched in such physicalistic terms as *energy, displacement, charge*. The farther metapsychological speculations move away from the plateau of observation of the psychoanalytic method, the less such observation will be able to substantiate or to refute the speculative superstructure. The distance between practice and theory can be measured by the terminology: the richer the physicalistic-neurophysiological language of meta-

71

psychology becomes, the more difficult it is to determine its psychological nucleus. The metapsychological points of view can nevertheless be of practical help in orientation, depending on how explicit the rules of correspondence have been made. It could be said in general that meta-psychological assumptions have an empirical scientific significance only if they can be linked to observations by rules of correspondence (Carnap, 1950). Such rules do not furnish a complete definition of the theoretical concepts through the language of observation, but they give an empirical content that is good enough for applicability and examination. When one considers the dynamic, topographic, structural, genetic, or economic assumptions of metapsychology, along the lines of Rapaport's summary (1960), it becomes clear that their proximity to observation varies widely. Their "survival potential" (Rapaport) depends on their nearness to the plateau of observation; without rules of correspondence, they atrophy, even if they seem to be unchanged. Their unchanged state can be a sign that they are not at all basic, but, on the contrary, have been discounted in practice or have not been current or proven practical from the beginning.

The clincal research that led to the so-called Hampstead Index (Sandler et al., 1962) showed how important it is to establish rules of correspondence. The task of relating the observational data of an individual case with the clinical theory of psychoanalysis (and possibly with its metapsychology) makes conceptual precision mandatory as a prerequisite for validation or falsification studies. The therapeutic flexibility of the psychoanalyst will not be narrowed by this; to the contrary, it will rather be widened, because alternatives will be defined and systematized. But mainly, it will become possible to determine more accurately which observational data agree with a clinical hypothesis and which ones refute it. Though the testing of alternative hypotheses is the mark of the psychoanalytic interpretive process, it is not its aim definitely to refute one or another clinical-theoretical explanation of a given case. The analyst, for technical reasons of treatment alone, has to keep himself open to the possibility that a psychodynamic hypothesis considered as refuted in the present phase of the treatment could be revalidated later. Freud's *A Case of Paranoia Running Counter to the Psycho-Analytic Theory of the Disease* (1915b) points up casuistically some problems of falsification of theory in a single case, from which general refutations have to be derived.

The problems of falsification gave rise to an informative discussion between psychoanalysts and theoretical scientists (Hook, 1959), in which Waelder (1962) later took part with a critical review. Hook (p. 214) asked some psychoanalysts what kind of evidence they would deem valid for ascertaining that a child has no Oedipus complex. Hook's question derives from a position within the theory of science that Popper (1959, 1963) introduced as "falsification theory." In his arguments with the logical positivism of the early Vienna Circle, Popper arrived at the conclusion that inductive logic does not provide a "criterion of demarcation" that would facilitate differentiation of the empirical, the metaphysical, the scientific, and the unscientific systems. On the basis of detailed arguments that we cannot take up here (nor can we go into critical considerations of the falsification theory by Kuhn, 1962; C. F. von Weizsäcker, 1971; Wellmer, 1967; or Holzkamp, 1970), Popper concludes that the "criterion of demarcation" is not the verification, but the falsification of a system. Popper demands that the logical form of the system "shall be such that it can be singled out, by means of empirical tests, in a negative sense: *it must be possible for an empirical scientific system to be refuted by experience*" (1959, p. 41; italics Popper's).

Psychoanalysts can agree with this definition of empirical sciences, as shown by a representative quotation from Waelder's (1962) critical review: "if no set of observations is thinkable that would disprove a proposition, what we have is not a scientific theory but a prejudice or a paranoid system" (p. 632). In the light of this agreement in principle, it is rather surprising that psychoanalytic theory has been scientifically criticized from the point of view of the theory of falsification. This comes from demands for the creation of experiments of falsification. The theory of falsification grants scientific status only if *experimenta crucis* can be performed. According to Wellmer (1967, p. 27), the criterion for falsification consists in the fact that only those theories are empirically valid that expose themselves to the risk of experimental refutation. Those would be theories that would "permit" only a genuine subclass of all possible experimental results, while they would "forbid" all the others. Though Popper has shaken the foundations of the scientific theories of the logical positivists of the Vienna Circle with the theory of falsification, he has — although in critical distance from them — followed the same interests, namely, to enthrone the method of experimental natural science as the only valid one. "The 'explanatory theories' or the 'theoretical explanations' of empirical science, according to Popper, should be proven empirically independently from the experiences that they explain. The type of theory that satisfies this requirement is the statement of universal laws. Statements of universal law can be useful for the deduction of limited prognoses that can be proven by planning new experiences, independently of any former ones" (Wellmer, p. 13).

73

We are coming back to Hook's question and hope that by our remarks on the theory of falsification we can explain why the answers of the psychoanalysts could not satisfy his requirements for scientific theory. The given, fictitious, diagnostic description of a child without any signs of an oedipal experience or behavior possibly still contains a minimal percentage of the Oedipus complex. Waelder rightly pointed out that the scientifically and experimentally oriented falsification theory neither recognizes the logical structure of the Oedipus complex as a concept of types[12] nor values the possibilities of clinical refutations of theories, because of its restrictively normative conception of science. Besides absolute refutations, there exist other ones, especially in the applied sciences, which are so highly probable that, for all practical purposes, one can call them refutations. The clinical theory of psychoanalysis, particularly in its special part, contains descriptions of pathogenesis in autistic children or in preoedipally disturbed grownups, who "practically refuted the Oedipus complex." So one could say that the Oedipus complex was already refuted by the psychoanalytic method before Hook formulated his question on the basis of the theory of falsification. In fact, in testing clinical alternatives of pathogenic connections, considerations develop for conceiving a scale along which the Oedipus complex dissolves itself into its components and can thus be conceptualized as having zero effectiveness, as in the case of a paranoia of jealousy, "which went back to a fixation in the pre-oedipal stage and had never reached the Oedipus situation at all" (Freud, 1933, p. 130). It is evident that in a diagnostic and prognostic evaluation of the case — i.e., in the clinical validation of theory — positive and negative signs are compared and weighed against each other. Therefore, Hook's question is highly relevant because it could lead to a thoroughly necessary and desirable increase in the precision of the theory by its demand to provide a negative definition. It is, at any rate, not easy to explain, because of the different levels of abstraction in psychoanalytic theory, which one of its regions can be proved valid by interpretive practice.

In conclusion, we shall give a summary of the different levels of psychoanalytic theory, in order to mark the regions that are most relevant in empirical testing of the psychoanalytic theory. We will use Waelder's schema (1962) because of its clarity.

The schema differentiates:

1. *Data of observation.* These are the data the psychoanalyst receives from his patient and which, generally, are not available to others. These

---

[12] Compare the explanations of Hempel, 1952, and Kempski, 1952.

data form the level of observation. They become subject to interpretation relative to their connection with each other and their relation to other modes of behavior or to conscious or unconscious contents. Here we are at the plane of *individual clinical interpretation* (Freud's individual "historic" interpretation, 1916-1917, p. 270).

2. *Generalizations*. From the individual data and their interpretations derive generalizations, which lead to certain assertions in regard to patients, formation of symptoms, and age groupings. This is the level of *"clinical generalization"* (Freud's typical symptoms).

3. *Theoretical concepts*. The clinical interpretations and their generalizations permit the formulation of theoretical concepts, which can already be contained in the interpretations or which could lead to interpretations of, for instance, such concepts as repression, defense, return of the repressed, regression, etc. Here we have the *clinical theory* of psychoanalysis before us.

4. *Metapsychological concepts*. Beyond this clinical theory, without being able to draw a sharp line, are more abstract concepts like cathexis, psychic energy, Eros, death wish, i.e., psychoanalytic *metapsychology*. Especially in metapsychology, or rather behind it, is Freud's personal philosophy (see Wisdom, 1971).

The schema makes a hierarchy of psychoanalytical theories visible; their respective values for scientific theory vary in empirical content. Interpretations relate mainly to clinical theory. They contain explanations, which permit prognoses, as we will point out later. How far the technological aspect of this theoretical area and its theoretical and scientific position apply to the more abstract elements of psychoanalytic theory will be discussed in the following chapters.

In conclusion we want to say that the phenomena that were discovered and interpreted in the therapeutic dialogue have been objectified in a verifiable description by Freud and put into a causal, historical, and genetic connection.

IV. General and Historical Interpretations

Whereas in our last arguments we stressed the explanatory character of psychoanalytic theories, the prominent German sociologist of the "critical school of Frankfurt," Habermas, presents quite a different view of Freud's scientific achievements.

What Habermas sets as his task in his book *Knowledge and Human*

Interests (1971a) is concisely summarized by Nichols (1972) in a short review of that book[13]: "first, to provide a critique of science on the basis of self-reflection — a critique he develops by tracing the various alternatives to positivism provided by idealism, historicism, and phenomenology; and second, to lay some of the foundations for an epistemology which satisfactorily connects knowledge (as theory) with human interests" (p. 18). One of the sciences Habermas is dealing with in great detail is psychoanalysis, as a representative example of a social science that has not yet found its proper philosophical underpinning. Right at the beginning of his chapter "Self-Reflection as Science," Habermas characterizes the traditional self-understanding of psychoanalysis as a scientistic self-misunderstanding (p. 246).[14]

This wrong and misleading understanding of the metascientific status of psychoanalysis would especially concern the evaluation of psychoanalytic theory rather than its practice, i.e., it would regard in particular the research efforts to validate the theory. The origin of this misunderstanding is reconstructed by Habermas in the following way: The basic categories of psychoanalysis were "first derived from experiences of the analytical situation and the interpretation of dreams" (p. 252). The assumptions regarding the functional relations of the psychic apparatus and the origin of symptoms, etc., are "not only *discovered* under determinate conditions of a specifically safeguarded communication," but "they cannot be displayed independently from these" (p. 307). It follows from this that "psychoanalytic theory formation is embedded in the context of self-reflection" (p. 252). The connection of the structural model, which originally was derived from the communications between doctor and patient, with the model of energy distribution would then constitute the decisive and misleading step: that Freud "did not comprehend metapsychology as the only thing it can be in the system of reference of self-reflection: a general interpretation of self-formative processes" (p. 252).[15]

According to Habermas, "it would be reasonable to reserve the name metapsychology for the fundamental assumptions about the pathological

---

[13] During the preparation of this English translation of our paper, we realized that we are in considerable agreement with most of Nichols' critical remarks.

[14] *Scientism* means, according to von Hayek, "the slavish imitation of the method and language of science" (Popper, 1957, p. 105).

[15] A self-formative process signifies the cultural correlate to the biological process of development from childhood to adulthood. It comprises the process of education, of training, and of growing self-awareness that can be summarized also in a concept of growing psychosocial identity. The category of *Bildung* (self-formation) is central to the philosophical idea of enlightenment and played a great role in Germany's cultural development during the last centuries.

connection between ordinary language and interaction" (p. 254). A metapsychology thus conceived would be not an empirical theory but a methodological discipline, which, as metahermeneutics, would have to explicate "the conditions of the possibility of psychoanalytic knowledge." Whether Habermas has any use at all for the classical metapsychological points of view, remains obscure.

We have already dealt with the role of metapsychology in the process of psychoanalytic insight (*Erkenntnis*) and with the question of clinical verification of metapsychological viewpoints. The notion that, for many metapsychological viewpoints, it is impossible to set up rules of correspondence implies that vast areas of metapsychology belong to the speculative superstructure of psychoanalysis, which can hardly be verified by empirical-clinical methods.[16]

In any case, between the various chapters in the building of psychoanalytical theory, there exist, as we have seen, a great number of indirect connections, so that from the observations that can be made on the "ground floor," accessible to all, conclusions can be drawn for what is supposed to occur on higher or lower floors. Thus, on the one hand, metapsychology plays a much smaller role than Habermas ascribes to it, and, on the other hand, it can be scientifically verified to a limited extent, though it belongs mostly to the speculative superstructure. In this state of affairs, metapsychology does not lend itself at all to being used as a metahermeneutic approach.

The methodological discipline proposed by Habermas is not affected by this criticism of the misunderstanding, which, in our opinion, crept into Habermas' reception of the concept of metapsychology. We believe that the methodological position of general interpretations[17] would gain little if one gave it a superstructure (*like* metahermeneutics) that is in some way related to metapsychology. To this superstructure would adhere, in our opinion, all those obscurities that characterize the relationship between clinical theory and metapsychology. The methodological significance of general interpretations is sufficiently independent.

[16] Cf. Freud (1914a): "But I am of opinion that that is just the difference between a speculative theory and a science erected on empirical interpretation. The latter will not envy speculation its privilege of having a smooth, logically unassailable foundation, but will gladly content itself with nebulous, scarcely imaginable basic concepts, which it hopes to apprehend more clearly in the course of its development, or which it is even prepared to replace by others. For these ideas are not the foundation of science, upon which everything rests: that foundation is observation alone. They are not the bottom but the top of the whole structure, and they can be replaced and discarded without damaging it" (p. 77).

[17] As we will specifically show later, the concept of *general interpretations* comes from Popper, who introduced it for historical explanations.

With these, Habermas has described strategies of research that are simultaneously of self-reflection. On the level of self-reflection, as distinguished from the logic of the natural sciences and humanities, something like a methodology separated from its content is not possible, because the structure of the context of knowledge is one with that of the object under examination. The general interpretations, however, are also distinguished by Habermas from metahermeneutical statements: "For, like theories in the empirical sciences . . . general interpretations are directly accessible to empirical corroboration. In contrast, basic metahermeneutical assumptions about communicative action, language deformation, and behavioral pathology derive from subsequent reflection on the conditions of possible psychoanalytic knowledge. They can be confirmed or rejected only indirectly, with regard to the outcome of, so to speak, an entire category of processes of inquiry" (p. 255).

Habermas thus characterizes those laws, the metascientific status that we questioned in the beginning, as "general interpretations." It would be wrong to understand these to be psychoanalytic interpretations (*Deutungen*) in the technical sense in which the word is used in treatment. On the contrary, they can be conceived of as patterns of early childhood development that can be applied as interpretive schemas for individual life histories. They consist of "assumptions about interaction patterns of the child and his primary reference persons, about corresponding conflicts and forms of conflict mastery, and about the personality structures that result at the end of the processes of early childhood socialization, with their potential for subsequent life history. These personality structures even make possible conditional predictions" (p. 258). In this framework, general interpretations are developed that are the result of various and repeated clinical experiences. They have been derived according to the elastic procedure of hermeneutic anticipations (p. 259). The basic outline of the whole proposition developed here by Habermas, which alone makes possible the experiences outlined so far, is the consideration of the life history[18] as a self-formative process (*Bildungsprozess*), which, in the case of a patient, is characterized as disturbance. In line with this, the object of psychoanalytic treatment is "the interrupted self-formative process," which, by the experience of self-reflection, is brought to its end. Regarding general interpretations, we now must keep in mind that, contrary to interpretations in the technical sense used in treatment, as soon as an interpretation claims the status of

---

[18] Habermas places the reconstruction of the life history entirely in the center of his discussions. In fact, however, the working-through of the transference neurosis in the here and now plays a much greater role therapeutically than the reconstruction of the past.

"general," it is removed from the hermeneutic method of continuous correction of preliminary understanding by the text. Therefore, it is true of general interpretations that they are fixed, as distinguished from the hermeneutic anticipation of the philologist. With this Habermas means that general interpretations have a theoretical anchorage, insofar as they imply at least generalizing statements which must be demonstrable in the individual case and which therefore are exempt from the permanent change through the hermeneutic circle. Therefore, general interpretations must be verified by derived prognoses. If, further, one takes into account that the reconstructive postdictions (statements after the fact) — which, with the model of the general interpretation, can as narrative forms be derived for the individual case — also have for Habermas the character of hypotheses, which are fallible, then we have found thus far in these discussions clear indications that the aforementioned sentence of Popper (*"it must be possible for an empirical scientific system to be refuted by experience"*) is also valid for psychoanalysis (1959, p. 41; see also p. 73).

So far, Habermas' clarification of the metascientific position of psychoanalysis seems to offer the following advantages: uncovering of the scientistic misunderstanding leads to the question of how far an imitation in psychoanalysis of the methods of the natural sciences that are not appropriate for their object has brought empirical research to an impasse. Insofar as the verdict of scientistic self-misunderstanding concerns many a metapsychological viewpoint — the model of energy distribution,[19] for instance — Habermas' critique corresponds well with similar conceptions held by quite a few psychoanalysts (i.e., Rosenblatt & Thickstun, 1970; Holt, 1962, 1965). The problems involved in the concept of "psychic energy" are, of course, discussed by many more authors than we can refer to in the context of this paper (see esp. Shope, 1971).

From Habermas' argumentation, it follows, as from similar discussions (like those of Rosenblatt and Thickstun, and Holt) that it would be misleading to look for the great X of psychic energy, which, as Freud (1920a) said, enters as an unknown into all our equations, by way of psychology. The conclusion that psychoanalysis belongs to the humanities and not to the natural sciences could contribute to the stimulation of

---

[19] We would have before us a law of natural science, if one succeeded in verifying empirically the psychoanalytic model of energy distribution, in showing measurable conversion (*Wandlung*) of energy, and in deducing prognoses with the knowledge of specific border conditions. There were fundamental reasons for the fact that the efforts undertaken by Bernfeld and Feitelberg in this direction had to fail. "The energy-distribution model only creates the semblance that psychoanalytic statements are about measurable transformations of energy" (Habermas, 1971a, p. 253).

empirical research appropriate to the object of psychotherapy. Following Habermas, this research should refer to the general interpretations covering the realm of the clinical theory of psychoanalysis.

The characterization of psychoanalytic clinical laws as "general interpretations," as systematized historical knowledge, doubtlessly facilitates the understanding of the specific situation of psychoanalysis. Moreover, if one sees as central that the general interpretations must be tested against derived prognoses, then a clear dividing line to the philological-hermeneutic procedure has been drawn and empirical research has been secured to the extent of establishing expected behavioral changes — hopefully, in accordance with the theory. It is tempting to turn with this understanding to the verification of psychoanalytic theses. Habermas would then, a difference in terminology aside, come close to Popper. To be sure, Habermas moves again in another direction, when he deduces the degree of validity only from the patient's self-reflection.

In contrast to the instrumentalistic viewpoint of the purposive-rational organization of means or of adaptive behavior, the elementary events of a psychoanalytic dialogue are processes in a drama: the functional relationship of disturbed self-formative processes and neurotic symptoms must be understood in the light of a dramatic model. "That is, the elementary processes appear as parts of a structure of interactions through which a 'meaning' is realized. We cannot equate this meaning with ends that are realized through means, on the model of the craftsman. What is at issue is not a category of meaning that is taken from the behavioral system of instrumental action, such as the maintenance of the state of a system under changing external conditions. It is a question, rather, of a meaning that, even if it is not intended as such, takes form in the course of communicative action and articulates itself reflectively as the experience of life history. This is the way in which 'meaning' discloses itself in the course of a drama" (Habermas, 1971a, p. 260).

In the drama of the self-formative process, the subject is at once both actor and critic. The goal of the process is the capacity of the subject to relate his own history and comprehend the inhibitions that blocked the path of self-reflection. "For the final state of a self-formative process is attained only if the subject remembers its identifications and alienations, the objectivations forced upon him and the reflections it arrived at, as the path upon which it constituted itself" (p. 260).

While on the one hand Habermas restores the relation to Freud's empirical-scientific thinking through the concept of general interpretations borrowed from Popper, on the other hand certain romantic elements, which are far removed from Freud's sober notion of education, seem to enter into the goal-conception of the self-formative process. Albert's (1971, p. 55) plea for a critical rationalism could include Freud's intention insofar as he justly indicates a certain linking of hermeneutics and dialectics as "German ideology," and opposes this to Freud's natural-scientific maxims. In the following discussion, we shall take a look at the consequences that result from Habermas' argument for the verification of general interpretations. The minuteness with which we refer to Habermas' philosophical exegesis of psychoanalysis is justified by the radical consequences of the announced verification of the "general interpretations," which, according to Habermas, result from it.

The metapsychologically founded, systematically generalized history of an infantile development enables the psychoanalyst to make "interpretive suggestions for a story the patient cannot tell" (Habermas, 1971a, p. 260). Because of this, the interpretation of a particular case proves itself "only by the successful continuation of an interrupted self-formative process" (p. 260). On the basis of this, Habermas can conclude that "analytic insights" possess validity for the analyst only after they have been accepted as knowledge by the analysand himself. For the empirical accuracy of general interpretations depends, not on controlled observation and the subsequent communication among investigators, but rather on the accomplishment of self-reflection and the subsequent communication between the investigator and his "object" (p. 261). With this, the general interpretations are marked off from statements regarding an object domain that are made in the context of general theories. While the latter remain exterior to the object domain, the validity of the former depends on the fact that "statements about the object domain [are] applied by the 'objects,' that is, the persons concerned, to themselves" (p. 261). The distinction between the empirical validity of general interpretations and that of general theories is characterized by Habermas as follows: In the behavioral system of instrumental action, the application of assumptions to the reality remains the concern of the inquiring subject. In the behavioral system of self-reflection, the application of statements is possible only via the self-application of the research object that participates in the process of insight. In short: general interpretations have validity only to the degree "that those who are made the object of individual interpretations know and recognize themselves in these interpretations" (p. 261).

Only now it becomes evident how clearly Habermas tries to draw the dividing line between general theories — which can be falsified — and general interpretations — which must be tested by the reflexivity attained by the patient. This effort to draw a dividing line cannot, however, be maintained by Habermas himself, nor are psychoanalytic practice and research in agreement with him. The contradictions in which Habermas becomes entangled can be traced back to the fact that the general interpretations on the one hand move too far from such evidence as is required for general theories, and on the other hand must prove their value in the distribution of clinical success and failure. These, however, following Habermas, evade intersubjective evaluation: "The criterion in virtue of which false constructions fail does not coincide with either controlled observation or communicative experience. The interpretation of a case is corroborated only by the successful *continuation of a self-formative process,* and not in any unmistakable way by what the patient says or how he behaves. Here, success and failure cannot be intersubjectively established, as is possible in the framework of instrumental action or that of communicative action, each in its way" (p. 266; our italics).

We cannot understand how Habermas relates the distribution of clinical success and failure to the patient's experience of reflection. Introspection and reflection are, precisely as psychoanalysis has shown, subject to serious self-deception. Whether the force of an unconscious motive is broken reveals itself objectively exactly there where it can be ascertained intersubjectively: in symptoms and changes in behavior. Besides, free association at first leads away from goal-oriented introspective reflection and expands it when it overcomes resistances. There is probably no analyst who bases the way in which he conducts his treatment only on the reflection of the patient, on his self-formative process, or takes it as the only proof of interpretive hypotheses. The experience of the patient, which he accumulates in the course of a psychoanalytic treatment, and as a result of which he arrives at a new interpretation of his life situation, is one aspect in which the success of the treatment manifests itself to the patient. On the other hand, there is an evaluation of the success of the treatment in the sense of objective proof of a successful psychic change, which can be fairly well operationalized and subjected to scientifically controlled testing. Habermas' discussion introduces the leading utopian idea that an enlightened subject disposes of the history of his "becoming himself"; this is, in our opinion, overestimation of self-reflection. It is easily overlooked that the emancipatory character of psychoanalysis is documented not only by the gained or regained insight into oneself, but also by changes in the capacity for human relationships. Many patients are unable, at the end of psychoanalytic treatment, to give account of which changes and which self-formative processes have taken place in them: They are aware of a change in the immediacy of their experience and actions, without being able to reflect philosophically on it in an adequate way. The maxim "Where id was there shall ego be" cannot be understood to mean that the dynamic unconscious, repressed, which unfolds its power behind the back of the subject, lies, after analytic treatment, permanently at the conscious disposal of the subject. We find Gadamer's (1971a) criticism concerning this matter to apply here: "The idea of the elimination of a natural determination in rational, conscious motivation, is in my opinion a dogmatic exaggeration inappropriate to the *'condition humaine'* " (p. 312). Habermas fails to appreciate the necessity that, psychoanalytically, the developmental process of the individual consists basically of psychic structures and functions that safeguard the ability to work and love. With this we do not mean a conforming adaptation to an ahistoric reality principle. This principle in our view has a regulatory function and is prone to historical change, which finds its respective sociocultural content in historical change. In the practice of psychoanalysis, therefore, we aim at a reasonable equilibrium between those poles that can be characterized as the pleasure principle and the reality principle. Ideally, the blind autoplastic subjection to the contents of the reality principle that are passed on by sociocultural tradition and its internalization in ego and superego functions should be replaced by reasonable alloplastic solutions. Here, a concept of the theory of therapeutic technique assumes significance, namely, "acting out." Acting out signifies such alloplastic, outward-directed efforts of change as are unconsciously drive directed. Insofar as the demands that only the environment should change are not accompanied by the willingness and ability to change oneself, one can usually assert psychoanalytically that in these one-sided alloplastic actions we often are dealing with acting out. That such acting out can often have vast social and historical consequences is one of the tragic paradoxes of the history of mankind. One could almost say, then, that, often, petrified situations can be changed only when, through certain misunderstandings of reality, forces of "acting out," which do not seem to know any limits, are liberated. The tragic fact is that the changes then regularly take place through aggressive-destructive forces, which soon lead to similar disturbing countermovements (see Waelder, 1967). Thus, important insights into collective processes can be gained from the psychoanalytic method, since one can clearly discern in the acting out of the individual the disharmony in society: it is fought there instead of beginning with the individual's own self-formative processes.[20]

Giegel's (1971) analysis of the "self-formative process" mediates between the poles of "reflection" and "practice" as they are developed here in a somewhat extreme form. "The single elements of knowledge about which a subject disposes are related to one another in a system, which can be structured in different ways.... When such structures, which organize the system of knowledge, are changed in such a way that a more comprehensive and compulsion-free organization of the elements of knowledge becomes possible, we speak of a self-formative process" (p. 253). After an illustration of such a structural change, taken from the domain of cognitive developmental processes in the child, Giegel continues: "At first the new structures develop without the control of the reflection of the developing subject. In order to be effective, the new structures must, however, be constructed out of the old ones with a certain continuity, for only so can the logical operations available in the earlier stage be carried on through a different context. The structures of knowledge are therefore always corrected only on particular points, and in no way are whole sections replaced by others" (p. 255).

In this change, Giegel attributes to the reflection of the subject a stabilization of the new organization of knowledge, from which result influences that stimulate the self-formative processes and possess a dual character: "On the one hand, they push on behind the subject's back, on the other hand, reflection on this passage is indispensable for its success" (p. 256). This interpretation is quite compatible with the structural model of psychoanalysis, which in its ego-psychological aspects has decisively influenced the technical theory. For a semantic clarification of the concept *formative process,* one can conclusively refer to Freud who, in his "Introductory Lectures" (1916-1917), presents the change of structure as an essential achievement: "Through the overcoming of these resistances the patient's mental life is permanently changed, is raised to a high level of development and remains protected against fresh possibili-

---

[20] Weiss (1965) has the Marquis de Sade say just this on the stage: That's how it is Marat / That's how she sees your revolution / They have toothache / and their teeth should be pulled ... / Their soup's burnt / They shout for better soup / A woman finds her husband too short / she wants a taller one / A man finds his wife too skinny / he wants a plumper one / A man's shoes pinch / but his neighbour's shoes fit comfortably / A poet runs out of poetry / and desperately gropes for new images / For hours an angler casts his line / Why aren't the fish biting / And so they join the revolution / thinking the revolution will give them everything / a fish / a poem / a new pair of shoes / a new wife / a new husband / and the best soup in the world / So they storm all the citadels / and there they are / and everything is just the same / no fish biting / verses botched / shoes pinching / a worn and stinking partner in bed / and the soup burnt / and all that heroism / which drove us down to the sewers / well we can talk about it to our grandchildren / if we have any grandchildren (pp. 60-62).

ties of falling ill. This work of overcoming resistances is the essential function of analytic treatment; the patient has to accomplish it and the doctor makes this possible for him with the help of suggestion operating in an *educative* sense" (p. 451).

The consequence of Habermas' effort to present psychoanalysis as the only tangible example of a science incorporating methodical self-reflection that furthermore should be a model for social reflection would be that the technology of clinical interpretative work would have to be rejected. Its methodological particularity, however — that it can be an explanatory science as well as an emancipating reflection — must be, in our opinion, the central issue in determining its epistemological status. The multiplicity of psychotherapeutic-intervention techniques that can be derived from psychoanalytic theory and practice indicates an instrumental aspect, of which no clinician is ashamed. "The very fact that, since Freud's time, the psychoanalytic method has been used in treating both children and psychotics — to neither of whom Habermas could really grant the capacity for self-reflection — would seem to substantiate this in an important way" (Nichols, 1972, p. 267).[21] Habermas' assertion that success and failure cannot be ascertained intersubjectively in treatment, that justifications based on the disappearance of symptoms are not legitimate, fails when confronted with psychotherapeutic practice. Also, Freud's emphasis that only the process of the analysis can decide the usefulness or uselessness of a construction does not exclude the confirmative force of changes in symptoms and behavior, but comprises an expression of the self-formative process more than only the self-reflection of the patient. Habermas himself says elsewhere (1963, p. 482) that one of the suppositions for the testing of theories is that repetitive systems can be made accessible to controlled observation. Just such repetitive systems are present, however, for instance, in stereotypes of behavior which, through the repetition compulsion, manifest themselves in the various forms and contents of transference neuroses. Repetition and change, both manifest in behavior, can be observed, and these observations are reflected in the practice and theory of psychoanalysis. Habermas (1967) admits that "single hypotheses can be taken out of the metapsychological context of interpretation and be tested independently" (p. 189). "Herewith is needed a transposition into the theoretical frame of strict empirical sciences. . . . In any case, Freud's theory contains

[21] As for the rest, the devaluating qualification that presents instrumentalism as the only knowledge of interest to the "real" sciences is pointed out by Albert (1971). According to him, such a reproach has, in the history of knowledge, always served the screening of specific articles of belief against criticism made possible by the natural sciences (p. 110).

assumptions which can be interpreted as lawful hypotheses in a strict sense; from this it follows that it also comprehends causal relations" (p. 190). What Habermas seems to admit here is the content of the general and specific theory of neuroses; its confirmation by the experience of the reflection of the patient alone, however, seems to us insufficient. With this, there is a task assigned to self-reflection that patients, again according to clinical experience, cannot accomplish.

We agree with Rapaport (1960) that proving the validity of the psychoanalytic theory is a task of the scientific community, which has to agree on the practical procedure of empirical science. Contrary to the restrictive limitation of the confirmation of general interpretations, psychoanalytic research and practice cannot be satisfied with a concept of the self-formative process that is as philosophically vague as it is rich in content, and from which confirmation of the theory should result. In any case, the logic of the explanation through general interpretations points toward the specific way in which the confirmation of psychoanalytic statements can alone be obtained: this becomes clear in the linking up of hermeneutic understanding with causal explanation: "Understanding itself gains explanatory power" (Habermas, 1971a, p. 328).[22] With regard to symptoms, constructions take the form of explanatory hypotheses with the aim of analyzing modes of behavior in causal terms. The dissolution of a "causal coherence" through interpretive effort illustrates the efficacy of psychoanalytic therapy. The constructions are to be applied to the single case; they thus become theoretical statements from which singular prognoses can be derived. Generally speaking, these prognoses identify the conditions causally responsible for the neurotic state and claim that the therapeutic process must dissolve these conditions in order to induce change. The disappearance of the efficacy of the supposed internal conditions — e.g., pathogenic unconscious fantasies — demonstrates itself in changes of symptoms and behavior.

In its logical form, however, explanatory understanding differs in one decisive way from explanation rigorously formulated in terms of the empirical sciences. Both of them have recourse to causal statements that can be derived from universal propositions by means of supplementary conditions: that is, from derivative interpretations (conditional variants) or lawlike hypotheses. Now the content of theoretical propositions remains unaffected by

[22] The reconciliation of the methodological antithesis between understanding (*Verstehen*) and explaining (*Erklären*) can be found *in statu nascendi* in Max Weber, in an "understanding explanation" or an "explaining understanding." According to Albert (1971), Weber tried, with his concept of theoretical sociology as an understanding science, which aims at an understanding explanation of the phenomena of cultural reality, to overcome the long-standing antithesis of explaining and understanding and with it the position of extreme historicity as represented by Dilthey (p. 137).

operational application to reality. In this case we can base explanations on *context-free laws*. In the case of hermeneutic application, however, theoretical propositions are translated into the narrative presentation of an individual history in such a way that a causal statement does not come into being without this context. General interpretations can abstractly assert their claim to universal validity because their derivatives are additionally determined by context. Narrative explanations differ from strictly deductive ones in that the events or states of which they assert a causal relation are further defined by their application. Therefore general interpretations do not make possible context-free explanations [Habermas, 1971a, p. 272, our italics].

From this follows, in our opinion, in regard to the methodology of research, that it is of the utmost importance to examine the individual case in its concreteness. Both the self-formative process, as experienced by the subject of treatment, and his objectively recorded changes in conduct and behavior must and can be examined on verbal and preverbal levels and thus become the criteria for testing the clinical hypotheses. In order to clarify still further the concept of general interpretation, which plays such a central role in Habermas' conceptualization, we shall now look for its original frame of reference. Popper (1944) introduced the term to distinguish between scientific and historical theories, to make a qualitative difference:

Now it is important to see that many "historical theories" (they might perhaps be better described as "quasi-theories") are in their character vastly different from scientific theories. For in history (including the historical natural sciences, such as historical geology) the facts at our disposal are often severely limited and cannot be repeated or implemented at our will. And they have been collected in accordance with a preconceived point of view; the so-called "sources" of history only record such facts as appeared sufficiently interesting to record, so that the sources will, as a rule, contain only facts that fit in with a preconceived theory. And since no further facts are available, it will not, as a rule, be possible to test that or any other subsequent theory. Such untestable historical theories can then rightly be charged with being circular in the sense in which this charge has been unjustly brought against scientific theories. I shall call such historical theories, in contradistinction to scientific theories, "general interpretations" [pp. 265-266].

The verifiability of these historical general interpretations is restricted insofar as there are no *experimenta crucis* in historical research and in psychoanalysis as there are in the natural sciences. Popper gives an elaborate argument for this, which leads him to give up the naïve view "that any definite set of historical recordings can ever be interpreted in one way only" (p. 266). Hereby it becomes clear how closely Popper's falsifications theory is connected with the axiomatic sciences. He then introduces a number of relative proofs for historical interpretations, which suffice to determine probable and relative validity. (1) There are false interpretations that do not agree with the acknowledged recordings.

(2) There are interpretations that need a number of more or less plausible auxiliary hypotheses to avoid falsification by the data. (3) There are interpretations that do not succeed in connecting a series of facts which are connected by another interpretation and are explained to that extent (p. 266). Accordingly, considerable progress would also be possible in the area of historical interpretations. Besides, all sorts of intermediate stations between more or less general points of view and specific or singular historical hypotheses would be possible, which, in the explanation of historical events, play the role of hypothetic initial conditions and not the role of general laws (see Klauber, 1968).

It is obvious that the considerable qualitative distinction Popper makes between scientific theories and general interpretations is no longer present in Habermas. In Habermas, general interpretations claim the same degree of validity as general propositions in the empirical sciences. Their decisive difference lies in the logical procedure of validating research. In order to become more acquainted with these differences, we now consider the problem of which relations exist between the general model of scientific explanation, general interpretations, and single forms of explanation as they occur in psychoanalytic work and research.

V. Description, Explanation, and Prognosis in Psychoanalysis

Allport (1937) characterizes scientific activity as the effort "to understand, predict, and control." Of this triad, the role of understanding is likely to be underestimated; it bears too close a relationship to philosophical speculation, whereby one easily overlooks the fact that understanding as a hermeneutic principle is in every scientific activity the condition of further progress. In the preceding pages we have already dealt at length with the role that understanding has in the scientific process. The procedures of prediction and control as represented in Allport's viewpoint presuppose explanations. In its daily decisions, clinical practice deals with this immanent coherence as a matter of course. For our discussion, however, it seems useful to clarify here once again the principle of this coherence, before we continue with a discussion oriented toward psychoanalysis. From a logical point of view, scientific predictions have the same structure as explanations. The event to be expected is deduced logically from given laws and auxiliary conditions, whereas explanations are a sort of post-hoc reconstruction of how an event has come about. This deduction of the prediction goes back to

Popper's (1959) description of the logical structure of causal explanations. Hempel and Oppenheim (1953) have systematized the relationship between prediction and explanation in the model of scientific explanation named after them (the HO-model of scientific explanation). In order to facilitate the discussion, we will repeat the relationships.

In an explanation, an *explanandum*—that is, a specific fact that has occurred—is presented. In order to explain it, one has to look for (at least) one law and the accompanying initial conditions. In a prognosis, however, the explanandum is not given; we know only the laws and the initial conditions. The following outline clarifies this difference in graphic form:

Explanation		*Prognosis*
sought	law	given
sought	initial conditions	given
given	explanandum	sought

In the explanation as well as in the prognosis an explanandum is deduced from (at least) one law and the initial conditions belonging to it. The only difference is that in each case different elements are sought and given. On the basis of our discussion in the section on "General and Historical Interpretations," it is clear that the HO-outline implies a type of explanation, which in psychoanalysis is only applicable by corresponding extension of the definition. Before we occupy ourselves with other forms of explanation, which, according to Stegmüller (1969), can likewise come under the concept of scientific explanation, we must come to grips with a contrary position. It is often said from various quarters that a great deal of Freud's achievements lie in his brilliant description of many aspects of human behavior. The most prominent representative of this position must be Wittgenstein, who, according to Moore (1955), emphasized: "There are so many cases [in Freud's writings] in which one can ask oneself how far what he says is a hypothesis, and to what extent [it is] only a good manner of presenting the facts" (p. 316). MacIntyre (1958), with whom we have already argued, arrives, in his effort to explain the concept of the unconscious, at a similar conclusion in this matter: "For Freud's achievement lies not in his explanations of abnormal behaviour but in his redescription of such behaviour" (p. 61). When one tries to fathom where the basis for such judgments lies, as Sherwood (1969)[23] has done, then one finds that Wittgenstein refers to *The Psychopathology of Everyday Life,* and that MacIntyre predominantly considers

[23] See also the discussion of Sherwood's book by Eagle (1973), Rubinstein (1973), and Sherwood (1973).

The Interpretation of Dreams. Both works indeed contain anecdotic material, given to illustrate ways in which the psychic apparatus functions. Causal remarks, taken out of the clinical context, appear thereafter only as ways of presenting the facts and easily lose their explanatory character. If, however, the clinical context is restored, then what Sherwood says is true: "It is of course true that Freud described certain acts of the patient in a new way. But the important thing is that he tried thereby to explain them. . . . To give a new description in given contexts can indeed come close to an explanation. The distinction between these two procedures is not always sharp, and, in each case, it depends on the context, the situation in which it takes place" (1969, p. 187).

Even though MacIntyre acknowledges elsewhere (1958, p. 79) that a clarifying description can indeed count as a way of explaining, he feels that he has to again deny the title of explanation to Freud's efforts to explain the significance of dreams, which have to do more with a deciphering than with explanation (p. 112). The discrepancy that here comes clearly to the fore concerns the scope, the concept of explanation. Different types of explanation are certainly at the base of Freud's clinical presentations.

Sherwood points to the fact that Freud's explanations in the case histories of patients — he illustrates extensively with the example of the Rat Man — always concern, first of all, an individual patient, a specific case history. The object of research is not a class of certain psychiatric symptoms, not a class of people who have a certain illness, but a single person. Like the historian, Freud is interested in the particular outcome of events, in order to perceive the typical. Accordingly, Freud uses generalizations about compulsion neurotics as a class. In the same way, there is a general theory of human behavior beyond the explanation of particular life histories (see Waelder, 1962). A presupposition for generalization is that the explanations have been tested in a particular case. The other condition is self-evident: that the explanations tested in the particular case are present in a group of cases, whereby they become typical. The typical coherences are always only part of a case history; the particular explanations are woven into the whole. This context, which represents the comprehensive integrating moment, is characterized as "psychoanalytic narrative." Within this narrative, various types of explanations can be isolated, which occur in different distributions. Hereby the narrative, however, is to be regarded not simply as the sum (total) of these various explanations, but as the integrating framework: "In short, giving an account of the resolution of a single symptom would in fact amount to the task of relating an entire case history" (Freud, 1896, p. 197).

According to Danto (1965), representations, which present events as elements in a history, are called "narrative statements." Since psychoanalytic explanations lie within the totality of a life history, the denotation "psychoanalytic narrative"—which as far as we know was first used by Farrell (1961) in philosophical discussion—underlines the historical character of psychoanalytic explanations, which soon led Freud to remark that it was not his fault if his case histories read like short stories (Breuer & Freud, 1893-1895, p. 160).

In Stegmüller's (1969) fundamental elaborations on the concept of scientific explanation—the most complete overview on the status of present-day analytic philosophy in the German language—he first of all singles out scientific explanation from a multiplicity of everyday usages of the word. The explanation of the meaning of a word, which can also be called "definition," the explanation as text interpretation or as instruction on how to act, as detailed description and moral justification—these numerous meanings of the concept of explanation show hardly anything in common, and Stegmüller calls them at best a concept family in Wittgenstein's sense. For the analytic philosophy of science, only the explanation of a fact has the rank of scientific explanation.

In the psychoanalytic models of explanation, as Sherwood (1969) shows, all those forms and explanations that are known from everyday language occur. It is a question of discovering the source of a feeling, of "explaining" as it were, the origin of something strange. Herewith nothing is yet explained in the sense of the HO-explanation—only a more precise knowledge of the facts is achieved. The explanation of the genesis (origin) of a symptom already poses difficult problems of demarcation. If the observed transference behavior is reduced to an infantile attitude to the mother, then not only are facts that appear as disparate brought together, but also, by way of trial, genetic explanations are accepted that must prove themselves as retrodiction. The multitude of phenomena and processes in the psychoanalytic situation requires different explanatory operations, which should not be, a priori, designated as scientific or unscientific. Sherwood concludes his illustration of the various types of explanation with examples from the case history of the Rat Man: "A psychoanalyst is called upon to answer a wider range of questions on human behavior, and his explanations can therefore be of very different sorts" (Sherwood, 1969, p. 202).

Indeed, the demarcation of different types of explanation from explanation in the strict sense of the HO-model, as is partly reflected in Sherwood, does not take into regard the fact that, according to Stegmüller, "the concept of scientific explanation was introduced in such a way that it could claim for itself general applicability in all *empirical* sciences" (p. 336). To be sure, the form of the construction of the concept of explanation decides whether it is applicable: a narrow conception corresponds to the HO-model as we have briefly outlined it in the passages above (under an explanatory argument should be understood a deductive conclusion, among the premises of which is at least one deterministic or statistic law hypothesis); if, however, the concept is taken in a larger sense, that of Stegmüller, then not only the search for grounds in reality, or causes, but also quite generally the search for a basis in reason can enter into the search for an explanation.

This enlargement of the concept of scientific explanation draws particular historical and, consequently, also some psychoanalytic explanations into its scope. The language of the historian, as well as of the psychoanalyst who reports on his case, is full of expressions that indicate an effort to explain. Logical or inductive arguments of many a thesis, instead of causal arguments, are often given. The selective description of the historian becomes an initial explanation because the description is governed by hypotheses. To be sure, in historical explanations regularities that have a statistic or trivial character are often drawn; the explanatory argument is therefore often not mentioned. Stegmüller lists other qualities of historical initial explanations, which cause the historical scientist not to interpret his statements as explanations in the sense of the HO-model. As a superior point of view, he introduces thereby, following Hempel, the incompleteness of such explanations. Incomplete explanations, which are also called "explanation outlines," can be reduced to the following four roots:

(a) The explanation has dispositional character (see below).

(b) The explanation contains self-evident generalizations from the commonplace, which are not specifically mentioned.

(c) The explanation is incomplete because further derivation of a law must be explicitly renounced because its range would be exceeded.

(d) The explanation is incomplete due to insufficient experiential material.

According to Stegmüller (1969), for the aforementioned reasons, high demands on historical explanations cannot be materialized; he therefore proposes a broadly conceived definition of historical explanation in the sense of the HO-outline: "An explanation of E on the basis of antecedents data A_1. A_n would accordingly be present, when the event-to-be explained is to be expected on the basis of its antecedents-event, and to be expected either in the sense of a purely intuitive and not further defined, or in the sense of a formally specified 'confirmative concept' [*Bestätigung*]" (p. 348). The genetic statements of psychoanalytic theory can be covered, that is to say with this form of historical explanation the present efforts to explain psychoanalytic developmental psychology can be so classified, at least formally. That hereby the degree of confirmation is attained with different precision is clearly shown in the various results of the longitudinal studies by Benjamin (1950), Kris (1951), Escalona (1952), and others. Interestingly enough Langer, as early as in 1957 when he was president of the American Historical Association, advocated "the use in the future, for the purpose of historical explanations, to a much greater extent than before, of ideas of psychoanalysis and related theories of depth psychology" (quoted in Stegmüller, 1969, p. 423). Langer pleaded in particular for the use of dispositional explanations, because the model of conscious-rational behavior could not suffice for the historian.

Let us now discuss in greater detail this concept of dispositional explanation, because, like functional explanation, it is of great importance for psychoanalysis. Statements such as "the glass breaks because it has quality X" are dispositional explanations. Because the dispositional quality of an object or individual has consequences in the nature of a law, Ryle (1965) classifies such explanations as "lawlike" statements. Dispositional explanations concern that "category of cases in which the activity of the acting persons should be explained with the help of character traits, convictions, goal projections, and other dispositional factors" (Stegmüller, 1969, p. 120). The patient brings to treatment certain modes of behavior and certain qualities based on subconscious conflict constellations, which we explain by dispositions. Since the patient unconsciously seeks a repetition of his infantile traumata, he constructs the transference situation in an analogous manner. The formation of the transference neurosis can be interpreted as the transposition of such dispositions in object relationships that are experienced anew. The overcoming of the transference neurosis will then lead to the dissolution of the unconscious conflicts that previously determined his behavior, and, with it, of the disposition of those conflicts as a lawful way of reacting. Dispositional statements are often not regarded as explanations, because their relation to basic laws is, as a rule, not made explicit.

The logic of functional explanations must still be discussed separately. Freud speaks of the dream as the guardian of sleep. Are we dealing here with a scientifically legitimate mode of explanation, or is the finalistic consideration here only a veil over an as-yet-unknown causal phenomenon? Or does the functional presentation represent only a descriptive coherence, without the claim of explanation? As a prototype of a functional explanation in psychoanalysis, we propose Freud's (1926) theory of

93

symptom formation. "Since we have traced back the generating of anxiety to a situation of danger, we shall prefer to say that symptoms are created in order to remove the ego from a situation of danger" (p. 144).

The manner in which Freud expresses himself here is teleological. It seems almost as if what happens in symptom formation should be included in the outline of conscious goal-oriented action. But, as Stegmüller shows, the logical outline of the functional analysis provides an appropriate representation of the relations. System S is the individual in whom pathological symptoms form. Disposition D is the pattern of compulsive behavior that impresses like a symptom. The effects of disposition D can be indicated by N, which is, in the case of symptom formation, the binding of anxiety. Herein, the functional explanation would be that, condition N is deemed necessary for a normal functioning of S, which in this case means that S can continue to live without serious psychic crises. As Stegmüller shows in his further examination, the testing of the empirical significance of such functional explanations presents considerable difficulties. These lie in the exact definition of the various parts of the explanation model. For the purpose of verification, *that* class of individuals must be specified for whom a defined disposition D lawfully has the effects N; that is to say, an empirical difficulty lies in the empirically meaningful definition of the system S for which the functional explanation is claimed. A further difficulty arises for empirical testing procedures when not only the disposition D_1, but also another disposition D_2 shows the same effects of the nature N, for the system is thus functionally equivalent to disposition D_1.

Let us put this problem in psychoanalytic terms. Not only the defense mechanism of denial, but also that of isolation, of reversal, etc., can be utilized for the binding of anxiety of someone suffering from compulsion neurosis. The introduction of additional dispositions weakens, however reciprocally, the explanatory value of the original one. Thus, for instance, Malinowski's thesis that the effect of magic is necessary for the functioning of primitive society is reduced in its explanatory value because no proof is given that only this magic enables primitive man to overcome existential anxiety. The weakness of the functional analysis thus lies in its great range of descriptive applications, concerning which the heuristic character is easily overlooked. If, in psychoanalysis, it can be shown that different dispositions are effective for different categories of individuals, then the functional explanation can also claim explanatory value.

After this orientation regarding different forms of explanation and their use in psychoanalysis, we ask ourselves what the position of prognosis is in psychoanalytic theory and research. Although not all of science lies in proof, and prognosis is not its only purpose, the prognostic power of a theory has acquired an important place in psychological research. Historically, this evaluation is related in particular to the practically useful results of psychometric studies in research on training (see Kelly & Fiske, 1950, 1951; Holt & Luborsky, 1958).

In the history of psychoanalysis, prognosis has not been held in high esteem — neither as instrument nor as goal. Indeed, we must here distinguish between unreflexive-automatic clinical everyday use and theoretic reflection. "Every interviewer who exercises any kind of interpretative technique, predicts from one moment to the next," writes Meehl (1963, p. 71). Thus, in the practice of psychoanalysis clinical experience and suggestions of therapy derived from it are from the very beginning practiced as applied prognostics. "To be sure, we know very little about the frequency of their success and their reliability, and in how far the course of the interview depends on them," Meehl continues. The theoretical skepticism of the psychoanalyst was based on an opposition, pointed out by Freud (1920b), between analysis and synthesis, which proved to hamper the adequate reception of the prognosis as an instrument of scientific effort.

> But at this point we become aware of a state of things which also confronts us in many other instances in which light has been thrown by psycho-analysis on a mental process. So long as we trace the development from its final outcome backwards, the chain of events appears continuous, and we feel we have gained an insight which is completely satisfactory or even exhaustive. But if we proceed the reverse way, if we start from the premises inferred from the analysis and try to follow these up to the final result, then we no longer get the impression of an inevitable sequence of events which could not have been otherwise determined. We notice at once that there might have been another result, and that we might have been just as well able to understand and explain the latter. The synthesis is thus not so satisfactory as the analysis; in other words, from a knowledge of the premises we could not have foretold the nature of the result. . . . Hence the chain of causation can always be recognized with certainty if we follow the line of analysis, whereas to predict it along the line of synthesis is impossible [pp. 167-168].

This presentation from the case report on female homosexuality appears to demonstrate convincingly that it is in principle impossible to predict the future development of a personality, hence the range of genetic psychoanalytic statements is reduced to the *post-festum* analysis of the development of the personality. When at this point we apply the outline on explanation and prognosis reported above, then the question presents itself whether in fact, with exactly the same border conditions, the explanandum could have been something other than (as in the case under discussion) female homosexuality. We believe that if one follows the pathoetiological road in the directions Freud has recorded, other possibilities of development emerge in retrospect, because other border conditions occur at the horizon of thought. Then it seems as if the development did not necessarily have to lead to female homosexuality. Moreover, the "complemental series," the etiological outline developed by Freud (1905, pp. 239-240), contains border conditions which, if they are or were known, permit explanation. We are therefore confronted here with a problem that can perhaps hardly be solved in empirical ways but is not insoluble in principle. Freud's formulations can lead to misunderstanding insofar as the knowledge of the presuppositions or, more precisely, the knowledge of all presuppositions must make the nature of the event predictable. In the aforementioned article, Freud himself explains the pessimistic result — that synthesis is impossible with the lack of knowledge about further causes. These causes are, however, nothing other than alternative border conditions, which can, of course, looking back at the pathogenesis, never be known. Only a psychoanalyst endowed with the *Weltgeist* of Laplace could perhaps name all possible border conditions retrospectively. An illustration of the relation between the knowledge of possible border conditions and the prognostic results is given by Benjamin (1959) in his excellent work on the role of prediction in developmental psychology.

Although Freud's resignation concerns prediction only in the context of genetic psychology, we must remember that the claim of conditional predictions has been formulated with much reservation in other fields of psychoanalytic theory and practice as well. According to Rapaport (1960), this is related to the central position of the principle of overdetermination in psychoanalytic psychology:

> The psychoanalytic concept of *overdetermination* implies that one or several determiners of a given behavior, which appear to explain it, do not necessarily give its full causal explanation. This is not per se alien to other sciences, though *a principle of overdetermination* did not become necessary in any of them. Psychoanalysis' need for this principle seems to be due partly to the multiplicity of the determiners of human behavior, and partly to the theory's characteristic lack of criteria for the independence and sufficiency of causes. The determiners of behavior in this theory are so defined that they apply to all behavior and thus their empirical referents must be present in any and all behavior. Since there is usually no single determiner which constantly assumes the dominant role in a given behavior, other determiners can hardly be neglected while a dominant determiner is explored. When favorable conditions make one determiner dominant, the investigator is tempted to conclude that he has confirmed a predicted functional relationship — as he indeed has. Regrettably, the attempt to repeat the observation or experiment in question often fails, because in the replication either the same behavior appears even though a different determiner has become dominant, or a different behavior appears even though the same determiner has remained dominant [pp. 66-67].

On the basis of such considerations, it seems logical to Rapaport that Freud overestimated the role of postdiction, and underestimated the role of prediction in the construction of the theory. Waelder (1963) has subjected the principle of overdetermination to a critical analysis, which brings a logical as well as a semantic clarification. With reference to a pregnant place in Freud's (1909a) text, he points out that the principle of psychic determinism and of overdetermination must be understood as a heuristic concept, which for methodological reasons requires for all psychic processes—whether they appear as unpretentious, arbitrary, or accidental—sufficient motivation: "As you already see, psycho-analysts are marked by a particularly strict belief in the determination of mental life. For them there is nothing trivial, nothing arbitrary or haphazard. They expect in every case to find sufficient motives . . ." (Freud, 1909a, p. 38).

The introduction of determinism had, therefore, first of all the function of providing a secure methodological foundation for Freud's analyses. From the "belief" in the determination of psychic life, a series of methodological principles of the psychoanalytical technique of research can be derived. Besides, it follows from the citation that "to be determined" was for Freud equivalent with "to be motivated"; this permits Waelder (1963) to reject the philosophical debate about the question of determinism and free will. From here on the farther-reaching concept of overdetermination must also be considered. Let us first examine those places where Freud introduces the concept of overdetermination; in the *Studies on Hysteria* we find in the discussion of etiological questions the following references: "Almost invariably when I have investigated the determinants of such [hysterical] conditions what I have come upon has not been a *single* traumatic cause but a group of similar ones" (Breuer & Freud, 1893-1895, p. 173). What he illustrates here casuistically in the case of Elisabeth von R. is further explained in the theoretical chapter "The Psychotherapy of Hysteria": "He [the physician] is aware of the principal feature in the etiology of the neuroses—that their genesis is as a rule overdetermined, that several factors must come together to produce this result" (p. 263). In the same way it is true for the symptoms of hysteria: "We must not expect to meet with a *single* traumatic memory and a *single* pathogenic idea as its nucleus; we must be prepared for *successions* of *partial* traumas and *concatenations* of pathogenic trains of thought" (pp. 287-288).

The clearest definition of the extent of the concept is found in Freud's (1895b) discussion of Löwenfeld's critique of the anxiety neurosis: "As a rule the neuroses are *overdetermined*; that is to say, several factors operate together in their aetiology" (p. 131).

What can be summarized from these citations and what functions as "the principle of overdetermination" is therefore the idea that there is for the neurotic disorders and their symptoms not a single cause, but many causes working together, the relationship among which cannot be seen as simply cumulative. The structural totality of this set of causes produces together the necessary and sufficient conditions. This principle of a multifactor genesis was new neither in philosophy (see, for instance, John Stuart Mill) nor in psychology.

In *The Psychopathology of Everyday Life*, Freud (1901), in the discussion of promises, quotes Wundt, who in his *Völkerpsychologie* (psychology of nations) claims for slips of the tongue a series of psychic influences that raise doubt about a single causal motivation of promises: " 'In some cases, too, it may be doubtful to which form a certain disturbance is to be assigned, or whether it would not be more justifiable, in *accordance with the principle of the complication of causes*, to trace it back to a concurrence of several motive forces' [Wundt, *Völkerpsychologie*, 380-381]. I consider these observations of Wundt's fully justified and very instructive" (Freud, 1901, pp. 60-61).

Even if the principle was not new, and is, especially today, recognized in all sciences that occupy themselves with more complex systems, it is nevertheless of special credit to psychoanalysts who as pioneers have consistently applied it. Sherwood's (1969, p. 181) criticism of psychoanalysts who claim to have "newly discovered" this principle and who want it understood as an essential concept that distinguishes psychoanalysis from other sciences, passes by, to that extent, the heart of the matter. Psychoanalytic explanations have too often been criticized for their pasticity and vagueness. To no small degree, these criticisms stem from efforts on the part of psychoanalysts to take into account the multiple conditions and functions of psychic acts.

In any case, Sherwood justly indicates a misunderstanding of the concept of overdetermination, to which Waelder also addressed himself. If one means thereby that there are several causal "constellations," independent of each other, necessary and sufficient, as Guntrip (1961) seems to say, then a logical impossibility is the result.[24] Waelder (1963) tries to clarify the content of the concept of being overdetermined, which starts from the above-mentioned logical untenability. The historical perspective Waelder gives in his reference to the origin of the concept is

---

[24] Anyway, as Stegmüller (1969) indicates, self-directed behavior-flexible systems can reach a similar goal along roads that are causally independent of each other (p. 5).

interesting. Freud's effort to conceive of psychic processes and results in neurophysiological concepts brought the model of psychic causality into analogy with the processes of a single neuron: stimulus-accumulation with threshold values was an adequate concept for the manner in which neurological processes are effective. The overdetermination necessary for neurological processes — namely, to reach threshold values — was borrowed for psychic processes. Waelder corrects the basic misunderstanding by bringing out the meaning of the situation and introducing a new concept: the principle of the multiple function of a psychic act implies no contradiction with regard to logic causality; it expresses the psychoanalytically central fact that any psychic act can simultaneously serve different needs and problem solutions.

While the confusing "overdetermination of the psyche" was one limitation of the possibility of prediction, still, even after clearing away this misunderstanding, the question remains why we are incapable of predicting the nature of the result from knowledge of the presuppositions. In answer to this, Freud alleges that only qualitative, not quantitative etiological relationships are known. Only at the end of a developmental process could one say which of the psychic forces were the stronger ones, because only the outcome can inform us about the relationship between the forces. Particularly obscure relationships are present when human behavior is the result of a conflict of almost equal inner forces, and this makes possible different end results. Conflict solutions and steps of development are therefore decisive processes. The greater the number of border conditions, the more degrees of freedom exist, and the factors of uncertainty in the prediction increase proportionately. On the other hand, predictions become reliable in those cases wherein there is no conflict or wherein one side is clearly stronger than the other.

In regard to this, Waelder (1963) mentions two marginal cases that render predictions possible: first, those in which the behavior is exclusively governed by the mature ego; or, second, those under completely opposite conditions in which the governing by the mature ego is practically entirely eliminated and the action is therefore exclusively ruled by biological forces (drives) and the primitive efforts of solution of the immature ego — that is, when the wealth of determinants of human behavior is diminished (pp. 90 f.). Anna Freud (1958) further pointed out that predictions are possible not only in these two extreme cases, but also in the numerous cases in which the components — primitive inner forces and sense of reality — exist in a stable relation characteristic for the individual concerned. Such stable mixtures would then constitute the essence of character (p. 92). More or less stable relations, that is, limited "degrees of freedom," exist always in the circumscribed range of psychic disturbances within the total personality. Psychoanalytic explanations and predictions concern these relatively closed systems.

With respect to the difficulties mentioned so far of deriving the possibility of prediction from the theory of psychoanalysis, the question now arises whether we have here conceptional obscurities or fundamental objections. The question is of particular interest in regard to practical necessity: "Thus prediction, or predictability, is in analysis not accidental but belongs to its essence. And it is obviously true . . . that our technique is constantly based on such tentative predictions. Without it a rational technique would be impossible" (Hartmann, 1958, p. 121).

For clarification, we should first distinguish between different areas in which prediction can be used, in order to examine, in each case, whether and to what extent predictions are possible. In its present form, psychoanalytic theory has hypothetic explanations ready for a wide range of social phenomena. Systematic verification of such explanatory efforts with the help of predictive techniques will be discussed here only for the therapeutic situation.

Escalona's (1952) skepticism whether prediction is possible in clinical psychoanalytic research finds its origin in two considerations: the one, which refers to the conclusive force of an applicable prediction, does not directly belong here and will later be discussed separately; the other consideration compares the psychoanalytic therapeutic situation to the laboratory experiment and finds that in the therapeutic situation, for instance, the environmental variable cannot be controlled sufficiently to be able to make meaningful predictions concerning the behavior of the patient. "According to Bellak's critical objection, with which we would agree, Escalona overlooks that in psychoanalysis one has to do with *relatively* stable and permanent structures, which guarantee a high degree of evenness in the reaction to stimuli" (Thomä & Houben, 1967, p. 678). Bellak and Smith (1956), in an experimental study, were able to show not only that they have introduced an argument into discussion, but that the meaning of the environmental variables is, in fact, considerably reduced by the reaction-readiness of the patient.

From the effort to make predictions concerning the next step in treatment—short-term predictions—one can reasonably distinguish the effort to make prognostic assertions concerning the outcome of treatment. For this, goals of treatment have to be formulated and written down at the beginning. To illustrate this with the model of the prediction study of the Menninger Clinic, changes in behavior, adaptive changes (in Hartmann's sense), intrapsychic changes such as insight, changes in drive defense,

100

constellations, or structural changes of the ego can be indicated. As Sargent and her co-workers (1968) have shown in detail, the use of predictions as scientific instruments requires, in any case, a more precise explanation of the formal nature of predictions. Based on Benjamin's (1950, 1959) fundamental longitudinal studies of children, in which he specified prediction as an instrument to validate psychoanalytic-genetic assertions, they outlined a prediction model that permitted empirical testing of predicted changes after psychoanalytic treatment (see also Luborsky & Schimek, 1964, for a thorough study of these issues).

As we have been able to show — without specific reference to any of the studies mentioned — prediction as an instrument of examination can also be used in psychoanalysis. The stability of neurotic processes permits us to regard the psychoanalytic treatment situation temporarily as ahistoric, even if it is embedded in the framework of systematically generalized history. In conclusion, one question must still be raised that puts the significance of prediction in a larger context. Hempel and Oppenheim's outline of scientific explanation (1953) leads to the plausible conception to which we referred above, "that explanatory and prognostic arguments are similar in regard to their logical structure" (Stegmüller, 1969, p. 153). This would mean that we can only be content with an explanation when we can turn it around, as it were, and use it as an instrument of prediction. On the other hand, we know examples of correct predictions in which the explanatory coherence was not always already known. This theoretical self-evidence, as suggested by the HO-model, was annulled by Scriven (1959). In his analysis of the role of explanation and prediction in the theory of evolution, he shows that the explanatory force of Darwin's hypotheses is not reduced by the lack of prognoses of similar scope: "Darwin's success lay in his empirical, case by case by case, demonstration that recognizable fitness *was* very often associated with survival and that the small random variations *could* lead to the development of species. He did not discover *an exact universal law* but the utility of a *particular indicator* in looking for explanations" (p. 478). To a great extent, similar conditions seem to exist for psychoanalysis. Complete explanatory sets of laws and border conditions are seldom enough available that could be transformed into valid predictions. But very often psychoanalysis can demonstrate the explanatory power of particular indicators that sediment into the well-known "rules of thumb" of which the daily clinical work draws its predictive capacity.[25]

[25] A detailed discussion of the thesis of the structural identity of prognosis and explanation is found in Stegmüller, 1969, pp. 153-198.

101

VI. Circularity and Self-Fulfilling Prophecy [26]

In the discussion on predictions in psychoanalysis, the question must be examined whether interpretations fulfill themselves therein. We have to occupy ourselves, therefore, with the problem of circularity. To make the theme explicit, let us look in the text of our work for references to circle and circularity. First we hit upon the hermeneutic circle, then on circularity in historical explanations. We can further perceive a circular movement in the psychoanalytic art of interpretation, where certainly, to pick up a thought of Dilthey, one could speak of a "circularity of experience, understanding, and representation of the mental world in general concepts: — if we include under the latter the clinical theory of psychoanalysis" (Dilthey, *Collected Works,* VII, 145, as quoted by Apel, 1967).

Let us first maintain with Apel that the hermeneutic circle signifies, "that we always must have understood already, in order to understand at all and to be able to *correct,* however, our preliminary understanding through the *methodic* endeavor of understanding" (p. 147, our italics). In this definition the demand for methodic correction of preliminary understanding seems to us essential, because by it the common bond of scientific proceedings is assured.

Apel thus sees in hermeneutics a "methodic" circle. With Gadamer, who follows Heidegger, the circle has lost this meaning. If one simplified somewhat, one could say that in the philosophical hermeneutics of Gadamer and Heidegger the incomplete preliminary understanding is replaced by the "anticipation of completeness." In this anticipation of completeness the totality seems always to be already known, so that parts become understandable only when they appear in a complete unity of meaning. The philosophical-hermeneutic anticipation of completeness (Gadamer, 1965, p. 277) presupposes that hermeneutics is freed from the restrictions of the scientific concept of objectivity, as Gadamer emphasized (p. 250). The important thing for us is a correction of the psycho-analytic-psychotherapeutic preliminary understanding, which is in

---

[26] The expression *self-fulfilling prophecy* was coined by R. K. Merton in 1957. He refers to the theorem of W. I. Thomas, the Nestor of American sociologists, which is basic to the social sciences: "If men define situations as real, they are real in their consequences." Merton (1968) adds: "Were the Thomas theorem and its implications more widely known, more men would understand more of the workings of our society. Though it lacks the sweep and precision of a Newtonian theorem, it possesses the same gift of relevance, being instructively applicable to many, if indeed not most, social processes" (p. 475).

agreement with the empirical sciences and can be made objective. Thus, Gadamer's anticipation of completeness takes the place of an antithesis that cannot be regarded in an empirical-scientific way, because it is from the very beginning outside of its terrain and enjoys, therefore, a kind of extraterritorial immunity. Here, one could say, to simplify, that the circle is completely closed from the beginning.

Circularity in a general sense exists in every scientific inquiry because a selective preliminary understanding enters into the formation of hypotheses. Radnitzky (1973) has discussed those aspects of the circle that one can render visible outside of hermeneutics (p. 215). In the natural sciences descriptions are governed by anticipated explanations. Before something can be explained, that which is to be explained (the explanandum) must be expressed in the language of the theory with which one hopes to achieve the more exact explanation. For instance, in order to explain planetary movements with Newton's theory, one must set the descriptions in a relevant form, but in order to do this, one must possess a certain preliminary understanding.

Preliminary understanding and correction, formation of hypotheses and verification, characterize every science and therefore cannot imply circularity in the sense of a vicious circle. Also, the process of knowing is itself a circular process. It proceeds from ideas (hypotheses) to the facts and back again. To conceptually distinguish general circularity from its incorrect forms, we indicate the latter, from now on, as *vicious circle*, as faulty conclusion, or the like. When, then, does preliminary understanding become faulty circularity?[27] When is the reproach of circular conclusion justified? What proof can be found in the above-quoted assertion of Popper (1944, p. 265) that it is unjust to accuse scientific theories of circularity, while in general interpretations, thus in historical explanations, circularity can be present in the pejorative sense of the word. With Popper's compilation of the correction possibilities of historical interpretations through manuscripts and other source material, a delimitation has been expressed. It is a question of eliminating faults which necessarily still characterize the preliminary understanding — by testing hypotheses with facts. Hereby one should take care that the immanent faults in the preliminary understanding do not remain hidden by a pre-established choice of material, which would lead to an apparent confirmation. The fact that theory and method move in the same frame of reference would have to lead to a vicious circle only when the research directions were such that they could give answers that are already given

[27] In a recently published book by Göttner (1973), we found a most comprehensive discussion of the relevant aspects of the vicious circle — begging the question, etc.

by the theory. Theory and method must therefore be independent from each other to the extent that the observations can say "no" to the theory (see Meehl, 1973, pp. 114 ff.). A theory constructed according to the well-known proverb: "When the rooster crows, the weather changes or it remains the same" cannot be contradicted.

That it is possible for theory and method to move in the same frame of reference, while sufficient independence remains, is illustrated by Popper in a comparison of research and legal processes. Investigating a specific problem that need not concern us here, namely, the establishment of so-called basic sentences, Popper shows, in the example of a classic trial by jury, the jury members' and judges' dependence on and independence from the penal system, where the rules of procedure and jurisdiction, one could say plural controls, protect against errors (1959, pp. 109-110). Rules of procedure according to which the verdict is arrived at are, it is true, not identical with the legal norms to be applied to the case, but both belong to the legal system. To this extent a dependence exists on the legal system, and the process moves within this circle.

It is not surprising that precisely this analogy of the research process with a legal process — likewise discussed by Radnitzky (1973, p. 216) — played a role in the discussion between Habermas (1969) and Albert (1969) on the occasion of the so-called dispute on positivism (see Adorno et al., 1969, pp. 242, 278). Albert refers to the fact that in the relationship of rules and manner of procedure to the legal system one does not find a circle "in the relevant sense of the word." A "relevant circularity," as we may in any case understand Albert, would be a faulty conclusion implicit in the system or procedure. Of greater importance, however, is what Habermas concludes from the analogy between research and legal process: "Something like experimentally established facts at which empirical-scientific theories could fail, are constituted first in a preliminary context of interpretation of possible experience" (1969, p. 243).

The reason we presented Popper's analogy[28] and the following discussion between Albert and Habermas is because there the all-around relationship to the legal system must result just as little in faulty judgments as do faulty conclusions in psychoanalysis. They occur because their interpreting practice depends on its explaining theories. To the contrary: all precautions serve to avoid, to respectively correct, faulty judgments in the one case, faulty conclusions in the other. Since in the

[28] Since Popper (1972) otherwise illustrates the methodology of the empirical sciences almost exclusively with the natural sciences, this analogy has special significance: it shows that Popper himself cannot maintain the restriction of the concept of empirical science.

section on general interpretations we have already established that the testing of psychoanalytic theory takes place by the standard of changes that can be predicted under certain conditions, we can now turn to a further, more fascinating problem. Let us assume that a patient suffering from anxiety neurosis would, in the course of psychoanalysis, show changes in his symptoms conforming to the theory. Since the theory, as we have shown, has influenced the technique of interpretation, the self-confirmation could be produced along this way (self-fulfilling prophecy). At this point one usually quotes what F. Kraus[29] is supposed to have said: The psychoanalyst finds the Easter eggs that he has first hidden himself (as quoted by Wyss, 1961). Thus, it is supposed that psychoanalytic observations are not related to the real facts, but owe their existence to the imagination of the psychoanalyst. Here, one attributes to the imagination a power which it does, in fact, possess: it produced reality long before Sigmund Freud discovered its constructive and destructive potential, and it was illustrated with a document that was completely independent from psychoanalytic technique—the Oedipus saga as described by Sophocles. As we read in Jones's biography (1953), Freud's discovery was connected with the fact that he had recognized oedipal wishes and fears in a personal form. The discovery that the theme of self-fulfilling prophecy is explicit precisely in the Oedipus complex is obvious not only because of its central position in psychoanalytic theory. After all, the Oedipus myth proves that the power of prophecies extends to their tragic fulfillment. It is for this reason that Popper (1963, pp. 35, 38, 123; 1957, p. 13) proposed to speak always of an "Oedipus effect" in those cases where one wants to indicate the influence of a prognosis on the predicted event. Popper substantiates his proposal with the oracular pronouncements that set the "causal chain" (thus Popper) of events in motion precisely by their prophesizing: Laius arranges for Oedipus to be murdered after having his heels pierced, to prevent the prophesied patricide and incest. We may here assume familiarity with Sophocles' *Oedipus Rex* and turn to the context on which Popper founds his proposal. He emphasizes that the driving force of the oracle's pronouncement has escaped the psychoanalysts, and he believes he can prove this. According to Popper, Freud has overlooked the influence of the psychoanalyst on the patient and his communications—as well as the related methodological problems in theory testing—in the same way as he over-

---

[29] Although this ironical remark could as well have come from the antipsychoanalytic and anti-Semitic mind of K. Kraus, who allegedly said that psychoanalysis is the illness that it pretends to cure, it was the German internist F. Kraus who, on the whole, was less antagonistic to psychosomatic medicine.

looked the role of the oracle in the Oedipus saga. Thus Popper suggests that psychoanalytic interpretations come close to the pronouncements of the oracle. At the same time, he diagnosed a partial reduction of the field of vision of the psychoanalyst, which prevents him from recognizing the proper interpretations of the "causal function."

This much is true: oracular pronouncements are not set at the beginning of the causal chain in psychoanalysis. Insofar as one cannot credit the oracle with omniscience, one will have to raise the question where, then, the oracle can have got his information. We do not hesitate to answer: from Laius, Jocasta, and Oedipus. It is not the oracle that sets the law of destiny in motion: it is father, mother, and son who speak through the oracle. But how does Laius know that Oedipus may kill him? From himself, and his own unconscious destructive desires, directed against his son. At the hand of Laius', Jocasta's, and Oedipus' fate, Freud has illustrated that human reality can be determined by conscious and *unconscious* psychological wishes—to a degree of complete necessity. In the first discussion of the Oedipus complex, on dream interpretation (Freud, 1900, p. 263), one can, however, also read that oedipal conflicts can have a different outcome and that the complex in question, then, is structured by different specific initial conditions—for instance, in the area of family and social culture. One could say, in short, that man, on the basis of his psychophysical constitution in the oedipal phase, lawfully gets into conflicts whose outcome is decided by initial conditions. In discovering the Oedipus complex in his patients, Freud was impressed by the biological lawfulness of its structure, although its dissolution took various forms. He described the psychodynamic efficacy of these various forms of dissolution as registered in the experience and behavior of man. That the "initial conditions" responsible for these conflicts occupy so important a place was then revealed in experiences with neuroses, perversions, and psychoses in the various diagnostic categories and—last but not least—in anthropological field research (see Lindzey, 1967). Besides, in psychoanalytic therapy it is not of primary importance to dissolve the particular form of the Oedipus complex into its components and to provide historical-genetic explanations. Rather, its influences on ways of feeling and behaving should be delimited from those of other unconscious dispositions. For instance: inferiority feelings and ideas of insignificance, as well as impotence representing possible forms of a fear of castration that has become unconscious, can be distinguished from the development of the same triad on the basis of disturbances in the oral phase or on the basis of narcissistic disorders. We have here one of those certainly still insufficiently solved problems of the clinical theory of psychoanalysis, namely, to determine typical pathogeneses more precisely. It is here that the difficulties that we discussed in the section on general interpretations operate. It is a matter of indicating or refuting covariants in those areas for which, according to the theory, there must exist a broader context—for example, repetition compulsion and its dissolution. The discovery of no matter which wishes and fears related to the total complex means little at first. The decisive criterion in a given case is whether the hypothesis of a causal relationship between unconscious oedipal death wishes and experiences, for instance, and apparently unfounded and totally unintelligible guilt feelings can be proven or not (if X, then probably Y). Similar or content-wise different correlation statements are of the greatest importance for clinical theory and practice. In the steps from secured descriptive correlations to explanations, motives in their dissolution prove to have been causes that operated. While correlation statements about typical symptom or character configurations are not prognoses in the scientifically relevant sense, their dissolutions are predictable under certain initial conditions, and therefore they are not *ex post facto* explanations. The former, namely, the correlation statements, make a diagnostic orientation possible and follow the proverb *ex ungue leonem* [by his claw we know the lion]. To conclude from the claw to the lion is therefore, as Waelder (1962) notes—in opposition to Arlow—not a prediction, because from the occurrence of a specific sign one can only conclude the existence of another symptom, while predictions concern future changes in a situation. These are determined by conditions, which is why one also speaks, in short, of "conditional prognoses."[30]

Scientific prognoses are conditional in contrast to prophecies (Popper, 1963). Albert (1968, p. 130) has given, in line with the distinction stressed by Popper in particular, the following summary of the logically contrasting structures of prognosis and prophecy: a presupposition for the prognostic application of a theory would be an appropriate description of the end situation of the event-to-be-predicted (including the different interventions possible for the acting person) in the language of the theory in question. Such a description of the initial conditions of the proceedings would result in specific statements which, in contrast to the general

---

[30] The opposite of conditional prognoses are unconditional prophecies, while unconditional prognoses are those in which the conditions can with certainty be regarded as fulfilled. Popper (1963) mentions the following example: "If a physician has diagnosed scarlet fever then he may, with the help of the conditional predictions of his science, make the unconditional prediction that his patient will develop a rash of a certain kind" (p. 339). Here, however, it appears rather to be a variation of *ex ungue leonem*.

hypotheses of the theory itself, concern a well-defined area in space and time.

Let us to this end consider once again the extremely simplified psychoanalytic example that has been given. End situation: guilt feelings. Explanatory hypothesis: unconscious oedipal death wishes. Determination of specific initial border conditions, namely, forms of resistance, which could annul the influence of psychoanalytic "interference" (interpretations), that is to say, make them ineffective. (The resistance argument obviously does not serve the *correctness* of the psychoanalyst, but it qualifies various end situations with different prognoses.) The positive or negative result of the prediction has, first of all, significance only for this particular case at this particular time.

We have dealt generously with the concept of initial conditions, which refers to the validity of a universal natural law and concerns its specific application. There is now no need for us to clarify which psychoanalytic assumptions can have a nomological character. The deductive method of causal explanation is, according to Popper (1957, p. 146), also applicable when, in the uniqueness of events—and the psychoanalyst has to deal with these first of all—the typical can be discerned as it is generalized in psychoanalytical theory. Thus, statements of probability can be derived from the theory and can be tested. For the rest, Albert (1972) does not hesitate either to grant to the alternatives of action, that is, to the possible interferences, the role of causally relevant circumstances, or to designate them as initial conditions (p. 130). When it is a matter of determining the influence of these initial conditions, of the operations of the acting person on the proceedings, then alternative influences can be checked against the presuppositions, that is, they can be either verified or falsified. To apply this logical structure in an empirical scientific manner means to test in the context of the particular theory, after the principle of trial and error, alternative interventions against the predictions. The psychoanalytic procedure follows this rule whereby the place of manipulative interventions in experimental arrangements, which are independent from the experimenter as a person, is taken over by technical interpretations which are insolubly connected with the participating person.

Our comparative discussions can be summarized as follows: that psychoanalysis as technique and theory fulfills presuppositions to interrupt apparent vicious circles, that is, to recognize faults in the definition of the initial conditions (psychodynamic situational diagnosis) as well as in the influencing operations (initial conditions are the techniques of interpretation). One could even say that the course of treatment is characterized by a constant correction of these faults. Since in every case the conditional prognosis is changed accordingly, a systematic testing of it is possible only when the conditions remain somewhat constant over a certain period of time. Sudden blows of fate, totally independent of the psychoanalytic process, can create a new situation, just as intervening exterior events can be suitable to call forth a fluctuation of themes in psychoanalytic sessions. Sooner or later, however, those relatively stable situations with which psychoanalytic theory concerns itself in particular will again exist, because they constitute the core of nosologically and psychopathogenetically different disorders. We mean the repetition compulsion. That the repetition compulsion is a superordinate essential characteristic of psychic disorders is unquestionable. No theory deserves to be taken seriously that does not present testable hypotheses for the psychogenesis of the repetition compulsion, which characterizes all psychopathological symptoms. Freud's greatest methodological discovery is, in our opinion, that he has discerned the repetition compulsion in the transference neurosis. Popper (1963) cannot escape expressing in this connection his agreement with psychoanalysis: "Psycho-analysts assert that neurotics and others interpret the world in accordance with a personal set pattern which is not easily given up, and which can often be traced back to early childhood. A pattern or scheme which was adopted very early in life is maintained throughout, and every new experience is interpreted in terms of it; verifying it, as it were, and contributing to its rigidity" (p. 49).

Popper then gives his own explanations—based on his theory of neuroses—for the repetition compulsion; most neuroses come about through the prevalence of a dogmatic attitude because a partial fixation of the development of a critical attitude has taken place. Their resistance against changes could perhaps on some basis—with this, Popper terminates his considerations of his theory of neuroses—be explained as follows: on the basis of an injury or shock, anxiety emerges, and there is an increased need for confirmation and security. This process would be analogous to the injury of a limb. From anxiety one no longer moves it, and it becomes stiff. One could even maintain that the case of a stiff limb is not only similar to the dogmatic reactions, but an example of it.

We must deny ourselves the opportunity to translate Popper's theory of neuroses into psychoanalytic concepts and subject it to Popper's own demands for refutations. This much can parenthetically be mentioned. The trauma to the limb[31] implies castration anxiety, and the stiffness

---

[31] We invite the reader's attention to the German pun: limb = *Glied*, *Glied* = Penis. Furthermore, *stiff* and *stiffness* are the most frequently used German terms for erection. Certainly Popper knows this pun, perhaps without "knowing" what role it unconsciously played in his theory of neurosis.

refs (in Popper's own words) to character deformation, i.e., to the results of unconscious, defensive processes. Here it is essential to note the agreement regarding the presupposition for psychoanalytic explanations and prognoses. Their presupposition is that in the repetition compulsion a repetitive system is present in which the conditions of its origin are conserved, and strengthened—even via feedback (Popper here appropriately described psychoanalytic experiences).[32] At the pivotal point of the transference neurosis, repetitions can be observed as nowhere else. This pivotal point is methodologically of particular interest. Given the case wherein the explanatory hypothesis says that a dogmatic attitude has come about as a protection against castration fear: from the hypothesis a technique of interpretation can be deduced which has the purpose of making the unconscious castration fears conscious. With this abbreviation of technical terminology, a complicated procedure is described that leads to an intrapsychic change of the, thus far, operative motivations. The conditional prediction that the dogmatic attitude will loosen when fears of castration no longer have their causal (motivating) power confirms or refutes the explanatory hypothesis concerning this relation. That psychoanalytic interventions address themselves to causes in order to change them leads to a peculiar situation. Their disappearance becomes proof of their previous causality. With the annulment of the repetition compulsion, psychoanalysis justifies itself therapeutically and scientifically. This thesis means that explanations of psychopathological phenomena in neuroses, perversions, addictions, psychoses, and character disorders are verified and falsified (proven to be true or false) by the predicted change. If one tries to arrange the explanatory steps formally according to the many possible meanings of explanation, we can say that the repetition compulsion on the observational level refers to a latent (unconscious) disposition as a theoretical concept; then we can describe the repetition compulsion in the first place as an essential characteristic of a disposition. This description provides, if confirmed by the case, the presupposition of a dispositional explanation. In the therapeutic dissolution of the disposition for a "repetition compulsion," typical relationships as they are systematized in clinical theory become observable relationships which, according to their logical structure, belong predominantly to the historical-genetic and probabilistic-genetic explanations, as well as to the functional analysis (see above section V).[33] In historical explana-

---

[32] An interruption of the repetition compulsion can therefore be effected by psychotherapeutic work on the strengthening of the ego.

[33] To avoid misunderstanding, we draw attention anew to the fact that although psychoanalysts in general do not give patients a logical explanation of one kind or another, their rational manner of conducting treatment does, indeed, observe logical laws.

tions circular errors can be particularly great, in Popper's opinion. For psychoanalysis, however, these problems should be easier to solve than for historical science, as Freud (1937) showed in a comparison with archaeology (p. 259). It is the repetitions in the transference of reactions from life history, originating in the early years, that permit the psychoanalyst to correct his explanatory outlines. This correction is accomplished in the practical application of life-historical constructions in the present and in prognostic testing, as we have described earlier. Historical interpretations are not verified by the fact that men in the present learn a lesson from history or do not. Genetic-psychoanalytic constructions, on the contrary, address themselves to the repetitive systems of man, who himself represents his history. If the goal of a limited change in the empirically examined case (symptom-bound repetition compulsion) is not reached, and if this was deduced historically and genetically from an unconscious fear of castration, then the construction must be regarded as refuted for this case and during this phase of treatment.

We conclude with a few remarks concerning the problem of suggestion, which will be discussed in greater detail at some other time. In the context of circularity and self-fulfilling prophecy, we must first set straight Popper's assertion that psychoanalysts have overlooked their own influence on the patient in the same way as the role of the oracle in the Oedipus saga has been overlooked. The opposite is true: Freud (1921, p. 89; 1916-1917, p. 448) has frequently concerned himself with the theme of suggestion. That the objectivity of the findings that are brought out can be questioned because of possible suggestive influencing has been denied with good reason. The psychoanalytical method itself, as is known, originated in the failure of suggestive practices and of cases wherein these had proven to be ineffective. Most patients who come into psychoanalysis have behind them frustrating autosuggestive efforts, as well as all kinds of unsuccessful influences from others against their symptoms. It can, therefore, not be the usual suggestions that lead to a change in a structure that so far has remained stable (repetition compulsion). Besides, the "suggestions" of the psychoanalyst are not aimed at the symptoms but at their motivations. For this reason, Freud has distinguished hypnotic and other kinds of suggestions from the psychoanalyst's sphere of influence, though he has stressed that the latter obviously also depends on the capacity of being influenced as an essential characteristic of man; if such were not the case, psychoanalytic interference would also be impossible. Technical interpretations in treatment can be compared to operations in experimental arrangements without which the theory cannot be verified. In the objection that the psychoanalyst finds the Easter eggs that he himself first has hidden, one

111

supposes a *vicious circle*, a self-fulfilling prophecy. Now, nobody will contest that symptoms are real and manifest themselves as the consequences of a psychopathogenesis. We allude to Merton's theory and maintain: the patient defined his emotional experiences, wishes, and fears as "real" long before a psychoanalyst appeared on the scene. The psychoanalyst discovered the definitions, he did not create them. It seems to us that, otherwise, one must make an absurd assumption: one would have to start from the fact that, in connection with the predicted symptomatic changes, freshly discovered pathogenesis was neither operative nor did it remain operative in the present via repetition compulsion: in other words, that the elimination of the repetition compulsion takes place independently from its pathogenesis through suggestions of one kind or another. Nobody will seriously want to maintain such a complete separation. The fact that the psychoanalyst as a person has positive and negative influences on his patient should not be indicated by the loaded term *suggestion*.

Freud's often misunderstood recommendation that the psychoanalyst should conduct himself in regard to his patient as a mirror which only reflects is in particular directed against uncontrolled suggestions. It is an invitation to observe countertransference and to burden the patient neither with one's own personal problems nor with one's own ideologies. To this extent, the recommendation serves the interest of the patient. In it, however, is also expressed the scientific ideal of the experimenting researcher who would have his method entirely independent from the person. The precise quotation and its context are the basis for the following assumption: "The doctor should be opaque to his patients and, like a mirror, should show them nothing but what is shown to him" (Freud, 1912, p. 118). Freud wanted to purify the psychoanalytical method of all undesirable elements, and if one takes the quotation to the letter, of all personal elements. It is clear that this summons should not be taken literally. All witnesses tell us that as a physician Freud himself provided another example. If the psychoanalyst behaves only like a mirror and adds nothing to what is shown, then the psychoanalytic process can never get started (see Stone, 1961). The explanatory psychoanalytic theories pass their tests of verification as far as the elimination of the repetition compulsion. That it is interrupted must be attributed to *new* experiences which the patient has in communicating with the psychoanalyst and which he tries out and enlarges. Verification and falsification of the theory are thereby complicated, particularly since the conditional prognoses depend on the question of whether or not new experiences take place.

Thus, no testing of psychoanalytic theory is possible without considering that the method is embedded in human interaction. The transference onto the mirror characterizes *one* side of this interaction. What takes place in the psychoanalytic situation is more than the testing of a theory that refers to the psychopathogenesis up to the immediate present. The very title of the study on technique, "Remembering, Repeating, and Working Through" (Freud, 1914b), permits us to perceive that the working-through leads via remembering (past) and repeating (present) to the future. That the psychoanalyst, precisely in this working-through, acts as mediator to new experiences and makes positive identifications possible, is self-evident. This is essential and constitutive for therapy, though it complicates the testing of the theory. There is no reason, however, to speak of suggestion where the psychoanalyst is acting as a person.

Summary

In preparing our empirical research, we have reviewed the discussion about the scientific-systematic position and about the logical status of psychoanalysis so as to determine our own position within these controversies. Our work mediates between the attempts at methodological clarification that have been made by psychoanalytic authors and the debate about the character of psychoanalysis — whether it is science or hermeneutic-dialectic procedure — which has been carried on by non-analysts. The conception of psychoanalysis as "depth hermeneutics" has been criticized along the lines of Popper and Albert. In our opinion, the grounding of all psychoanalytic knowledge on the basis of a strict psychology of *Verstehen* would limit the empirical basis of psychoanalysis. Objectifying methods are an indispensable corrective in this regard. We have considered the relationship between psychoanalytic theory and therapy. Psychoanalytic data collection must be made reliable, the theoretical concepts sharpened, and the rules for translating them into empirical tests of falsification defined. According to Freud, metapsychological concepts belong to a "speculative superstructure" whose relevance diminishes with increasing distance from clinical experience. In agreement with Waelder (1962) and Wisdom (1971, 1972), we distinguish the following steps in psychoanalytic theory: (communicated) observational data; clinical generalizations; clinical theory; metapsychology, Freud's "personal philosophy." Objectification and falsification apply chiefly to "clinical theory."

113

We have discussed the dovetailing of general theories (chiefly the theory of neurosis) with interpretations as they occur in psychoanalytic therapy and with the theory of such interpretations. The concept of repetition compulsion refers to a psychic apparatus as a relatively closed system that is embedded in life history and in whose frame motives become effective in the guise of causes. The proof of any hypothesis under consideration consists in the elimination of those initial conditions that potentiated the repetition compulsion. Whereas Habermas contends that the patient's self-reflection is the sole criterion for the revision of disturbed formative processes, we criticize this view as a utopian-dogmatic overestimation of the role of knowledge. We have discussed the role of description, explanation, and prediction in psychoanalysis, and have dealt with the problem of circularity of reasoning and self-fulfilling prophecy in psychoanalytic practice and its consequences for clinical research.

REFERENCES

Abel, T. (1953), The operation called *Verstehen*. In: *Readings in the Philosophy of Science*, ed. H. Feigl & M. Brodbeck. New York: Appleton-Century-Crofts, pp. 677-688.

Adorno, T. W., et al. (1969), *Der Positivismusstreit in der deutschen Soziologie*. Neuwied & Berlin: Luchterhand.

Albert, H. (1968), Theorie und Prognose in den Sozialwissenschaften. In: *Logik der Sozialwissenschaften*, ed. E. Topitsch. Cologne: Kiepenheuer & Witsch.

_____ (1969), Im Rücken des Positivismus? In: Adorno et al., 1969.

_____ (1971), *Plädoyer für kritischen Raionalismus*. Munich: Piper.

_____ ed. (1972), *Theorie und Realität*. Tübingen: Mohr/Siebeck.

Allport, G. W. (1937), *Personality: A Psychological Interpretation*. New York: Holt.

Apel, K. O. (1955), Das Verstehen. *Archiv. für Begriffsgeschichte*. 1:142-199.

_____ (1967), *Analytic Philosophy of Language and the Geisteswissenschaften*. Dordrecht: Reidel.

_____ (1971), Szientistik, Hermeneutik, Ideologiekritik. In: *Hermeneutik und Ideologiekritik*. Frankfurt: Suhrkamp, pp. 7-44.

Bellak, L., & Smith, M. B. (1956), An experimental exploration of the psychoanalytic process. *Psychoanal. Quart.*, 25:385-414.

Benjamin, J. D. (1950), Methodological considerations in the validation and elaboration of psychoanalytical personality theory. *Amer. J. Orthopsychiat.*, 20:139-156.

_____ (1959), Prediction and psychopathological theory. In: *Dynamic Pathology in Childhood*, ed. L. Jessner & E. Pavenstedt. New York: Grune & Stratton, pp. 6-77.

Bernfeld, S. (1934), Die Gestalttheorie. *Imago*, 20:32-77.

Bonaparte, M. (1945), Notes on the analytic discovery of a primal scene. *The Psychoanalytic Study of the Child*, 1:119-125. New York: International Universities Press.

Breuer, J. & Freud, S. (1893-1895), Studies on Hysteria. *Standard Edition*. London: Hogarth Press, 1955.

Bühler, K. (1927), *Die Krise der Psychologie*. Jena: Fischer.

Carnap, R. (1950), *The Logical Foundations of Probability*. Chicago: University of Chicago Press.

Cremerius, J. (1971), *Neurose und Genialität*. Frankfurt: Fischer.

Danto, A. C. (1965), *Analytical Philosophy of History*. Cambridge: Cambridge University Press.

Deutsch, H. (1928), Ein Frauenschicksal: George Sand. *Imago*, 14:334-357.

Devereux, G. (1951), Some criteria for the timing of confrontations and interpretations. *Internat. J. Psycho-Anal.*, 32:19-24.

Dilthey, W. (1894), Ideen über eine beschreibende und zergliedernde Psychologie. *Sitzungsbericht der Kgl. Preuss. Akad. d. Wiss.*, 29:1342.

———— (1900), Die Entstehung der Hermeneutik. In: *Gesammelte Schriften*, 5:317 ff. Stuttgart: Teubner, 1964.

Eagle, M. (1973), Sherwood on the logic of explanation in psychoanalysis. In: *Psychoanalysis and Contemporary Science*, 2, ed. B. Rubenstein. New York: Macmillan, pp. 331-337.

Eissler, K. R. (1968), The relation of explaining and understanding in psychoanalysis: Demonstrated by one aspect of Freud's approach to literature. *The Psychoanalytic Study of the Child*, 23:141-177. New York: International Universities Press.

———— (1971), Death drive, ambivalence, and narcissism. *The Psychoanalytic Study of the Child*, 23:25-78. New York: International Universities Press.

Escalona, S. (1952), Problems in psycho-analytic research. *Internat. J. Psycho-Anal.*, 33:11-21.

Farrell, B. A. (1961), Can psychoanalysis be refuted? *Inquiry*, 1:16-36.

———— (1964), The criteria for a psychoanalytic interpretation. In: *Essays in Philosophical Psychology*, ed. D. Gustafson. Garden City, New York: Anchor Books.

Freud, A. (1936), *The Ego and the Mechanisms of Defense. The Writings of Anna Freud*, 2. New York: International Universities Press, 1966.

———— (1958), Child observation and prediction of development. *The Psychoanalytic Study of the Child*, 13:92-116, with discussions by R. Spitz, 117-119, H. Hartmann, 120-122, R. Waelder, 123-124. New York: International Universities Press.

Freud, S. (1895a), Project for a scientific psychology. *Standard Edition*, 1:283-397. London: Hogarth Press, 1966.

———— (1895b), A reply to criticisms of my paper on anxiety neurosis. *Standard Edition*, 3:123-139. London: Hogarth Press, 1962.

———— (1896), The aetiology of hysteria. *Standard Edition*, 3:191-221. London: Hogarth Press, 1962.

———— (1900), The interpretation of dreams. *Standard Edition*, 4 & 5. London: Hogarth Press, 1953.

———— (1901), The psychopathology of everyday life. *Standard Edition*, 6. London: Hogarth Press, 1960.

———— (1905), Three essays on the theory of sexuality. *Standard Edition*, 7:125-243. London: Hogarth Press, 1953.

———— (1909a), Five lectures on psychoanalysis. *Standard Edition*, 11:9-56. London: Hogarth Press, 1957.

———— (1909b), Analysis of a phobia in a five-year-old boy. *Standard Edition*, 10:3-149. London: Hogarth Press, 1955.

———— (1912), Recommendations to physicians practicing psycho-analysis. *Standard Edition*, 12:109-120. London: Hogarth Press, 1958.

———— (1914a), On narcissism: An introduction. *Standard Edition*, 14:73-102. London: Hogarth Press, 1957.

———— (1914b), Remembering, repeating and working through. *Standard Edition*, 12:147-156. London: Hogarth Press, 1958.

———— (1915a), Instincts and their vicissitudes. *Standard Edition*, 14:109-140. London: Hogarth Press, 1957.

———— (1915b), A case of paranoia running counter to the psycho-analytic theory of the disease. *Standard Edition*, 14:261-272. London: Hogarth Press, 1957.

———— (1916-1917), Introductory lectures on psycho-analysis. *Standard Edition*, 15 & 16. London: Hogarth Press, 1963.

———— (1918), From the history of an infantile neurosis. *Standard Edition*, 17:3-122. London: Hogarth Press, 1955.

———— (1920a), Beyond the pleasure principle. *Standard Edition*, 18:3-64. London: Hogarth Press, 1955.

_____ (1920b), The psychogenesis of a case of homosexuality in a woman. *Standard Edition,* 18:145-172. London: Hogarth Press, 1955.

_____ (1921), Group psychology and the analysis of the ego. *Standard Edition,* 18:67-143. London: Hogarth Press, 1955.

_____ (1925), An autobiographical study. *Standard Edition,* 20:7-74. London: Hogarth Press, 1959.

_____ (1926), Inhibitions, symptoms and anxiety. *Standard Edition,* 20:77-172. London: Hogarth Press, 1959.

_____ (1933), New introductory lectures on psycho-analysis. *Standard Edition,* 22:7-182. London: Hogarth Press, 1964.

_____ (1937), Constructions in analysis. *Standard Edition,* 23:255-269. London: Hogarth Press, 1964.

Gadamer, H. G. (1965), *Wahrheit und Methode: Anwendungen einer philosophischen Hermeneutik.* Tübingen: Mohr/Siebeck.

_____ (1971a), Replik. In: *Hermeneutik und Ideologiekritik.* Frankfurt: Suhrkamp, pp. 283-317.

_____ (1971b), Rhetorik, Hermeneutik und Ideologiekritik. In: *Hermeneutik und Ideologiekritik.* Frankfurt: Suhrkamp, pp. 57-82.

Giegel, H. J. (1971), Reflexion und Emanzipation. In: *Hermeneutik und Ideologiekritik.* Frankfurt: Suhrkamp, pp. 244-282.

Glover, E. (1947), Basic mental concepts: Their clinical and theoretical value. *Psychoanal. Quart.,* 16:482-506.

Göttner, H. (1973), *Logik der Interpretation.* Munich: Fink.

Greenson, R. R. (1960), Empathy and its vicissitudes. *Internat. J. Psycho-anal.,* 41:418-424.

Guntrip, H. (1961), *Personality Structure and Human Interaction.* New York: International Universities Press.

Habermas, J. (1963), Analytische Wissenschaftstheorie und Dialektik: Ein Nachtrag zur Kontroverse zwischen Popper und Adorno. In: *Zeugnisse: Theodor W. Adorno zum sechzigsten Geburtstag.* Frankfurt: Europ. Verlagsanstalt, pp. 473-501.

_____ (1967), *Zur Logik der Sozialwissenschaften.* Tübingen: Mohr/Siebeck.

_____ (1969), Gegen einen positivistisch halbierten Rationalismus. In: Adorno et al (1969), p. 235.

_____ (1971a), *Knowledge and Human Interests.* Boston: Beacon Press.

_____ (1971b), Zu Gadamers "Wahrheit und Methode." In: *Hermeneutik und Ideologiekritik.* Frankfurt: Suhrkamp, pp. 45-56.

Hartmann, H. (1927), *Die Gundlagen der Psychoanalyse.* Leipzig: Thieme.

_____ (1958), Discussion of Anna Freud's "Child Observation and Prediction in Development." *The Psychoanalytic Study of the Child,* 13:120-122. New York: International Universities Press.

Heimann, P. (1969), Gedanken zum Erkenntnisprozess der Psychoanalytikers. *Psyche,* 23:2-24.

Hempel, C. G. (1952), Problems of concept and theory formation in the social sciences. In: *Science, Language and Human Rights.* Philadelphia: University of Pennsylvania Press, pp. 65-68.

_____ (1965), *Aspects of Scientific Explanation.* Glencoe, Ill.: Free Press.

_____ & Oppenheim, P. (1953), The logic of explanation. In: *Readings in the Philosophy of Science,* ed. H. Feigl & M. Brodbeck. New York: Appleton-Century-Crofts, pp. 319-352.

Holt, R. R. (1962), A critical examination of Freud's concept of bound vs. free cathexis. *J. Amer. Psychoanal. Assn.,* 10:475-525.

_____ (1965), A review of some of Freud's biological assumptions and their influence on his theories. In: *Psychoanalysis and Current Biological Thought.* Madison, Wis.: University of Wisconsin Press.

_____ & Luborsky, L. (1958), *Personality Patterns of Psychiatrists.* Vol. I. New York: Basic Books. Vol. II, Topeka, Kan.: Menninger Foundation.

Holzkamp, K. (1970), Wissenschaftstheoretische Voraussetzungen kritisch emanzipatorischer Psychologie. *Zschr. Sozialpsychol.,* 1:5-21, 109-141.

Hook, S., ed. (1959) *Psychoanalysis, Scientific Method, and Philosophy.* New York: New York University Press.

Jaspers, K. (1948), *General Psychopathology.* Chicago: University of Chicago Press, 1963.

Jones, E. (1953), *The Life and Work of Sigmund Freud*, 1. New York: Basic Books.

Kelly, E. L., & Fiske, D. W. (1950), The prediction of success in the VA training program in clinical psychology. *Amer. Psychol.*, 5:395-406.

_____ (1951), *The Prediction of Performance in Clinical Psychology*. Ann Arbor: University of Michigan Press.

Kempski, J. von (1952), Zur Logik der Ordnungsbegriffe, besonders in den Sozialwissenschaften. *Studium Generale*, 5, pt. 4.

Klauber, J. (1968), On the dual use of historical and scientific method in psychoanalysis. *Internat. J. Psycho-Anal.*, 49:80-87.

Kohut, H. (1959), Introspection, empathy and psychoanalysis. *J. Amer. Psychoanal. Assn.*, 7:459-483.

Kris, E. (1950), *Introduction to: S. Freud, Aus den Anfängen der Psychoanalyse*. London: Imago.

_____ (1951), Ego psychology and interpretation in psychoanalytic therapy. *Psychoanal. Quart.*, 20:15-30.

Kuhn, T. (1962), *The Structure of Scientific Revolutions. International Encyclopedia of Unified Science*, Vol. 2, no. 2. Chicago: University of Chicago Press.

Kuiper, P. C. (1964), Verstehende Psychologie und Psychoanalyse. *Psyche*, 18:15-32.

_____ (1965), Diltheys Psychologie und ihre Beziehung zur Psychoanalyse. *Psyche*, 19:241-249.

Levi, L. H. (1963), *Psychological Interpretation*. New York: Holt, Rhinehart & Winston.

Lewin, K. (1937), Psychoanalysis and topological psychology. *Bull. Menninger Clin.*, 1:202-212.

Lindzey, G. (1967), Some remarks concerning incest, the incest taboo, and psychoanalytic theory. *American Psychologist*, 22:1051-1059.

Loch, W. (1965), *Voraussetzungen, Mechanismen und Grenzen des psychoanalytischen Prozesses*. Bern/Stuttgart: Huber.

Loewald, H. W. (1971), On motivation and instinct theory. *The Psychoanalytic Study of the Child*, 26:91-128. New York: Quadrangle Books.

Loewenstein, R. M. (1951), The problem of interpretation. *Psychoanal. Quart.*, 20:1-14.

Lorenzer, A. (1970), *Sprachzerstörung und Rekonstruktion*. Frankfurt: Suhrkamp.

Luborsky, L., & Schimek, J. (1964), Psychoanalytic theories of therapeutic and developmental change: Implications for assessment. In: *Personality Change*, ed. P. Worchel & D. Byrne. New York: Wiley, pp. 73-99.

MacIntyre, A. C. (1958), *The Unconscious: A Conceptual Analysis*. London: Routledge & Kegan Paul.

Malan, D. H. (1963), *A Study of Brief Psychotherapy*. London: Tavistock.

Meehl, P. E. (1963), *Clinical Versus Statistical Prediction*. Minneapolis: University of Minnesota Press.

_____ (1973), Some methodological considerations concerning some problems of psychoanalytic research. In: *Psychoanalytic Research* [*Psychological Issues*, Monog. 30]. New York: International Universities Press.

Meissner, W. W. (1971), Freud's methodology. *J. Amer. Psychoanal. Assn.*, 19:265-309.

Merton, R. K. (1957), The self-fulfilling prophecy. In: *Social Theory and Social Structure*. New York: Free Press, pp. 421-436.

_____ (1968), Die Eigendynamik gesellschaftlicher Voraussagen. In: *Logik der Sozialwissenschaften*, ed. E. Topitsch. Cologne: Kiepenheuer & Witsch.

Meyer, A. E. (1967), Die Interbeobachter-Übereinstimmung: Ein psychologisches Methoden-Kriterium und seine Bedeutung in der Medizin. *Mat. Med. Nordmark*, 19:196.

Moore, G. E. (1955), Wittgenstein's lectures in 1930-33. Reprinted in: *Philosophical Papers*. London: Allen & Unwin.

Nichols, C. (1972), Science or reflection: Habermas on Freud. *Phil. Soc. Sci.*, 2:261-270.

Perrez, M. (1971), Zur wissenschaftlichen Theoriebildung und zum Bewährungsproblem in der Psychoanalyse. *Z. f. Klin. Psychother.*, 19:221-242.

Popper, K. (1944), *The Open Society and Its Enemies*. Princeton: Princeton University Press, 1963.

_____ (1957), *The Poverty of Historicism*. Boston: Beacon Press.

_____ (1959), *The Logic of Scientific Discovery*. New York: Basic Books.

117

_____ (1963), *Conjectures and Refutations*. London: Routledge & Kegan Paul.

_____ (1972), Die Zielsetzung der Erfahrungswissenschaft. In: Albert (1972).

Radnitzky, G. (1973), *Contemporary Schools of Metascience*. Chicago: Regnery.

Rapaport, D. (1960), *The Structure of Psychoanalytic Theory: A Systematizing Attempt* [*Psychological Issues*, Monog. 6]. New York: International Universities Press.

_____ & Gill, M. M. (1959), The points of view and assumptions of metapsychology. *Internat. J. Psycho-Anal.*, 40:153-162.

Ricoeur, P. (1970), *Freud and Philosophy*. New Haven and London: Yale University Press.

Rosenblatt, A. D., & Thickstun, J. T. (1970), The concept of psychic energy. *Internat. J. Psycho-Anal.*, 51:3, 265-278.

Rosenkötter, L. (1969), Über Kriterien der Wissenschaftlichkeit in der Psychoanalyse. *Psyche*, 23: 161-169.

Rubinstein, B. B. (1973), On the logic of explanation in psychoanalysis. In: *Psychoanalysis and Contemporary Science*, 2. New York: Macmillan, pp. 338-358.

Ryle, G. (1965), *The Concept of Mind*. New York: Barnes & Noble.

Sandler, J., et al. (1962), The classification of superego material in the Hampstead Index. *The Psychoanalytic Study of the Child*, 17:107-127. New York: International Universities Press.

Sargent, H., et al. (1968), *Prediction in Psychotherapy Research* [*Psychological Issues*, Monog. 21]. New York: International Universities Press.

Schmidl, F. (1955), The problem of scientific validation in psychoanalytic interpretation. *Internat. J. Psycho-Anal.*, 36:105-113.

Scriven, M. (1959), Explanation and prediction in evolutionary theory. *Science*, 130:477-482.

Seitz, P. F. D. (1966), The consensus problem in psychoanalytic research. In: *Methods of Research in Psychotherapy*, ed. L. A. Gottschalk & A. H. Auerbach. New York: Appleton-Century-Crofts.

Sherwood, M. (1969), *The Logic of Explanation in Psychoanalysis*. New York: Academic Press.

_____ (1973), Another look at the logic of explanation in psychoanalysis. In: *Psychoanalysis and Contemporary Science*, 2, ed. B. B. Rubinstein. New York: Macmillan, pp. 359-366.

Shope, R. (1971), Psychical and psychic energy. *Philosophy of Science*, 38:1-12.

Stegmüller, W. (1969), *Probleme und Resultate der Wissenschaftstheorie und analytischen Philosophie*. Vol. I: *Wissenschaftliche Erklärung und Begründung*. Berlin: Springer.

Stierlin, H. (1972), Review of: *Sprachzerstörung und Rekonstruktion*, by A. Lorenzer. *Internat. J. Psycho-Anal.*, 53:422-425.

Stone, L. (1961), *The Psychoanalytic Situation*. New York: International Universities Press.

Thomä, H. & Houben, A. (1967), Über die Validierung psychoanalytischer Theorien durch die Untersuchung von Deutungsaktionen. *Psyche*, 21:664-692.

Truax, C. B., & Mitchell, K. M. (1971), Research on certain therapist interpersonal skills in relation to process and outcome. In: *Handbook of Psychotherapy and Behavior Change*, ed. A. Bergin & S. Garfield. New York: Wiley.

Uexküll, T. von (1963), *Grundfragen der psychosomatischen Medizin*. Hamburg: Rowohlt.

Waelder, R. (1962), Psychoanalysis, scientific method, and philosophy. *J. Amer. Psychoanal. Assn.*, 10:617-637.

_____ (1963), Psychic determinism and the possibility of predictions. *Psychoanal. Quart.*, 32: 15-42.

_____ (1967), *Progress and Revolution: A Study of the Issues of our Age*. New York: International Universities Press.

Weber, M. (1951), *Gesammelte Aufsätze zur Wissenschaftslehre*. Tübingen: Winckelmann.

Weiss, P. (1965), *The Persecution and Assassination of Jean-Paul Marat as Performed by the Inmates of the Asylum of Charenton under the Direction of the Marquis de Sade*. New York: Atheneum.

Weizsäcker, C. F. von (1971), *Die Einheit der Natur*. Munich: Hanser.

Wellmer, A. (1967), *Methodologie als Erkenntnistheorie*. Frankfurt: Suhrkamp.

Wisdom, J. O. (1967), Testing an interpretation within a session. *Internat. J. Psycho-Anal.*, 48: 44-52.

_____ (1971), Freud and Melanie Klein: Psychology, ontology, and Weltanschauung. In: *Philosophy and Psychoanalysis*, ed. C. Hanley & M. Lazerowitz. New York: International Universities Press, pp. 327-362.

_____ (1972), A graduated map of psychoanalytic theories. *Monist*, 56:376-412.

Wyss, E. (1961), *Die tiefenpsychologischen Schulen von den Anfängen bis zur Gegenwart*. Göttingen: Vandenhoeck & Ruprecht.

September, 1972

II

CLINICAL STUDIES

The Parent's Psychic Reality
as a Part of the
Child's Psychic Reality

AUGUSTA BONNARD, M.D., F.R.C. Psych. (*London*)

Pleased as I am to pay tribute to Dr. Sterba, my chief qualification for doing so would seem to be that, although my published output is far smaller than his, its subject matter is no less diversified. Since my principal current preoccupation is with the ordering of a wide range of clinical material from two follow-up research studies,[1] I would like to extract an offering that should prove pertinent to one of Dr. Sterba's published themes. I do so also for the purpose of exemplifying the two-way feedback advantage accruing from working in private practice as a psychoanalyst and in a clinic, as a child psychiatrist, with case material from both.

In a communication "On Hallowe'en," Dr. Sterba (1948) shows very clearly how differently this occasion is [consciously] understood and cele-

---

Dr. Bonnard died on October 11, 1974.

This paper was originally written in honor of Dr. Richard Sterba, on the occasion of his 75th birthday.

[1] Each of these studies is of one hundred of my own diagnostic, etc. child cases from my part-time career of 25 years as the Consultant Psychiatrist of the East London Child Guidance Clinic, situated in the London Jewish Hospital. One of these studies is likely to be unique in that it represents a personal second follow-up investigation by the original diagnostician (myself) covering a total time span, since the first diagnostic encounter, of 25 or more years. The group of one hundred *unselected* cases were originally drawn from a much bombed area of London, i.e., one with major ongoing changes in its population. Nevertheless, thanks mainly to the skill and devotion of Miss K. Lewis, now a retired Divisional School Care Officer, only 20 of these cases have proved wholly untraceable. Of the rest about whom we have information, no less than 44 cases have been personally interviewed by me, and another eight by my deputies. Twelve have emigrated and two have died. In my view and that of others familiar with this changed area, this is a remarkably high "recovery" rate. Both this second follow-up study and the other five-year-plus follow-up, i.e., a recent one (of one hundred cases *selected for their clinical merits*) are sponsored by "my" North Eastern Metropolitan Regional Hospital Board, i.e., they are the beneficiaries of governmental support. Fortunately, these studies have proved extremely interesting and instructive.

123

brated in Austria, the land of his upbringing, and in America. He describes how, in Austria, a predominantly Catholic country, it retains its solemn religious preoccupation with the dead, as the eve of All Souls' Day. Dr. Sterba postulates that its intrinsic connection with death is "overlooked," i.e., denied, in its American variant. Instead, it is transmuted into a "fun" festival, with the roles of malevolent-looking black witches being played out for the adults by the children. Other deathly representations occur in the form of skull-like cut-out pumpkins with lights inside. It is the children's prerogative at Halloween to confront the adults in playful ways with these emblems of death, the relevant significance of which is consciously (or culturally) denied. Thereby, the children confront their parents with their adult (repressed) fears of death and so reinstate the psychic significance to them of this seemingly jolly occasion. No doubt Dr. Sterba would agree that this interpretation of Halloween as celebrated in America (and in some of the northern parts of England, where its manifestation of witches is regarded as pagan) would be one type of example (Dr. Sterba's being of a boomerang order) illustrative of a psychoanalytically couched concept of mine: that "part of a child's external reality is comprised of the psychic reality of its parent(s)." This concept was first publicly cited and attributed to me by Anna Freud in her Address to the Sixteenth International Psycho-analytical Congress, held in Switzerland in 1949. Unfortunately, her presentation seems not to have been published, so now I can reinstate it here, both literally and relevantly, in its actual clinical matrix.

The concept finally crystallized out of consecutive studies of seven children exhibiting school phobia whom I treated at the clinic. Their case material was presented at the First International Congress of Psychiatry held in Paris in 1950, under the title "School Phobia: Is It a Syndrome?" (Bonnard, 1950). The syndromal link among all these cases came from my realization that each of these children had at least one paranoid parent. While, thanks to further extensive experience with this symptomatic condition, I no longer consider it always to be specifically syndromal, as I tentatively did then, it may be of interest that the presence of a paranoid parent has continued to figure in subsequent case material of mine and of others, as the single most common parental factor associated with this condition.

These and allied symptomatic conditions are, of course, strikingly illustrative of this comprehensive concept. It is, therefore, curiously pleasurable to me to be able to present an actual example from this series of seven early cases, one I recognized long ago as germinal to the concept in question: a patient who not only "fell" luckily into the *unselected* first follow-up study but who has, to my further enlightenment, been personally interviewed by me recently. His case was a pathological variant and obverse of Dr. Sterba's theme. However, the knowledge gained from this germinal case was to fortify me in my subsequent under-standing and dealings with this and other allied symptomatic conditions, including a work phobia in an adult analytic case (with a pseudo scientist, i.e., a paraphrenic mother).

There may be those who regard the kind of clinic material here presented as psychoanalytically wanting in that it does not emanate from the validating consonance of deductions derived from analytic treatment. Even so, it would be a mistake to regard this as either shallow inquiry or "inspired guesswork." Let us begin with the fact that, except under the conditions and practices of child analysis, real opportunities are rarely granted to us as analysts for direct observation and evaluation of at least one of the patient's parents. Nor is informed elicitation from a relevant adult, including statements in regard to other relevant adults, or sibs or others, a routine possibility in psychoanalytic practice. To be so excel-lently served as by one's colleagues in a child psychiatric clinic, furnished with a social history, with the psychologist's findings, with a school report where relevant and sometimes invaluable data from other agencies are provided, is indeed a rare opportunity.

In other words, in a clinic setup, we usually do not have to lose considerable diagnostic time in groping for significant "leads" and data; or, if we do have thus to grope under the facilitating conditions of clinic inquiry, we are usually drawn into other aspects of the clinical picture. Nor in analytic practice would it be feasible, other than by exception, even with child cases, to interview the patient effectively, whether separately or together with the parent, on the same diagnostic occasion — an over-all procedure for which a minimum of one and a half hours was allocated in the clinic.

Then, too, the fact of having interviewed both parent and child with no gap in time can bring enormous observational advantages;[2] with some children, the situation of sitting and waiting in the clinic premises, knowing that they themselves are the subject of discussion, can of itself sometimes provide remarkable facilitating consequences. (This would not, however, be recommended as standard procedure, since it can also have serious drawbacks, especially in private practice.) Furthermore, at the end of these diagnostic encounters in the clinic, a psychiatric report was routine, even if it was stated to be incomplete, hypothetical, or

---

[2] This was of pathognomonic significance in the case about to be outlined.

125

otherwise lacking. Since all these reports would be read by others, known or unknown, this was a tough discipline, with uneven literary and other outcomes, dependent as these were on many other factors, such as the time left available, or fatigue, or presence or absence and quality of secretarial help. These reports and my subsequent notes of the follow-up cases, which of necessity have the finiteness of being limited, and which cover a total time span of not less than 25 years, can be peculiarly and unequivocally instructive precisely because they are so stonily sketched. The case material from the clinic is, therefore, proffered as being not shallow, but, at worst, if only very occasionally, incomplete or tentative, as most of these follow-up outcomes have reassuringly and instructively confirmed.

With this digression, we begin with the — for me, "historic" — case of a boy of fourteen and a half years of age, who as a school phobic had already absented himself from his ordinary school for six months. He was then attending a special class of five children.[3] As he was entitled in those days to leave school at the end of the following three-month term, the likelihood of transforming him back into a regular school pupil seemed small, particularly in view of the possibly psychotic nature of his disquieting rationalization for disliking the masters and pupils of his school. He had said that he refused to attend there because "they all sniffed at him." The logic of this possible "idea of reference," however, was no less disquieting. It devolved from his having come back from a school camping holiday where the teachers had led the way in being shirtless on warm days. Thereafter, he totally refused to wear a shirt. Instead, even during the winter term and until he had refused school attendance, he had insisted on wearing his overcoat in the classroom, beneath which was his bare torso. The fact is that, after months of this mode of dressing, his coat might well have become smelly. So, even if his remark of being sniffed at was not necessarily suggestive of incipient schizophrenia, his coat-wearing was.

This boy was the eldest of four children. His locally born and bred mother, having married a northerner, left London with her family when wartime bombing continued. She remained in the provinces with her husband's family during the war years. Until she left London, she and her

---

[3] Mr. J. C. Hill, the author of *Teaching and the Unconscious Mind* (1971), was that remarkable London County Council Divisional Inspector of Schools with whom I had the good fortune to be cooperating locally, who was the inaugurator of the initially experimental classes of five pupils to one gifted teacher for children with inhibitions of learning. He instituted these on the correct assumption that such children were likely to be emotionally disturbed or deprived. These "special tutorial" classes, now quite numerous in London, continue to prove their observational and therapeutic worth.

husband, he being largely unemployed and sickly, had continued to reside, together with her first two children, in her parents' small house. Therefore, my patient's upbringing had also been in the hands of his grandparents up to his seventh year. It seems he was very attached to them, especially to his grandfather. As his mother told both the psychiatric social worker and myself, when the war was over and her mother, having been widowed a year previously, became the sole occupant of a house, she decided to return to London.

In order to do so, she had asked if she and the baby could come and spend a holiday with grandma. Once there, as she put it, the other members of her family could gradually be inserted and remain. She said her mother dared not refuse because at that time, habitable dwellings were so few as a result of the bombing that some premises were being requisitioned by the local authorities on behalf of the homeless. She said that this fact had enabled her to threaten her mother into acquiescence.

Her mother, as she described her to me, was a snob who expected her daughter to care for every stick of furniture in the place (a daughter who was subject to a cleaning mania, as it turned out, and who had been a problem, as another agency informed us, throughout her youth), and was rarely to be found in her own home. Instead, over these last years, grandma consorted increasingly with her older child, another daughter, who lived luxuriously in an outer suburb, and who was married to a "posh" bank manager, her second husband. Indeed, as my patient's mother told me with flashing eyes, this sister of hers had the impertinence to invite her with her husband and family to visit at Christmas, only to insult them with gifts, as if to humiliate or make them envious. As I listened to this bedraggled creature's diatribes, it became clear that here was a case of paranoic jealousy. When it was the boy's turn to be interviewed by me, after a discussion with him of his schizophrenic type of (sniffing, etc.) accusations against his rejected school and his suffering from nightmares, he then launched into what sounded just like a gramaphone repetition of his mother's withering abuse of her own mother and sister. The only difference was that he did so in a north-country accent (his father's), one that he should have "lost" long ago, after he returned to London, the consequences of which he also complained about—i.e., of being quipped about his speech at school by other pupils.

As the clinical situation seemed so hopeless—i.e., the referral had come shortly before school-leaving age and I had a firm conviction that this hostile woman would never again set foot in the clinic—it seemed to me there was nothing to lose, other than the risk I had decided to take, based on my evolving rationale of school phobia. I therefore told the boy

127

that I had not been listening to him speaking to me, but only to his mother. He was telling me her jealous thoughts just as if he were a parrot. Surely he knew, as well as I did, that he had every reason to be grateful to his kindly aunt and uncle and to his grandmother and deceased grandfather. It was they who had mainly brought him up before he left London. And now he was in the position of almost having reached school-leaving age and was only attending a "special class." When he went out to find a job to earn for the family, as he told me he intended, he would discover that employers are interested in scholastic records. He must, therefore, hurry up and get back into school and show that he was a capable boy.

At the end of these statements, he looked at me with contempt and wanted to stalk out of my room. However, I went out with him to his mother and made an appointment for him two weeks hence, knowing that his (tutorial or special) class teacher would do her best to insure that he came to see me. Two weeks later, that is, three days before the Christmas holidays, a member of the office staff brought me an ultimatum from my patient. He had come and had allowed precisely five minutes of his time for the clinic, to which he had brought a friend, en route to an outing. When he came into my room, he told me that, in effect, I was impertinent and that he shared his mother's dislike of me. He informed me that this would be the last time he would see me, and so it was to be until 25 years later, in my home, for the follow-up interview. Intermediately, however, at the beginning of the next school term, he told his tutorial-class teacher that he was now considering his possible return to school, and he did so three weeks later. He stayed on to complete his last term, some weeks beyond the minimum leaving age, having acquitted himself there excellently in every respect. It was his special-class teacher who for years remained in touch with him and who obtained his first job for him as an office boy with a stockbroker. Here, too, he gave complete satisfaction, leaving in some kind of huff a week before being conscripted into the Royal Air Force. He remained voluntarily in the Air Force for an extra period, with great wisdom, although he was billeted part of the time at home. All of this I knew long before the follow-up encounter, i.e., a second follow-up, this last being perhaps my oddest meeting with him, but one to which he had readily agreed, having refused in the past when asked by his special-class teacher to see me.

The oddity lay, for me, in his breezy friendliness of manner, as if two erstwhile chums were meeting. It is true that he had a "success story" to tell as an earner and as a husband and father, which could give some semblance of logic to his good cheer, but the real oddity belonged to quite another quarter. From first to last, he spoke to and of me with friendly knowingness, of my being the "one who had understood it all from the word 'go.' " He did also say, under pressure, that I was the only one who had spotted what his trouble at home really was. So, too, I found it disconcerting that he spoke of his special-class teacher and long-term benefactress merely with offhand tolerance. Indeed, I found his fixed notion of my "cut-and-dried correctness" of the past so peculiar that I reminded him of his actual behavior with me, especially of his second and last brief visit. At this, he gazed at me incredulously and said, "But you knew perfectly well that I wasn't meaning one word. What else could I say to you then?" He was also able to give me the clearest accounts of the pathological features, past and present, presented by his mother and siblings. All three have remained unmarried and live with her and their nonworking father under her total domination.

Each sibling is employed in a menial capacity and with no will to self-betterment. My ex-patient described how often he had vainly pleaded with them to leave the mother and to strike out for themselves, but of this they were quite incapable. It was also interesting to be told, in view of what followed, that his wife was a "civilian employed in Scotland Yard" when he courted her and was an ex-grammar-school girl, i.e., one of probably superior intelligence and education, who regarded him as an amazingly shrewd and confident person. She found it hard to associate him with his peculiar family setup, and she disliked his mother, seeking actively to avoid them all. As for himself, he told me that he did not regret his strange upbringing. It had enabled him to have a kind of sixth sense in divining people's intentions and weaknesses, which was invaluable to his employers. Thus it was that there were few labor troubles among the workers for whom he was responsible, for if any were a nuisance, either in their views or in their eligibility for severance pay, whether for good or bad reasons, he knew how to "ease them out" of their jobs in advance, just as if they thought this had been their own idea. Of course, I finally had to wonder whether his mode of breezy assertion of my omniscience in the past might not have been an example of these supraparanoid aptitudes, but if so, then it was in its manner rather than in its content, in that he told me that his wife had been informed of my spell-breaking role for him.

The relevance of this case is that, presenting himself as he did initially as a potential schizophrenic or as a *folie à deux* (or maybe both), there can be no doubt that an all but paramount part of his external reality seemed to be comprised by the psychic reality of his mother, albeit as a form of adaptation. Yet, as my subsequent experience has taught me, the symptomatic condition of school phobia, while exemplifying the "spell" by which *some* of these children are held by their parents, also signals to external society their need for help.

Expressed otherwise, with certain of these cases or those with allied symptomatologies, the emergence of such a "nuisance" symptom, i.e., one that does not brook being ignored, may well prove to be the mark of (reality-testing) ego-resilient struggle: it may be indicative of potential health and not the opposite, as tends to be assumed. The positive connotations of the symptomatologies of children constitutes a major topic in its own right. What does need to be stressed, however, is that, inasmuch as the dynamic function of a symptom such as school phobia is to mislead (*including the patient*), the child's behavior and those subjected to it can, therefore, become no less misleading or misled.

As I now know, neither the officials concerned with this patient nor his father attributed his return to school to my intervention. This was not only because it was so short and sharp (its disconcerting effect on the boy having immediately been realized by his teacher) but also because he dissembled defensively with respect to the nature or source of his change of attitude toward school attendance. So there, too, is another small item that could have had great significance and which is pertinent to the fact that the psychic reality of each parent constitutes a part of the child's external reality.

We, or maybe the special teacher, did succeed in having this weakling husband call in at the clinic. There he agreed that "his wife lives and breathes her sister and mother." If he had indicated this opinion to his son at that period, then this, too, would have provided a strong therapeutic spur to his return to school, since in these cases, it is usually the lack of a confrontatory dissident parental figure (i.e., who encourages a capacity for normal reality-testing) that is so pathogenically denied to these children in question.[4] All in all, it was the special teacher whom this passive father regarded as having cured his son, a success that his amour propre would prefer to concede to her. While every analyst must be aware of many examples among their patients of the consequences of their parents' psychic reality on the tenor of their lives (especially when this is unfavorable), the cases here to be cited would seem to me to have a more transparent quality, particularly if the word *trans-parent* is noted to be a pun — its choice in this sense having been unintentional.

The next example is also of a boy patient, one of nearly nine years of

---

[4] My presentation is highly condensed, as this case shows. For example, the fact that this boy had retained a northern accent of itself indicated an obstinate allegiance to an area where his mother had been in the minority.

age, brought to the clinic by his mother, mainly with the determination to have him permanently institutionalized. She made no secret of the fact that her husband had divorced her on his demobilization at the end of World War II because she had given birth to an illegitimate child. He was then to take custody of the two eldest children, apparently abandoning his two younger ones to her to bring up along with the bastard child. Consequently, she had to make many moves, including positions in and out of domestic service. Her living conditions were, therefore, difficult and uncertain. She claimed that her chances of remarriage had been ruined two years previously by my patient through his rudeness and defiance to the man then in question. He had also become a determined wanderer from home, especially at night. She said she was convinced that he kept bad company, that he pilfered and was well on the road to delinquency. In any event, she claimed that she *must* dispose of him again, owing to overcrowding. The fact was that he had already experienced separation from her in having been placed in a wartime residential nursery between the ages of three-and-a-half to five years, where, she said, she had to assume he must have been a nuisance, although one member of the staff had later corresponded with him for a while. (My arithmetic told me that it was during this period that she gave birth to the illegitimate child.)

When I interviewed this good-looking and upstanding youngster, who had scored the absurdly low I.Q. level of 69, he answered me in the firmest tones. I asked why it was that his mother wanted to place him in a residential school. Somewhat to my surprise, he answered that this was because he was a thief. I, therefore, asked him to inform me of some of the articles he had stolen. This he did forthwith, and as the list and its nature developed impossibly, I decided that here was a bitter child "out-Heroding Herod," who was no thief, as I was to tell him. I explained that his mother just could not manage to earn enough and look after three children in their overcrowded conditions and that, as he was the eldest, we would do our best to place him in a nice residential school, maybe a bit like the nursery of which he had had experience, except that this would be a school for older children. He further informed me that his younger half-brother was the son of his mother's neighbors, both of whom had been killed in an air raid, a fact that accounted for his different surname.

His, too, was an unselected follow-up case that was part of the first study. We did not meet again after this single encounter until our follow-up interview in my home 25 years later. However, thanks to his nine-years' institutionalization in one school, I had been able to learn a

131

good deal about him at the first follow-up, and, subsequently, about his after-history.

Because he was the responsibility of an official organization, my sleuthing colleague was able to trace him to a quite far-off city, where his mother, having remarried, resided, as did his legitimate and now married sister. At the time he was finally reached via his mother's cooperation, she was dying from secondary carcinoma, as she tactfully conveyed to me by phone. Indeed, she must have been an individual with a remarkable personality in that the other (illegitimate) son also turned out to be nearby, having returned from the other side of the world where he had emigrated. The legitimate half-brother was to inform me that he came back as soon as he knew of his mother's dire condition, bringing a wife of clearly non-European stock. In my few dealings with this mother in the past, and then again years later by phone, she presented herself as a person of exquisitely refined manners and diction, quite a mystery woman, one who was also aware of her ongoing untruthfulness and yet had a becoming frankness. From what has already been indicated and from what follows, it is clear that her capacity for forging libidinal ties with her three children and creating a need to please her must have been quite remarkable.

When this attractive man of good attire and presence came to see me (as did also his emigrant half-brother on another occasion, he too having been my patient briefly and thus included in this follow-up study), I was confronted by someone whose profound and unshakable sense of inferiority was as understandable as it was undeserved. Not only did his childhood experience include relegation to an institution for nine years, but when his stay there had to end and he had sought to rejoin his mother, then remarried, she had again refused to have him with her. He was therefore placed by the authorities with foster parents. He told me that he had felt quite lost with them and his work-mates, having no common life experiences to be able to share or even talk about. He described how, when at last he did rejoin his mother, his stepfather could barely tolerate him, a rejection that caused him to move elsewhere in the area. He then married and settled in the same town as his sister, where he had responsible employment in an engineering works.

He spoke of the sense of horrible unworthiness by which he felt himself imbued. (I knew his entire school and work records had remained impeccable throughout.) He said that only such a sentiment could explain how it was that his otherwise generous and loving mother needed to relegate him to an institution. Clearly, it was because he must have been a horrible kind of child. I asked him to be more specific. He told me that something remained of his past that had always puzzled him. While he was well aware that he had been a wanderer and a thief, yet, no matter how much he tried, he was never able to recollect an item he had stolen. It was most gratifying to be able to read to him verbatim the relevant part of my ancient psychiatric report. In it was the statement that this upstanding boy was no thief but was listing the articles he had stolen as a way of proffering a bitter excuse for his mother in ridding herself of him (again).

However, I broke no evil spell thereby, not even when I pointed out to him that his major preoccupation and curiosity ought to be in regard to the fate of his own father. Indeed, I went so far as to tell him that if he cared to come to see me again in due course, i.e., after his mother's demise, I might then be entitled to convey some items of personal information to him, but that, meanwhile, he should tactfully ask his mother about his paternal family. He did come to see me again after his mother's death, having gained very little information from her, because his questions, meager as these were, had upset her and, therefore, himself. When I could then tell him that he had two older siblings who might prove eager to know him, he showed total indifference, also to the prospect that his father might still be alive. Nor did the reiteration of my statements from the past, setting out that he had been no thief but an upstanding oedipal son, grant him much assurance or self-esteem. Instead, he told me that he could not be an affectionate father and that whereas both he and wife worked "Box and Cox" (she in the evenings) in order to be able to afford no less than the best, he got little joy out of life. He described how the employees under him seemed to think of him as a confident person, an appearance he was able to maintain provided people kept their distance. Nor had he any real friends, partly because he was so busy at home. This man was indeed an institutional creature of the best kind, in that he was an asset to his employers and to society at large, but he remained the rejected boy, unable to be lovable to his children, feeling it more prideful to be blameworthy, as his mother insisted to me that he was, rather than be merely nonsignificant to both his parents.

There are many other features of interest in his case, such as his "twinship" choice of wife, i.e., one who, like himself, although a manifest "success," could never claim to be superior to him on the score of her antecedents.[5] As can be deduced, the cruelty of this man's superego com-

---

[5] It may be of interest, not only that he told me at our first follow-up meeting that he was thinking of emigrating to the country of his half-brother's choice, but that this half-brother was the allegedly adopted child whom his mother had retained, but who now had moved far away from her. The step-brother, who, it will be recalled, also saw me, was much less intelligent and more banal and was

prised his mother's derogation of him as a child fit only to be institutionalized. Yet, to complicate the issue, it was also my guess, long ago, that part of the reason for his listing of crimes was to enable his return to a *reliable* environment. Indeed, his insistence that his nine years in the well-conducted boarding school "were the happiest of my life" fit in with my knowledge that the staff regarded him as a paragon. There, in an impersonal, i.e., emotionally neutral atmosphere, as in the engineering works where he is employed at present, by his reliability and high institutional standards, his superego could refute his idealized mother's banishment of him as an unwanted Jocasta's son.

The case of yet another boy patient will be cited in order to underline similarly the factor of falsification of memory and thus of the self, as a consequence of the parents's psychic reality. When he was nine years of age, he was brought by his widowed mother to the clinic, chiefly on account of "being oversensitive, crying too readily, and having temper tantrums when he wished his relatives dead." He was a highly intelligent child of parents of different ethnic and religious origins, who was being brought up by the mother and her parents in determined ignorance of his paternal identity and of his father's depressive past, which had ended some years previously.

When I interviewed him, I had the benefit of one of the routine

---

subjected to his stepfather's ongoing contempt. It was not he, however, who revealed that his wife is non-European nor that she dominates him. Such marriages in his adoptive land are uncommon and, as other allied material indicates, such marital choices tend to be associated either with a sense of basic inferiority or with a "frontal" rebelliousness. This man told me that he had always supposed himself to be illegitimate, although his birth was alleged to be otherwise. Then, too, perhaps his emigration enabled him to ignore the fact that his sibling had been "put away," as this procedure continues to be termed.

The account of this mother given by three devoted children whose lives were greatly traumatized by her surprisingly provided a study of charm and of an "idealizable" personality. Each knew her to be untruthful and with a past to hide, yet each regarded her as "a perfect lady" of kindliness and refinement. The fact would seem to be that some children accept the identificatory validity of the fantasy expressions of their parent's psychic reality, although its (usually) grandiose content can sometimes be discerned and even realized by the child. These fantasies, therefore, can continue their wishful destiny via the child's ego ideal.

Thus, for example, it turned out with a girl in analytic treatment with me that her ambition to be a ballet dancer devolved from one of her Lesbian mother's (borderline-psychotic) variations of her past. In this case, her career as a ballet dancer, as she told me, had been brought to an end when both her big toes had been fractured on rising up on her (ballet shoe) "points," when her toes penetrated right through the rotted floorboards of the stage. In fact, her nearest approach to this kind of past had been her employment as a cinema usherette. Had Freud left the two invaluable concepts of the ego ideal and the superego intact, these two pillars of our psychic reality would have allowed for the highly instructive differentiation of their constituents, such as, in this instance, of the child's ego-ideal implementation of her mother's psychic "irreality." Adelaide Johnson somewhat similarly described the enactment by the child of parental impulses, wishes, or fantasies as long ago as 1953.

advantages to hand with this kind of diagnostic work—the psychologist's report. She had commented on his reluctance to end the test situation, and his expression of surprise that it had not proved more difficult. She therefore accompanied him back to his mother, whom he delightedly told of the interesting activities he had enjoyed. The psychologist intervened to remark that he had worked hard and had done very well. Thereupon the mother looked incredulous and said she was surprised, "as he doesn't take in many things at school," thus indicating that his intellect did not appear to her to be good enough to justify such a complimentary statement. In fact, however, his school report was also excellent.

When I talked with the boy, he spontaneously informed me that he knew a great deal about his father's origins. For example, he told me that when an "outside lecturer" at his school had given a travel talk to his class, he had risen to point out to the visitor the very island whence his father had come. He also urged me to study it carefully in a large atlas, emphasizing that, despite its seeming smallness and the ugliness of its shape, and in contrast to the place where he was currently living, it was really an island of great variety and beauty, with its own religion. Indeed, he was eventually to ask whether the manner of which he (correctly) told me of his father's death could have been caused by mere inadvertence. When later I pleaded with his mother to desist from blocking the boy in his capacity for comprehension of his true identity and thus depriving him from gaining a well-founded sense of poise, she totally rejected my suggestion. The next and last time a visit was scheduled, she sent her mother and sister to the clinic without the boy to tell me my ideas were impossible.

Because of my interest in the evolution of his case (hence his inclusion in the second research series), reports on him covering a period of years were obtained from his school, as well as from another individual. Thanks to a special talent, he was undertaking a somewhat unusual university career. I therefore wrote him a very careful letter indicating my research interest in him, couched in terms of my desire to learn what it is that children are able to recall of their clinic experiences. He replied immediately to say that he recalled some kind of puzzling disagreement at the clinic that he would gladly come and discuss with me. Meanwhile, he asked me to let him know precisely for what reasons he had been originally brought to see me, emphasizing that he was aware of, and had fully concurred with, his mother's decision not to come to the clinic any more. He also wrote that he recalled having undertaken some tests there, which *"were not much good."*

For our present purposes, the feature of this response of relevance here is his apparently negative recollection of the clinic, which amounted to a faithful rendering of his mother's reactions and a reversal of those that had been his own. The fact is that in my report I stated my initial interview with the child to have been so unusually rich, fascinating, and dramatic that it ought to have been tape-recorded. I described how he had eagerly asked question after question, each as the prelude to the next, often exclaiming, "So, when can I come again?" At the end, I had commented that maybe next time I could give him some clearer explanations, as I would in the meantime be asking his mother to answer anything he chose to ask her, to which he had responded, "In fact you have answered quite a lot of these questions already." So, too, his present-day derogation of the tests consisted of a transposition of his mother's attitude toward them and her remark to the psychologist about him. In other words, the statement that he had worked and done well at these tests could not have been a valid compliment ("because the tests were no good," i.e., invalid). In this context, it should be recalled that he had urged me to give a fair-minded look at his father's island of origin so that I would appreciate it, despite its usual misleading and unfavorable representation. This was a plea he now disallowed on his own behalf, in accordance with his mother's viewpoint of himself and of the person (myself) he had been so keen to meet with again.

It should prove of great interest to those who may follow up this research in the future, to discover what he had retained of the question he put to me when he spontaneously informed me of the precise mode of his father's death, about which I had been obliged to dissemble. Maybe a future follow-up encounter could still prove of belated value to him, just as certain of the interviews with these long-term cases have proved to be to their subjects. Thus, for example, it was a boon to be able to tell a man that he was illegitimate and consequently not the son of the (later acquired) brutal and criminal (deserting) spouse of his mother. Or to be able to reveal to another that the "dark" secret of his paternal origins was not that his paternal aunts were prostitutes, but that he had colored blood, the awareness of which the boy had been able to convey to me years ago as his secret knowledge of his deceased and "unmentionable" father, the fact of his awareness unguessed by his mother. Nor can the self-declared (non)-thieving thief have been any worse off for being shown that his criminality had been no more than the manifest invention of an unhappy nondelinquent child. A future follow-up interview with the university student might still usefully inform him about some of the well-documented parental sources of the sense of sadness to which I know from another quarter he is prone, pertaining as this does both to the psychic realities of his parents and to his consequent external reality and history. It requires little imagination to realize the psychic burdensomeness, in this and allied cases, of the split enforced in his ego by his mother's psychic reality, of the knowing yet not knowing of basic truths that are debarred from consciousness, much as if these were but (his own) disallowed or forbidden notions or impulses.

We come now to a female clinic patient whose case is in broad keeping with my view that some symptomatologies bespeak potential ego strengths. (I might add that the gender ratio of the cases from the clinic reported thus far reflects the referral ratio, i.e., three males to one female.) At the age of exactly eight years, this patient was brought by her mother, who was convinced that the young child was already soliciting passing men on the street, both by exposing herself and by asking for food, and that her whole manner and style were precociously those of a full-blown prostitute. Her available school report stated, however, that she was a normal and pleasing child, happy in school and showing no evidence of the complaints made against her by her mother (which also included thieving). Both the contents of the social history obtained by our psychiatric social worker and the passionate verbosity of the mother at interview made it clear that this woman was some kind of pseudologic psychopath of a borderline psychotic order. Her three children were not the offspring of the alleged husband of the past, nor were they presumed to have the same father. A social agency had given us the information that although she had no known employment, her living conditions approximated the luxurious. She was, therefore, regarded as either a prostitute or else a "kept" woman. As a deliberate diagnostic maneuver, I interviewed this mother and child together for part of the time.

Not for one moment were the mother's accusatory statements regarding the little girl's debased behavior toned down in her child's presence. The child was a very pretty little person with a gaily ingratiating yet anxious air, with eyes that flickered merrily but did not leave her mother's face for an instant. It was obvious that her so-called flirtatious manner was universal, i.e., unrelated to the gender of the recipient, and generally placatory or beguiling in its purpose and, of necessity, ever watchful toward her mother. Despite my efforts to beguile her, this mother attended only twice more and refused to meet further with the psychiatric social worker, even on her own premises. It was my conviction that this borderline psychotic woman was set on materializing a precocious prostitute out of her defensively winsome child. Nor could this mother be persuaded, either by myself or the welfare authorities to whom my psychiatric report and warnings were directed, to allow the girl to enter a residential school. Because this woman was also quite cunning, it did not prove possible to "pin" on to this mother what was then the only feasible designation applicable to such a case — "loss of parental rights" — on the grounds of her being the source of "exposure of the child to moral danger." In fact, as this young married woman was to tell me 25 or more years later at our follow-up meeting, a curiously eager occasion for her, no official interventions of any kind were ever made on her behalf.

It was most touching for me to realize, all these years later, how significant her few visits to the clinic had proved to be (and how much this significance had since been actively sustained by her "news" letters to me). Somehow, she had remained keenly aware that there in the clinic she had had a true ally. Her life story was as curious as it was unexpected by me, prefaced as it was by her mother's statements about her when she was called on for follow-up purposes by my sleuthing colleague, Miss K. Lewis. She told Miss Lewis that her daughter, married and training to be a hospital nurse in the West of England, had led a life of total promiscuity and that, having already had no less than fourteen abortions to date, she was now disgracefully cohabiting. She stated that she herself was sickened by her daughter's life style.

When I then wrote to this young woman to explain the nature of my research, I made it clear that I was the psychiatrist "with whom her mother had not seen eye to eye." She was offered her traveling expenses if she would agree to make the long journey to see me. But at the end of the interview that finally transpired, she rejected monetary payment, stating how much the visit had meant to her. She informed me that she had remained a virgin until her engagement to her fiance and that the three miscarriages she had experienced were all "legitimate" and deplored.

It was true, however, that she had left her husband and that she was cohabiting on a steady basis with a young man who was an adopted son, now a university "drop-out." Her marriage, she said, had broken up because her husband had turned out to be homosexual. This she did not realize for the first years. She described how he had increasingly brought young men home, some to stay as guests. Gradually, he explained that all were homosexuals who had despaired of cure. She, with her interest in caring for people, was the *one* who could best help them to overcome their fears of women by proffering them coitus with her. She said that, having acceded to this request increasingly, she came to enjoy it and welcomed the promiscuity, knowing by then that her husband was likewise a homosexual. The background of her nursing career, however, was most creditable. Needing a roof over her head to get away from her

138

mother, she had taken employment in a home for old ladies. In due course, the matron told her that a person with her disposition and talents ought to have a professional training as a hospital nurse, a course that she then agreed to undertake.

She told me that it was her present lover and his ideals, which came to include her conversion to his religious cult, which had weaned her out of promiscuity and her casual attitude to sexuality. Then, in the manner of an afterthought, she told me that there had always been a special relationship between herself and her senior half-brother, who had also moved to the part of the country where she then lived, though she did not often see him.

The fact was that she knew him to be a bitter person still deeply in love with her. For many of her years at home, her mother often being out (when not occupied with a client in her bedroom), she and her brother engaged in every kind of erotic practice other than coitus. She knew that she had been partly afraid and yet had partly enjoyed these experiences, because their lives were so lonely and their mother so hard to endure. She said that she regarded it as difficult to believe that her mother was not completely aware of what was going on between them. In the end, however, she repudiated her brother, and, although she went to many parties, her behavior was strictly virginal. It was this that had attracted her future husband. To this account can be added the observation that she was a person of exceptional elegance of body and charm of manner. I told her of my fears over the years that she would become the prostitute her mother had inculcated her to become, a role that did, in fact, take a special twist in the belated obedience to her mother that characterized her relations with her husband.

Since this interview, she has kept in irregular touch with me by letters, each time declaring her wish to phone or visit me, but doing neither. Once she informed me that she had passed her final exams; later she wrote to say that she had changed her first name. Since then, she has informed me that her married name was now also different, since she had remarried and was pregnant and hoped soon to visit me. But if that was really so, I wondered, then to whom was she married? Was she married to her previous lover, or to another non-earner, or to someone else?

While I have no idea what her gradual change of names represents, beginning rather unusually with her first name, I do know that her mother had also subscribed to name-changing of the following order. Let us say that her mother's maiden name was stated to have been "Bing." It then became "Ling," (by marriage), which she then preferred to change, on behalf of her daughter and herself, to that of "King." The actual name changes, for which I am unable to find a suitable counterpart, were of a kind whereby she could claim that whoever used one of the names was doing so mistakenly from mishearing the (currently) correct one. As to whether my ex-patient, a very pleasing and frank person, and one who had undertaken a hard-working training in the service of others, was now burgeoning into a fantast, it was impossible to tell from her cryptic letters to me.

But that she longed for love objects with integrity and ideals as permanent models by which to expunge her antecedents, there was no doubt. Her case has been outlined because, in many identificatory and other respects, her idealistic standards of refinement of manner and interests were most baffling, as was her mother's continuing ability to live above her economic station. It would seem to me that my once-upon-a-time patient had identified herself, somewhat as in the other female case, with her mother's self-ennobling pseudologic statements and her averred ideals, of which the means justified the end, but with a remarkable difference in that my ex-patient was prepared to work hard under somewhat self-effacing conditions to attain these as deserts. Were this the story of an actress or dress model, careers for which she is exceptionally well endowed, then this might read as being nicely consistent in the sense of a compromise achievement. Instead, she has obtained her qualifications as a nurse and midwife, and she adheres to a modern idealistic cult, which she did say was of a somewhat secret nature and required its members to shun publicity.[6]

The only consistency that can here be attached to her life style is

---

[6] On the night this manuscript was corrected and finalized, she phoned me. She has married her former lover's friend, who knows all of her history, as is incumbent in the mystic cult all three share. Hence, too, she said, the change of her first name, chosen for her by their religious leader, since the name she carried (Mary) did not accord well with her personality and was proving a hindrance to her ready communion with their divinity. She described with enthusiasm how her husband is set on spoiling her, which, with the enterprises he already owns and his studies for a high-level speciality, he can well sustain economically. She spoke with delight of their charming cottage set remotely in the woods, where her ex-lover is a weekly guest for supper and to which her taciturn older brother has agreed to come and stay at Christmas for several days. Never has she seen him so happy. Nor does she allow her training to be a waste, for already she has a place in the lives of the nearby villagers as a friendly advisor. Yes, her mother has been informed of her remarriage, but not of her advanced pregnancy, for she is afraid of her mother's "peculiar mouth." She having spoken of her husband's "aristocratic" family ties, I suggested that at that distance she was well placed, henceforth, for side-stepping her mother. She immediately said that this she would never do because she *is* her mother, and at her mother's age life becomes ever more lonely. She also admitted that she had paid recent flying visits to London without taking the time to call on me.

I am inclined to believe the present fairytale-like outcome of her life story, with herself as the endearing hyphen at Christmas between three "informed" lovers, two now being interchangeably fraternal and she pregnant by the third. In her home, none of the three siblings had known who the three fathers were.

140

clinically derived from my research study and is of a wholly unexpected and readily disputable order. It is a finding that emerged from the long-term follow-up group, to which she belongs, of the 44 cases I personally interviewed. Among these cooperative individuals—out of a total of 56 possibles for interviewing—there are, in my view, a remarkably high number who concern themselves with the welfare of others. Of these 44 people, mainly of lower-middle-class origins, five, including this young woman, are engaged in full-time professional careers of an idealistic nature, while another five donate their part-time services to welfare aims. One of these five full-time workers (a regional youth-club organizer) had full psychoanalytic treatment in the clinic, while three others were suitably institutionalized on my recommendation. Therefore, one concludes, no doubt with narcissistic aplomb, that their mitigating experiences in, or promoted by, the clinic helped to fire their imaginations and to add substance to their ego ideals.

It is, of course, well known that many individuals are drawn to different kinds of social service or other altruistic occupations by the pull of their own therapeutic needs. It could possibly be argued that these altruistic follow-up examples illustrate this psychopathological aspect. Nevertheless, within their own family or sibling setting, theirs represents a high or the highest level of achievement therein, an outcome that surely can lay claim to a positive significance in terms of its likely correlation with favorable psychiatric intervention in their childhoods. Nor do almost all of the after-histories of the followed-up cases do other than enhance (when one excludes mental defectives or other such gross conditions) the general upward trend of the population into the middle classes, for which the superior *cultural* standards and ideals of these persons equips them well, this last being a circular phenomenon, as shown by Freud's concepts of the ego ideal and the superego.

My final example illustrating that the psychic reality of the parents comprises part of the external reality of the child is taken from my analytic practice. A professional man with a history of turbulent aggressivity, including verbal, within the home and in gang play, was characterized in adulthood by a very restrained and deferential tone of voice. There is more than one explanation for its adoption. However, an important element of his childhood experience, his father's depressive states, had never been consciously conceptualized by the patient, although these had often been made descriptively apparent by him in the analysis. It therefore proved startling to him (in the context of his own plaintive tone of voice) to hear me speak of his father as "a depressed man, too wretched when in these states to assert himself vocally as a

141

response to your (dissocial) goadings." As the patient later put it, in that instant, when he gained a new comprehension of his father, a lifetime of his own nagging antagonism became meaningful. So, too, this made sudden sense of the exercise of his own saccharine (plaintive and defer-ential) "best voice," which at any rate helped to keep the peace with his mother. The depressive nuances of this "best voice," which largely remained to the present day, were, for many, indistinguishable from a deprecatory or gentle tone.

His father was an uneducated immigrant with poor powers of verbal exposition, prone on occasion to punitive rages. In the country of my patient's childhood, great store was set on cultural conformity. A wide gulf was therefore increasingly created between this depressive father and his better-educated children. Part of my patient's conscious perceptions of his father's depressive states devolved on this noncommunicating aspect of the "foreignness" between them. Nevertheless, much of my patient's quasi-dissocial behavior was engaged in as a means of removing the affect of depression by which he was imbued and by which he could recognizably delineate a father who was subject to apathetic depression but who also unleashed his son's sadistic impulses. These broke out whether to enliven and engage this man by prodding or else to retaliate, or both. In certain respects, my patient's failure to be able to "put a name to" (conceptualize) his father's depressive states was of itself a reflection of his father's lack of vocabulary (by which to know how to "express oneself").

Finally, from an overcondensed analytic case, an example of a psycho-pathological background that is becoming a social rarity. It is one in which a child can be deprived of access to the psychic reality of its parents although they reside on the premises. I refer, in this instance, to a girl brought up during much of her first seven years by strict and unintelli-gent nannies, in the Spartan conditions of a large establishment geared to the Calvinistic requirements of an impeccably able, righteous, and successful, if rather silent, father, whose decorative wife of much less intelligence was intimidated by all these circumstances. The keynote of these circumstances — also translatable into class distinctions — was that original sin could be kept at bay indefinitely by duties and discipline, even in those situations of indulgence created by wealth, provided that spontaneity of response, i.e., instinctual gratifications, be exorcised.

My patient was the eldest of quite a large family, through the quick arrival of which she had been suddenly and irrevocably separated from her breast-feeding (pregnant) mother at about fourteen months of age with the coming of the first nanny. This shy, inhibited, depressed patient, herself the highly perceptive and solicitous mother of several non-nannied children, proved a difficult analysand in that her anhedonia seemed for a long time to be as ubiquitous as it was impenetrable. Whereas much of this served as the continuation of the negativism she developed at the loss of her mother's presence—her mother later dubbed her "the vinegar girl"—the more baffling elements of her anhedonia were finally understood as belonging to the complexities of her enforced voyeurism. She used the comments of employed staff (not forgetting the young nursery maids whom the nannies also sought to domineer) as her "go-between peep holes" or stethescope (the unexpected fact being that this word is derived from the Greek word for breast, this being *stethos*) to her Olympian parents. In the process, she identified herself empathically with their lowly selves as with their revealing grumbles and ambivalent dicta. Suffice it to say that in these constrained and anger-laden ways, this highly intelligent child, fixated as she was to the symbolic mechanism of "sour grapes," was also in search of the psychic-reality mainsprings or core of the parental duo of mutuality in which neither shame nor disgust could play an exclusionary part. These last were the ways she learned, and emulated when herself a mother, from the loving and lovable nanny who arrived—as always, without the explanation of whatever was of emotional significance—when she was seven years old.

Through her empathic lowly identifications with grumblers, whose ranks (as grumbler) her mother eventually joined, she was always to react as an "as if" eternal servant and as a would-be lady. She could only feel herself to be real and worthwhile when pregnant, and as long as her babies remained inalienably dependent, i.e., until they became toddlers in a (to her) threatening universe, when she again became overpowered by her envy of what she gave so perfectly but never was able to savor in return.

This overcondensed account illustrates the paradox of the human condition: in Western society, or where nuclear families prevail, whereas part of the external reality of the child is comprised of the psychic reality of the parents, which may be pathogenic, the traumatized and sustained exclusion of this reality can prove no less so.

REFERENCES

Bonnard, A. (1950), La Phobie de l'école est-elle un syndrome? *Enfance*, 4:183-185, 1951.

Hill, J. C. (1971), *Teaching and the Unconscious Mind*. New York: International Universities Press.

Johnson, A. M. (1953), Factors in the etiology of fixations and symptom choice. *Psychoanal. Quart.*, 22:475-496.

Sterba, R. F. (1948), On Hallowe'en. *Amer. Imago*, 5:213-224.

March, 1974

Sacrificial Parapraxis—Failure
or Achievement?

PAULA HEIMANN, M.D. (*London*)

In his paper "The Multiple Determinants of a Minor Accident," Richard Sterba (1972) presents an intriguing inquiry into a parapraxis which he concludes by pointing to a gap in our theoretical understanding. As he will remember, I was so fascinated by his paper that I wrote to him about it, yet I did not know then what it really was that held me so much in its grip. When invited to contribute to this Festschrift, I knew without a moment's hesitation that I had to return to this paper, to take up the challenge of the questioning note on which it ends and to find out what it was that so exercised my mind about it. I am thus doubly grateful for the invitation.

I

PARAPRAXES

Like so many psychological facts, parapraxes were generally neglected until Freud turned the torch of his scientific exploration on this pheno-menon and brought to light its hidden meaningfulness and psychic function. The first generation of psychoanalysts was obviously fired by *The Psychopathology of Everyday Life*, followed Freud's example by analyzing slips and bungled actions that came their way, and sent him instances to swell his collection. Later generations of analysts, however, have neglected the problem parapraxes pose. We seem content to look

---

This paper was originally written in honor of Dr. Richard Sterba on the occasion of his 75th birthday.

145

for the hidden meaning, as Freud has shown, but so far as I know, there has been no attempt at correlating parapraxes to specific aspects of psychoanalytic theory. All the more welcome is Sterba's paper, that points to this gap, explores the part which the ego and regression play in parapraxes, and offers an answer, albeit tentatively.

The publication of *The Psychopathology of Everyday Life* followed that of *The Interpretation of Dreams* by one year, but as Strachey[1] pointed out, Freud had already mentioned the solution of a parapraxes in 1898 in a letter to Fliess. He was thus preoccupied with this psychic phenomenon at the same time as he was struggling with the problem of dreams and of neurotic illness, and when discussing parapraxes, he showed their similarities with both the dream and neurotic symptoms.

Yet Freud made only a very modest claim concerning the scientific stature of *The Psychopathology of Everyday Life*. He said in a footnote: "This book is of an entirely popular character; it merely aims, by an accumulation of examples, at paving the way for the necessary assumption of *unconscious yet operative* mental processes, and it avoids all theoretical considerations on the nature of this unconscious" (p. 272).

The book was written before most of his major psychoanalytical and cultural works, but Freud was obviously content to have it reissued without link to his new discoveries, and with additions only of new examples, so that essentially the book remained as it was originally. In a sense this highlights its importance.

In my view, *The Psychopathology of Everyday Life* is twin to *The Interpretation of Dreams* — true, lighter in weight, but twin none the less. In his interpretation of parapraxes Freud shows that they serve the same function for psychic economy in the wakeful state that dreams serve in the condition of sleep. Impulses which we suppress and repress or have never allowed to reach consciousness can be lived out with impunity in the parapraxis, because the slip has been only transient and thus can be made good instantly, and in the dream where, so to speak, higher charges are at stake, because it occurs during sleep, whilst the motor apparatus necessary for action in the outer world is switched off. Thus we are all psychotic in our dreams, albeit not necessarily to the same degree in every dream, and we have a transient neurosis in our parapraxes. Here, too, not to the same degree in every one, and some slips, like losing or mislaying things which we need; or forgetting names, dates and intentions; or certain bungled actions which damage other people as well as ourselves, we cannot afford with impunity. Both the dream can fail and the

---

[1] Editor's Introduction, p. xii.

parapraxis can fail. The hallucinatory experience of a dream may continue into the wakeful state of a psychotic condition, and too many, too frequent, or enduring parapraxes lead over into an open neurotic condition. Symptomatic acts can transcend into neurotic symptoms.

By and large, however, it might be said that those people remain healthy who can restrict their most primitive impulses and primary-process thinking to the hallucinatory dream psychosis and their ambivalence conflicts to mild and transient parapraxes. I think we rightly worry about patients who never report dreams, never talk about their somatic processes or never express hostile aggression or ruthless love demands. They are a caricature of normality.

Another exceedingly important trait that *The Psychopathology of Everyday Life* has in common with *The Interpretation of Dreams* is the demonstration that, contrary to the opinion current at the time, the frontiers between mental health and mental illness are not hard and fast. By diminishing the sharp divisions between mental health, neurosis, and psychosis, both works open new dimensions to the understanding of psychic life.

Freud named and grouped together the various parapraxes according to the specific function that was at fault. A look at his chapter headings shows this clearly. He inquired into the individual motivations that determined the occurrence of each slip. In his chapter on bungled actions, however, Freud gave a few examples which he named in accordance with the motive that prompted them. He called them "sacrificial acts." Here is the example that Sterba quotes as similar to his own slip action. Freud flung a slipper at a beautiful little marble statue of Venus and broke it into many pieces. Surprisingly for a collector, he remained utterly indifferent to the loss he had inflicted on himself. But we soon understand this as we read his analysis of the event. Preceding his bungled action he had received the news that the illness of one of his daughters was improving and not fatal, as he had dreaded. In smashing his little Venus statue, he had made a sacrifice as a thank-offering. The determining motive for another sacrificial act was to avert worse disaster. Instead of breaking a friendship, he broke his latest acquisition, an Egyptian figure. He added that both could be mended!

When commenting on his smashing of the little Venus, Freud stated that it still was a mystery to him, even at the time of writing about it, how he decided on a sacrificial act so quickly, chose his target so appropriately, and aimed so accurately, feeling sure that had he set out with the conscious intention to hit only the little statue and none of the articles nearby, he would have failed.

Another type of sacrificial parapraxis mentioned by Freud relates to an old custom: on certain festive occasions some articles were broken deliberately, whilst a phrase was spoken to invoke good luck. This link with tradition is particularly pertinent to my ideas, and I shall return to it later. But I may here point to the need to distinguish between a fault in our mental functioning and an act of preserving a tradition that originates in a significant cultural event in the remote past. We need to reconsider our notion of regression.

These sacrificial parapraxes are clearly of a very different order from those slips that give transient relief in conflictual object relations, as in the example of the assistant asking his colleagues to "belch" instead of "clink their glasses" in honor of their revered chief.[2]

DR. STERBA'S ACCIDENT

Dr. Sterba dropped the rear door of a Volkswagon station wagon on his forehead. The impact gashed the skin and cut a chunk out of it. The bone was not touched. He reacted with equanimity to the accident and was at first unwilling to recognize it as a parapraxis. Later, however, the true analyst's urge to analyze his actions asserted itself, and he found his mind particularly lucid whilst flooded by memories and thoughts.

I shall briefly summarize his findings.

Freud's discovery of the similarity between a parapraxis and a dream is beautifully borne out by Sterba's interpretive procedure, when he first mentioned the event of the day preceding the day of the parapraxis.

This event was his daughter's marriage. He was delighted with her choice of a husband; he greatly liked his son-in-law and the new family. What crowned his happiness was the fact that his son-in-law was Jewish. It was one of the happiest days of his life.

Thus his first interpretation of his slip action was that it was a sacrificial act, a thank-offering, which he compared with Freud's smashing of the little Venus. However, he was unwilling to attribute very great significance to this meaning, and looked for other and more infantile unconscious determinants (again, similar to the way we regard a dream) and recognized the self-injury as an equivalent of circumcision, indicating impulses of rivalry with his daughter's husband. When telling a friend about the accident, he made a slip of the tongue, saying that a piece of his foreskin—skin of his forehead—was taken out. The whole and rich

---

[2] Strachey's translation of Freud's works is inspired and inspiring. In this instance, however, I feel that his word "hiccough" is milder than the German word *"aufstossen,"* whereas "belch" conveys the coarseness better, and that "drink" is not close enough to *"anstossen"* (Freud, 1901, p. 54).

history of his relationship with Jewish people came into his mind, interwoven with his relationship to his family.

He grew up in a family who shared the general Austrian hostility against Jews which, after Hitler's advent, increased to violent hatred, particularly on the part of his older brother. In his schooldays he had no contact with his two or three Jewish classmates, who were mediocre and dull. Yet he greatly appreciated the attitude of the priest who taught religion, who included the Jewish boys in all his extracurricular activities, who never used the word "Jew," already then a word of scorn, but instead spoke of *"de gente electa."* (We may recognize here a forerunner of the guiding figures whom Sterba later collected in contrast to those who by kinship or convention were his mentors.)

Memories moved to young manhood, when for the first time he met Jewish young men whose intelligence and culture attracted him, and whom he found superior to his gentile colleagues. This was during his military service, in the officers' school. The Jewish companions were older and had more experience of life. From them he heard for the first time of Freud and his work. By contrast the gentile Prussian major disgusted him with his cruel vulgarity. Sterba claims that it was largely due to a Jewish friend that he came out alive from the holocaust of the First World War.

On returning to civilian life and his medical studies, he decided to train in psychoanalysis, a decision that made his gentile colleagues recoil in horror.

The incident of his membership paper was remembered and led to the interpretation of initiation rites and castration fear. Further determinants belonging to the oedipal constellation and sibling hostility came up, as he went on remembering how he increasingly associated himself with Jewish people and increasingly alienated himself from his family and their values, i.e., their growing enthusiasm for Hitler and Hitler's Germany. In view of these factors the instrument of the injury was meaningful: a German car became the punishing agency.

There are two outstanding events that proved his sense of belonging with his Jewish friends. One was his rejection of the invitation to read a paper to the Berlin Psycho-Analytical Society, which by then had been swallowed up by the German Psychotherapeutic Society after all Jewish psychoanalysts had been outlawed. Sterba accepted on the condition that he read a paper after a Jewish Viennese colleague. This, of course, put an end to the invitation. The other and most poignant event was the last time he saw Freud. A day after Hitler's army invaded Austria, the Board of the Vienna Psycho-Analytical Society met at Freud's house and every member was asked about his plans. Sterba, like all Jewish analysts, declared that he would emigrate—the supreme test of his electing to belong with the Jews. This memory continues to the—amazing—fact that the President of the International refused to help him since, as a gentile, he could have remained in Vienna. Without help, a refugee in Switzerland (notorious for her hostile attitude to refugees), exposed to persecution, and a repetition of this later in the United States—these experiences gave to the self-inflicted "circumcision" an added meaning of defiance and self-assertion against injustice and persecution. The Sterbas learnt in their own personal lives what generations of their elected people had suffered.

Having explored the determinants of his slip action, Sterba turned his attention to the role his ego played in it. And here he encountered the same problem which Freud had called a mystery. To achieve only a fleshwound, a "circumcision," and to leave the bone unharmed, this bungled action must have been controlled by superb ego functioning, an incredibly sharp gauging of the distance of head from door, and of the impact of that door on the head. Such precision without repeated careful practice does not occur under normal circumstances.

To account for the phenomenon Sterba looked for regression to an infantile capacity that might have been lost in the process of growing up. It is known that a child may have greater intellectual sharpness, greater sensitivity and creative imagination than later as an adult, but this is not the case with sensory-motor skills. They are not the prerogative of childhood; they have to be acquired. Ontogenesis thus did not seem to provide the answer.

Sterba then thought of one other situation in which such unusual excellence of ego functioning occurs. Quoting Pfister, he refers to mountaineers who, threatened by falling to their apparently unavoidable deaths, were able to save their lives by acting with incredible speed and skill to stop the fall. They report that they felt no fear and could marshall all their capacities for the task of survival.

Sterba himself reports a similar observation concerning a workman who was standing on a platform fixed by ropes to the roof. Suddenly one rope broke, and the platform swung into the vertical position. The man would have fallen to his death had he not in a split second dropped his tools, grabbed the bannister, and held on to it so that Dr. Sterba and his patient could pull him inside the consulting room.

Since, however, in the incident with the car door, Sterba was not in mortal danger, nor was Freud in the slip action with the little Venus statue, the explanation that maximal ego efficiency is available when survival is at stake did not apply.

150

Mild pressure by id and superego extracting a mild sacrifice, loss of an *objet d'art* in Freud's case and a harmless injury in Sterba's own, does not constitute a situation of emergency, releasing superperformance on the part of the ego. A "purely speculative hypothesis" makes Sterba return to the notion of regression. This time, however, not to a stage in ontogenetic development, but to the phylogenetic past. There are observations concerning primitives whose natural motor-sensory dexterity with their primitive tools far exceeds what civilized man can achieve, even with effort and practice.

I should like to quote Sterba's last paragraph in full. "Culturalization seems to make these faculties recede. May we assume that under the special circumstances mentioned above, the Ego has the possibility to reach into the phylogenetic past and be enabled in this way to acquire for a moment what seems to be superhuman motor and sensory faculties?" Let us note that he ends with a question.

It is the paradox that Sterba's consideration throws into relief so clearly. A parapraxis, a faulty action, is by definition due to a failure on the part of the ego. Yet at the same time, it reveals an unusual excellence of ego functioning. We know that psychoanalysis is full of paradoxes — "*Ça n'empêche pas d'exister.*" Nevertheless they present an irresistible challenge.

To start with, I feel reluctant to give up the connection with mortal danger. True, as Sterba states, neither he nor Freud were actually in any danger when they made the bungled actions described. However, we cannot dismiss the role of death in their thoughts. I have little doubt that the news of the improvement in his daughter's condition was very fresh in Freud's mind and that he still felt the dread of her impending death.

As regards Sterba, his powerful memories of his relations with Jewish people — the mortal danger threatening Freud and the other Jewish analysts and friends, when Hitler came into power, the many murders committed by Hitler, the war, and his own near death, the hardship the Sterbas suffered in Switzerland, and later the full persecution by people swearing to annihilate the Sterbas — death looms very large in the history of his rejoicing in his daughter's marrying a Jew, the day residue of his parapraxis.[3]

Next, the phylogenetic regression tentatively considered by Sterba is

[3] I hope Dr. Sterba will not compare me with the German Professor of Literature who annotated Goethe's autobiography, and corrected Goethe's statement that his greatest love had been Lily, with the remark (in excruciating language): "Here Goethe is in error. This was the case for him with Frederika." In the train of ideas which Sterba's paper has set going in me, I must give a significant place to the theme of death. I hope to justify this idea.

151

not pathological, it is exceedingly healthy. We remember here Kris's concept of regression in the service of the ego, which is helpful for certain ego interests. A broader concept of normal regression has been presented by Anna Freud (1966), who allocates to regression a regular function in development, alternating with obvious spurts of progression. Particularly germane to my ideas is her example of the sixth-form girls who were serious students in the early lessons but, when overburdened by a crowded timetable, "regressed" into silly giggles. The male teachers who took the lessons when they were overtired called them "a flock of silly geese." In fact they were not. Their "regression" was a healthy self-assertion against unreasonable demands which turned a learning situation into intellectual paralysis.

I conclude my present brief excursion into regression by underlining the normal forms of regression and their protective and productive functions. We might distinguish between regressing to an earlier mode of thinking and acting which would be pathological, and reactivating and reliving an earlier experience that contributes to maximal benefit to oneself.

Now a few comments on the incident with the workman. It made me think of many dreams encountered in analysis. If a patient had told me that he dreamt he fell from heaven, was in extreme danger of dying, could just hold on to an insecure support and was finally saved by being pulled to safety through an opening, I would think that he had presented a birth fantasy, and images of very early life would float into my mind. Although this was not a dream, but a real event, I found myself thinking of early life, and this leads me to my section on narcissism.

II

NARCISSISM

The supreme feat of survival in mortal danger presupposes that mind and body, all mental and bodily systems, work in unison. When this is the case, the theory of the three structures, different in their functions with complex dynamics revolving upon conflict, seems not the best framework for the observation under discussion, since intrapsychic conflict would detract from the individual's marshalling all his capacities to achieve survival. In other words, I want to consider a regression to the state of undifferentiation, the very early infantile state. Absence of fear, as reported by mountaineers who saved themselves from almost certain death, points to the revival of certain elements of narcissism.

To return to the question of the theoretical framework, I would like to refer to Kohut (1971), who prefaces his erudite book with a comment on theory formation and distinguishes between experience-near and experience-distant abstractions. The theory of the systems id, ego, superego is less experience-near and denotes a higher level of theory-formation than the abstraction "Self."

Whereas many analysts consider the concept "Self" as not sufficiently scientific, I find it most useful because it is closer to immediate experience and more comprehensive than the terms "Subject" or "Ego." The former is contingent on the reciprocal concept "Object," the latter on the connections with Id and Superego. Winnicott (1971) liked to work with the Subject-Object antithesis and combination and coined the term "Subjective Object." In my view this does not hold for the most primitive stage. The occasions which demand the application of the three structures with their inter-and-intrastructural conflicts are the analyst's daily bread, so to speak, when working with the transference problems of neurotic adult patients. Erikson's concept of "Ego-Identity" (1950) is highly meaningful, but again bound to a higher phase of development, one in which recognition of other identities has long been achieved and recurs with renewed intensity.

Thus to my way of thinking, the term "Self" is more fitting for earliest stages of development. It seems to me best in accord with Freud's description of primary narcissism (1911, 1914, 1925).

Mahler (1969), drawing on extensive researches concerning psychotic children and normal development, adheres to Freud's view of early narcissism. She describes an early "normal autism," preceding the infant's symbiotic relationship with his mother, which gradually gives way to the separation-individuation process.

Early infantile thinking is dominated by the pleasure principle. Pleasure is good, and good is Me. Pain is bad, and bad is Not-Me. We may extend this to: "Me—mine—good (pleasurable)—allowed to exist—Yes," and "Bad (painful)—Not-Me—not mine—existence refused—No." It is an error, which I too made years ago, to think that Not-Me equates with the recognition of another person, a Not-Self. What it denotes is merely the omnipotent negation of pain, employing the mechanism of negative hallucination. This is possible thanks to the reality of the maternal figure (Freud, 1911, pp. 219-220). However short-lived this omnipotence may be, its existence leaves traces which later experiences may revive.

153

In objective reality the infant survives the caesura of birth and long stretches of babyhood and childhood by virtue of other persons' love, sensitivity and responsiveness to his needs, coupled with realistic judgments. In the infant's reality helplessness and dependence have no place; he lives in a global philosophy of an all good world that is of his doing and belongs to him.

Favorable physiological and psychological endowment will intensify this philosophy; unfavorable endowment, early physical illnesses or environmental distresses detract from it and give more weight to its interruptions by pain, hunger, tensions of any kind.

Such favorable endowment includes what Greenacre (1957, 1958) describes as the capacity for forming "collective alternates," a basic characteristic of the artist.

I have elsewhere (1962) suggested that narcissism should not be regarded exclusively as an early position of the libido, but should be appreciated in the wider context of an experiential orientation with which the young infant meets all incoming stimuli. Like all psychic formations, narcissism is subject to the processes of maturation and development.

At least three types of narcissism can be distinguished: primary, naïve narcissism, the prerogative of the dawn of thought before the existence of Others than Self is appreciated; secondary, object-hostile narcissism, based on real or imagined wrongs perpetrated against the Self;[4] and creative narcissism, which, in addition to forms of narcissism specific to the creative person and the creative process (which I do not attempt to explore here), includes both the naïve, omnipotent narcissism and the object-hostile narcissism, the latter, particularly pronounced, if there are objects who oppose the creative act.

All forms of narcissism persist throughout life. Naïve narcissism is often met in highly sophisticated persons. Its hallmark is the surprise with which they react, when they meet with a view different from their own. The ease and interest, however, with which they can consider the new, divergent opinion, are free from object-hostility. Equally, secondary narcissism with the propensity for feeling wronged is compatible with advanced thinking and mental health. It is hardly necessary to state that the extreme forms of narcissism like hypochondriasis and paranoia belong to the realm of pathology. This fact, however, does not contradict the view that narcissism is subject to development and compatible with

---

[4] Some authors define secondary narcissism with regard to the source of narcissistic feelings, i.e., narcissistic supplies offered to the infant by the parental objects. I am here, however, concerned with the quality of the narcissistic condition, not with its sources.

154

health. A final mature form does not interfere with mature object relations; on the contrary, a certain amount of mature narcissism encourages object relations and makes for positive enjoyment in encountering another Self with different qualities, felt as enriching, complementary and congenial to one's own Self.

III

COLLECTIVE ALTERNATES

Greenacre (1957) lists several basic characteristics for the artist, covering with this term all creative persons who are capable of expressing their creativity in real activities in any field of human endeavor.

These characteristics are a greater than usual sensitivity and responsiveness to sensory stimulation, unusual awareness of relations between various stimuli, which includes an unusually quick grasp of gestalts, unusual width and depth of empathy, and unusual intactness of the sensory-motor systems necessary for the actual performance of the creative act. Thanks to these capacities the artist forms collective alternates, finding or creating them from contemporary life, or history or imagination.

In a net that spans eight centuries Greenacre comes up with several poets, a saint, and an explorer who, thanks to this gift for finding and creating collective alternates and identifying with them, were supreme achievers.

We might regard the mountaineers and the workman mentioned earlier as belonging to the category of "artist" as defined above. Their "superhuman" faculties that saved their lives include some of the characteristics attributed by Greenacre to the creative person, such as the unusual sensory response, the rapid perception of gestalt, the intactness of the sensory-motor apparatus: the branch on the route of the fall, or the bannister of the swinging platform to hold on to, the bit of glacier into which to thrust the pickaxe, are perceived and used in split seconds. Connoisseurs of sport will be able to point to artists in the area of physical prowess, not only in unusual situations of extreme danger.

What, however, do we know about the more than averagely gifted person from our work as analysts? In my experience it is less the achiever than the persons who, despite being highly gifted have failed to achieve, who turn to analysis for liberation of their talents. This request as motive for seeking analysis turns up surprisingly frequently in assessment interviews of patients applying for treatment at the London Clinic of Psycho-Analysis. It may be that the old fear that analysis would destroy talent has been overcome, but there may also be other motives, like shame about putting suffering from symptoms first and the expectation of having a better chance, when laying stress on cultural problems.

Amongst the factors that limit the potential artist from becoming an achiever, the obverse of their specially intense sensitivity and responsiveness to stimuli appears as paramount. This is their unusually intense and easily stirred narcissistic vulnerability. I should like to illustrate this with an example.

This was a woman, very gifted in her profession and in several forms of art. It appeared in her analysis that wherever she had worked, she had been immediately acknowledged as above average and had received offers of quick promotion. She either had not taken these up, realizing that they were not what she really wanted, or she had suffered, equally quickly, severe narcissistic hurts, and the flames of success rapidly turned into ashes.

Her childhood history was full of violence and tragedy, of physical and mental neglect and rejection. She had the capacity for forming collective alternates. In fact, her self-image revolved upon her having had a little basket into which she collected all the good things that her primary object(s) did not give her, but which she did obtain from other people—the maids in the house, visitors, people in the neighborhood, including the strange men who were called farm hands—from beautiful sights in a landscape, and later from art in its multiple forms.

But she also had an overaverage narcissistic vulnerability which so far had prevented her from having the success in her career to which she was entitled by virtue of her talents.

Her analysis with me started in a favorable way, although she might easily have construed an early rejection. That she did not do this, and that we were able to establish a solid working alliance that survived many a storm, was essentially due to two factors: one, in the preliminary interview she was enchanted by a vase with a little red rose on a table in my consulting room (as indeed I was too), and these little red roses and I, associated with them, were added to her collective alternates, her collection of good things; second, at an early stage in the analysis I presented the hypothesis that her distress at being put into the "last room" and left alone and helpless in her cot was mitigated by having within her field of vision a tree with its branches and leaves and seeing these in movement against a sky with changing colors. This reconstruction was in part based on her actual experience in the analysis: she could see from the couch a bit of sky and branches of a tree, which acted as a comfort for her disappointment that I did not live in a beautiful house, and that opposite my flat there was another nondescript block of flats. The equation between my consulting room and her nursery was clearly expressed when she suggested one day that I should paint my bookshelves and furniture white, and imagined with delight how good they would then look.

In a complex interaction of inner changes and external gratifications she became increasingly productive in her work. In her personal relations she discovered the pleasure from feeling kindness and fondness for and from other people, and the tendency to react with narcissistic hurt diminished. Further, she developed a sense of self, of justified self-assertion and claims, and could plan a future that would offer her scope for her talents, work satisfaction, and social and material rewards. I felt it as very significant that she now had developed a healthy narcissism and therefore could envisage making appropriate demands for respect and external acknowledgement as well as being ready to give on her part.

Earlier she had rushed into love affairs which could not give her the needed assurance of her value as a woman and a person, since she had never allowed herself the time necessary for an appraisal of the real person and of her motives for instant gratification.

These attempts at healing narcissistic wounds, therefore, had resulted in short-lived relationships, which she broke as easily as started, to discover later in the analysis how very little of herself had been engaged.

Now she was ready to allow time for the natural growth of a potential love relationship, but she was not willing to give up vital interests for the man's sake, as there were serious doubts about his ability to become a real partner in love.

Greenacre points out that the gifted infant will enrich the relationship with the primary object with the experiences from the wider fields of his sensitive responses. But the capacity for collective alternates has also the opposite effect, i.e., of achieving a greater than usual independence of the original objects and finding others outside the original milieu that correspond better and are more congenial to the gifted person.

This presupposes the capacity for undisturbed self-assertion.

IV

SELF-ASSERTION

With the recognition of the importance of a healthy and creative

157

narcissism is correlated the notion of self-assertion.[5] Inability to develop the sense for self-assertion plays a crucial part in psychic illness. These patients either use what might be called corrupt or perverse forms of self-assertion, promiscuous relationships without affection, uncalled-for derogatory criticisms of other people, including those for whom they care, and on whose good will they depend, or they confuse self-assertion with hostile aggression and impose inhibitions on themselves which they attribute to their parents, indulging in a permanent sulk.

These patients, though, maintain areas of solid ego functioning, of satisfactory object relationships, and of sexual potency, although interspersed with actual perverse sexual activities or compulsive perverse fantasies. They feel, and certainly in analysis convey, personality restrictions and weaknesses or gaps in rapport.

It is obvious that the artist in Greenacre's sense must be capable of asserting himself and his talents despite the obstacles that might oppose him. The gifted person does overcome these obstacles and moves from his original milieu, if this is not congenial to himself, into another milieu of his choice.

We often see how our patients, incapable of healthy narcissism and healthy self-assertion, use phoney devices which of course do not succeed and may lead to a form of "false Self." Originally Winnicott (1971) designated with this name persons who could show achievements, but only at the price of inner estrangement from their real selves. I have found false Selves in patients who were unable to express their feelings of love or of admiration or their striving for warmth and color in their lives and relationships. In a defensive way they espied whatever possible weakness another person might have and, playing on these weaknesses in subtle ways, attacked these people and deprived themselves of the chance of a gratifying relationship, or they clung to a list of wrongs that their parents and later parental figures like former analysts had done them.

Here is one of many examples. Mr. E.'s analysis could roughly be divided into four phases. The first comprised the preliminary interview and the first two analytic sessions. In this first phase the basic elements of the analytic relationship were laid down and I shall summarize them briefly. I made it clear to the patient that I was not willing to let him have another interminable and fruitless analysis, and that I expected him to take his share of responsibility for the analysis. I ended the preliminary

---

[5] I am aware that by stressing the importance of self-assertion I am not talking about an entirely new concept. The notion of healthy aggression has been indigenous in psychoanalysis from its very beginning. Yet with the associative links to our widened understanding of narcissism, my use of "self-assertion" is wider, although overlapping with the old concept of healthy aggression.

interview by saying to him: "You have now seen me and we have discussed times and fees. It is now up to you to decide whether you want to have analysis with me." The patient was very surprised. He had obviously expected that I would make the decision without his sharing in it.

In the first analytic session we had a repetition of his uncommunicative talk of the preliminary interview. After listening in a baffled way, I realized that the patient was not addressing himself to me at all, but that he was performing a ritualistic incantation of which I was not meant to be a participant. And this is what I told him. In the next session without such an incantatory preamble, he told me that he felt in a dilemma. This amounted to something like this: if he talked about his external life, he did not give analysis its due, but if he talked about matters appropriate to analysis, he neglected his real problems. (What he said was in fact far more confused than I have been able to reproduce it here. To me it was a phoney dilemma.) I said something like his denying that he was one and the same person in different aspects of his life.

In the following session the next phase of the analysis started, that is to say, he talked with involvement about his very serious problems. Ritualistic incantations did, of course, occur repeatedly, but he was himself now alerted to this form of escape and defense. The analysis proceeded in the usual way until a cataclysmic event occurred that threatened his business, his good name, and his livelihood. It was possible to make him realize that homicidal and suicidal wishes were no means of solving the problem. He realized also that he could not just throw his worries into my lap and expect magic solutions from me. He began to work very hard and continuously, and he was rewarded by saving his good name. Materially he incurred severe losses. The next phase of the analysis was characterized by his talking in great detail about his attempts to find new work and to acquire the necessary knowledge for the new undertaking.

Practically from the beginning there ran through the fabric of this analysis like a red thread the problem of self-assertion. The patient showed that neither had he ever been able to form the notion of self-assertion spontaneously nor could he grasp it responsively. Instead he could only think in terms of violent actions. He complained to me that he never had been able to express aggression. This was an ever-recurring item in his ever-recurring complaints about his parents. Since practically in the same breath in which he depicted himself as incapable of expressing aggression (attributed to his traumatic upbringing by his parents), he expressed wildly sadistic fantasies occurring at the slightest provocation, and even without any discernible provocation, I tried to clarify what he meant by "expressing aggression," and suggested that he protested against the injunction not to act on his aggressive impulses which he obeyed for fear of retaliation. I also, when it seemed appropriate, spoke of his distress about his inability to assert himself in constructive ways. My patient remained tone deaf to these interpretations, despite his well-developed intellectual capacities and artistic leanings. He often explicitly appreciated my comments and interpretations; he liked the sessions and positively erupted with delight: "But you listen to me; you let me talk!" Nevertheless, he regarded me as a nice old thing who, in contrast to his first analyst, did not persecute him, but he did not attribute any professional or intellectual acumen to me. I never gave him such erudite interpretations as his first analyst (a man) had done, and although they had done him no good, I came off badly in comparison. (That I did interpret his homosexual impulses and contempt for the penisless woman may be accepted without my producing the credentials.)

The third phase of this analysis was determined by his hard work to regain a viable position. Whilst in the preceding phase the sessions were filled by his anxiety-ridden descriptions of the oncoming disaster (always interspersed with infantile material of having been wronged), in this phase he spent most of the time telling me in detail about his new business undertakings which met with success.

Only in the following phase did the analysis reach greater depth. He now began to report dreams, often very bizarre, and frightening, with open homosexual and heterosexual incestuous contents which disturbed him deeply. He no longer liked coming to his sessions, nor did I continue to be the nice old thing. But he became very punctual and did everything possible not to miss any session.

It was in this last phase that he began to understand the notion of self-assertion and to distinguish it from that of destructive actions against other people.

The point I am trying to make is that in this case, actions based on self-assertion, following very serious threats to his existence, preceded his conscious appreciation of this psychic process. Correlated with this insight, significant changes in his outer conduct of life occurred that took into account his wish to give expression to his cultural interests.

V

SACRIFICE

Looking for a phylogenetic prototype of a sacrificial act valid for our

Western culture, I turned to Genesis and the story of Abraham being "tempted" by God to sacrifice Isaac, his only son left to him.

I make no claim to base my ideas on Bible research, but allow myself to approach the story as a psychoanalyst. (What remnants of unremembered reading may be at work, I do not know.)

It may well be that several highly important steps in development took place in a relatively short period or are presented in a condensed way in symbolic and poetic language. Amongst these are the termination of slavery and the lesson that a servant has the same standing with God as his master. This is expressed, we may surmise, in the covenant which God made with Abraham, when he asked him to carry out the circumcision on himself, on all of the men in his employ, and on the "men bought" as well.

Still more momentous is the step to abolish the sacrifice of human life. There is an impressive build-up to depict the horror of human sacrifice. Abraham is shown as a good person as he pleads with God to save Sodom from destruction, if there are some righteous living in that town. He engages in a veritable bargaining with God, starting with 50 innocent persons and coming down to 10, as the condition on which God agrees to spare the wicked town.

There is the moving narrative of the aging couple, Abraham and Sarah, being childless, and how Sarah, giving up all hope of having a child, suggests to Abraham to make her handmaiden pregnant so that his seed should bear fruit; how later, envy and jealousy between the women and the triumph which the master's mistress feels over her mistress cloud the former domestic happiness.

We are told of the wondrous promise of God's messengers, which God himself repeats, that Sarah will bear Abraham a son; how neither of them can believe it since she has ceased to menstruate. There is now some tension between God and Abraham, with Abraham quickly repenting. The miracle comes to pass, and Isaac is born.

The narrative gains in drama. Abraham arranges a feast for Isaac's weaning. This provokes the stepbrother's mockery. Sarah, now having a son of her own who healthily overcame the dangers of earliest infancy and proved her value as a mother, feels safe enough to give vent to her long-standing wrath about Hagar's arrogance. She demands that the maid and the maid's son be expelled. Abraham, albeit with grief in his heart, complies, begging God to take care of Ismael and receiving God's promise that He will do so.

The scene now seems set for the old parents to end their lives calmly, assured that their son will take over when the father retires. But as this event approaches with Isaac having outgrown his childhood and ready for his task, Abraham again hears God's voice, and this voice orders him to sacrifice his son.

The Biblical narrator succeeds in making us imagine vividly the horror and sadness in the old man's heart, his guilt toward his trusting son, his dread of telling his wife when the dreadful deed is done, the despairing outlook of an empty future. The drama ends as, at the last moment, God forbids Abraham to slay his son. Abraham puts a ram in his place.

I have ventured to depict the phylogenetic development of the concept of God and to show that this process started with a deity that found pleasure in blood sacrifices and thus justified the cruel strivings of the primitive mind. To use a term of an Oxford physicist friend of mine, "God-mindedness" is the prerogative of the human being. It undergoes vicissitudes and produces concepts in accordance with cultural progress. How difficult it was to give up the lust of killing is well described by the author of Genesis when he tells that Abraham killed a ram to please God.

From Abraham's time it took centuries until "God-mindedness" designed a God whose injunctions were of an ethical nature and demanded love and justice as guiding principles.

How tenuous this advance in "God-mindedness" is, how easily it can be reversed to the worship of barbarism in our "enlightened" times needs no documentation.

If I am right to regard the relinquishing of human sacrifice as the phylogenetic prototype of the sacrificial parapraxis, this would explain that this parapraxis is in a class by itself: it occurs only on unusual, profoundly moving occasions; it harms no other person than the individual himself who commits the bungled action; and this damage is slight. As a commemoration of a momentous step in cultural development, it bears witness to achievement rather than failure—as the analysis of its determinants shows: the life of a daughter being saved; a friendship being mended; a daughter moving into a new phase of life with all prospects of happiness.

The history of the last instance given in detail demonstrates the rejection of injustice and cruelty and the election of ethical values which includes our profession itself.

REFERENCES

Erikson, E. H. (1950), *Childhood and Society*. New York: Norton.

Freud, A. (1965), *Normality and Pathology in Childhood: Assessments of Development. The Writings of Anna Freud,* 6:93-107. New York: International Universities Press.

Freud, S. (1900), The interpretation of dreams. *Standard Edition*, 4-5:1-621. London: Hogarth Press, 1953.

_____ (1901), The psychopathology of everyday life. *Standard Edition*, 6:1-279. London: Hogarth Press, 1960.

_____ (1911), Formulations on the two principles of mental functioning. *Standard Edition*, 12: 213-226. London: Hogarth Press, 1958.

_____ (1914), On narcissism: An introduction. *Standard Edition*, 14:67-102. London: Hogarth Press, 1957.

_____ (1925), Negation. *Standard Edition,* 19:235-239. London: Hogarth Press, 1961.

Greenacre, P. (1957), The childhood of the artist: Libidinal phase development and giftedness. In: *Emotional Growth,* Vol. II. New York: International Universities Press, 1971, pp. 479-504.

_____ (1958), The family romance of the artist. In: *Emotional Growth*, Vol. II. New York: International Universities Press, 1971, pp. 505-532.

Heimann, P. (1962), Notes on the anal stage. *Internat. J. Psycho-Anal.*, 43:406-414.

Kohut, H. (1971), *The Analysis of the Self.* New York: International Universities Press.

Kris, E. (1952), The image of the artist. In: *Psychoanalytic Explorations in Art.* New York: International Universities Press, pp. 64-84.

Mahler, M. (1969), *On Human Symbiosis and the Vicissitudes of Individuation.* New York: International Universities Press.

Sterba, R. F. (1972), The multiple determinants of a minor accident. *Israel Annals of Psychiatry and Related Disciplines*, 8:111-122.

Winnicott, D. W. (1971), *Playing and Reality.* London: Tavistock Publications.

March, 1974

Dreams and the Latent Negative Transference

SANFORD M. IZNER, M.D. (*La Jolla, Calif.*)

To recognize, understand, and permit working through of the negative aspects of the transference neurosis often poses difficult problems in psychoanalytic treatment. This is especially true for negative elements that remain latent and obscure throughout the course of analysis.

Sterba (1927), among others, has demonstrated very lucidly the difficulties in recognizing and managing the latent negative transference and has emphasized that the progress of analysis may often be impeded by hostile feelings that have not been brought to light and interpreted. Freud (1925a), in summing up the vicissitudes of transference, had this to say: ". . . so long as it is affectionate and moderate, it becomes the agent of the physician's influence and neither more nor less than the mainspring of the joint work of analysis. Later on, when it has become passionate or has been converted into hostility, it becomes the principal tool of the resistance" (p. 42).

Freud (1915b) has also pointed out that the only way we have of recognizing unconscious processes is "under the conditions of dreaming and of neurosis" (p. 187). I shall here confine the discussion to elements of the transference that are principally negative and latent in character and their relation to dreaming.

We will assume that negative or hostile feelings during analysis may be characterized by expressions of direct and overt hostility, avoidance, denial and negation, some instances of acting out, and overt and conscious breaches of the fundamental rule, along with more subtle forms of expression too numerous and varied to require mention. Many

---

This paper was originally written in honor of Dr. Richard Sterba on the occasion of his 75th birthday.

of these forms of expression retain a quality of latency during analysis, in the sense that the feelings associated with them do not obtain direct conscious expression, and even the unconscious derivatives of the affect seem to obtain discharge largely through indirect means. In these situations we recognize most clearly many of the characteristics of primary-process functioning, in which the elements of displacement, condensation, symbolic representation, and other forms of distortion appear to predominate.

Which leads directly to a consideration of the dream as one of the best-defined avenues for expression of ideation and affect. Freud (1900) demonstrated that dreams could be understood only by undoing the dream work, with the help of the patient's associations, so as to discover the latent thoughts responsible for producing the dream. He pointed out that manifest content could only be considered and interpreted in this light. The importance of latent expressions in all analytic work, and particularly in relation to dreams, is well recognized and generally acknowledged. In analysis, dreams take on the form of a communication between the patient and analyst, and to presume knowledge of what a dream might signify to the dreamer without considering the additional latent associations might be compared with attempting to spend only one surface of a coin — symbolic interpretation notwithstanding (Freud, 1923, 1925b).

A phenomenon commonly observed in the dreams of patients during analysis is the analyst's recognition that the most significant and pertinent interpretation of a given dream or series of dreams depends on a reversal, or a representation of the situation (or affect) by its opposite in the manifest dream (Freud, 1900).[1] It becomes evident from the latent associations (latent in the sense that the conscious connection between the manifest content and the associations has not been made prior to the verbalization of the expressions) that, in the dream, the patient has actually reversed what he is really experiencing or might wish to express at that point in the analysis. This seems to be especially true in relation to feelings and events most directly concerned with the transference neurosis. In his discussion of distortion in dreams, Freud described this phenomenon as a wish-fulfillment. He also took up the question of some possible exceptions to the rule.

Freud illustrated that even "counterwish" dreams (which, because of their unpleasant contents or the desire for punishment, might at first

---

[1] We are concerned here only with the reversal of manifest dream content and not with chronological reversal in dreams.

glance be considered at odds with the theory) actually comply with the rule of wish-fulfillment. To illustrate this principle further, he utilized dreams that were opposite in manifest content to what was really desired, as determined by the expressions of the patient, stating, "that the non-fulfillment of one wish meant the fulfillment of another" (p. 151). This sort of reversal was most clearly demonstrated in what he termed "contradictory dreams." He noted that the most frequent occurrence of this type of dream followed directly upon his own attempts, during the analysis of some of his patients, to formulate for them the basic expression in the dream: that of a wish-fulfillment. After he had tendered his explanatory remarks to the patient, the dream that frequently followed, when subjected to analysis of the latent content of the associations, expressed the patient's desire to contradict Freud's previous explanation. Among his examples, the following, taken from his analysis of a female patient, is most illustrative:

One day I had been explaining to her that dreams are fulfillments of wishes. Next day she brought me a dream in which she was travelling down with her mother-in-law to the place in the country where they were to spend their holidays together. Now I knew that she had violently rebelled against the idea of spending the summer near her mother-in-law and that a few days earlier she had successfully avoided the propinquity she dreaded by engaging rooms in a far distant resort. And now her dream had undone the solution she had wished for: was not this the sharpest possible contradiction of my theory that in dreams wishes are fulfilled? No doubt; and it was only necessary to follow the dream's logical consequence in order to arrive at its interpretation. The dream showed that I was wrong. *Thus it was her wish that I might be wrong, and her dream showed that wish fulfilled* [Freud, 1900, p. 151].

Freud added that the contradictory wish represented the dreamer's attempt to deny another inference Freud had made concerning important latent memories which had not yet come clearly to light in the analysis, but which, apparently, were quite true — as if to express the wish that these suspicions were unfounded because the events in question had never occurred at all. The transference character of all this material is clear. Although Freud did not utilize the term transference in this instance, there is little reason to question his awareness and understanding of the relation of the patient to the analyst during the therapeutic process, even at this early stage of psychoanalytic development. Freud emphasized the defensive aspect of the contradictory dream as an additional form of dream distortion.

It might be of importance at this point to mention Freud's earliest references to the transference: his discussion in the *Studies on Hysteria* (Breuer & Freud, 1893-1895) of "the transference onto the physician" of distressing ideas, in the sense of making a "false connection." Another very early use of the term "transference" is to be found in his discussion of the Dora case (1905), where it is used in a sense more closely allied to our present application of the term. In Chapter VII (1900) Freud uses the term in reference to an economic problem. He discusses the energy shift from unconscious wish-fulfillment and the attachment of the disturbing affect to a rather innocuous conscious thought in order to obtain discharge. From the economic standpoint, this sort of energy transfer remains as a component of the mechanism of displacement, which plays such a prominent role in the phenomenon of transference.

But it is in his discussion of "contradictory" dreams that Freud made some of his earliest references to the thought that his patients might desire, in an unconscious way, to express hostile or negative feelings about their relation with him as an analyst. At the same time, he pointed out that the patient's need to oppose what had been communicated by the analyst is actually directed at an intensive warding-off of certain unpleasant memories or experiences that have a latent connection to the material under discussion. This fear that the analyst might infer what has been repressed in association to a relatively innocuous thought coincides with the economic element of the energy transfer mentioned above.

To recapitulate: through an understanding of the latent meaning behind the associations of the patient whose dream was chosen as an illustration, it was made clear that a reversal of the manifest dream content was in order, if one were to grasp what the patient was attempting to convey to the analyst. Freud demonstrated that a reversal of the manifest dream corresponded to what underlay the patient's associations to that dream. It was clear that both the latent material and reversed manifest content pertained to the same idea: that of the wish to prove the analyst wrong. The latent hostile impulse in the phenomenon was directly concerned with the transference neurosis and, in the example given above, seems to represent one of Freud's first expressions regarding latent negative transference feelings.

It is my purpose to demonstrate that the phenomenon of reversal in dreams may be related to specific levels in the defensive organization of the ego, structured as a form of distortion in order to ward off the expression of latent negative feelings in the transference. Dreams of this nature, then, might be considered a distinct clue to the existence of latent hostile feelings and could be interpreted on this basis. At the same time, such an interpretation would provide additional confirmation for the theory that all dreams represent the fulfillment of a wish—and, for the patient in analysis, a wish directly referrable to the transference figure of the analyst as the object choice of that particular level of development and associated with that period of the evolving infantile neurosis. Although reversal or representation by its opposite occurs under many other conditions and, in certain situations, might be utilized to ward off positive feelings, the discussion here will be confined to the use of reversal of manifest dream content as a representation of a regressive form of defensive activity on the part of the ego, in order to provide a distorted presentation of hostility that cannot otherwise be expressed. We might speculate that the dream reversal would be most apt to occur when specific levels of the defensive stratification predominate, especially at times when the patient is anticipating communication of the dream to another, or possibly in situations of self-communication, when he is making an attempt to analyze his own dreams (Beres, 1956; Anna Freud, 1946).

As further illustrations of the relation of dream reversal to the latent negative transference, the following situations in analysis may serve to clarify the thesis.

A 44-year-old married woman returned to analysis preoccupied with feelings of depression and unworthiness because of her desire to act on sexual impulses that had in the past led to extramarital affairs. She felt she had benefited from her former therapy, in that she had brought many of her disturbing impulses under temporary control, but now sought further help. In addition to her need to depreciate her former analyst for "his excessive talking," she was considerably disillusioned with the analysis because of her impression that the analyst's guidance had led her into divorce proceedings and almost ended her marriage. She had dropped the attempt at divorce when she terminated the analysis, which she felt no longer afforded the protection and control she had sought for her disturbing sexual and aggressive impulses.

The patient, a very bright and competent woman, was employed in a semimanagerial capacity. She worked in order to provide funds for the education of her two daughters, an opportunity she herself had been deprived of because of her mother's feeling that "only boys should go to college"—that girls did not require this background for marriage. Her feeling that her husband was unable to provide the necessary funds seemed to recapitulate many of her attitudes in relation to her parents: she had always experienced her mother as the aggressive and controlling parent, and her father as weak, incompetent, and a poor provider. She described her older brother, an unsuccessful salesman, as similar to her father, whereas her younger brother, whom she had "mothered and taken under her wing," became a physician and a well-trained specialist in his profession.

Soon after her entry into the second analysis, the patient developed a strong positive transference marked by many expressions of her regard for the analyst and colored by numerous dreams that seemed to confirm these feelings. She spoke of her desires to act out some of the libidinal impulses arising out of the transference with men she met at work, but she managed to keep the desire for displacement on a fantasy level. Most of the hostility for both her mother and father in the transference remained latent, except for an occasional reference to her former analyst or a disparaging remark about one of her superiors. While the patient was experiencing fairly intense and overt libidinal feelings in the transference, she decided she would like to increase the number of her analytic visits. Although she repeated this desire on several occasions, her request was not granted. At the same time, she had also felt rejected in her attempt to act out her libidinal impulses with a business acquaintance who did not seem to respond to her interest in him. She became depressed, and, although her overt expressions to the analyst remained positive enough, she presented a dream of the night when her last request had gone ungratified. In the dream, a man is trying to get the patient to go with her, but the patient refuses and wants, instead, to go with her husband, who is nearby.

In associating to the dream, the patient described the intense depression that followed the rejection by her business acquaintance. She was made aware of the reversal of the manifest dream content: that she had really felt rejected by the analyst, who had been so inconsiderate with regard to her request for more analytic time. She realized that she was angry and did not want to be either with the man in the dream or her business acquaintance. In addition, she was expressing in the dream her wish that the rejection in the analysis had never happened at all. Her anger at feeling disregarded was followed by intense hostility to the analyst. The interpretation of her anger was then made in relation to her desire to be cared for and attended to by the analyst as she had once wished to be cared for by her mother. This was clearly a defensive regression from the position of feeling angry with and rejected by the analyst as father in the transference, feelings that had been distorted and mastered by reversal in the dream. In the interval following these interpretations and prior to her next analytic visit, she recalled a dream concerned with a most disturbing repressed memory from early childhood. It involved a primal-scene situation, and the repressed memory recapitulated the patient's depression and anger at being moved out of her mother's bedroom, where she had slept for a considerable part of the first eight years of her life. She recalled being made to sleep in another room at times when her father and mother slept together. She could still remember "those sounds in the night that triggered this fear," accompanied by intense anger and depression. The patient's anger at the analyst, latently present in her associations and manifested by reversal in the dream, seems clear. That this phenomenon is structured to distort and disguise these feelings, enabling the patient to ward off the return to consciousness of the associated repressed and disturbing childhood memory, also seems evident.

Another example taken from the analysis of the same patient further illustrates the thesis of dream reversal. While discussing something in the presence of her family, it occurred to her that her older brother seemed inattentive. She mentioned this to the analyst, and, as usual, there was little comment. At her next appointment she presented a dream: A boy friend of her daughter's is making sexual advances to a girl friend of the patient's. The patient asks, "How can you do this sort of thing?" and he replies, "It's the natural thing to do."

Her associations revealed that her daughter was visited by a boy friend at home that evening and that the patient had gone upstairs to sleep, leaving them alone. She recalled thinking that the boy might make sexual advances to her daughter after the patient had gone to sleep, and then recalled a thought she had had during her previous analytic visit, one she had suppressed. After expressing many positive feelings for the analyst, who gave no evidence of a response, she had had the fleeting thought that he must have fallen asleep. Later, after the visit, she felt very irritable and angry, but was not aware of the reason. When the reversal in the dream was pointed out, the patient became aware that, "it is not the natural thing to do — to react to sexual overtures by going to sleep." This resulted in her feeling quite angry that one should withdraw in this way from her advances, and she related it to the fear that her daughter might be the one who would make sexual advances to her boy friend "in a most natural way," after the patient had gone to sleep: thus the patient had the impulse to make advances to the analyst if she felt he was asleep.

When her latent anger in the transference had been interpreted and expressed, she remembered the older brother's inattentive attitude of a few days before, which brought forth the recall of her intense repressed rage at him. For some time when she was a small child, she had slept in the same bedroom with him. She had often felt angry because of her desire to be involved in sexual play with him and his tendency to ridicule her for these feelings or to ignore her and go directly to sleep. She also recollected a most humiliating thought that had occurred to her at that time — her desire to make sexual advances to her brother (and probably her father too) as he slept. Her latent anger, in defense against re-experiencing the disturbing memories and impulses from childhood, became manifested in the reversal of the dream content. It is of particular interest that latent negative transference feelings of this nature be directed toward the rejecting love object of the oedipal period as the result of the feelings of narcissistic mortification (Eidelberg, 1959) resulting from such experiences.

Another case involved the situation of a 29-year-old divorced professional man who entered analysis a short time after the disruption of his marriage. At that time he was terribly anxious and depressed, and blamed himself for his wife's breaking up the marriage. In his seven years of marriage, the patient had never been capable of consummating the marriage sexually. His wife had finally decided to go out with other men, which the patient experienced as a devastating injury to his self-esteem. He had been deeply hurt by her leaving. The patient was the only child of a marriage between a successful business woman and a man twelve years her junior. The patient's father had been taken into the mother's women's apparel business and was considered by everyone in the family to be her employee.

The patient was very closely attached to his mother, whom he described as a dominant and overprotective woman who argued violently with her rather immature husband. On several occasions she drove him out of the house. The parents were divorced when the patient was twelve years of age, and after that he saw his father on only a very few occasions. For most of his early life, the patient slept in the same room with his mother, even at times when his father was at home. He always felt that his mother was much more closely bound to him than to his father, and he was very dependent on her in return, although he also resented his dependent position.

From the time he began his schooling, the patient was always the best student in his class. His mother took pleasure in his achievement, but he felt her pride resulted from the gratification she experienced from the recognition and admiration of her friends, rather than from a real interest in him. He recalled that in earliest childhood he took considerable interest in women's undergarments and used to wear some of mother's "underthings and corsets" when he masturbated. This masturbation was accompanied by a fantasy of lying in bed dressed as a girl and being masturbated by a fully clothed woman lying alongside of him.

His interest in women's undergarments persisted after he entered analysis. Since early childhood he had pilfered or purchased and worn women's "panties."

When he began analysis, he was employed in research work, but was not very productive. He was driven to exposing his genitals at night to women on the street, and his intense anxiety because of these impulses, coupled with his extreme loneliness, led him to seek analysis. Another element of importance seemed related to the patient's realization that he had married shortly before his discovery that his mother was critically ill and might not survive the illness. He had the impression that his mother wanted him to get married, as if she knew she would not be there to take care of him. He realized that after she became ill he no longer had the desire to return home from school to visit her, and avoided seeing her as much as possible.

In any discussion of this patient's productions, it is important to take into account his "sexual reversal" and accompanying feminine identification. His fetishism was present throughout his marriage, and he continued to wear women's underclothes through the early years of analysis. For this patient, almost everything seemed to be "reversed," and for many months all of his dreams were of this nature. In the main, his defenses were characterized by reversing, turning on the self, undoing, isolation, and numerous reaction formations, accompanied by ambivalence in connection with most of his aggressive and sexual impulses. Characterologically, the patient was also immobilized by his parsimoniousness and strong need for self-denial. Although much could be said concerning his productions and symptomatology in relation to the importance of his tendency toward "sexual reversal," we will confine ourselves to the significance of the reversal of manifest dream content as evidence of his latent negative-transference feelings.

The early months of analysis were characterized by compliance and superficial cooperation interspersed with occasional sarcastic or hostile expressions—evidently a re-enactment of his early relation with his mother. His dreams, which were all "reversed" in content, expressed this clearly. A rather typical situation in the analysis relevant to the latent negative transference can be described as follows.

The patient had been out of town for a professional meeting and felt guilty for being away from the analysis. On his return, he became aware that he had completely forgotten the material discussed at the meetings. This was uncharacteristic for one with such an excellent memory. After arriving home and before his return to analysis, the patient decided to write a check in payment for his analytic visits for the previous month. He wondered why he felt it was so imperative that he write the check. He experienced difficulty in deciding on the correct total for the check, which also was uncharacteristic for an expert in mathematics who made a practice of calculating things well in advance. He realized that he must have felt "guilty about something." He related the following dream of the night before his return to analysis: He is unable to complete a mathematics examination in time, looks out of the window at the school across the street, and notices a flood in front of the school. He is concerned because he fears the parents will be unable to visit the children there.

It was clear from his associations that the patient felt anxious about returning to analysis, and this feeling, coupled with his intensely ambivalent attitude, was reflected in his strong impulse to write the check and his difficulty with the calculations. When he experienced the impulse to write the check, memories from the meetings returned to consciousness. When the reversed content of the dream was revealed as a fear that, because of anger, "the child could not visit the [analyst] parent," the patient suddenly experienced and expressed his anger about returning to the analysis. Only after he discussed his need to write the check and his guilt about going away was he able to express his anger at the analyst for not struggling with him about his going away as a mother would have been expected to do.

While he was out of town, he had the sudden impulse to "look at women," a desire he had not experienced in years. At the same time he felt a strong impulse to return to dressing in women's undergarments. He recalled how in childhood he used to slip on one of his mother's girdles and masturbate. This brought to mind many of his mother's prohibitions against masturbation and the anxiety and anger they aroused in him. He recalled a dream he'd had, which he dated as having occurred before he was four years old — the earliest dream he could remember. In the dream, he is in bed and his mother is there. She tells him that a friend is coming to visit, and the patient immediately thinks she must mean his father — but then an elephant walks in. The patient felt that this dream must have been related to his childhood desire to "visit his parents" in their bed and his feeling of exclusion and anger when he was not able to do this.

On another occasion, the patient dreamed of being on a train. He was in a dining car, and the waiter brought him five choices of dessert. The patient selected a little brown one and spilled some of it on mother's skirt. He tried hard to wipe it off.

He was immediately aware of the transference reference in the dream, relating the five desserts to the number of analytic visits per week. At the same time, he complained that the times of these visits placed a significant hardship on him and interfered with his recreational activities. He would have chosen other appointment times. The reversed quality of the dream was then interpreted: The patient was angry at not getting his choice of appointment times. In addition, he had evidently experienced this lack of choice as a punitive sort of activity on the part of the analyst, that of getting his "dessert." The patient then expressed his anger at feeling that he did not get what he wanted and was being forced by the analyst to do things on schedule, just as his mother had demanded of him when he was a child. He recalled that she would interrupt his play and insist that he spend a regular time every day on the toilet, attempting to overcome his childhood constipation. As a result, he would be so enraged that with every bowel movement he would make certain that most of the feces would be smeared all over the toilet seat and his clothes. Instead of trying to clean it up as in the dream, he would really rub it in as retaliation for his mother's "rubbing in" his obstinate attitude toward her demands. This was the uncomfortable, repressed memory that his latent hostile feeling in the transference was structured to defend against, in order to assist him in suppressing this impulse in the analysis.

To summarize, an attempt has been made to provide an explanation for the rather frequent clinical experience of the phenomenon of dream reversal and its association to elements of the latent negative transference. The defensive function of reversal in relation to the latent negative transference has been explained, and the connection to repression of unpleasant memories and impulses from the period of the infantile neurosis with the resultant amnesia has been made. The hostile nature of the impulse directed at the love object of the oedipal period has also been described.

In "Instincts and Their Vicissitudes," Freud (1915a) indicated that the defensive phenomenon of reversal must be considered from two separate standpoints: the alteration of the instinctual aim and the change in instinctual content. Alteration of the instinctual aim involves the replacement of active strivings by passivity; alteration of content is limited to the substitution of hatred for love. The situation of dream reversal in relation to the latent negative transference seems to clearly trace this process. A substitution of rage against the frustrating or rejecting love object of the oedipal period develops, along with a regressive return of feelings of childhood helplessness. The accompanying state of passivity results in the need to further distort any activated disturbing impulses by representing them as reversed.

Several questions come to mind. First of all, why, in a dream, does no direct denial of what has been said or done become a major determinant?

Secondly, why, in a person who has been previously capable of expressing overt and direct hostility toward the analyst, do we now find a need to resort to a dream, with the additional distortion of reversal? The explanation offered by Freud (1900) that " 'No' seems not to exist as far as dreams are concerned" (p. 318), an explanation later confirmed by Fliess (1953), seems to apply. In addition, as analysis proceeds, the state of regressed functioning of the ego results in the utilization of defensive reactions associated with earlier developmental periods. These reactions are directed at warding off feelings associated with experiences of childhood helplessness, feelings that seem to preclude the expression of hostile impulses, especially in response to the control and influence of the transference figure in analysis, who represents the object choice of that developmental period. A stratification of defensive operations is then set into motion, which is directed at the control of anxiety arising in relation to regressive activities utilized in the flight from the threatening negative feelings connected with the oedipal problem in the transference (Beres, 1956; Anna Freud, 1936). Anna Freud (1965) has referred to the existence of anxiety in association with different developmental levels. She has pointed out that the earliest form of anxiety is concerned with the fear of annihilation, which is followed developmentally by the anxiety related to separation from the love object of the preoedipal phase. Castration anxiety arises with the oedipal problem, and she views the appearance of this form of anxiety in the treatment of children in whom it has not existed as evidence of the forward motion of the analytic work. The change in object relations on which this observation is based seems clear. The shift in object choice as a defensive reaction to the transference figure of the analyst seems, in a large measure, to be based on the regressive reversal of this developmental phenomenon. Negative feelings directed at the frustrating or rejecting love object of the oedipal phase and the associated castration anxiety of this period lead to defensive activities that reverse the entire developmental process. As an added result, the anxiety more closely associated with earlier periods of development predominates and constitutes an attempt to totally avoid negative feelings in the transference. The trauma and resultant "scars" of the early object relation contribute to this stratification of defensive operations, which functions to ward off the "narcissistic mortification" so clearly described by Eidelberg (1959).

In the interests of clarity and brevity, no attempt has been made to discuss sexual reversal or reversals of affect in dreams, in connection with latent negative transference. Nor can absurdity in dreams (Freud, 1900) and the connection to latent hostile feelings be taken up here. These topics might provide a basis for further investigation of this problem.

REFERENCES

Beres, D. (1956), Ego deviation and the concept of schizophrenia. *The Psychoanalytic Study of the Child*, 11:164-235. New York: International Universities Press.

Breuer, J., & Freud, S. (1893-1895), Studies on hysteria. *Standard Edition*, 2. London: Hogarth Press, 1955.

Eidelberg, L. (1959), The concept of narcissistic mortification. *Internat. J. Psycho-Anal.*, 40: 163-168.

Fliess, R. (1953), *The Revival of Interest in the Dream*. New York: International Universities Press, pp. 75-76.

Freud, A. (1936), *The Ego and the Mechanisms of Defense. The Writings of Anna Freud*, Vol. 2. New York: International Universities Press, 1966.

_____ (1965), *Normality and Pathology in Childhood. The Writings of Anna Freud*, Vol. 6. New York: International Universities Press.

Freud, S. (1900), The interpretation of dreams. *Standard Edition*, 4 & 5. London: Hogarth Press, 1953.

_____ (1905), Fragment of the analysis of a case of hysteria. *Standard Edition*, 7:3-112. London: Hogarth Press, 1953.

_____ (1915a), Instincts, and their vicissitudes. *Standard Edition*, 14:109-140. London: Hogarth Press, 1957.

_____ (1915b), The unconscious. *Standard Edition*, 14:159-215. London: Hogarth Press, 1957.

_____ (1923), Remarks upon the theory and practice of dream interpretation. *Standard Edition*, 19:109-121. London: Hogarth Press, 1961.

_____ (1925a), An autobiographical study. *Standard Edition*, 20:7-70. London: Hogarth Press, 1959.

_____ (1925b), Some additional notes upon dream interpretation. *Standard Edition*, 19:125-141. London: Hogarth Press, 1961.

Sterba, R. (1927), Über latente negative Übertragung. *Internat. Zeitschrift Psychoanal.*, 13: 160-165.

February, 1974

Affect Tolerance

HENRY KRYSTAL, M.D. (*Detroit*)

From her six years of experience in the British Emergency Medical Services during World War II, Elizabeth Zetzel (1949) has distilled observations pertaining to individual differences in the capacity to bear anxiety. Special characteristics of wartime experience focus attention on this variability. As the soldier responds to realistically appraised danger, it is necessary for him to function in a state of anxiety. He cannot afford to have his anxiety "blocked," for it is vital to his survival that he be kept alert to threats in his life and ready for instant life-preserving action. He must not, however, become overwhelmed with his anxiety or it will interfere with his effectiveness. The function of the army psychiatrist is to improve or restore the overwhelmed soldier's ability to bear his emotional responses to the imminent danger situation in order to enable him to return to a life-threatening situation.

There is, in fact, an optimal level of anxiety for all activities, and, in some, the "fine tuning" that is necessary becomes especially conspicuous. In psychoanalysis, for example, we are fundamentally committed to the evocation of affective responses. Once these emotions make their appearance, the patient must "handle" them. If the patient permits his emotions to build up to uncontrollable, threatening proportions, the analyst is confronted with a potential psychoanalytic emergency that may interrupt the therapeutic work (Peto, 1967). On the other hand, if the patient's fear of his emotions has led him to develop extensive disassociations of affect, or widespread affect inhibitions, psychoanalytic interpretation remains a mere cliché and its therapeutic potential is limited (Krystal, 1973).

Part II of a study of "The Genetic Development of Affects and Affect Regression." Part I appeared in *This Annual*, 2:98-126, 1974.

The attention of the psychoanalyst thus inevitably shifts from the intrapsychic sources of affects and their form to the patient's degree of success in handling or "having" his emotions. The positive value of the ability to tolerate anxiety impressed Zetzel early on: ". . . the presence of anxiety symptoms, both in childhood and in adult life, is often of good prognostic significance" (1943, p. 30), and "in that individuals who have been capable of tolerating relatively great amounts of anxiety during the course of development proved on the whole less liable to develop relatively irreversible neurotic reactions in the face of traumatic war experiences" (1949, p. 33).

One of the observations that alerted Zetzel to the function of affect tolerance as an independent variable was the discovery that individuals who successfully handled the reality of long-term danger could be overwhelmed by a relatively minor incident. For instance, a fireman who functioned well "during the worst London fires" became demoralized and "suddenly developed acute and inhibiting anxiety symptoms after receiving a very slight injury to his hand when a falling beam in a burning building touched him" (Zetzel, 1949, p. 7).

In reflecting upon these observations, Zetzel not only surmised that the capacity to bear anxiety was valuable in the face of danger, but also arrived at a far-reaching conclusion: "Not only . . . do I believe that the capacity to develop and tolerate secondary anxiety is decisive in the achievement of mental stability and health, but also I should like to suggest that this capacity is important to an allied subject of vital clinical significance: the limitations of analysis as a therapeutic process" (p. 50).

The "function" of anxiety tolerance may be seen in broader perspective in Zetzel's book (1970). Her statement is so germane to contemporary thinking that I will quote it:

For neurotics the capacity to recognize and tolerate the existence of an internal, unconsciously determined danger situation by developing secondary anxiety is decisive. This capacity is very closely linked to the problem of psychological insight. If anxiety is defined as the response to an internal danger situation, the capacity to develop and tolerate anxiety, associated as it must always be with an unconscious conflict, is very closely related to the capacity to recognize and tolerate the instinctual conflicts and tension which constitute the threatened internal danger situation. This means that *the more an individual has been able,* in an internal, unconsciously produced danger situation, *to develop and tolerate anxiety, the more one finds in analysis that he is capable of facing and resolving the conflicts which determined it* [p. 51; italics added].

This statement is especially pregnant with clinical and theoretical implications when we keep in mind that during the intervening years, Zetzel (1965) had studied the capacity to bear depression with equal perspicacity. She observed that the ability to tolerate depression was an indispensable condition of "optimal" maturation and an important ingredient in the ability to withstand disappointment, loss, frustration, illness, retirement, and many other "painful though inevitable, experiences." She brought together these separate observations in a statement regarding the effect of early object relations on basic ego functions and the tolerance of affects. Similarly, in the introduction to *The Capacity for Emotional Growth* (1970), wherein she summarized her work, Zetzel extended the prognostic significance previously attributed to anxiety alone: "Patients who cannot tolerate anxiety or depression will seldom prove capable of working through a transference neurosis. Many such patients cannot terminate any form of therapy successfully" (p. 11). Thus, Zetzel's writings contain a capsule history of her development of the concept of affect tolerance. But whereas her work evolved through the study of war neuroses and depressive patients, my investigations on this subject have developed in a different context.

In working with drug-dependent individuals, my colleagues and I have found it necessary to postulate that a major cause of their use of a drug as an affect-blocker was their basic impairment of affect tolerance (Krystal & Raskin, 1970). We have felt that this disturbance was caused by severe (cumulative) trauma in infancy and early childhood. And in working with individuals who were massively traumatized in adolescence and adult life, we have also found that perhaps the most disabling sequel was their impairment of affect tolerance (Krystal, 1968; Krystal & Niederland, 1971).

Both of these groups of patients dreaded their emotions so severely that they could not bear the affective responses to psychoanalytic psychotherapy. Accordingly, we found it helpful to recommend a "preparatory phase of treatment serving to increase affect tolerance" (Krystal & Raskin, 1970, pp. 99-101). Inasmuch as such disturbances in the ability to bear emotions are quite prevalent in a variety of syndromes, I will set forth a basic description of affect tolerance.

The ability to bear emotions in their totality, without isolating the cognitive from the "expressive" aspects is acquired relatively late in one's growing up. It is not encompassed in a single ego function, but is a composite of the attributes of one's personality in relation to multiple functions and factors. We have to speak carefully about the quantitative element of affect, for it is not helpful to concretize our economic metaphors in this area. It can be said only that the degree of intensity of an affect that can be tolerated by one person at any given time is finite. Whenever the intensity or duration of affect causes one to experience the

181

threat of being overwhelmed, signal anxiety is provoked, initiating some modification of the affect experience.

This process of the ego regulation of the affect experience is usually part of the normal handling of affect, and the defenses are in the interest of the ego. In fact, in the long run, the ready availability of many and varied "resources" makes for increased ability to tolerate affect. Some of those positive processes and reactions will be described later. While on the one hand affects can be utilized by the ego for a variety of purposes, they also may, and do, pose a threat to the ego.

Jaffe (1969) has commented that affect tolerance varies greatly in different individuals, with multiple factors at play, and Zetzel (1970b) especially emphasized that the development of affect tolerance is a lifelong process. Let us return to the observation of some of the events and developments by which some of the ego functions related to affect tolerance come to their maturity. Freud (1917) gave us the classical description of a maneuver that helps to increase the tolerance of a painful affect when he pictured the mourner as periodically distracting himself and returning to the painful work of mourning only for a limited period of time. He also implied that current love objects and the denial of loss of the object (with flight into fantasy and temporary denial of the reality) were "resources," as it were, which the mourner could use to keep grief within tolerable limits.

Each affect has its individual problem and history in a given individual. For example, an emotion that was overwhelming at some earlier time is subsequently experienced as dangerous. When affects threaten to become unbearable or seem about to overwhelm the ego, it is advantageous to have a number of temporary strategies, devices which ease the distress momentarily and permit a later return to the full conscious attention to one's own painful living. Among those commonly used self-help devices are: transient consciousness modifications, shifting of attention cathexes (self-distraction), eliminatory or cleansing fantasies, compensatory acting-out. There are also a variety of self-administered or "object-involving" methods of comforting or "mothering" oneself. Where such modes of behavior are experienced as prohibited and therefore inaccessible, objects, drugs, or placebos may have to be used to circumvent inner barriers (inhibitions) resulting from repression (Krystal & Raskin, 1970). The effectiveness of the various ego functions and resources that may be utilized for affect tolerance are often noticeable by their conversion of an affect from its acute form to an extended one, so that they become moods (Jacobson, 1957). Thus, anxiety may be converted into worry.

182

In permanent blocking of affectivity by relatively long-lasting defenses, the emotions are experienced as physiological "attacks" and may break through intermittently. Even recurring periods of depression or anxiety are experienced as "attacks." During such attacks, the affects may not be consciously recognized as such (e.g., in hyperventilation syndromes). This subjective experience is the cause of the tendency, found in both patients and doctors, to experience their emotions as if they were illnesses. The patient's attitude toward an emotion may compound his difficulties with it. The fear of an affect may set up a self-perpetuating circular reaction such as "being afraid of being afraid."

This entire process may vary in degree of consciousness and capacity for reflective self-observation: defenses against emotions, such as "affect-lameness," isolation, or drug abuse, may become important aspects of character development.

While there has been no disagreement with Freud's (1923) statement that the "ego is the actual seat of anxiety" (p. 57), there is some dispute about the nature of the relation between the two. Engel's (1962) view was the following:

Affects originate in infancy as the communicative and behavioral expressions of drive. As the psychic apparatus evolves they come to acquire the qualities of ego function as well. Affects have two essential characteristics: they are felt subjectively and are expressed nonverbally, indicating to oneself and to others one's current state of need.... As the mental apparatus develops these processes progressively come under the aegis of the ego. The perceptual processes whereby one knows *how* one feels are functions of the ego, as are the processes whereby one learns *what* one feels [pp. 123-124].

Structural theory, which, after all, is but a means of classifying mental contents according to their relation to drives and conflicts, creates some clumsiness in our consideration of affects. Affects are described by psychoanalysts as both drive-derivative and possessing characteristics of ego function. They are both "physiological" and ideational. As Novey (1963) puts it: "The very structural models we employ in our consideration of personality and its development expose us to the potential for a peculiar aberration of thinking. For example, we are apt to conceive of the ego as something having a psychic structure which 'experiences' emotions . . . as being of the essence of what we speak of as ego" (p. 295). I do think that Novey's point is well taken. However, we have to acknowledge that affects also "reflect differing aspects of drive, ego, and self-object activities" (Schmale, 1964, p. 288). It is useful to consider the interactions between ego and affect, even if *these considerations represent to some extent an artificial opposition of intrasystematic elements.*

What has been discussed elsewhere as the genetic history of affect development (Engel, 1962; Schmale, 1964; Krystal, 1962, 1970; Krystal & Raskin, 1970) has its parallel in the ego's recognition of, and reaction to, affects. This process is analogous to the development of the ability to bear pain (Krystal & Raskin, 1970). In the transition of affect experience from "attacks" as they appear in infancy (and the affect-regression problems known as psychosomatic diseases) to the adult form of affect experience, there is also a process of ego development in regard to affect tolerance.

One comes to acquire insight, comfort, and familiarity with affects as states of one's self. One develops a multitude of modes of action, defenses, and patterns for keeping affect within tolerable limits of intensity and duration. In addition to these developmental patterns of dealing with pain, the mother plays a vital role in helping the child to "interpret his experiences, as well as to organize them and internalize them, even to the point that tension can be experienced as pleasurable" (Panel, 1968, p. 640).[1] What are involved, then, are evaluation and regulation of affect by the ego. Probably, "affect attacks" in the adult are complex reactions reached with the complicity of the ego, at times unconsciously motivated and at other times representations of a panic in the face of an evaluation of the affect as possibly overwhelming, flooding, disorganizing (destroying) the ego.

Affect Storms as a Psychoanalytic Emergency

It should be made clear that affect storms represent a very specific type of psychiatric and psychoanalytic emergency and should be distinguished from the more commonly understood fear that certain impulses and drives, such as self-destructive wishes, will "get out of hand" and cause one to destroy oneself.

Fenichel (1941) is in error when he treats both dangers as if they were the same: "that which is sometimes described in the literature as the 'fear of the strength of the instincts' really ought to be called 'fear that intense affects may appear and overwhelm rational behavior' " (p. 220). The more familiar fear experienced in connection with intense emotions is

---

[1] In a paper in preparation I present evidence that the quality of pleasure and distress is not an intrinsic quality of affects, but becomes secondarily (albeit quite closely) related to emotions through experience.

184

that cognitive elements of the affect contain an undesirable wish that the subject fears will "come true": that death wishes for the object expressed in anger, rage, or hate may "break through" and result in harm to the object or to the self. With libidinally derived wishes, other dangers are feared: the wish-fulfillment of incestuous strivings, exposure to rejection, humiliation, or, as in borderline states, the merging of the self-representation with the object representation.

But the dread of being *flooded with affect* is less frequently noted or understood, and the common psychoanalytic and psychiatric emergency it presents has to be handled by a specific interpretation related to the ego's experience of the affect. Correct interpretations in states of crisis due to the fear of affects can increase the ego's recognition and tolerance of the affect. Proper therapeutic management consists in helping the patient to re-establish his feeling of security and self-control.

CASE ILLUSTRATION

Mrs. H., a woman in her early thirties, had been in analysis for three years in another town. Her professional position required that she move to a small town in Michigan. This created an intense problem for her, because throughout her analysis she was subject to overwhelming emotional reactions, which occurred either during her analytic hours or at some other time. As a result, her analyst had to be available to her for emergency calls at all times. She had had to call him a number of times since coming to Michigan.

Her referral to me was preceded by one such occasion when, overwhelmed with her emotions and uncontrollably crying, she had called her analyst in her home town, long distance, several times a day. On this occasion, her emotions built up to the point where she panicked, fearing that she was going to lose her mind or be permanently flooded with unbearable feelings. When she reached my office (after driving almost 100 miles), she was quite heavily sedated, having taken about a dozen different drugs, including tranquillizers, narcotic derivatives, antihistamines, and even some "stimulants." She expected that in talking to me she would be overwhelmed with her "hysterics," and, before she did so, she wanted to discuss with me the "emergency aspects" of her case: namely, that the night before, because of her panic, she had taken several capsules of a hypnotic drug and had managed to fall asleep for a few hours only to wake up in terror at 4 A.M., tempted to take more drugs. She was afraid that at this rate she was going to overdose herself.

When it became necessary for her to leave her analyst, he had given her a supply of medication. In addition, she was taking a variety of drugs

185

for asthma, eczema, and other psychosomatic symptoms of anxiety. She had a history of colic, and a very traumatic childhood. At present, she felt that she had to control her emotions at all costs, even including an increase in the use of medication to dangerous proportions, in order to maintain her professional position.

After discussing her mental problems, I pointed out to her that she was using her emotions to control the significant objects in her life, including the remote analyst, and therefore had missed the chance to observe that her emotions were signals *to herself* which she could utilize and live with. The patient protested that she had not been manipulating her analyst "until it was time to leave," but she did allow that her parents did not care for her, except for her "attacks," which included, besides those already mentioned, "attacks" of migraine and essential hypertension. I then proceeded to explain to her the nature of emotions, and how, unless she became frightened and/or angry about having them, they would run their course and could be utilized by her to her advantage.

The patient said, "This is the strangest thing anybody has ever said to me. Nobody has ever talked to me like that!" She left the hour quite composed and never did unleash her "hysterics." In subsequent visits, the work was virtually exclusively concerned with her *handling* of her emotions, before a complete history of her other problems was ever obtained. Later, it was possible to deal with the "psychosomatic diseases" of this patient as affect regression and storm.

One of the serious problems illustrated by this case is the necessity for the psychoanalyst, psychiatrist, one can even say for the physician, to be able to tolerate his patients' intense emotions without panic. When the therapist is overimpressed or frightened of the patient's emotions and proceeds to block them or to hospitalize the patient unnecessarily, the patient not only fails to increase his ability to bear his emotions, but, on the contrary, compounds his dread of them. I have emphasized elsewhere (1970; Krystal & Raskin, 1970) that the psychiatrist may be of great help, especially to some patients, by assisting them in their handling of affects. The success of the self-help group known as "Recovery, Inc.," which bases its work on the writings of Dr. Abraham Low (1950), derives from the help members give each other in learning to tolerate anxiety. Patients need to get acquainted with their emotions as signals, often unpleasant, but manageable and essentially self-limited.

In this respect, the psychiatrist supplies, belatedly, a function the patient's parental and familial background has failed to perform. To be able to function in such capacity, however, one had to appreciate the nature of the subjective experience of a patient whose affect tolerance is impaired. They are individuals who have been traumatized in childhood, whose affects were allowed to flood them. Among the residues of such experiences is a life-long dread of affects. In such patients, the genetic development of the affects themselves has often suffered, causing the affects to be mostly somatized, poorly verbalized, and poorly differentiated.

Affects as a Challenge to the Self

What is the affect experience of more "normal" individuals who have not had serious childhood trauma and for whom at times affects may still be burdensome? Schafer (1964) has pointed out that: "Whether a particular emotion is 'dangerous' or 'painful' or not is jointly determined by existing intrapsychic conditions, the nature of the emotion itself, and the structure-building potential of the interpersonal or social context" (p. 296). A good deal of one's reaction to an affect will depend on the nature of the affective element itself (i.e., whether it is a minimal, mostly cognitive signal affect, or whether it is somatic, undifferentiated, and related to primary-process thinking), and the nature of the ego's familiarity and comfort with it. Affects, however, always represent a challenge and burden for the ego. Eissler (1953) has described the nature of the process:

Every emotion has the tendency to enfold and to engulf the whole ego and to exclude the presence of any other emotion. When I speak of the tendency to take possession of the whole ego I do not mean this only in terms of excluding other emotions. Aside from its tendency toward finding a discharge by means of the psychomotor system, an emotion will also lead to the cathexes of the body image and of the representations of objects. An emotion also has the tendency to accumulate new energy by activation of all memories which are closely related to it and whose contents support it [pp. 203-204].

Eissler's statement illustrates how difficult it is to discuss affect, and especially the burden it places on normal ego functions, without being swept into a mechanistic orientation or a reification of our metaphors. In fact, even to talk about "affects and their impact upon the ego" is to create an artifact. Affects are ways of living and experiencing that cannot be separated from other functional aspects without doing violence to the wholeness of the living individual. Schafer (personal communication) has taken the view that, if we view affects as an experience rather than as an expression, it becomes necessary to reconsider just what about the affect could be possibly "threatening or dangerous to the ego."

187

The accretions of metaphors that have been useful through the years have contributed to our difficulties in dealing with affects. The greatest obstacle to our clinical and therapeutic conceptions have been metaphors that refer to the "discharge" of emotions. I have held that anal analogies involved in our conceptions of affects, especially anger, confuse our theoretical and therapeutic vision (Krystal & Raskin, 1970; Krystal, 1970). Although so much is said nowadays, especially by nonanalytic therapists, about the need for patients to "express" their anger, the only possible help the patients can obtain is to learn to tolerate it. The ideas of riddance, and the inevitable anal analogies, are completely misleading here.

Among those who have advocated dispensing with economic theories, Schafer has addressed himself directly to the problems of affects. He found that a source of difficulty in the effort to conceptualize affect stems from the prevalent inclination to think in spatial terms—trying to locate affect "inside" oneself as a quantity with a propensity to discharge to the "outside." Schafer (1972) advocated that affect be considered an adjective, a way of acting, thus eliminating the difficulties resulting from reification and the anal and spatial analogies.[2] Jaffe (1969) has observed that affect tolerance varies greatly in different individuals and that multiple factors are at play, and Zetzel (1970b), as noted previously, has especially emphasized that the development of affect tolerance is a lifelong process.

Psychic Trauma

Affects become threatening and impossible to handle comfortably when psychic trauma is experienced. In Freud's earliest writings about trauma, he defined it as "Any experience which calls up disturbing affects—such as those of fright, anxiety, shame or physical pain" (Breuer & Freud, 1893-1895, p. 6). In 1926, Freud emphasized that the essence of danger in trauma was affect, namely, helplessness on the part of the ego in the face of accumulation of excitement of either external or internal origin that cannot be dealt with. If we avoid the quantitative explanation of the

---

[2] The observation that when affects reach a certain intensity they may interfere with other ego functions does not imply that they are separate or different or inherently "opposed" to other functions. The situation is analogous to some electrical developments, wherein an electrical current carried by a given device may become excessive, overheat some part of the circuit, and thereby interrupt it. Thus, it is more accurate to say that certain mental events may be inherently so exciting, or meet with such intense emotional reactions, as to threaten operation of the entire system.

economic theory, we have to question whether there is a qualitative difference in the nature of affect triggering the traumatic situation. It is usually taken for granted that automatic anxiety is traumatogenic,[3] and is distinguished from signal anxiety in its intensity and its association with helplessness. The response of helplessness as a reaction to the perception of danger has been highlighted by Stern (1951), who has pointed out that reactions to danger can be classified in three progressive stages: (a) a state of excitation related to increased discharge, as seen in gross anxiety states; (b) catatonoid reactions related to inhibitions in function, with rigidity, psychomotor retardation, and loss of all purposeful and self-saving behavior and ideation; (c) shock, with annihilation of the organism resulting from the failure of the homeostatic mechanism.

The catatonoid reaction to danger (playing "possum") is of ancient phylogenetic derivation. Neal Miller (1951) states that there are two basic effects of fear: "One is a tendency to remain motionless, which reaches its extreme form in death-feigning in certain animals and sometimes produces results suggestive of waxy flexibility of catatonics. The other is the pattern of startle, withdrawal, running and vocalization. Both of these incompatible patterns seem to be activated by fear, and behavior may shift rapidly from one to another, or when a frightened animal just freezes, then suddenly scurries for shelter" (p. 441). Catatonoid reaction can be induced experimentally in most, if not all animals (Tomkins, 1962), and in many it becomes the end reaction of a chronic anxiety-producing situation from which the animal cannot escape (Liddel, 1967).

To "freeze" and lie still is the first reaction of young vertebrate animals to danger, especially when the mother is away. It may be an interesting preamble to the study of the development of affects in man to observe that the human infant has lost this fundamental life-preserving reaction. The immaturity and helplessness of the infant is such that, unless the mother is there to respond to his need at all times, he cannot survive. In the tragic circumstances when families were hiding from persecution (e.g., during the Nazi period), the uncontrollable crying of a child frequently jeopardized the whole group. Among the kinds of traumatization that assume a nightmarish quality are those of some survivors who, as infants and little children, were choked, almost to death, by their mothers to keep them from betraying their presence.

My experiences with the survivors of Nazi persecution indicate that a progression from an excited anxiety to a passive surrender and catatonoid

[3] K. Eissler (1966) does not agree; he feels that "anxiety cannot traumatize the psychic apparatus, any more than the defense mechanisms can" (p. 26).

189

reaction does indeed take place in the state of unavoidable and life-threatening danger (Krystal, 1968). In this state, a condemned person may even cooperate with his executioner. The survivors of Nazi persecution who escaped being killed spent years in a condition closely akin to the catatonoid state (Krystal, 1968; Lifton, 1967). Many years after liberation, these survivors still show an overreaction to anxiety and a tendency to somatization. Thus the effects of an overwhelming of the defensive and expressive function of anxiety to the point of inhibition, with a surrender to destruction, are traumatic and cause a disturbance in affect handling and tolerance similar to that described by Greenacre (1958).

Stern (1953) contended in his early work that the specific danger of automatic anxiety was that it could produce a severe state of stress — of neurogenic shock and death. That there is such a possibility cannot be questioned. For our purpose, it is important to interpolate that it is the *feeling* of *impending* shock and death that is traumatic. I am inclined to postulate that at times its is the intensity or nature of the affect experience that may be traumatic — at others it is the cognitive content (e.g., the inevitability of destruction). Freud (1926), of course, believed that to confront the danger of destruction would be traumatic, but he felt it necessary to elaborate the *meaning* to the ego of such disaster: namely, that the ego reacts to "being abandoned by the protecting super-ego — the powers of destiny — so that is has no longer any safeguard against all the dangers that surround it" (p. 130).

In his later writings, Stern (1968a, 1968b) emphasized the *meaning* and the physiological aspect of that ultimate in anxiety which we tend to think of as fear of death, but which actually is deadly fear. He pointed out that that was the sense in which Freud (1923, 1926) used the term *Todesangst*. He postulated that the mental representation of the danger of dying was based on the infantile experiences called "biotraumata." These were ordinary, commonly occurring failures of the mother's nurturing and stimulus-barrier, supplementing functions. When exposed to intense stimuli and unfilled needs, the child responds with rage, fear and somatization. This physiological reaction, and the accompanying distress form the mental representation of the ultimate danger — a suffering so terrible that it is experienced as a fate worse than death.

The nature of infantile affects, as discussed earlier (Krystal, 1975), being totally somatic, massive, and undifferentiated, do create a clear and present danger to the survival of the infant. The mother's intervention before the situation becomes unbearable rescues the child from the self-destructive "forces" within himself. From the experience of these infantile

190

affects stems our fear and reluctance to gain control over autonomic functioning, which I will discuss in greater detail later.

These traumatic situations of childhood leave us with a special dread of our affects' developing to the intensity of a "fate worse than death," i.e., to the intensity of the infantile traumatic situation. Depending on the extent and severity of the trauma in childhood, and the resources and assets of the ego, the apprehension of one's emotions determines one's characterological patterns of affectivity. In individuals who suffered excessive traumatization in infancy and childhood, the mortal dread is linked with feelings of helplessness, immobility, and suffocation that are considered to be reasons for the overwhelming nature of automatic anxiety, castration anxiety, fear of dismemberment, losing one's mind (Stern, 1968a, 1968b). Perhaps this dread is also what Melanie Klein (1946), linking it with the ideation of "falling to bits,"[4] called "psychotic anxiety." *This unbearable feeling is what causes, or, more properly, is, the first part of the traumatic process.* It initiates a series of unconscious pathogenic reactions that represent the trauma syndrome. The adult's mortal dread — with the feeling of impending annihilation, immobilization, suffocation — Stern interpreted as the re-experiencing of the infancy panic and total stress reaction that resulted from the absence of the indispensable mother. Extraordinary traumatization, with the infant experiencing a hostile rejection, morbidly reinforces the commonly occurring biotraumata resulting from normal frustrations and separations (Stern, 1968a, 1968b). Under these circumstances, the reaction to affect becomes permanently excessive.

In addition to the residual childhood influences, intense affects are also disruptive to adult functioning. Magda Arnold (1950) argues that "Intense anxiety interferes with thinking as well as action because of its physiological (sympathetic nervous system) affects. Anger is disruptive because it represents intense parasympathetic stimulation which results in incoordination" (p. 30). What do we mean when we talk about "the ego being flooded" or "overwhelmed" with affect? Solnit and Marianne Kris (1967) have characterized the traumatic situation as one in which there is a "paralyzing, immobilizing or rendering to a state of helplessness, ranging from numbness to an emotional storm in affect and in behavior. This includes disorganization of feelings, thoughts and behavior as well as depriving the ego of certain autonomous functions . . . followed by regressive phenomena, severe inhibitions, physical symptoms

---

[4] This alludes to the danger of the disintegration of the coherent self and the overriding of emotional integrative functions of the ego.

191

and characteristic recovery patterns" (p. 212). The pathological defenses are often avoidance and, in regard to affect, the above-mentioned blocks, which create a permanent impairment of affectivity.

Brierley (1937) has stressed that affects are mainly "tension rather than discharge phenomena" (p. 259), but, as I have already mentioned, the "discharge" concept of affects requires careful rethinking, for affects are not vectors directed "outward," but physiological reactions, which have to be endured and which run their self-limited course unless they become involved in some circularly causal reaction (e.g., becoming afraid of one's fear, and thus becoming more afraid).

What of the idea of abreaction? Its phenomenology cannot be contested, nor can the subjective experience be questioned. But an understanding of psychic trauma can give us a different view of the help to be derived from it. From the above description of trauma, it is fair to assume than an individual can find himself overwhelmed with such intense affect that it has to be warded off by massive repression and other dissociative reactions, such as fainting, depersonalization. When the patient is in this state, he lives in terror that the affect will break through and overwhelm him. *When we help the patient bring back his memories and affects gradually, we help him to re-establish his comfort vis-a-vis the affect, and his tolerance of it.* It follows, then, that the development of comfort in dealing with emotions, and the rich repertoire of patterns with which this can be achieved, is perhaps the most important single element in trauma prevention (Krystal, 1970).

The Development of Affect Tolerance in Childhood

The best-known, and most conspicuous, educational efforts on the part of the parents that help the child to acquire affect tolerance take place during the latency period. Yet latency is underestimated as a developmental stage, and the importance of the role of the parents in promoting the essential maturational task of developing affect tolerance is taken for granted. However, even minimal reflection alerts us to the fact that the task of "upbringing," in which parents, teachers, counselor, and even siblings and peers are involved, focuses on the development of skill in the handling of emotions, and, in effect, the development of affect tolerance. Many kinds of inducements, such as "I can take it" clubs, are used — rewards as well as punishments.

But one key operation, which is reserved primarily for the mother, is begun in infancy: her role as an "auxiliary stimulus barrier." While permitting the child to experience both pleasurable and painful affects *to an intensity that he can bear*, she stops and interrupts further increment in excitement before it overwhelms his ego.

What methods stand at her disposal? Her very presence and response is already reassuring to the anxious child. She may be able to offer herself (her ego) as an auxiliary organ for the child in that she is not herself perceptibly anxious. In the child's necessity to accept her evaluation of the world lies the foundation of his suggestibility. The young have no choice but to accept the mother as omnipotent. They will therefore exercise their imagination to support this belief, even when the mother cannot relieve their distress. And so, in areas of pain, or painful affect, the child is inclined to allow the mother to distract him, or to *compensate* him for the discomfort. If the child is to acquire this soothing function for himself, he must feel he has permission to "take her place," as a source of succor. Such compensations may be actual gratifications, such as foods, which make one feel better, or they may be symbolic, as when some act of absolution or riddance is performed to deal with feelings of shame or guilt. As an individual grows, it is the ready access to such techniques and resources within himself that makes it possible for him to take in his stride a variety of unpleasant feelings and states in the course of an ordinary day of work or study.

Only when protected from trauma can the child in latency and adolescence gradually build up his ability to bear his affects with increasing comfort and security. With Raskin (1970, pp. 25-29) I have emphasized that the educational maternal efforts that help the latency child to better tolerate pain also apply to his learning to tolerate painful affects. Anna Freud (1952) made the following observation:

According to the child's interpretation of the event, young children react to pain not only with anxiety but with other affects appropriate to the contents of the unconscious fantasies, i.e., on the one hand with anger, rage, and revenge feelings; on the other hand with masochistic submission, guilt, or depression.... Where anxiety derived from fantasy plays a minor role or no part, even severe pain is borne well and forgotten quickly. Pain augmented by anxiety, on the other hand, even if slight in itself, represents a major event in the child's life and is remembered a long time afterward, the memory being frequently accompanied by phobic defenses against its possible return [p. 272].

In the process of teaching the child to control affect, the parent also serves as an example and in fact will often consciously and verbally encourage the child to identify with him (her) and to exercise that monitoring function in the future himself. When the child shows that he can take over, the parent expresses approval and rewards the child's use of a mode of dealing with one's emotions previously demonstrated by the parent. Many such patterns evolve around going to doctors, dentist, school, etc., and the good mother will offer her emotional support as long as necessary, but be ready to leave the child to his own resources as soon as possible.

The mother's interventions in the emotional state of the infant are many and varied. The infant experiences his affects passively, as if they were emanating from the mother. When he has good feelings, he experiences them against the background of his maternal object-representations, which (he feels) must signify that it is all right for him to have the good feelings. When he feels distress, he must turn to his mother for an evaluation of the *meaning* of his discomfort.

Because affective expression is the infant's only form of communication, the mother promotes a certain kind of reaction in the child by the way she responds to it. Therese Benedek (1956) has described in some detail how the child, perceiving pain, comes to the mother first to find out if he has been hurt, and then if necessary to get succor. The mother may respond to the child's need by talking to him gently as she attends to whatever injury is involved, thereby offering him an example to follow in managing his feelings. Or, responding to her own needs at the moment, she may become excessively upset, show panic, and thus contribute to the child's fear of his injury, and also *to his anxiety*. Alternately, the mother may scold or punish the child for getting hurt, adding guilt to fear and burdening the child's feeble affect tolerance. The examples of the parent's efforts in the direction of improving the child's ability to handle his affects comfortably and securely are virtually endless. The child seems to include such goals in his ego ideal at an early age and will often describe a recent situation (say, at the doctor's) the way he wishes he had acted rather than withstand the shame of not being able to live up to his own ideal.

The child's ability to develop a gradually improving degree of verbalization and desomatization, as well as the various ego functions that produce affect tolerance, will depend not only on the kind of help he receives from his parents in this regard, that is, what the parents *do* and *say* about it, but also what the parents *are*. Quite likely, identification with the parents, and imitation of their way of dealing with their emotions becomes the most important determinant of the patterns the child will develop for himself. "Liberal" or authoritarian patterns prevail in certain families in regard to the handling of anxiety, and the attitude toward one's emotions seems to be workable (within limits) as long as the

194

parents can be *consistent* about what they teach and what they do about their own feelings. Because of the dual process of acquisition of affect tolerance (by learning and by identification), children whose parents have difficulty in handling affect have difficulty in developing advantageous ways of dealing with their own emotions. A. Katan (1961) has pointed out one instance of such difficulties, in " . . . the type of parents who not only are unable to show their own emotions but also do not permit emotions to show in the child. If such parents speak about their feelings which they are unable to show, or speak about the child's feelings, it is clear that their words are used not to further the expression of emotions but to ward these emotions off. If this is the case, the words are not a bridge, as they ought to be, but are a defense against the emotions. The child may now take over the example set by the parents and also use words defensively (p. 187).[5]

Related to the interactions between mother and infant around affect is a fateful development in regard to self-representation or, as used to be said, "body ego." For all parts of the body related to affect expression are experienced by the infant as controlled by, and belonging to, the maternal object-representation and not to the self. This is so because the infant seems to experience the entire affect experience as emanating from the object. If the mother is unable to convey to the child the feeling that it is all right for him to assume the consciously recognized possession of these autonomically controlled parts of himself, serious difficulties may arise. Finkelstein (1973) reported a case of a patient who experienced his penile erections as being entirely controlled by his female partner. His lack of ability to consciously acknowledge control of his sexual excitement was a contributory cause of his premature ejaculations. Raskin and I have described in detail (1970) the ways in which the inaccessibility of affect regulatory functions can be a major factor in the tendency to drug addiction. Kohut (1971) has stated that certain narcissistic individuals suffer a serious impairment in their ability to regulate their skin temperature and maintain a feeling of warmth: "They rely on others to provide them not only with emotional but also with physical warmth" (p. 64).

We are just beginning to look for those times and signals when the mother conveys to the child the permission to comfort himself, as in the

---

[5] A. G. Green (personal communication) has expressed concern that a similar self-defeating situation is set up by the analyst who verbally encourages the patient to experience his emotions consciously, while he himself sits like a wooden Indian. For the patient who suffers an impairment of affect tolerance, the analysis must provide an opportunity to gain greater comfort in relation to bearing his emotions. Otherwise, he receives his interpretations on an intellectual level, in a state of isolation of affects, and converts the interpretation to a cliché.

195

use of a transitional object. Some mothers, apparently feeling jealous, may take the transitional object away from the child (Bush, 1974). We have to wonder whether this action represents a prohibition of the kind of self-soothing that, cumulatively, would lead to the psychopathology we observe in drug-dependent patients.

The mother who is capable of consistent nurturing supports the feeling of trust and active mastery that permits the tolerance of pleasurable feelings that are basically *proleptic* (Spitz's [1963] term referring to the anticipation of gratification). In contrast, individuals who have suffered severe disappointments during infancy cannot tolerate any hopeful expectation of feeding or love. Schmale (1964) has considered this development from the point of view of the infant, who, from the age of 12 to 16 months, becomes aware of his symbiotic relationship with his mother, becomes aware of the need for help, and with undue deprivation is subject to the feeling of helplessness: "Helplessness, which reflects psychic immobilization, is an expression of the infant's inability actively to pursue gratification along with the awareness of a need to be taken care of by external other-than-self object" (p. 294). But I am concerned here not with the traumatic potential of such feelings of helplessness, which no doubt can be real, but with the effect of such experiences upon the individual's comfort with positive "proleptic" feelings in his life. It is my conviction that individuals such as those mentioned by Atkin (1973), who dare to have no feelings except anger, are ones whose maternal contacts were consistently disappointing and for whom the expectation of gratification provokes an anticipation of hurt and helplessness. Thus, the quality of nurturing by the mother becomes the crucial experience in regard to the development of tolerance of proleptic affects.

Similar inferences can be drawn about the maternal reaction at other points in the child's psychosexual and psychosocial development. Here I will follow Schmale's (1964) outline, which highlights certain affects in connection with key developments. In the second year of life, when the child becomes aware of prohibitions, he not only contributes to his evaluation of himself but also learns whether it is permissible for him to expect to be good, to expect to find himself virtous, or whether he must expect himself to fail and be guilty. Although other skills may be learned at this age, for example, the ability to "handle" objects, there may be a lack of ability to tolerate the hopeful expectation of what is required. In connection with the establishment of bodily self-control, the child has occasion to feel either pride or shame, and the mother can be helpful in allowing him to gain a degree of comfort with both of these feelings.

In the oedipal stage, along with the awareness of sexual identification, there is a reintensification of feelings of pride, shame, and envy, among others. A key question is involved: whether the child may entertain hopes for sexual and generative wishes. This is a matter not just of the fate of the Oedipus complex itself, but of the child's feelings about the permissibility of his strivings and the associated feelings of hope. If the child is not helped to feel that his hopes are permissible, he is pushed in the direction of hopelessness (Schmale, 1964).

An illustrative case was the patient whose mother could only accept a pre-Oedipal relationship with him as her extension — an adored phallus. Her inability to tolerate any potent men caused the young boy to experience his phallic strivings as prohibited, resulting in impotence and narcissistic character problems. In analysis, he kept asking me to "fix him up" with one of my patients.

Since affective expression is the infant's only form of communication, the mother promotes a certain kind of reaction in the child by the way she responds to it. Most mothers are able to handle the emotions of the very young child as requests for their services and willingly fulfill the child's needs. However, the infant's distress state assaults her ideal of being a loving mother of a contented, "good" baby; increasingly, as the child progresses, she responds to his emotional outbursts with irritation. In later childhood, "Overt emotional expression tends to bring disapproval or punishment" (Jones, 1967).

This development has three major results: (1) It tends to promote verbalization and formulation of self-observation in the child, since it becomes necessary for him to formulate his demands in words. (2) Internal responses to affects assume a greater role (Jones, 1967). This process thus favors the establishment of psychosomatic patterns as substitutes for chronic affective states. One can trace here a "bifurcation" of affect development into verbalization on the one hand and formation of "psychosomatic" (disease) patterns on the other. (3) In identification with the parents, the child responds with guilt and shame to the self-observation that his affects have manifested themselves in an overt and uncontrollable way. For instance, the little boy who cries in fear suffers further mortification upon observing his own "childish" response and attacks himself for it. Blushing betrays an emotion, and the reflective self-awareness of it is responded to with more shame. This secondary reaction adds to the fear of the affect. The child first learns to respond to his affect from the maternal and familial reactions and, later, from his peers. He is thus introduced to the social norms for his affective behavior.

Social influences on the *reactions to having an emotion* are potent forces in the development of affect tolerance, and even pain tolerance (Tunky & Sternbach, 1967). The interpretation of bodily states is, according to all available evidence, strongly influenced by the social attitudes toward a given emotion that were acquired in childhood (Schachter, 1967). Although, in the main, early psychoanalytic writings emphasized oppressive attitudes toward sexuality, they inspired writers such as D. H. Lawrence to observe that our society was just as repressive in regard to all affectivity. More recently, it has become clear that the antiemotional attitudes of our culture have created a problem with regard to affective reactions that cannot be ignored by present-day analysts (Sterba, 1960, 1969). As I have indicated, in dealing with patients who have little ability to bear their emotions, a preliminary phase of treatment may be necessary, in which the analyst addresses himself directly to the nature of feelings, and the way he handles them (Krystal, 1973b).

The Development of Affect Tolerance in Adolescence

The acquisition of the patterns of handling affects by learning and identification that plays such a significant part in the child's emotional growth always poses the question: under what circumstances may he exercise the role that the parents have been taking during childhood? This question is an extension of the crucial point mentioned above, namely, that the individual needs, in addition to learning ways to comfort and control himself, to acquire the *feeling* that it is permissible for him to take over all parental functions. That this task is rarely accomplished completely is demonstrated by the common need for religion, inspiration, magic, superstition, and drugs, all of which have one common ingredient: they are ways of overcoming the inner repressive barriers by which essential self-caring functions have become inaccessible by being reserved for the object representation (Krystal, 1973b).

Whereas the fundamental operations related to this freedom to use one's own resources take place in the establishment of the separation of the self-representation from the object representation in early childhood, they are subject to repeated revisions. The time such revisions occur most frequently and conspicuously is adolescence, when it is necessary for the youngster to practice assuming an adult role and to function with increasing self-sufficiency. Each such opportunity, whether minor or

198

major, such as going away to school, presents a challenge and tests the degree to which a young person has been able to assume the exercise of functions hitherto reserved for his parents. Pleasurable affects must be kept within manageable bonds, which may be conceptualized as the adequate function of paternally derived aspects of the superego. With regard to painful affects and related states (e.g., tiredness and boredom), in addition to the need for controls, the youngster needs the freedom to assume self-comforting attitudes derived from the identification. A failure to take over these functions represents a serious handicap, which manifests itself clinically as part of a variety of syndromes.

CASE ILLUSTRATION

Mrs. J. presented herself as a person with a variety of difficulties, many of which were related to her narcissistic personality organization. In addition, she was practically crippled by her impairment in affect tolerance. As a child, she had handled her emotions in an isolated manner, with somatic "attacks," which took the form of severe migraine headaches with days of vomiting. As a student, she could bear neither the tension required for concentrated study nor the anxiety of examinations, and so she failed in high school. Eventually, she tried to study nursing but discovered that she could not stand the "bad smells" of sick people; so she quit, rather than force herself to acquire the usual tolerance for unpleasant smells or tasks. She then tried to become a teacher, but, when confronted with some children who were difficult, she decided that she could not bear the stress and gave that up too. She married, essentially expecting to function as a naughty child and hoping that her husband would be an ever-forgiving, indulgent mother, who would be impervious to her rages. Her inability to tolerate bad smells and fear of dirt, combined with her feeling that she could not bear the self-discipline and deprivation involved in work, made it most difficult for her to function as a homemaker. Her idea of work was derived from certain clichés about enjoying one's work. It became necessary in the therapy to ask her such simple questions as: "If work was fun, why would they pay one to do it?"

Her resulting inability to function adequately intensified her problem of envy. All of these problems made it most unlikely that she could either *work* in the analysis, or be able to tolerate the affect necessary to progress in it. For instance, she had a severe phobia of snakes. However, her attitude was that the way to handle this phobia was for the whole world to conspire to protect her from any exposure to snakes — not only real live ones, but even pictures of them — for the mere representation of a snake filled her with dread and horror. The idea of becoming a mother filled

199

her with so many types of fears that she rejected the possibility categoric-ally. Thus, early in her analysis, the dealing with affect tolerance became, of necessity, the major interest and activity.

It may be said, with Kohut (1971, p. 49), that the defect in the above patient represented a failure to successfully establish the kind of trans-muted internalizations that would make it possible for her to exercise certain adult functions. Thus some aspects of her problems were handled as part of the narcissistic transferences. However, it was also necessary to interpret her feeling that she did feel free in assuming these "forbidden" roles, and she wanted me to assume the role of the permission-granting mother. In addition, it was essential that she accomplish the major task of adolescence that had not been carried out at the appropriate time: the work of mourning for her infantile attachment to her parents and to her childhood self-representation.

For adolescence to be successful, one has to be able to bear such mourning, a process that enables one to begin to tolerate depression (a task that is, however, completed later). Failure to do so makes it impossible to change self-representations from ideal to realistic ones, and establishes a tendency to use denial and projection. Petty and I found, in working with patients who had lost an organ or an aspect of themselves, that if they could not go through the process of grieving for the loss, they became stuck in denial, or some form of self-compensatory compulsion (Krystal & Petty, 1961). Zetzel (1965) has underscored that depressive re-sponses are temporary and reversible in those whose previous self-esteem did not depend upon absence of "subjective" (secondary) anxiety. The development in adolescence of the ability to mourn is but one of the landmarks in the development of affect tolerance, albeit a monumental one. Wolfenstein (1966) has likened adolescence to "a trial mourning, in which there is a gradual decathexis of the first love objects, accompanied by sad and painful feelings, with reality testing of memories confirming the irrevocability of the childhood past. It is only after this initiation into mourning has been undergone that the individual becomes able to perform the work of mourning in response to later losses" (p. 122).

The renunciation of the mother-child relationship, which takes place in adolescence, makes possible the advancement of conscious self-inte-gration, self-possession, and *self-awareness of one's affects as signals to oneself.* This development is neither easy nor satisfactorily accomplished by even a majority of people. Such an extension of one's "owning his soul" is often acquired only in an analysis. It is the key step in the development of adult affect and affect tolerance. Zetzel (1965) refers to this very process: "However slight its overt expression may be, the experience of depression is a prerequisite for optimal maturation. Depressive affect comparable to contained anxiety occurs in response to loss, disappointment, frustration, illness, retirement, and other painful, though inevitable, experiences" (p. 87). This developmental approach to both anxiety and depression highlights the effect of early object relations on basic ego functions and the tolerance of affect.

In addition to learning to bear grief, the adolescent is confronted with challenges and opportunities to practice tolerating a variety of other affective states. Doing work and experiencing nongratification also require that one tolerate some boredom, or even muscle discomfort and pain, and that one "give oneself credit" for accomplishments, major and minor, and thus adopt the role of an appreciative parent. Such ability is a "cushion" in facing failure or simply lack of recognition. This process is intimately related to the ability to tolerate anxiety and shame. The counterphobic and exhibitionistic tendencies of the adolescent are resources that permit temporary relief but should become less necessary as he goes along.

Another temporary device is the adolescent's feeling of narcissistic invulnerability. Optimally, as one progresses into young adulthood and maturity, one reaches the point where one can tolerate depression. Only *some* people in their maturity or old age are able to renounce enough of their need to deny their own death to be able to mourn the loss of parts and eventually all of themselves. Erikson (1959) makes this point in terms of the psychosocial crisis of "integrity vs. despair," in which one develops the ability to face not being. Schafer has recently (1973) discussed some of the struggles of the adolescent in relation to the re-experiencing of affects related to separation-individuation, pointing out that adolescents are especially prone to experience their feelings as "substances," often fecal ones, which "accordingly may be withheld or expelled and gotten rid of or destroyed; or they may fill one up and either explode or leak (or spill) out. Or perhaps they are oral substances (milk, poison, vomitus) or psychosexual things (urine, semen, babies)" (p. 46).

These primary-process-mediated conceptions of affect are ubiquitous, making it necessary for the analyst working with adolescents (and adults in therapy) to proceed with elucidation in the way that sex education is handled in child analysis. The discovery of unconscious fantasies about affect is often the key to understanding some adolescent activities, whether drug-taking, counterphobic exploits, or sexual promiscuity. The adolescent's attitude to emotions and the manner in which they are handled may be perhaps the single most important hindrance to the completion of his developmental tasks.

I have already alluded to the fact that affect tolerance requires lifelong development. Adolescence is not the last opportunity, or crisis, in relation to emotions. Young adulthood presents renewed challenges and opportunities to become fully independent, assume a parental role, etc. Every life crisis presents such opportunities: calamity is opportunity in work clothes. But it may be startling, perhaps, to consider middle age and old age as developmental phases as well: we are used to thinking of developmental epochs as preparations for some future time when life begins in earnest. But the simple fact remains that every single event of one's life, including dying, presents one with a new combination of affects, which we can learn to handle with grace. For, in the last analysis, what is commonly taken as a fear of calamity, disaster, or even death can be discovered to be the fear of one's own affects. Affect tolerance is the ability that permits us to take our reaction off the signal and put it on to the meaning, the import, of that signal.

Psychoanalytic Psychotherapy and Disturbances in Affectivity

Most of the time the affective component of mental events is subliminal and in the nature of a signal, but this represents the culmination of many years of successful development. In this "subliminal" state, affects are our chief motivators and automatic regulators (Leeper, 1970; Izard et al., 1965). Still, the fact is that our emotional state does not require a conscious "reading" at all times. This situation lends itself to two phenomena with which we are familiar in everyday life: (1) We tend to experience emotions as periodic outbursts only, ignoring the fact that all of our life takes place against the background of moods, and is accompanied by ever present and constantly changing emotional responses to all perceptions, impulses, conflicts, and every other form of living. (2) When the emotion becomes intense enough to dominate our consciousness and can no longer be denied, we still tend to externalize it in the sense of experiencing it as if it were emanating from the object. The tendency to externalize is a residual of the infantile experience of affects: Anna Freud (1965) considered it a subspecies of transference. Giovacchini (1967) has correlated the use of externalization to infantile techniques of adjustment, a point also emphasized by Schafer (1964), when he emphasizes that even such feelings as "self-loathing and pride are experienced as *emanating from* internalized objects" (p. 283).

202

Although externalization of one's emotions and object representation is an acceptable convention in everyday life and language patterns, it still does represent a manifestation of repression. In an analysis it becomes part of a significant resistance. It is a last-ditch effort to ward off the self-confrontation with one's transferences, including the affective aspects of the repressed or otherwise defended material. An interpretation received in this isolated fashion is turned into a cliché and completely misses its therapeutic potential. The problem has been well summarized by Watkins (1971):

> When psychoanalytic therapy has failed, the failure has often been caused by the intellectualization of the therapy. It has dealt only with ideas and has not elicited feelings, emotions, affects. Thus the forgotten or pathogenic experiences which lie at the basis of some conflict are not revealed in their true, living, experiential colors. They are seen like a movie film in black and white instead of technicolor. To be understood, integrated, controlled, a forgotten experience must be lifted from repression in all of its original vividness, its original "feelingness": or, as the existentialists hold, its "beingness." "Insight," to be genuinely therapeutic, must be total and must involve full visceral and muscular, as well as cerebral responses. An understanding must be "felt" as well as "known" [p. 21].

Thus, prior to giving an interpretation, every analyst must consider whether or not the patient is ready to deal with the affective component of a given idea. If it appears that the patient could not bear all the affects related to the integration of the potential insight, perhaps it may be best not to utter this intervention. Instead of piling up interpretations, we might well devote ourselves to the exploration of the patient's degree of affect tolerance.

It is frequently necessary to point out that the patient has certain preconceived notions about affects (such as we have noticed in the adolescent) and that his attempts to handle affects are dominated by a fear of them. Every patient needs to distinguish, early in his analysis, between his emotions and his *handling* (*having*) of them. Just as we concern ourselves with the defenses against affects, and the uses of affects as protection against other emotions or as object substitutes (Seton, 1965), so must we work with the patient's attitude to his feelings and the defensive operations involved. Thus, all of the developmental history of affect tolerance should be subject to interpretation.

When affects cannot be experienced freely and with full self-awareness, they may become incorporated in character structures, object relations (Knapp, 1963), or symptoms. It follows, therefore, that in giving up these defensive structures, the analysand has to be able to experience feelings that he at one time warded off as too dangerous. The patient's experience of his affects and the analyst's interpretation of the meanings of the affects play a crucial role in the progress of the analysis.

A Therapeutic View of the Ego's Reaction to Affects

Clinically, we find anxiety to be the most frequently dreaded affect. It is different from all the other human predilections in that the fear of it can produce it and perpetuate it. Anxiety is also "special" in the sense that it represents the reaction to the perception of danger, even if that danger refers to the development of other affects. The form of anxiety with which we are so familiar, however, is just the first in a series of reactions to the perception of danger. In order to appreciate the dimension of the challenge anxiety may present to the ego, it is necessary to recall that, as Stern (1968a, 1968b) pointed out, one's reaction to danger may progress from an agitated to a catatonoid ("paralyzed"— *Schreckstarre*) state, which represents an acceptance of the danger as hopeless and unavoidable—an archaic surrender (Krystal, 1970; Krystal & Raskin, 1970). This view of the catatonoid reaction to the perception of danger as being part of a continuum of anxiety is in harmony with Bibring (1953), who believes that depression, like anxiety, is an ego experience of an event of catastrophic significance; but in the case of depression this event is perceived as unavoidable (p. 35).

The next step in the progression of such overwhelming perception of irresistible danger might be psychogenic shock and death (Stern, 1968a, 1968b). Thus, the clinically observable fear of affect may refer to the intuitive perception of the lethal potential of emotions. It is possible for affects to develop a destructive, overwhelming intensity, and for the ego to be in a position of such "weakened" defenses that it would become overwhelmed, flooded and disorganized by some affects. While the normal person can make a correct evaluation that at a given time and circumstances there is no danger that his ego will be flooded with affect, he also takes for granted the hope that it will never happen. This hope is a form of denial, but one that is supported by the past experience. In any person who has experienced traumatization, this hope is not unequivocally self-evident, and to maintain it requires a constant effort. The influence of benign introjects, the use of object representations and achievements, are helpful in the support of the feelings that because one is good, worthy, intact, and in good self-control, the danger of trauma is not eminent. These defenses can serve to cancel the aftereffects of moderate and fairly short-lived trauma. But when individuals have been severely traumatized, especially those whose belief in orderliness, fairness, and rational causality has been destroyed, they are never able to rebuild their self-confidence, optimism, or basic feeling of security. They live in constant expectation of the return of the traumatic state and affects (Krystal, 1968; Krystal & Niederland, 1971; Krystal & Raskin, 1970). When this happens, the individual endeavors to suppress any and all emotions. If the affects do "break through" despite the ego's defenses, they often come through in an incomplete way and are experienced as attacks from "outside."

As I have said, in the treatment of patients who dread their affects, block them successfully, or are subject to such "attacks," there is need for a special preparatory therapeutic task, which cannot be considered interpretation but involves explanation, elucidation, and (overt or covert) reassurance.

The task is to demonstrate to these patients their fears of their emotions, and to help them to discover the way in which they block their affects and the way in which their affects "break through." If we consider, for instance, the drug-dependent patient as engaged in blocking his affects pharmacologically because he cannot tolerate them, how can we suddenly expect him to do so in his treatment? It becomes necessary to establish what having the emotion *means* to the patient, in order to be able to proceed to give "affect education" as a corrective measure. Only after we deal with the meaning of affects as magical punishment, signs of weakness or effeminacy, or similar fantasies, can we demonstrate to the patient the use of feelings as signals. In addition to the explanation that feelings are self-limited, not dangerous, but useful, the patient needs the experience to test the validity of such assertions. The analyst thus finds himself in a role analogous to the mother's in permitting the patient to live his emotions as fully as possible, but stepping in before they overwhelm the patient and repeat childhood traumatization.

CASE ILLUSTRATION

Mr. J.'s heavy use of drugs was preceded by his discovery at about age 15 that he was impotent. All later opportunities for sexual relations panicked him and filled him with shame. This produced a vicious cycle in which, out of fear of emotions, he was constantly drugged. We soon discovered that sexual excitement and shame was not the only feeling he had trouble handling. He also had much difficulty with anger, especially in relation to his father; thus he was driven to the acting out of a cycle of defiant behavior, remorse, and forgiveness, without consciously recognizing the emotions motivating his behavior. In addition, he could not tolerate the simple tensions of doing work. When he and his younger brother undertook to paint a house, he was surprised to find that his younger brother was able to put in a day's work, whereas he could not stand the boredom and physical effort for more than about an hour.

In the analysis, the only modification of technique necessary was the emphasis on the nature of his affects and his handling of them. We found that his affects were for the most part somatic in nature, poorly verbalized, and undifferentiated. In relation to work, for instance, we knew only that there was some discomfort about it he could not stand — as if he had a physical disability. However, putting his words in a slow and meticulous fashion eventually made it possible for him to recognize that his inhibitions caused him to feel very disturbed when trying to do "man's work," but that this experience was in the nature of an ur-affect, which was an undifferentiated form of the painful affect precursors. Gradually, his feelings evolved to the point where he could experience more closely the adult type of anxiety as separate from anger, guilt, shame, envy, etc.

At the same time, we paid much attention to his *handling* of affects, which included his conception of his emotions and his reaction to them. His infantile trauma history had made it impossible for him during his adolescence to handle the excitement and anxieties of sexual relations. The progress in handling his affect (augmented by the undeterminable degree of a "transference cure") made it possible for him to accomplish successful sexual relations after a couple of months of treatment. This development, in turn, lessened the intensity of his conflictual affects and encouraged him to continue with the work. By the time he had to leave for college, I felt confident that he could handle the emotional stresses of a psychoanalysis.

While an educational process is involved in this preparatory phase of the treatment, one has to exploit the positive transference deliberately in order to make it possible for the patient to take another look at his affects. This task is in fact a belated version of the process that, as we have noted, ordinarily takes place under the protection of a good mother. However, this task is more difficult for the therapist, for unlike the child, the patient experiences strong negative transferences in this sphere. We are concerned with individuals who have suffered severe childhood trauma and have experienced their mother's failure to function as a temporary stimulus barrier (or auxiliary ego), as an act of abandonment and punishment. In the transference they expect disappointments of similarly global dimensions. Their ambivalence, their cannibalistic impulses, and their intense envy and guilt make it difficult for them to be patients, or even experience the passivity of being "good learners."

We have previously pointed out (Krystal & Raskin, 1970) that for some patients the transference becomes too threatening, making it necessary for them to be treated in clinics where they can "split up" their ambivalent transferences. Vaillant (1973) has been so impressed with the disruptive potential of the transference in alcoholics that he has set up a clinic which effectively diffuses all contacts with the staff. His goal is to prevent the development of transference to any single therapist.

Assuming that we are dealing with individuals who may be able to handle their transferences if they are interpreted, the related emotions would surely threaten to disrupt the treatment if ignored. Thus, it becomes apparent that even during this stage of treatment one cannot be purely "didactic" or even "giving." As a matter of fact, in those cases where the therapist finds it necessary to give the patient medication, he may discover that the patient experiences, and reacts to, his ministrations as if they were poisonous. Although at this point in the treatment the analyst wants to encourage the development of a positive transference and avoid interpretations that provoke intense affective reactions, at times he has to give transference-resistance interpretations, in order to assure the continuation of the treatment.

The patient needs to observe that there is a double process: first he develops the emotion in question, and then he reacts to having it. He becomes either frightened of it and/or angry about it, thus building it up into a panic, rage, or other affect storm. We have already seen that the self-help group known as Recovery, Inc., which bases its works on the writings of Low (1950), emphasizes the increasing tolerance of anxiety as its major task. In group meetings, anxiety is repeatedly described as "painful but not dangerous," and the point is made repeatedly that anxiety will be "self-limited" for those who do not get upset about having it.[6] Most, if not all, of the considerable success of this group has to do with the success its members have in helping each other to increase affect tolerance.

By simultaneously paying attention to the nature of the affect as a response to experiences, ideas, etc., and at the same time highlighting the ego's responses to *having* the affect, it is possible to help the patient to discover how he has been working himself into feelings of panic.

---

[6] I find that only Low's attitude toward anxiety is applicable here. In regard to anger, he has taken a repressive attitude, with the idea that mentally ill patients cannot afford to indulge in "temper."

Frequently, the explanation alone will not change the patient's attitudes. He will often refuse to help himself and will insist in the transference that the therapist take care of him, relieve his bad feelings, prevent their future development and, like an idealized mother, guarantee his comfort and safety from his bad feelings. The idea that it is necessary for the patient himself to develop *more affect tolerance* is not at all clear to him, and he insists on complete freedom from all unpleasant states. Besides, as he sees it, if any part of his personality needs to be developed, it is up to the doctor to do it. So, again, it becomes necessary to engage in transference interpretation, albeit with extra caution.

Sometimes these explanatory interventions about the nature of affects as a state of oneself are inadequate and have to be supplemented by additional interpretations. The following are examples of situations in which additional aspects of affects have to be dealt with:

(1) When the inability to experience the affect comfortably is due to the fact that the affect is taken as a "sign," in magical terms. In certain types of intersystemic constellations, affects such as anxiety and guilt are experienced as a sort of "doomsday signal," which has to be stopped if a whole chain of unimaginable disasters (punishments) is not to befall the patient. Clearly, this type of reaction is a repetition of the destructively punitive way in which such patients interpreted their object representations. Recognizing that this anticipation is a memory, its reconstruction is the first step in the psychotherapeutic process. The second step consists in the recognition that one is dealing not with an object relation, but with a cognitive-affective pattern related to self-representation and object representation — and that of course is what resolving the transference is about.

In reconstruction, one may find that this type of fantasy may be related to the "internalization" of a parental pattern of repressive dealing with aggression. When this view of the world is established, the patient may experience any misfortune, including his own pain or painful feelings, as a sign that the "wrath of God" unleashed upon him will go on to terrible ends. In this type of masochistic personality, there is a special tendency to link a series of untoward events, in order to "prove" that the day of judgment is here. Such theories are common in the precipitation of affective disturbances, especially depression, and each of the elements involved in the preclinical "buildup" has to be identified, and its lack of relationship with the others demonstrated. Murphy (1961) has indicated that the accumulation of such depressive feelings represents a serious predisposition to trauma. Under these circumstances, any event that can be experienced as conforming to the "doomsday pattern" may create the traumatic situation. Interpretation of the pattern serves to prevent this type of psychoanalytic emergency.

(2) When as a result of traumatization in the past, which threatened to overwhelm and destroy him, the patient has a tendency to have a "catatonoid reaction" to intense affect. This problem commonly is manifested in the patient by a feeling of being "dead," or by a variety of dissociative reactions, from depersonalization to psychosis. It is essential to identify the affect that is being warded off, as well as to discover why it progresses to the point where the patient repeats a pattern of feeling hopeless and surrendering himself.

CASE ILLUSTRATION

Mrs. F. suffered explosive, overwhelming emotional outbursts which were so severe that on several successive admissions to the psychiatric hospital she was given the diagnosis of virtually every type of schizophrenia. I have described her affective disturbances in Part I of this study (Krystal, 1975). She had a history of childhood traumatization, with colic eczema and asthma. After two and a half years of treatment, the last two years of which were spent in analysis, five times a week, she was functioning quite well, without a single episode of overwhelming affect. But then, a number of things coincided that caused her to develop increasing anxiety. Two of the situations that developed at this time provoked her guilt and called forth an expiatory ritual. The latter was a common feeling among college students: She felt that she could not take her exams or write her term paper unless she put herself through the ordeal of building up her anxiety to a pitch. On top of all that, she developed a symptom related to an area of narcissistic hypercathexis. This development was an intense mortification and led to a "relapse," in the transference, to experiencing the analyst as endowed with magical powers. When her pleadings did not produce the result she desired—that I should instantly relieve all of her distress—she experienced rage, which in turn frightened her even more.

As a result, at this time, after experiencing intense anxiety, she began to be aware of feeling "dead," with vague feelings of depersonalization as well as immobilization. Every movement was becoming difficult for her, despite the fact that "inside" she felt as if her "engine was racing." She was afraid she was having a "complete relapse" and kept reproaching me that she couldn't be getting any better if, after all this time and work, she was still so disturbed and upset. I simply said that there was no evidence that she was going to have a relapse, and I pointed out her many achievements and the ways in which she was functioning quite well. She

209

then *became able to cry* and, after expressing her concern about current matters, she felt "alive again." She went home and took care of all her pressing problems, including the writing of her term paper.

The next day, however, she brought back the "affect crisis" in retrospect, with much relief; and at this time it was possible for me to show her that in the past she had been involved in similar affect storms but with a different outcome. Usually, there had been a combined problem of anxiety and anger. Whenever she was anxious, she used the affect communication to try to control her love object and obtain relief instantly. If that did not happen, her anger and anxiety would mount. She used to reach a point where she felt hopeless, and her affective response used to change from an agitated response to anxiety to a catatonoid state, in which she developed a general inhibition of conation and muscle function and felt dead.

The patient's reaction resembles the "psychic closing off" described by Lifton (1967), Niederland (1961) and Krystal (1968), in which the individual massively suppresses all feelings and functions like a robot. In most of the early treatment of patients such as Mrs. F., this process takes place quickly, automatically, and silently, and the analyst has to look out for it. A history of severe trauma in childhood should alert the analyst to the possibility that an affect related to phase-specific conflicts will be especially threatening to the ego, and at the same time will be close to the core of the problem. In a patient whose mother developed a postpartum psychosis, for example, the affect that was most threatening was related to his conscious recognition of attachment to another person and the yearnings, hopes, and expectations it aroused. What he feared most was the pain of disappointment, which had been nearly lethal to him in his early childhood.

It is commonly believed that the most threatening affect is always aggression. This is not the case. In severely traumatized individuals who are threatened by the prospect of taking a chance on another human being anger and hate may be the only affect experienced. Under these circumstances there is an unconscious fear of love or warm, tender feelings. In his work with concentration camp survivors, Hoppe (1962) identified this situation as a "hate addiction." This is another illustration of the fact that dealing with disturbances of affectivity leads us invariably into the nature of object representation and self-representation, psychic structures in which the affective memory (Arnold, 1969) represents a dominant aspect.

In addition to the patient for whom the development of certain affects is experienced as catastrophic, many more fear certain affects enough to run from analysis just prior to their development. A patient who had terminated her two previous analyses in the middle was warned by me repeatedly that her fear of intimacy and feminine yearning would prompt her to stop the analysis for the purpose of going off somewhere to accomplish some "important achievement," which she could then (in fantasy) present to me for admiration, as she had done twice in her previous analysis and in adolescence in relation to her father.

If I may be permitted to paraphrase Freud's (1937) statement about the nature of the "rock bottom" of resistance in men and women, I would put it in terms of the fear of affects. As is well known, the affects that are experienced as most threatening to women in analysis are, in general, shame, humiliation, and envy; whereas in men the most threatening affect is the anxiety related to fear of loss, and fear of dependency and passivity toward another man, i.e., castration anxiety. In some cases it is necessary to prepare the ground by increasing the ego's knowledge and familiarity with the affect that is so threatening, thus supplementing the inadequate affect tolerance that should have been accomplished, mainly in latency and adolescence, with the help of the parents. Forewarning a patient about forthcoming intense affect experience is a helpful procedure. Novey (1963) sketched the problem in this area: ". . . the more intense my emotional state becomes the less am I capable of maintaining the necessary distance of the observer and the less capable am I of describing it in verbal terms" (p. 267). Acquiring familiarity with affects in advance permits recognition of them under stress, and increases the likelihood that the patient's ability to bear them will not be exceeded.

The Technique of Dealing with Affect Regression

The therapeutic consideration in problems resulting from affect regression has already attracted some attention. The nature of the task has to be in accord with the genetic developmental history of affects I have described in the earlier part of this study (Krystal, 1975). Engel (1962) summarized that story as follows: "As mental apparatus develops, these processes [affects] come under the aegis of the ego. The perceptual processes, whereby one knows *how* one feels are functions of the ego, as are processes, whereby one knows *what* one feels. The latter involves the differentiation of affects into distinct qualities and their eventual identification in terms of language" (p. 123).

211

From a technical point of view, the verbalization of affects becomes a crucial step. Often one finds oneself in a role similar to that of a child analyst who has to supply words to his young analysand. Kligerman (Panel, 1968) felt that this function was analogous to that of the mother who helps the child to interpret, organize, and internalize feelings. Hence, "one often has to help patients who are very regressed to understand *what* they are feeling and to give their feelings a name" (p. 640). Novey (1959) has also stressed the importance of helping the patient to translate feelings into words:

Often the verbalization, by the therapist, of the existence of a given affective state in the analysand will serve as a channel for the emergence of feeling aspects of this affective state. When a given affective state which is in repression gains access to consciousness and thus to a feeling experience, its potential pathogenicity is sharply reduced. In addition, the act of translating this feeling into verbal terms and of then sharing it with the analyst further reduces its pathogenicity [p. 101].

In the process of verbalizing the affects, we are also helping the patient with affect differentiation; as Brierley (1937) put it: "In as far as we are able to unravel the tangled skein of a composite affect, we lay bare a fragment of developmental history. We can not only trace history, we can see history in the making. We can watch the process of affect modification going on under our eyes" (p. 267). The translation of affects into words requires that we use clues from various sources as to the meaning of the emotions involved. In almost every case, it is necessary to use the patient's dreams and associations to reconstruct the cognitive elements of the affects, and the "story behind them" — the drives, conflicts, and defenses that are involved — in short, the vicissitudes of the affect in relation to the rest of the personality. The following case illustration demonstrates several aspects of this work.

CASE ILLUSTRATION

In *Dr. B.*'s[7] previous hour he referred to a dream about his taking codeine. He actually *was* taking codeine, two tablets three times daily, originally to relieve pains in his leg, later for "burning" in the same leg, and now "just in case" it might develop later. The codeine functioned for him during the work day, but after returning home he used food and alcohol in a similar way. I questioned him about what results he desired from these things he "took in" and whether there was anything specific

[7] Another illustration of Dr. B.'s difficulties with affects appears in Part I of this study (Krystal, 1975).

from which he sought relief. Although the patient had a vague idea that his discomfort had to do with feelings, he was not able to verbalize them, or give any direct expression to them. Instead, during most of the hour, he continued to reproach me for not helping him to become professionally independent. I was just like his orthopedic surgeon, who left him with some "pain" so that he had to take codeine.

The next day, however, he opened the session by saying that through the day he had continually thought about his codeine dream. He realized that he had a tremendous need for love, that he tried to get it from his present senior associate, Dr. X., but was unsuccessful. He realized that he used me as a substitute and wanted to get love and attention from me, but that, although I attend to his thoughts and feelings, I am like codeine in being only temporarily relieving rather than making him free and independent.

I asked the patient what occurred to him about his *need* for Dr. X's love. He did not know, but observed that he had the feeling that Dr. X. does not like him and is angry with him "all the time." He has considered going up to Dr. X. and asking, "Why are you angry with me? I did not do anything to hurt you." He then proceeded to enumerate all the things he does for Dr. X. —such as doing his work every day. He did have "all kinds of different [critical and hostile] ideas, but never voiced them."

When he said that my treatment was like giving him codeine, I wondered what occurred to him about the idea that in the dream codeine represented me. I reminded him of some of his previous associations to this dream and, before that, to his conflict over oral impulses. My comments were couched in terms of the feelings experienced. At this point, the patient remembered that he had had a dream the previous night: "I was lying down and you came over and leaned over to kiss me; it was very uncomfortable and I woke up." The vague "bad feeling" continued upon awakening.

Associations: What frightened the patient about the idea in his dream that I was coming over to kiss him was that it seemed to him I was going to choke him. He recalled that in the dream he also had the feeling I was holding his hands. This reminded him of a traumatic event of his childhood, when he was forcibly removed from home and taken away. He thought he could recall how he must have felt then—enraged, kicking, and screaming. They "probably" had to hold him down, and maybe even choked him. He was afraid that if he started to scream, he would become very destructive. He then talked about how he felt deprived by me.

His wife was now a lot more interested in sex than he was, and he was uneasy about her interest and could not imagine that anyone would be physically attracted to him. But on the previous night he had awakened with the feeling he was licking his wife's genitals and did want to have sexual intercourse. However, when he tried to awaken his wife, she made noises indicating that she did not want to be bothered. He got very upset and masturbated. He thought his mother had breast-fed him because it was probably less trouble than mixing a formula. He went through many imagined details of faulty mothering in his infancy.

When the patient "ran out of thoughts," I asked him about the feelings he had had upon awakening from the dream, since he had described them only as "uncomfortable." The patient found that he had felt a vague uneasiness but was unable to put it into words. I then reviewed for him the affects referred to in his associations: oral deprivation, yearnings, fears, specifically of being choked, and helplessness, anger and fear of it. The hopelessness (cf. Schmale, 1964) was shown in his despairing inability to make his wife a willing partner and was reflected in his dream in my coming over to him. In reviewing his feelings, he became aware that he could not verbalize angry feelings and *concentrated* on feeling deprived. He reviewed the story of the childhood trauma, which left him feeling helpless and hopeless, with a fear of uncontrollable destructive rage but also with an underlying feeling of guilt related to the idea that his aggression had caused the whole destructive chain of events.

I then reviewed for the patient some of the reconstruction of his childhood, in which he had experienced intense oral frustration and a special problem related to his mother's inability to function consistently. The trauma of his childhood made him feel that his aggression had got out of hand and had caused terrible destruction. He was similarly afraid that he would destroy me if I were to feed him or to kiss him. I reviewed briefly the problem of oral ambivalence as demonstrated in his "codeine" dream.

At this point, the patient recalled that besides the "bad" feeling in the dream, the feeling was a very delicious one, which made him wish that I would "keep on." This idea reminded him that on the previous night he had seem a film with a reference to Bernini's statue of St. Theresa of Avila, in which she was portrayed "like in an orgasm." She described a vision of God piercing her heart with a fiery arrow. This statement involved a parapraxis, since it was an angel and not God who was alleged to have pierced Theresa's heart. The patient continued to elaborate on the transference experience of the dream in terms of the day's residue: that it must be "unbearably painful," yet it was such a wonderfully ecstatic feeling that "she asked that it go on forever." When he saw the film, he thought that the vision referred to sexual intercourse with the fiery arrows representing a penis penetrating the vagina.

214

My emphasis here is on affect verbalization and distinguishing the affect components. The degree of help with affect verbalization that is required *on the part of the analyst* will vary from patient to patient, and from one phase of the analysis to another. However, if the analyst does not recognize that the patient needs help with affect verbalization, the patient may experience his affects as forbidden and unspeakable, and his regression regarding affects may be aggravated. As with all aspects of the development of the personality, it is necessary for us to keep in mind the course of the genetic development of affects in order to recognize the regressions in them.

Still, the basic question remains: What "does the job" when the patient is finally able to work with his emotions? Conventional wisdom and linguistic usages would suggest that the curative act is the ability to "express" the emotion. These models of affects rest on anal analogies and conceptions, which are especially attractive in our dealing with aggression. These views have been given official sanction in the metaphors of the economic theory. The most cogent clinical criticisms of the economic theory are the problems resulting from the handling of affect. The idea of abreaction has been carried to extremes in such methods of "working off" feelings (especially anger) as smashing punching bags. Some of the currently popular groups (whether or not they call themselves "therapy") operate on the assumption that the "expression" of affect is automatically curative. Their methods, however, do not have lasting results, because affects are complex phenomena with an inseparable cognitive element. If I may be pardoned for using an economic metaphor for just a moment, these ideas, fantasies, and memories continue to surface with great urgency and "keep generating" the expressive aspects of feelings. The emotions are intimately related to their ideational contents, and are not easily displaceable by the mere fiat of a therapist.

However, it cannot be denied that people feel better when they can do something about a situation that bothers them, when they can "speak up" when they are wronged, when they can set things right or revenge themselves. How are we to understand this?

Two points can be made. First, the most uncomfortable aspect of feeling wronged or abused is the feeling of helplessness that develops when one can do nothing about it. Whenever one can do something about it, at least the helplessness is avoided. Being able to assert oneself in the face of some fear enhances one's self-respect and serves as an immediate palliative. Second, the act of revenge becomes relevant only in its ability to foster revenge fantasies, which in turn are relevant in their lending the stamp of reality to fantasies of undoing, and the kind of "balancing" that is so characteristic of obsessive-compulsive patients.

215

Magda Arnold (1950) has aptly summarized the effect of "release therapy":

> *Release therapy* would be effective because anxiety has to be reduced materially before the patient can dare to become angry and so recognize his denied organic sensations. The effect of this therapy would lie not in expression of his "repressed" emotion (which on this hypothesis is present organically, but acknowledged psychologically), but in his *recognition* of it which will lead him to a reevaluation of the original anger-producing situation.
>
> *Reeducation* of emotions can be achieved only if we can change our evaluation of the situation we find ourselves in. Fear or anger need not be suppressed or repressed; they need not be felt, if only we cease to regard a given situation as threatening or annoying [p. 31].

The temptation to ignore the cognitive aspects of affects is great; it manifests itself not only in the above approaches but in behaviorist and pharmacotherapeutic ones as well. What, then, is the most helpful, the most therapeutic approach to affect? It is the goal of helping the patient *to be able to experience his affects fully, without disassociation or displacement.* In order to do so, the patient may have to regain his comfort in regard to *having* his emotions. In addition, where there is regression in the nature of the affects themselves, the therapist will have his work cut out: he must help the patient to verbalize and differentiate his emotions.

Summary

The genetic development of emotion proceeds along the lines of verbalization, desomatization, and differentiation. Therapeutic efforts in affect regression are directed toward helping the patient to verbalize his emotions. Once the patient is able to put his feelings into words, there is a gradual and simultaneous desomatization. At the same time, the undifferentiated nature of his emotions is demonstrated, and the patient is helped to identify and experience progressively more refined nuances of his feelings.

Affect tolerance involves so many varied parts of the personality that it continues to improve throughout the analysis. However, in certain cases, it is necessary to attend to it early in the analysis, sometimes as a preliminary stage. Patients need to distinguish their emotions proper from their reactions to having them. They are often involved in a circular causation that converts an emotional reaction to a clinical syndrome.

The self-limited, signal nature of emotions is observed. The task is to help the patient to live with his affects and not to depend on "expression," abreaction, or any other form of riddance.

REFERENCES

Arnold, M. D. (1950), An excitatory theory of emotion. In: *Feelings and Emotions*, ed. M. L. Reynert. New York: Hafner, pp. 11-34.

––––– (1969), Emotion, motivation and the limbic system. *New York Academy School*, 159:1041-1059.

Atkin, S. (1973), Discussion of Krystal's paper: Therapeutic modification in impairment of affect tolerance. Fall Meeting, American Psychoanalytic Association, New York.

Benedek, T. (1956), Toward a biology of a depressive constellation. *J. Amer. Psychoanal. Assn.*, 4:389-427.

Bibring, E. (1953), The mechanism of depression. In: *Affective Disorders*, ed. P. Greenacre. New York: International Universities Press, pp. 13-48.

Breuer, J., & Freud, S. (1893-1895), Studies on hysteria. *Standard Edition*, 2. London: Hogarth Press, 1955.

Brierley, M. (1937), Affects in theory and practice. *Internat. J. Psycho-Anal.*, 18:256-268.

Bush, F. (1974), Discussion of a paper on: The nature of the primary transitional object. Michigan Psychoanalytic Society, February 14, 1974.

Eissler, K. R. (1953), Emotionality of a schizophrenic patient. *The Psychoanalytic Study of the Child*, 8:199-256. New York: International Universities Press.

––––– (1966), Trauma, dream anxiety schizophrenia. *The Psychoanalytic Study of the Child*, 21:17-51. New York: International Universities Press.

Engel, G. L. (1962), *Psychological Development in Health and Disease*. Philadelphia and London: W. B. Saunders, p. 124.

Erikson, E. H. (1959), *Identity and the Life Cycle* [*Psychological Issues Monog.*]. New York: International Universities Press.

Fenichel, O. (1941), The ego and the affects. *Collected Papers, Second Series*. New York: Norton, 1954, pp. 215-227.

Finkelstein, L. (1973), Awe and premature ejaculation: The role of an affect in the analysis of a sexual dysfunction. Paper read at the Michigan Psychoanalytic Association, September 13, 1973.

Freud, A. (1952), The role of bodily illness in the mental life of children. *The Writings of Anna Freud*, 4:260-279. New York: International Universities Press.

––––– (1965), *Normality and Pathology in Childhood. The Writings of Anna Freud*, 6. New York: International Universities Press.

Freud, S. (1917), Mourning and melancholia. *Standard Edition*, 14:243-258. London: Hogarth Press, 1957.

––––– (1923), The ego and the id. *Standard Edition*, 19:3-66. London: Hogarth Press, 1961.

––––– (1926), Inhibitions, symptoms and anxiety. *Standard Edition*, 20:77-175. London: Hogarth Press, 1959.

––––– (1937), Analysis terminable and interminable. *Standard Edition*, 23:209-253. London: Hogarth Press, 1964.

Giovacchini, P. (1967), Frustration and externalization. *Psychoanal. Quart.*, 36:571-583.

Greenacre, P. (1958), Toward an understanding of the physical nucleus of some defense reactions. In: *Emotional Growth*. New York: International Universities Press, 1971, pp. 128-144.

Hoppe, K. (1962), Persecution, depression and aggression. *Bull. Menninger Clinic*, 26:195-203.

Izard, C. E. (1965), Affect, awareness and performance. In: *Affect, Cognition and Personality*, ed. S. S. Tomkins & C. E. Izard. New York: Springer.

217

Jacobson, E. (1957), Normal and pathological moods: their nature and their function. *The Psychoanalytic Study of the Child,* 12:73-113. New York: International Universities Press.

Jaffe, W. G. (1969), A critical review of the status of the ego concept. *Internat. J. Psycho-Anal.,* 50:533-547.

Jones, H. E. (1967), The study of patterns of emotional expression. In: *Feelings and Emotions,* ed. M. R. Reynert. New York: Hafner.

Katan, A. (1961), Some thoughts about the role of verbalization in early childhood. *The Psychoanalytic Study of the Child,* 16:184-188. New York: International Universities Press.

Klein, M. (1946), Notes of some schizoid mechanisms. *Internat. J. Psycho-Anal.,* 27:99-110.

Knapp, P. H., ed. (1963), *Expression of Emotion in Man.* New York: International Universities Press.

Kohut, H. (1971), *The Analysis of the Self.* New York: International Universities Press.

Krystal, H. (1962), The study of withdrawal from narcotics as a state of stress. *Psychiat. Quart. Suppl.,* 36:53-65.

———, ed. (1968), *Massive Psychic Trauma.* New York: International Universities Press.

——— (1970), Trauma and the stimulus barrier. Read at the American Psychoanalytic Association Annual Meeting. San Francisco, Spring, 1970.

——— (1973a), A discussion of selected aspects of affect theory. In: *Festschrift in Honor of the 75th Birthday of R. Sterba,* ed. A. Grinstein, mineographed.

——— (1973b), Consideration of technique in affect regression and impairment of affect tolerance. Read at the Fall meeting of the American Psychiatric Association.

——— (1975), The genetic development of affect, and affect regression. *This Annual,* 2:98-126.

——— & Petty, T. A. (1961), The psychological aspects of normal convalescence. *Psychosomatics,* 2:1-7.

——— & Raskin, H. A. (1970), *Drug Dependence.* Detroit: Wayne State University Press.

——— & Niederland, W. G., eds. (1971), *Massive Psychic Traumatization.* International Psychiatry Clinics, 8:1.

Leeper, R. W. (1970), Motivational and perceptual properties of emotions. In: *Feelings and Emotions,* ed. A. M. Arnold. New York: Academic Press.

Liddel, H. S. (1967), Animal origins of anxiety. In: *Feelings and Emotions.* ed. M. L. Reynert. New York: Hafner.

Lifton, R. J. (1967), *Life in Death: Survivors in Hiroshima.* New York: Random House.

Low, A. A. (1950), *Mental Health Through Will Training.* Boston: Christopher.

Miller, N. E. (1951), Learnable drives and rewards. In: *Handbook of Experimental Psychology.* ed. S. S. Stevens. London: Wiley.

Murphy, W. F. (1961), Trauma and loss. *J. Amer. Psychoanal. Assn.,* 9:519-532.

Niederland, W. G. (1961), The problem of the survivor. *J. Hillside Hospital,* 10:233-296.

Novey, S. (1959), A clinical view of affect theory in psychoanalysis. *Internat. J. Psycho-Anal.,* 40:94-104.

——— (1963), Discussion of Engel's paper. In: *Expression of Emotion in Man,* ed. P. H. Knapp. New York: International Universities Press, pp. 294-299.

Panel (1968), Psychoanalytic theory of affects, L. B. Lofgren, reporter. *J. Amer. Psychoanal. Assn.,* 16:638-650.

Peto, A. (1967), Dedifferentiations and fragmentations during analysis. *J. Amer. Psychoanal. Assn.,* 15:534-551.

Schachter, S. (1967), Cognitive effects on bodily functioning: Studies of obesity and eating. In: *Neurophysiology and Emotion,* ed. D. C. Gron. New York: Rochester University Press.

Schafer, R. (1964), The clinical analysis of affect. *J. Amer. Psychoanal. Assn.,* 12:275-300.

——— (1972a), Internalization: Process or fantasy. Paper read to the Michigan Psychoanalytic Society, Detroit, May 20, 1972.

——— (1973), Concepts of self and identity and the experience of separation-individuation in adolescence. *Psychoanal. Quart.,* 42:42-59.

Schmale, A. H., Jr. (1964), A genetic view of affects. *The Psychoanalytic Study of the Child,* 19:287-310. New York: International Universities Press.

Schur, M. (1969), Affect and cognition. *Internat. J. Psycho-Anal.*, 50:647-653.

Seton, P. H. (1965), Uses of affect observed in a histrionic patient. *Internat. J. Psycho-Anal.*, 46:226-236.

Solnit, A. J., & Kris, M. (1967), Trauma and infantile experiences: A longitudinal perspective. New York: Basic Books, pp. 175-221.

Spitz, R. A. (1963), Ontogenesis: The proleptic function of emotion. In: *Expression of Emotions in Man*, ed. P. H. Knapp. New York: International Universities Press, pp. 36-64.

Sterba, R. (1960), Therapeutic goal a present day reality. *J. Hillside Hosp.*, 9:195-217.

_____ (1969), The psychoanalyst in a world of change. *Psychoanal. Quart.*, 38:432-454.

Stern, M. M. (1951), Anxiety, trauma and shock. *Psychoanal. Quart.*, 20:179-203.

_____ (1953), Trauma and symptom formation. *Internat. J. Psycho-Anal.*, 34:202-218.

_____ (1968a), Fear of death and trauma. *Internat. J. Psycho-Anal.*, 49:458-461.

_____ (1968b), Fear of death and neurosis. *J. Amer. Psychoanal. Assn.*, 16:3-31.

Tomkins, S. (1962), Affects, images, consciousness. In: *Positive Affects*, Vol. 1. New York: Springer, p. 395.

Tunky, B., & Sternbach, P. A. (1967), Further physiological correlates of ethnic differences in response to shock. *Psychophys.*, 4:67-74.

Valliant, G. E. (1973), The dangers of transference in the treatment of alcoholism. Paper read at Boston University Conference on Alcoholism, September 14, 1973.

Watkins, J. G. (1971), The affect bridge: A hypoanalytic technique. *J. of Clin. & Exper. Hypnosis*, 19:21-27.

Wolfenstein, M. (1966), How is mourning possible? *The Psychoanalytic Study of the Child*, 21:92-126. New York: International Universities Press.

Zetzel (Rosenberg), E. R. (1943), A clinical contribution to the psychopathology of war neuroses. In: *The Capacity for Emotional Growth*. New York: International Universities Press, 1970, pp. 12-32.

_____ (1949), Anxiety and the capacity to bear it. In: *The Capacity for Emotional Growth*. New York: International Universities Press, 1970, pp. 33-52.

_____ (1965), On the incapacity to bear depression. In: *The Capacity for Emotional Growth*. New York: International Universities Press, 1970, pp. 82-114.

_____ (1970a), *The Capacity for Emotional Growth*. New York: International Universities Press.

_____ (1970b), Psychoanalysis and psychic health. In: *The Capacity for Emotional Growth*. New York: International Universities Press, pp. 271-290.

March, 1974

219

On the Diagnostic Term, "Schizophrenia"

PING-NIE PAO, M.D. (*Rockville, Md.*)

Although it is generally taken for granted that there is a clear-cut, commonly understood definition of schizophrenia, unfortunately, such is not the case. Over 90 per cent of the patients admitted to Chestnut Lodge are diagnosed as schizophrenics by their referring psychiatrists or by a staff member of the hospital where they have previously resided for months or even years. Since all of these patients have been given tranquilizers, when first seen in the hospital, they appear "rational." Yet, when the drug is discontinued, a variety of clinical pictures emerge.

Brief descriptions of three such patients are typical. (1) *Patient A.* was not unusually anxious (although before her admission she had been hospitalized elsewhere for two years, following a period of acute excitement during which she had shaved her hair and burned her cottage in response to "voices"). Her eating and sleeping patterns were not disturbed. She was witty, charming, very creative in art, and reasonably sociable. She was even able to establish a reasonable alliance with her therapist. Only after prolonged and careful observation was it evident that she exhibited an extreme tendency toward control—especially of her emotions and thought processes: she was never spontaneously gay or sad; nor would she allow free-associative thinking. (2) *Patient B.* became very active physically and rarely engaged in any relaxed conversation with anyone. (Prior to her admission, however, this patient had been hospitalized for over two years. The hospitalization had been precipitated by aimless wandering, following several years of life in communes.) During the therapy sessions, a marked disturbance in her thought processes was noted. She talked in highly abstract terms. After listening to her for five minutes, one might have concluded that she had a philosophical bent, but, after a bit longer one found oneself utterly confused and exhausted

221

by the effort to make some sense out of her communications. (3) *Patient C.* (following an unsuccessful romance with a girl he hardly knew) had previously been in another hospital for eighteen months. He had "lost zest for living" and had preferred to sit all day in a shaded and darkened room. After drug therapy was terminated at Chestnut Lodge, he became instantly upset. He showed sleep disturbance, paced the floor, and before long was hitting people. And shortly after his admission, he was unable to control his sphincters and was catatonic.

Many other examples could be given, but the brief descriptions of these three patients illustrate our point: developmental data and previous course of illness aside, each of these patients had been considered schizophrenic. Patient A had exhibited an excess of control over her emotions and thoughts (different from obsessional patients); Patient B. had shown disconnected speech and thought processes; Patient C., catatonic behavior. The term *schizophrenia* was used to describe many combinations of clinical symptoms. But it is clear that to arrive at an accurate conceptualization we must determine whether the patient being referred to by a colleague, let us say, is like Patient A., B., or C. A more precise definition is thus an indispensable prerequisite for anyone writing about schizophrenia.

In this presentation, after a historical review, I shall first consider the criteria for a diagnosis of schizophrenia and second, I shall subgroup schizophrenia in terms of current psychoanalytic knowledge. I must state at the outset that in making this attempt I do not strive to work out a criterion that will be generally acceptable, but rather, I aim to delineate one that can be useful in assessing the various theories of schizophrenia and the divergent therapeutic recommendations for schizophrenia in the psychoanalytic literature.

The Origin of the Term

Attempts to define and classify the mental illnesses were made as early as the middle of the nineteenth century. But it was not until 1899 that Kraepelin's system brought order to the classification. According to this system, a psychosis is endogenous if it is not caused by a demonstrable anatomic lesion in the brain, by the existence of an identifiable toxic or chemical agent, or by metabolical or hormonal disturbances traceable in the human organism that could affect the function of the brain. This system subgroups endogenous psychoses into two broad categories:

namely, dementia praecox[1] and manic-depressive psychosis. While manic-depressive psychosis exhibits self-terminating episodes of an exaggeration of "normal" affects and behavior, dementia praecox is characterized by bizarre behavioral and affective manifestations and a steady deterioration of the psychic personality.

In the history of psychiatry, Kraepelin's contribution is important. As Bleuler (1911) put it, "Hand in hand with the elaboration of the dementia praecox concept, other disease-entities were defined, particularly the manic-depressive psychosis. In this way, dementia praecox was thrown into bold relief; and its delineations were no longer drawn unilaterally from within but also solidly from without" (p. 7). On the other hand, whatever advantage Kraepelin's contribution offered, it was outbalanced by its disadvantages. For, as Zilboorg (1941) said, Kraepelin's belief in the inevitability of deterioration inavoidably led to "the ultimate achievement of an attitude which expected little from man once he was mentally ill; it stood ready to take him into the kindly custody of a well-organized and well-conducted hospital where he could await his fate with the maximum comfort his psychological condition, social position, and financial ability would allow" (p. 461).

In 1903, Bleuler said of dementia praecox that "Twenty years experience has taught me to delineate the disease in the same manner as Kraepelin has done" (p. 113), but he noted that "dementia is not always an accompaniment of the disease, nor is the disease always praecox. To be sure, the name is not well chosen" (p. 120). Five years later, he suggested a new term, "schizophrenia," to replace it. In his monograph "Dementia Praecox or the Group of Schizophrenias" (for the most part written in 1908, but published in 1911), he listed his reasons for introducing the new term: (1) The term dementia praecox describes the disease and not the person who is afflicted with it. From the term, no adjective can possibly be derived. To write a differential diagnosis, one finds it extremely awkward and cumbersome to be writing about the disease and the person who is afflicted with the disease. (2) The term dementia praecox tends to lead to a misconception that the disease must begin during adolescence and end in a state of dementia. Clinically, this need not be so. And, (3) more significantly, the new term schizophrenic (from the Greek roots for *split* and *mind*) not only does away with the

[1] Zilboorg (1941, p. 458) has said that Kraepelin's use of dementia praecox differed from that of Morel, who had in 1860 coined the term to describe a clinical phenomenon with much delimited scope. Kraepelin, as Bleuler (1911) says, "subsumes the whole deteriorating group under the term [dementia praecox]" (p. 6). Following Kraepelin's usage, dementia praecox includes not only Morel's dementia praecox but also Kahlbaum's catatonia, Hecker's hebephrenia, Pick's simple deterioration, as well as the paranoia hallucinatoria or phantastica.

above problems, but also clearly reflects characteristics of the illness, namely, the phenomenon of a "splitting" of the mind or personality, characterized by Kraepelin as the "peculiar destruction of internal connections of the psychic personality" (1919, p. 1).

Because of its many advantages over dementia praecox, the term schizophrenia attained instant popularity. In fact, its popularity remained in spite of Freud's and Adolph Meyer's attempts to replace it. Although primarily interested in the function and the structure of the mind in the healthy and sick, Freud attempted to introduce the term *paraphrenia* to replace schizophrenia or dementia praecox. Partly because he never did attempt to convince others why paraphrenia was a better term, he was the only user of the term for a decade.[2] In the end, he accepted the term schizophrenia. Expounding a psychobiological (or a biological and adaptive) point of view, Meyer (1938) introduced the term *paraergasia* to replace schizophrenia or dementia praecox, in order to emphasize that mental illness is a reaction to the stress of life and not a "disease" that affects the brain. But despite the fact that he was once the dean of American psychiatry, Meyer's effort was as futile as Freud's had been.

According to Kraepelin's system, a diagnosis of dementia praecox is ultimately dependent on mental deterioration. Because dementia might take time to make its appearance, an instant diagnosis of dementia praecox can at times be difficult. By stressing that schizophrenia is to be diagnosed by the recognition of "the specific alteration of thinking, feeling and relationship to the external world which appears nowhere else in this particular fashion," Bleuler (1911, p. 9) readily remedied the shortcoming of Kraepelin's approach. At a time when psychiatry was still dominated by neurology, where an instant diagnosis was paramount, the importance of Bleuler's contribution was unequivocal. Later, when Freud and Meyer suggested their preferred new terminology, they were indeed striving to convey very important messages through their adopted terms. But because their contributions were made at a time when clinical diagnosis was considered vital, and because their contributions did not add much to facilitating the diagnosis, they had little chance of competing with Bleuler.

Notwithstanding the disagreement in nomenclature, Kraepelin, Bleuler, Freud, and Meyer seemed to be in agreement that dementia praecox, schizophrenia, paraphrenia, and paraergasia are different terms for one

---

[2] See Strachey's footnote No. 1 on p. 76 of Vol. 12 of the *Standard Edition.* The last time Freud actually used the term was in 1918 in a footnote added to "A Case of Paranoia Running Counter to the Psychoanalytic Theory of the Disease" (1915).

discrete clinical entity, which has its own boundary (e.g., it is distinguished from manic-depressive psychosis) and for which a definitive criterion for a diagnosis may be established.

The Usefulness of Diagnosticating

Before proceeding with the criteria for a diagnosis of schizophrenia, we must first consider the usefulness for diagnosticating. In recent years, many authors have raised an objection to the use of the term schizophrenia. Some feel that it is so misused that it is devoid of meaning. Some, like Szasz (1961) and Laing (1967), regard affixing a diagnosis of schizophrenia as equivalent to assaulting the personal integrity of the patient. Others, like Hay and Forrest (1972), feel that for a psychotherapist a formal diagnosis is a luxury. Their arguments are eloquent, convincing, and truly humanistic, but they do not seem to benefit the clinicians. From the clinician's point of view, in fact, a diagnosis can be very useful. It can enable professionals to communicate multilevel information in an economic way. For instance, a diagnosis of hysteria not only tells of phenomenological manifestations in the form of the patient's symptomatology, but also indicates a certain specificity of his conflicts, early object relations, etc. It informs us, in addition, that if psychoanalysis is to be recommended as the choice method of treatment, the therapist can be assured that the patient will be able to live through the anxieties aroused in the course of the treatment without experiencing a total collapse of his ego functions or a loss of a cohesive sense of self, beyond the therapeutic sessions. Similarly, a diagnosis of schizophrenia does not limit itself to the recognition of the fundamental and accessory symptoms that Bleuler spoke of. It informs us in addition that the patient had a disturbed early object relationship with resultant ego and superego defects which predisposed him to panic, a collapse of ego functions, and a loss of cohesive sense of self. It further informs us that psychoanalytic treatment cannot be profitably used without the adoption of parameters (Eissler, 1953), at least in the early phases of treatment.

Speaking as clinicians, Menninger et al. (1963) said, "our concern now is not so much what to call something as what to do about it" (p. 2), and "it is still necessary to know [the diagnosis] in advance, to plan as logically as we can" (p. 6). Very much in line with this viewpoint, Frosch (1964, 1970) has laboriously delineated "psychotic character," Kernberg (1967) the "borderline personality organization," and Kohut (1971) the "narcis-

225

sistic personality disturbances." Clinical reasons also prompted Anna Freud (1965b) to design the metapsychologycal diagnostic profile that studies pathology against the background of normal development, and Freeman (1972) to outline a profile for use in evaluating schizophrenic cases.

To these clinicians a diagnostic term seems to serve several purposes. It is used to transmit multilevel information economically; as the prerequisite for sound therapeutic planning; in the case of Anna Freud's profile, as a means to assess the various developmental lines and their deviations; and, as Freeman's case implies, as a basis for accurate diagnosis on which a theory of schizophrenia may be formulated and more consistent therapeutic endeavor can be recommended to the schizophrenic patients. To these clinicians, a diagnosis of schizophrenia is neither a luxury nor a derogatory label.

Criteria for a Diagnosis of Schizophrenia

DESCRIPTIVE AND SYMPTOMATIC APPROACH

We have indicated that, although Kraepelin differentiated dementia praecox from manic-depressive psychosis, Bleuler was the first to use symptoms as criteria for an instant diagnosis of schizophrenia. According to Bleuler, schizophrenic symptoms may be divided into two groups: fundamental[3] and accessory. The fundamental symptoms, which are essential and conclusive for a diagnosis, consist of "the specific alteration of thinking, feeling and relationship to the external world" (1911, p. 9). More specifically, they are disturbances in associative processes, dissociation between affect and thoughts, ambivalence and autism. Delusions, hallucinations, ideas of reference, the experience of being directed, the experience of bodily changes in the form of hypochondriasis, feelings of depersonalization and unreality, loss of a sense of past, merging of self with others, and so on, are conceived of as accessory symptoms. Although not prerequisites for diagnosis, the accessory symptoms may often dominate the clinical picture. "It is not often that the fundamental symptoms are so markedly exhibited as to cause the patient to be hospitalized in a mental institution. It is primarily the accessory symp-

[3] Bleuler's fundamental and accessory symptoms are not to be confused with his primary and secondary symptoms. Bleuler believed that schizophrenia is basically a disease of the brain that causes the associational disturbance. Thus, to him, associational disturbance is the primary symptom and the other symptoms are secondary to the associational disturbance.

toms which make his retention at home impossible or it is they which make the psychosis manifest and given occasion to require psychiatric help" (p. 94).

Today, if a diagnosis of schizophrenia is approached from the symptomatic and descriptive level, Bleuler's criterion of fundamental symptoms is still adhered to (see the A.P.A. DSM-11). Anna Freud (1965a) has demonstrated that deeper understanding of the patient can often be deduced from the surface data. But to rely on symptoms or surface data alone can be fraught with complications. Another patient at Chestnut Lodge, D., is an illustration of this diagnostic problem. She was deemed an ideal daughter by her mother until she was 16. But, as she became involved with boys, she no longer reported every detail of her daily life to her mother as she had previously. Distressed, the mother took the patient to a woman psychiatrist. After a seemingly promising start, the patient clammed up, which led to a change of therapists. With her male therapist, she repeated the same pattern. Because of the unbreakable silence and the general appearance of depression, hospitalization was recommended. Following an elopement, the patient was said to display bizarre behavior, such as hiding herself behind a chair in the doctor's office. With a diagnosis of schizophrenia, she was transferred to a second hospital, Chestnut Lodge, a long way from home. Now relatively free from the maternal influence, she was symptom-free. Her silence and bizarre behavior, which had presumably entitled her to the diagnosis of schizophrenia, were noted to be the result of a willful nonengagement rather than an autistic type of withdrawal. In line with Bleuler's (1911) statement that "definite schizophrenia disturbances of association alone were sufficient for the diagnosis" (p. 298), many cases that showed associational disturbance under no other circumstances except during the psychological testing process (cf. Rapaport et al., 1945-1946) were considered to be schizophrenic cases. To rectify this problem, later writers tended to subdivide schizophrenia into two classes: reactive vs. process schizophrenia, or schizophrenic-like psychosis vs. schizophrenia. The implication is that, although there are similar symptomatic manifestations, one class has a better outcome than the other. This approach, then, reintroduces Kraepelin's idea of using the outcome of the illness or the prognosis as a criterion. The feeling of hopelessness that often derives from such a view has already been mentioned.

A PSYCHOANALYTIC APPROACH

In concentrating their effort on the understanding of the hows and whys of the schizophrenic phenomenon, psychoanalysts do not as a rule concern themselves with the diagnostic criteria. When diagnosis becomes an issue, they simply accept the descriptive or symptomatic approach. Of extreme interest however, is the fact that the earliest analysts, such as Freud, Tausk, and Federn, perhaps less influenced by Bleuler, tended to use stricter criteria for the diagnosis of schizophrenia. The schizophrenic patients on whom Freud, Tausk, and Federn formulated their theories were distinctly sicker than those discussed in recent literature (e.g., Arlow & Brenner, 1969; Boyer & Giovacchini, 1967).[4]

Notwithstanding the lack of explicit effort to define the diagnosis, each psychoanalyst, in his theory formulation about schizophrenia, did, however, lay down his own criteria in one form or another. When Freud formulated his theory of schizophrenia in 1911, he ascribed all the schizophrenic symptoms to (1) libidinal decathexis from the outer world and from the representation of the objects, and (2) libidinal recathexis. The implication of the theory is that a "break with reality," consequent to decathexis, is an implicit criterion for a diagnosis of schizophrenia. The major drawback to this criterion is that the break often belongs to the history: we are then asked to rely on the history, rather than on the examination of the patient, to reach a diagnosis.

Tausk (1933) was the first to use the expression *loss of ego boundary* to describe the phenomenon that Bleuler called *merging of self with others*. Federn (1952) gave new meaning to the term *loss of ego boundary* by suggesting that it leads to misinterpretation of events, ideas of reference, delusional formation and so on. Thus, he seemed to have considered the loss of ego boundary an implicit criterion for a diagnosis of schizophrenia. As much as later observers like Nunberg (1920), Hartmann (1953), Jacobson (1954), Freeman & Cameron (1958), Searles (1968), and others all recognize that the loss of ego boundary is a consistent manifestation of schizophrenia, the fact is that the loss of ego boundary is a phenomenon more evident in the treatment setting than in the diagnostic setting. Talking to a stranger, the patient may not show any such disturbance at all. Furthermore, transient loss of ego boundary can often be witnessed in borderline psychotics and, sometimes, in neurotics in analysis—sometimes even in normal persons, as in states of ecstasy or states induced by consciousness-expanding drugs. If loss of ego boundary is to be used as a criterion for a diagnosis of schizophrenia, some qualifying phrase must be attached to it.

---

[4] Reichard (1956) suggested that two of the five cases Freud described in the *Studies on Hysteria* (Breuer & Freud, 1893-1895) could be diagnosed as schizophrenia. And in his recent review of the wolf man's childhood, Blum (1974) suggesta that Freud's "From the History of an Infantile Neurosis" would be more appropriately called "From the History of an Infantile Psychosis."

Melanie Klein (1946) identified the tendency of schizophrenic patients toward ego fragmentation and projective identification. Bion (1957) adds to the list of diagnostic criteria the patients' propensity for aggression and lack of capacity to maintain object relations. But all these observed facts, like loss of ego boundary, are more readily discernible in the treatment setting than in the diagnostic setting.

In 1917, Freud described how the thought process of schizophrenic patients is dominated by primary-process functioning. Unlike loss of ego boundary, or projective identification, this phenomenon does not require an analytic setting to be bared; in other words, it can often be discerned in a diagnostic situation where the patient and the doctor may meet for the first time. Hence, later writers tend to use "reverting to primary-process functioning" as one of the determining criteria for a diagnosis of schizophrenia. However, we must certainly not give a diagnosis of schizophrenia to these patients who, as Rapaport et al. (1945-1946) demonstrated, only show the primary-process functioning under stressful situations, such as during psychological testing. Therefore, as a diagnostic criterion, the circumstances in which primary-process functioning occurs and the duration of its existence must be specified.

AN EMPIRICAL APPROACH

At Chestnut Lodge, I interviewed each new patient shortly after his admission. This privilege has allowed me to learn, among other things, how to assess each patient diagnostically. Such assessment is by no means accurate; yet, it yields a significant guideline, though to some extent a highly personal one, for the criteria for a diagnosis of schizophrenia.

As I have already indicated, most "schizophrenia" patients have for many years now, been placed on psychotropic medications in other hospitals prior to their admission to Chestnut Lodge. Most of them were made "rational" by the drugs. The others, despite the rather large dose of medication they consumed daily, still demonstrated the fundamental or accessory symptoms described by Bleuler or the primary-process functioning described by Freud. During an interview setting, however, both the "rational" and "irrational" patients sooner or later exuded the same kind of aura.

Ordinarily, in such an interpersonal setting as an interview, we feel that we and the interviewee are in contact with each other if we are engaged in a conversation; there is an interaction of a live, lively, friendly, or unfriendly nature between us. But we feel very little of this in a similar setting with a schizophrenic. With him, we are never certain whether or not we are in contact emotionally; we intermittantly sense a wall or a barrier existing between us; we sometimes feel as if we are meeting with a robot; we may observe that his movements, facial expressions, and words are stereotypic; and we may find fragments of his interactional modes — his gestures, phrases, and manners — detached and disengaged from their cohesive purposiveness in human interaction. All this gives us the feeling that the patient is both there and not there. In other words, two people exchanging rituals, but their minds are miles and miles apart.

This peculiar atmosphere is created by the patient. Usually, it is created before he begins to talk; that is, its creation does not depend on the patient's speech. However, his stream of speech, his intonations, and his choice of words further enhance it. It may seem very thick in the beginning but appear to diminish in the course of the interview; or although it is not very obvious at the beginning, it may grow thicker as the interview goes on; or it may remain static throughout the interview. The fluctuation or lack of fluctuation could be due either to the degree of the patient's sickness or the interviewer's success or failure to elicit an emphatic trust from him. When the patient is gravely ill (i.e., acutely distressed and very self-engrossed), such as Mr. C. described above, the peculiar atmosphere tends to be maintained throughout the interview. Whenever the fluctuation does occur, it may be fair to say that the patient dispels the peculiar atmosphere because he considers the conversation with the interviewer worthwhile, or he hides behind the peculiar atmosphere because he distrusts the interviewer as he has distrusted others.

Speech, as indicated, helps to enhance the special atmosphere. For instance, after he has admitted that he needs to be in the hospital, the patient may then declare that nothing is wrong with him, or, after he has said he has been in various hospitals before, he declares that he never committed any crime and should not have been imprisoned. On the surface, the speech appears to be senseless. But on careful scrutiny, it seems clear that in either case a second thought tends to invalidate the first. The primary purpose for such speech is to simultaneously engage and disengage oneself in the conversation with the interviewer. That schizophrenic speech shows a special kind of peculiarity in itself has been beautifully described by Bleuler (1911), Storch (1924), Kasanin (1951), and others. A simple interpretation of these observations is that the patient's communicative language is also affected by his effort to simultaneously move toward and move away from the interviewer. The affected language takes the form of having crucial words replaced so that on the surface the patient's speech becomes completely irrelevant and impossible to comprehend. The word replacement is accomplished without the patient's awareness and subjected to the primary process. For example, upon entering the office for the first time, *Patient E.* (she was one of the rare cases who was not medicated) paced the room and screamed at the top of her lungs, protesting vehemently for having just been brought to the hospital against her will. Continuing to pace, she occasionally stopped her screaming, listened to the doctor's short comments on her distress at being rehospitalized (she had been in a hospital several years previously), on her complex emotions before the current need for rehospitalization, etc. She nevertheless kept up the pacing and screaming for over 25 minutes. At that time, she suddenly declared that she was tired. She readily accepted an invitation to sit down. Slouching in her chair, she closed her eyes and was quiet and motionless. Five minutes later, she opened her eyes, but otherwise made no movement. Fixing her eyes on a picture on the wall, she said, "The picture is very *peaceful*. I like it." Having followed her eyes to the painting of a countryside landscape, the doctor said, "It is. And you may find your inner peace around here, in this office." To which the patient responded clearly, "Yes." *Patient F.*, ten months after the initiation of treatment (he was not in treatment with me), lapsed into an apparent apathy following the doctor's summer vacation. Whereas he had earlier talked enough to make himself clear, now he was practically mute. The doctor, after having made a connection between his own vacation and the patient's behavior and having sat through many silent sessions with the patient, felt particularly irritated one day and told the patient of his dismay about the patient's silence and general attitude. For the rest of the session, although the doctor felt a bit relieved, the patient remained silent. The patient opened the next session, however, by saying desultorily that when he was in high school he was in love with Leslie. The doctor said nothing, and the patient, after pausing for a couple of minutes continued, again in a desultory manner, "I couldn't talk to Leslie."

Patient E. had said, "The picture is very peaceful," when she could have said, "You give me a very peaceful feeling." Patient F. could have said, "My anger or hatred for you, or even my attachment to you, has made me tongue-tied," but, instead, had to make his point via his long-past experience of being in love with Leslie. Phenomenologically, the word-replacement has been called schizophrenese (Hill, 1955). Talking schizophrenese, any patient may give the impression of what Bleuler (1911) described as "loose association" or "absence of hierarchical structure of goals" in his speech (p. 16). Patient F. also used intonation and affect to achieve his purpose of creating the described atmosphere.

231

By flattening his affect, talking in a desultory manner, and then pausing, he had told but had also untold his therapist why he had been silent.

It is perhaps not stretching a point to say that the special atmosphere I have described can be experienced only with schizophrenic patients. The special atmosphere is not created consciously; it is quite beyond the patient's awareness. Once created, it tends to make others feel estranged, bewildered, confused, and incapable of empathy for the patient's pre-occupation or mood. Consequently, in treating such a patient, the psy-chiatrist may resort to a technique or defense familiar to himself in order to remove himself from the patient; he might terminate the interview, keep his own thoughts unrelated to the interpersonal setting, etc. Judging from his own feelings and activities, he may conclude that his patient is extremely hostile and is making "attacks on linking" (Bion, 1959). But hostility explains only half of the phenomenon, even in the case of Mr. F. The doctor's long absence no doubt produced feelings in Mr. F., extreme feelings of being hurt and abandoned. As the result of his narcissistic rage, Mr. F. became silent. When frightened by his doctor's angry remarks, he felt compelled to talk, grudgingly and, therefore, crypt-ically. Nevertheless, the hostility would fail to explain the totality of the condensed act of telling and untelling (or getting together with and yet getting away from) the therapist. The act is not the result of ambivalence or ambitendency; it has transcended ordinary ambivalence—where the patient is still fully and completely related to the other person. In the act that creates this special atmosphere, the patient has sealed off his feelings, libidinal and/or aggressive; he simply turns on one of the defensive devices he originally adopted in order to simultaneously cope with two or more contradictory messages from his mother, and which he uses now in any ambiguous situation whenever he is reminded of con-frontations with his mother (cf. the concept of double-bind injunction by Bateson et al., 1956; and Kafka, 1971).

My emphasis is that the diagnosis should begin with the study of the interviewer's own emotional reactions in the interaction between the patient and himself. Here we may discover the patient's tendency to create a special atmosphere that conveys the patient's simultaneous expression of two diametrically opposite wishes—to move toward as well as to move away. This atmosphere interferes with the interviewer's empathetic understanding of the patient and often incurs a narcissistic hurt to the interviewer's ideal image of being a savior. Because of this hurt, the interviewer then thinks of the patient as being hostile, as having suspended his trust in the whole human race, and consequently as belonging only to a subhuman species.

The study of the interviewer's emotional response to the interaction between the patient and himself is subjective and personal. It should never be used alone as *the* diagnostic criterion; it must be objectified. To achieve this, the interviewer may need to spend more time with the patient. In a series of interviews, he may then have a chance to learn, among other things,[5] through the patient's report, the patient's inner experience. Such reports may reveal the first-rank symptoms (e.g., audible thoughts, experiences of impulses and volitional acts under outside influence, delusional perception, experience of thoughts as being controlled by others), as described by Schneider (1959). I do not, however, agree with Schneider's claim that a diagnosis of schizophrenia can be made with certainty in the presence of first-rank symptoms.

Anna Freud (1965a) says that when doing diagnostic work, the analyst

has to proceed as a comparative stranger to the patient, with no established transference coming to his help, and he has in his field of observation no more than overt behavior, conscious manifestations, descriptions of symptomatology and suffering often inadequate, in short the surface of the patient's mind. With child patients, with whom we are concerned here specifically, he has to proceed even without their cooperation or in the face of their opposition, which implies that these surface appearances, symptoms, etc. are also obscured by the subject's fears, distrust, avoidances, denials. To compensate for the paucity of material elicited under such conditions with child patients, the diagnostician finds himself forced to go beyond the subjective account which the patient is able or willing to give of himself and turn to allegedly objective sources as provided by information about the individual's historical and social background, the environment's or parents' descriptions and complaints, as well as to the technical help offered by a battery of tests" [p. 32].

This statement can easily be applied to schizophrenic cases. If we regard the diagnosis as being quite important (as the prerequisite for a sound planning of the treatment program), we must not only pay attention to symptoms and other surface data, but must also scrutinize carefully the patient's developmental history, his capacity to endure anxiety, his propensity for regression, his adaptive capacity, and his living environment. Such information may be elicited from all available sources—the patient himself, members of his family[6] the family physician, pediatricians, school reports, previous psychiatrists, previous psychiatric hospitals, etc.

If a diagnosis is approached in this fashion,[7] no differential diagnosis

---

[5] He may also observe loss of ego boundaries, reverting to the use of primary-process functioning, projective identification, etc.

[6] Empirically we know that the mothers of schizophrenic patients also have an air about themselves, which the mothers of borderlines do not have.

[7] The diagnosis of over 90 per cent of patients prior to admission to Chestnut Lodge was schizophrenia. Using our method of scrutiny, about 5 to 6 per cent of these patients were rediagnosed as borderlines.

is called for. In neither manic-depressives nor borderlines, does the "special atmosphere" occur. In the interview setting, the depressed patient tends to squeeze as much sympathy as possible from the other person; in the process he causes the interviewer to feel depleted and therefore irritated at the patient for his greediness. The manic patient often feels frustrated and attacks the other person—creating in the latter a feeling of outrage. Or, he tries so hard to entertain the interviewer as to overwhelm him, causing him to become bored and, consequently, irritated and eager to leave. Borderlines have a wide spectrum (Kernberg, 1970). Even the sickest cases do not not create the described special atmosphere. They may evoke a wide variety of emotional experiences in the other person, but they always make him feel he is *with* the patient. Aside from the transience of the "psychotic symptoms" and the identifiability of the cause of symptoms, the lack of "special atmosphere" in interpersonal relatedness is the most important characteristic difference between borderlines on the one hand and schizophrenics on the other.

Subgrouping of Schizophrenic Phenomena

As indicated in the beginning of this paper, many varieties of clinical phenomena may be diagnosed as schizophrenia. To produce a pinpointed effect, there has been a general tendency to subgroup the schizophrenic phenomena. Bleuler (1911), for instance, attempted to classify schizophrenia into subtypes such as catatonic, paranoid, hebephrenic, simple, and so on. Aside from specifying the predominance of certain symptoms at the time of diagnostication, this classification has no practical value. For, in intensive psychotherapy, every schizophrenic may show a predominance of each set of symptoms at various times during the course of treatment. The classifications adopted by the A.P.A. Diagnostic and Statistical Manual (1968) includes, in addition to Bleuler's subtypes, acute and chronic undifferentiated type, affective type, etc. But, despite those additions, the A.P.A. classification is, like Bleuler's subtypes, oriented to a descriptive and symptomatic viewpoint and therefore has limited usefulness.

In a recent paper, Fort (1973) summarizes the schema of subgrouping schizophrenia adopted at Chestnut Lodge. The schema is derived from a careful clinical study of a large group of schizophrenic patients (not borderline) admitted to Chestnut Lodge during the past fifteen years. The study included (1) the longititudinal data of maturational-developmental processes of these patients as supplied by their family members, family physicians, pediatricians, school reports, etc.; (2) a thorough follow-up of the unfolding of symptoms in these patients as reported by previous psychiatrists who had treated them before their admission to Chestnut Lodge; and (3) the clinical course from admission to discharge as observed at Chestnut Lodge. With this information, the schizophrenics are then divided into four subgroups: schizophrenia I, II, III, and IV. A schizophrenia I patient shows near-adequate ego development and functioning, including satisfactory sublimatory activities, until his late teens. In the face of final steps of second separation-individuation or reorganization of identity, the patient becomes acutely symptomatic. While the patient's early environment may not measure up to the average expectable environment, the personality of the mother or her surrogates shows little evidence of gross pathology of a schizoid nature. Now that he is sick, his family willingly rallies to help him to get well. Through psychoanalytic therapy, the patient will be able to improve his capacity for adaptation. In other words, the prognosis for such a patient is in general quite good.

A schizophrenic II patient shows consistent adaptive lag, with symptoms beginning in the middle teens. There is indication that the patient has struggled with his conflicts, though his efforts seem feeble and unsuccessful. Not only is his early environment more traumatic, but he is also still very much caught in the web of the highly pathological family drama. The prognosis for this patient is guarded; much depends on whether or not he can be extracted from the web of the family conflict. Therefore family therapy must be included as a part of the treatment program.

A schizophrenia III patient shows a highly pathological personality on the part of the mother figure and a distinctly defective ego functioning noticeable from the early developmental phases. Although he flourished during latency, he was swept off his feet at the slightest increase of drive pushes. He became symptomatic at the dawn of puberty. The prognosis for this patient is grave. For such a patient, psychoanalytic therapy requires many parameters, some of which may never be removed.

A schizophrenia IV patient may have begun as a schizophrenia I, II, or III. Because he had been neglected in treatment and had been kept for a long time in an institution, he is now utterly despairing and resigned to sickness and no longer belongs to the other subgroups. The prognosis for this patient is also grave, although a few may respond to a rigorous treatment program.

Fort has indicated that the classification of schizophrenia I, II, III, and

IV not only takes into consideration the dynamic, economic, structural, developmental, and adaptive points of view, but also facilitates the prognostic evaluation. This helps to determine the type of treatment. For instance, for schizophrenia I and II, psychoanalytic psychotherapy may be recommended, whereas, for those classified as schizophrenia III and IV, much modification of the psychoanalytic technique is required.

I believe that the classification of schizophrenia into I, II, III, and IV is a practical one and recommend that it be more generally adopted in order to do away with some of the existing confusion in the area of diagnosis and therapy. For instance, the current A.P.A. classification in the DSM-II comprises a very long list of subgroups, including acute and chronic undifferentiated schizophrenia, reactive and process schizophrenia, affective schizophrenia or schizo-affective disorder, pseudoneurotic schizophrenia, ambulatory schizophrenia, prepsychotic schizophrenia, latent schizophrenia, etc. All these terminologies seem to serve no function other than to qualify a better-or-worse-than-average outlook. In our classification, such prognostic distinction is clear cut. Furthermore, our classification takes into consideration the metapsychological viewpoints, in addition to descriptive and symptomatic factors. As of now, we are often at a loss when some of our colleagues speak of classical analysis for schizophrenic patients. We even wonder why, unlike our colleagues, we must introduce parameters. Our classifications could clarify this confusion at once. For, certainly, most of schizophrenia I (and many schizophrenia II) patients can be treated by classical psychoanalysis. But it would be highly doubtful whether any schizophrenia III and IV patients could be treated psychoanalytically without parameters.

Summary

From the clinician's point of view, the term *schizophrenia* can be used to transmit multilevel information among professionals, including sound planning for a therapeutic program for the patient who is designated a schizophrenic. Because the term has been overused, or even misused, it is necessary to give it a more definite boundary. I have offered my own criteria for a diagnosis of schizophrenia. Through the study of the general attitude of such patients (including speech) in relating to me, I have concluded that the schizophrenic patient is different from the manic-depressive patient or the borderline patient in that he tends to make others feel unable to establish contact with him. Incapable of developing empathetic feelings for the content of the patient's thoughts or moods, the other person may consider the patient hostile or sub-human. But, in fact, the special atmosphere is a defensive device designed to protect the patient against narcissistic wounds. I do not think the psychiatrist's personal emotional experience should be used as the sole criteria for diagnosis, however. Such personal experience must be supplemented by a careful scrutiny of the patient's background, the course of illness, the patient's ability to tolerate anxiety, etc.

However stringent the criteria may be for a diagnosis of schizophrenia, the term still covers a broad spectrum of clinical phenomena. For the sake of removing the existing confusion in nomenclature and therapy recommendations, I have proposed a schema, devised at Chestnut Lodge, dividing schizophrenia into four subgroups, namely, schizophrenia I, II, III, and IV. The classification takes into consideration the dynamic, economic, structural, developmental, and adaptive point of view, on the one hand, and prognostic and therapeutic guidelines, on the other. The classification may have further advantages by enabling us to encompass the many theoretical formulations of schizophrenia — some of which are based on the study of schizophrenia I and II and others on the study of schizophrenia III and IV.

REFERENCES

A.P.A. (1968), *Diagnostic and Statistical Manual of Mental Disorders, II.* Washington, D.C.: American Pyschiatric Association.

Arlow, J. A. & Brenner, C. (1969), The psychopathology of the psychoses: a proposed revision. *Internat. J. Psycho-Anal.,* 50:5-14.

Bateson, G., Jackson, D. D., Haley, J., & Weakland, J. H. (1956), Toward a theory of schizophrenia. *Behav. Sci.,* 1:251-264.

Bion, W. R. (1957), Differentiation of the psychotic from the non-psychotic personalities. *Internat. J. Psycho-Anal.,* 27:99-110.

———— (1959), Attacks on linking. *Internat. J. Psycho-Anal.,* 40:308-315.

Bleuler, E. (1903), Dementia praecox. *J. Ment. Pathol.,* 3:113-120.

———— (1911), *Dementia Praecox or the Group of Schizophrenias.* New York: International Universities Press, 1950.

Blum, H. P. (1974), The borderline childhood of the Wolf Man. *J. Amer. Psychoanal. Assn.,* 4:721-742.

Boyer, L. B. & Giovacchini, P. L. (1967), Pyschoanalytic treatment of character disorders. In: *Psychoanalytic Treatment of Schizophrenia and Characterological Disorders.* New York: Science House, pp. 208-234.

Breuer, J. & Freud, S. (1893-1895), Studies on hysteria. *Standard Edition,* 2. London: Hogarth Press, 1955.

Eissler, K. R. (1953), The effect of the structure of the ego in psychoanalytic technique. *J. Amer. Psychoanal. Assn.,* 1:104-105.

Federn, P. (1952), *Ego Psychology and the Psychoses.* New York: Basic Books.

Fort, J. (1973), The importance of being diagnostic. Read at the annual Chestnut Lodge Symposium, October 5, 1973.

Freeman, T. (1972), A psychoanalytic profile schema for the psychotic patient. *Brit. J. Med. Psychol.,* 45:243-254.

_____, Cameron, J. L. & McShie, A. (1958), *Chronic Schizophrenia.* New York: International Universities Press.

Freud, A. (1965a), Diagnostic skills and their growth in psycho-analysis. *Internat. J. Psycho-Anal.,* 46:31-38.

_____ (1956b), *Normality and Pathology in Childhood. The Writings of Anna Freud, 6.* New York: International Universities Press.

Freud, S. (1911), A case of paranoia. *Standard Edition,* 12:3-82. London: Hogarth Press, 1958.

_____ (1915), A case of paranoia running counter to the psycho-analytic theory of disease. *Standard Edition,* 14:261-272. London: Hogarth Press, 1957.

_____ (1917), A metapsychological supplement to the theory of dreams. *Standard Edition,* 14: 217-235. London: Hogarth Press, 1957.

Frosch, J. (1964), The psychotic character: Clinical psychiatric considerations. *Psychiat. Quart.,* 38:81-96.

_____ (1970), Pyschoanalytic considerations of the psychotic character. *J. Amer. Psychoanal. Assn.,* 18:24-50.

Hartmann, H. (1953), Contributions to the metapsychology of schizophrenia. *The Psychoanalytic Study of the Child,* 8:177-198. New York: International Universities Press.

Hay, A. J., & Forrest, A. D. (1972), The diagnosis of schizophrenia and paranoid psychosis: An attempt at clarification. *Brit. J. Med. Psychol.,* 45:233-241.

Hill, L. B. (1955), *Psychotherapeutic Intervention in Schizophrenia.* Chicago: University of Chicago Press.

Jacobson, E. (1954), Federn's contribution to ego psychology and psychoses. *J. Amer. Psychoanal. Assn.,* 2:519-525.

Kafka, J. S. (1971), Ambiguity for individuation. *Archiv. Gen. Psychiat.,* 25:232-239.

Kasanin, J. (1951), *Language and Thought in Schizophrenia.* Berkeley: University of California Press.

Kernberg, O. (1967), Borderline personality organization. *J. Amer. Psychoanal. Assn.,* 15:641-685.

_____ (1970), A psychoanalytic classification of character pathology. *J. Amer. Psychoanal. Assn.,* 18:800-822.

Klein, M. (1946), Notes on some schizoid mechanisms. *Internat. J. Psycho-Anal.,* 27:99-110.

Kohut, H. (1971), *The Analysis of the Self.* New York: International Universities Press.

Kraepelin, E. (1919), *Dementia Praecox,* trans. M. Barclay. Edinburgh: Livingstone.

Laing, R. D. (1967), *The Politics of Experience.* New York: Pantheon Books.

Menninger, K., Mayman, M., & Pruyser, P. (1963), *The Vital Balance.* New York: Viking.

Meyer, A. (1938), Proceedings of the 4th Conference on Psychiatric Education, Baltimore, Maryland, April 8-10, 1936. New York: National Conference for Mental Hygiene, p. 27.

Nunberg, H. (1920), On the catatonic attack. In: *Practice and Theory of Pyschoanalysis.* New York: Nervous and Mental Disease Monograph, No. 74, 1948, p. 3-23.

Rapaport, D., Gill, M. & Schafer, R. (1945-1946), *Diagnostic and Psychological Testing.* 2 vols. Chicago: Year Book Publishers.

Reichard, S. (1956), A re-examination of "Studies on Hysteria." *Psychoanal. Quart.,* 25:155-177.

Searles, H. F. (1965), *Collected Papers in Schizophrenia and Related Subjects.* New York: International Universities Press.

Schneider, K. (1959), *Clinical Psychopathology,* trans. M. W. Hamilton. New York: Grune & Stratton.

Storch, A. (1924), *The Primitive Archaic Forms of Inner Experience and Thought in Schizophrenia.* Nervous and Mental Disease Monog 36. Washington, D.c.: Nervous and Mental Disease Publishing Company.

Szasz, T. (1961), *The Myth of Mental Illness.* New York: Hoeber-Harper.

Tausk, V. (1933), On the origin of the "influencing machine" in schizophrenia. *Psychoanal. Quart.,* 2:519-556.

Zilboorg, G. (1941), *A History of Medical Psychology.* New York: Norton.

January, 1974

Aggression and Narcissistic Rage: A Clinical Elaboration

DAVID M. TERMAN, M.D. (*Chicago*)

After elucidating the clinical theory of the self in 1966 and in *The Analysis of the Self* (1971), Kohut (1972) defined another clinical entity—narcissistic rage—and placed it into the context of the newly developed theory.

Kohut calls our attention to a common, everyday phenomenon—the thirst for revenge. How well we all know it. Its tragic consequences have inspired some of the most gripping literature of our civilization. The paradigm might well be Captain Ahab in Melville's *Moby Dick*, as Kohut notes at the beginning of his paper on narcissistic rage. But Medea's revenge, too, can hardly be equalled for horror, nor Richard III for villainy; and the setting for the tragedy of Romeo and Juliet is also one of vengeance.

Yet, there is more to the clinical description. The thirst for revenge is not only the unrelenting need to right a wrong, it is also reactive. It is provoked by some injury to self-esteem—a narcissistic injury such as contempt, ridicule, or conspicuous defeat, or events which in any case are experienced as such by the injured party. Ahab, of course, was in relentless pursuit of the whale that had taken his leg. Medea had been rejected by Jason after having done everything possible to enhance his power and ambitions. And Richard III was

> Cheated of feature by dissembling nature,
> Deformed, unfinished, sent before my time
> Into this breathing world, scarse halfe made up,
> And that so lamely and unfashionable
> That dogs bark at me, as I halt by them.
>
> I: 1. 21-25

Freud (1916) had drawn our attention to this phenomenon in his paper on "Some Character Types Met with in Psychoanalytic Work." Quoting Richard's opening soliloquy, he pointed out that his wish for revenge was a reaction to the narcissistic injury he had sustained from nature. Freud noted that the wish to be exceptional stemmed from an "experience or suffering to which they [the patients] had been subjected in their earliest childhood, one in respect of which they knew themselves to be guiltless, and which they could look upon as an unjust disadvantage imposed upon them" (p. 313).

Kohut underlines the boundless, unrelenting quality of the wish to redress the injury. There is no empathy with the offender, no recognition of his separateness. He or it must only be blotted out, and there is no rest until the deed is accomplished, though in the process the avenger can also be undone.

Kohut makes further sense of the phenomenon by linking it with the vicissitudes of the infantile grandiose self. The rage is due to the need to insist on the absolute perfection of the self, arising when there is interference with the merger with an idealized self-object or if control over the mirroring self-object is lost. With greater economy, Kohut characterizes this rage as a reaction to the frustration of the *omnipotence* of the grandiose self. Its power over the self-object — either as the supplier of the idealized substance with which to merge or as the confirmation of one's own greatness — has become limited. This is then paralleled with the reaction of shame. Shame represents faulty discharge of the exhibition-istic wishes of the grandiose self, whereas rage represents the reaction to the frustration of the *omnipotence* of the grandiose self.

Interference with the merger with an idealized, omnipotent self-object may occur when either of two conditions is present: (a) when the self-object is unavailable, e.g., in a separation — like the weekend separation in an analysis; and (b) when the self-object is discredited — as in the discovery of flaws, death, defeat, or threat of defeat of the person or system within whose perfection one feels whole. The failure of a parent, the misunderstanding of an analyst, or the special and intense fear of opposing ideologies — the threat of Islam to medieval Christians, or of Godless communists to chauvinist Americans or capitalist imperialists to Russian communists — may all, with myriad implications and further qualifications, stand as examples of the latter condition.

The second area likely to stimulate rage is the failure of the self-object to provide the needed confirmation of the perfection of the self in whatever form and at whatever level the self needs to have such confirmation. I suspect this is necessary with every new acquisition of structure.

With every accretion to the self, there is insistence on the perfection of that new *part*. If the mirror does not provide the needed confirmation, it is smashed. Such was the wish of Ahab; such were the deeds of Richard and Medea. In the smashing of the offending mirror, one wipes out the flaw in the universe and establishes oneself as more powerful than any potential interference. In the clinical situation, this takes many forms, some of which I elaborate below.

Kohut discusses the therapeutic implications of this understanding of narcissistic rage. The gist of his position is that one cannot address oneself to the rage per se, but must deal with the archaic narcissistic matrix out of which it arises. That is, one must try to understand the way in which the archaic self is again damaged and in what the original damage consisted; then there will be a shift of such aggression in the service of realistic ambition. There will be neither unrelenting destruction nor vulnerability to narcissistic injury. (Neither education, the attempt to enlighten the individual so afflicted about the needs of others, nor the attempt to enlist the patient's momentarily detached observation is effective: the rage is only inflamed.) Kohut notes that the individual's increased capacity for empathy for his potential offenders may be a more certain sign of integration and repair of the damaged self than simply the eradication of all such tantrums. Of course, the development of such empathy could not take place without significant changes in the self, and hence the matrix out of which the rage arises is destroyed—or transformed. This process is like eradicating yellow fever by draining the swamps in which the mosquitos breed and maybe even converting the swamps to farmland.

The essentials of this formulation are, again, as follows: Narcissistic rage is described as the expression of a wish for unrelenting revenge, the need to right a wrong whatever the cost. Its origin is in the unmodified and split-off claims of the damaged grandiose self. It is the reaction to the frustration of the omnipotence of the grandiose self. It presupposes an earlier damage to the self, when the self could be whole only by virtue of the cooperation of the self-object. Its solution lies in the repair and integration of the damaged archaic self.

Clinical Implications

Kohut's formulation enables the analyst to approach such patients with less tendency to becoming angry or wishing to withdraw from them.

The Medeas and Richards of the world are not a savory lot. They treat those around them abominably. They tyrannize their "loved ones" and then self-righteously rage at their loved-ones' recalcitrance. And as the analyst becomes enmeshed in the patient's archaic narcissistic configurations, he too is subject to the same tyrannical and unempathic treatment.

As the treatment progresses, the amount of narcissistic rage decreases, the early self-damage is worked through, and the analyst becomes a "better" narcissistic object. For, as the analyst and patient understand more and more the vicissitudes of the transference—a dimension of which is the *correctness* of the patient's needs as they are understood in their *infantile* context—the analyst becomes empathic and hence completes the necessary self-experience required for the cohesion and subsequent integration of the archaic self-states.

It is both inevitable and essential that the patient experience the analyst as unempathic. This is, after all, a transference. Nonetheless, the degree of rage a patient experiences over what is, for example, an unavoidable and surely well-meaning misunderstanding of the precise reason for a current tension state may be bewildering to the analyst. The patient becomes unassuageable. No forgiveness is possible. The patient may demand an explanation for the error, but none will do. At such times the patient may experience attempts at genetic reconstruction—efforts to understand a crucial empathic failure of the parent in a context like the one being relived in the analysis—simply as devices to ward off the righteousness of his complaints. If ever an analyst feels like a pursued whale, it is at such times. The patient is relentless. Attacks on the weaknesses and defectiveness of the analyst are made with utter conviction, and they are accompanied by a feeling of enormous disillusion.

The nature of the analyst's perceived defects may derive from important aspects of the patient's own character that have been disavowed, or important aspects of the perceived parental character that have resulted in the patient's enmeshment in painful, inhuman, unempathic interactions. Most often, it is a combination of both.

What is the analyst to do at such junctures? It is tempting to confront the patient with the derivatives of his complaints. Confrontation alone, however, would interfere with the unfolding of the process of experiencing the analyst as part—a malfunctioning part—of the patient's self. Calling attention to any process that locates the source of the difficulty within the *patient* is experienced by the patient as a failure of empathy. For the essence of the experience is the failure of the analyst to function as part of the patient. And the fault, the blame at that moment, must be solely the analyst's.

When the patient's attacks center on defects in the analyst, they almost always include a real part of the analyst's character — or some aspect of his reaction to the patient. If one can find the portion in oneself that is, indeed, accurately perceived, and acknowledge both its existence and the distress it must have caused the patient, the patient's rage subsides, and he can recall the appropriate genetic situation; the analyst as idealized self-object is once more restored, and the reaction may eventually be seen as belonging more appropriately to the past. Much later, as a result of the experience of many such interactions, the self is less vulnerable, and the patient may look back and understand how much he has embodied the defect he has seen in the analyst — or how the perception of the analyst was grossly distorted by the experience of the parent in the past.

One patient, Mrs. A., made such vitriolic attacks on me frequently, but, in what has been a long and now apparently successful analytic effort, the number of such attacks has decreased. Two vignettes from her treatment will illuminate this discussion.

At one point she raged at some defect she had found in me and despaired at how sick and mentally confused I was. How could I have done such and such? I, as usual, confessed my ignorance of what might have set off the attack, but in doing so I was somewhat defensive. She then proceeded to tell me a parable about a leper who came to request lodging from a Samaritan. The man was dirty and repulsive and had running sores. He imperiously demanded to be fed, and the Samaritan reluctantly complied. After he had eaten, he demanded lodging — and so on — finally insisting that the host embrace him in bed because he was cold. As the host again reluctantly complied, the leper turned into Jesus Christ.

Both the patient and I realized that my understanding would not transform her into a savior, but might enable her to become an empathic person. Yet, it was only possible to maintain empathic contact with her leprous rage, and with the events that produced the cold, imperious grandiose self on the verge of fragmentation, if I understood the underlying process — and the narcissistic matrix out of which it arose.

The rewards of the understanding did come. Several years after that episode, she had again gone through a modified version of her despair over my inadequacy. This time it concerned my difficulty in maintaining my own self-esteem. When I acknowledged that, indeed, it could suffer under her attacks and that the suffering was irrational and a countertransference, she again became calm. But this time she said to me, "You know, my father always behaved so surely, and there could never be anything wrong with him. It was inconceivable that I should find him wanting—so I had to find things in you. Even if you were 99 44/100 per cent pure, I would have had to find the 56/100 to berate you with."

The remark indicated a growth in numerous capacities. When I was not needed to complete her archaic universe, I could be seen separately, and, hence, she could empathize with me. She could observe herself, distinguish between the present and the past, and test reality more accurately. The need to maintain archaic omnipotence was replaced by self-mastery and self-understanding. In this instance, my capacity to allow recognition of my defects permitted a real self-expansion and alleviated the necessity for maintaining a brittle grandiose self against an obdurate, autonomy-destroying, and primitive, idealized parental imago. Although the "defect" was understandable in adult functioning, it had to be regressively experienced as intolerable. Genetically, it was indeed the father's insensitive insistence on his own perfection while coldly damaging the patient's perfection that proved to be the central trauma.

Clinical Example

Mrs. R., whose central vulnerabilities were similar to the patient cited, was 42 when she came for analysis. Her husband had decided to divorce her several months earlier, and she realized that she was getting depressed even beyond what would have been appropriate in those circumstances. She had had a period of depression with considerable incapacity some fifteen years earlier, and a four-year period of treatment at that time.

She told in a rather garish and bizarre way of a very disturbed and chaotic life history. From the first, her appearance was not quite right. Her make-up was too heavily applied. She wore her hair long and tied it like a child's in a pony tail. Her dress was both a little too tight and too short for a woman her age. She looked like an older woman trying to look young and glamorous, but in her attempt to cover up her defects, she succeeded only in emphasizing them. She spoke in an exaggerated and exhibitionistic way about her sex life. She extolled its freedom and revealed, prematurely and without adequate restraint, some of its more intimate details. She matter-of-factly stated that she and her husband had had numerous affairs, the details of which they shared. Her first affair had begun when their only child, a daughter, was a young child, some eighteen years ago. A succession of lovers followed.

In addition to their sexual problems, the patient and her husband—an accountant—had had numerous interpersonal difficulties which had led to their divorce. In general, she had been angry, demanding, and frustrated; and he had been passive, reluctantly compliant, and withdrawn into himself or his work. The couple's daughter had many developmental problems, and though quite gifted, had not finished college, but was then married and working. Mrs. R. was aware of her daughter's difficulties and felt disappointed with her.

Mrs. R. came from a wealthy, Eastern family and was the oldest of five children. A sister was eighteen months younger and then three more siblings, two boys and another girl, followed every three years. Her mother was a flighty, overindulgent woman who greatly delighted in her bright, precocious and eager-to-please eldest child. She had nevertheless entrusted much of her daily, routine care to a young, conscientious maid.

Mother had felt that this arrangement was perfect until her second child was born; that she had managed to "arrange" for her elder daughter as though nothing had happened. She maintained this in spite of the fact that the maid who had cared for the patient married and left the household shortly after the sister's birth. She lived in a fey, make-believe world in which she could tolerate neither anger nor the absence of love. She tried to banish unpleasantness by cajoling, seducing, and denying it. When the patient began analysis, her attitude toward her mother was one of intense hostility—indeed, it was paranoid. She considered her mother responsible for her ills because of her diabolical need to keep her children dependent on her. She was seen as the center of the family she dominated by her wiles. On the other hand, Mrs. R. felt only sympathy for her benighted father, who felt trapped and went along with his wife's foolishness in spite of his better judgment.

Even at the outset it was clear that the patient's account was a gross distortion of the family situation. The father was hardly a milquetoast. In his work, he was a leader. Toward his family, he was dutiful but distant, disdainful, and intolerant. He scorned as sissys fathers who were affectionate with their daughters. He was given to public beratings of inferiors and often left his employees humiliated and tearful. He arranged the world in perfect harmony, and only fools interfered with his wisdom, which was exercised protectively only in behalf of his underlings. The patient recalled no such paternalistic attitudes toward her. She was the exemplary child. But she harbored no conscious rebellion or hatred for her father and did not complain of his treatment of others. It was especially difficult for the patient to grasp this aspect of her father, for in her early adult life he suffered a personality collapse and committed suicide.

It became clear, however, that although she appeared to have avoided her father's outbursts of intemperate bigotry, she did not escape the indignities of his "enlightened" childrearing practices. Reflecting his Prussian ancestry, he was concerned with cleanliness, toughness, and a "healthy" attitude toward the body. He subjected the family to cold showers and hot baths, and insisted on bathroom and bedroom nudity and openness. The children were to regard the body with proper clinical detachment, and exposure was expected to ward off "sick curiosity."

The further childhood history was one of primary investment in fairy-princess fantasy and the desire (successfully fulfilled) to please various authorities. Adolescence was marked by intense depreciation of her mother and premature sexual activity. She met her future husband in college. She then had few other boy friends, essentially clinging to the young man who passively permitted the dependence.

I shall summarize the transference vicissitudes from a distant, and, hence, wide perspective. In the early years, the imperium of self knew little else but the righteousness of its needs and its total right to have me, the omnipotent analyst, at its service. The patient's perception of the defects in my functioning was that I did not take her tensions seriously enough; whatever inadequacies I had in being able to relieve her tensions she felt as a deliberate withholding or selfishness. I could, but I just didn't want to, or I was too lazy, or cared nothing for her. Whenever she believed that I was able to understand her correctly, she felt wonderful; then she often had flying dreams, and I was correspondingly idealized. Inevitably and rapidly, the idealizations were followed by terrible disillusionments, as I inevitably failed to omnipotently or omnisciently fulfill some needed soothing function; and the disillusionment would be accompanied by rage and regression to early self-soothing mechanisms, including masturbation and ferocious eating. She felt so cold that she could not warm up. In the regressions, or on the way out of them, she often spoke of her mother's defects. Early in the analysis, the mother was seen as omnipotently withholding or punishing, or capricious; later the patient focused on her flightiness and insubstantiality, her lack of capacity to understand the seriousness and urgency of her tensions, and, quite surely, on her inability to aid the patient's autonomy with appropriate substitution of differentiated approval of her emerging separateness from engulfing oneness.

However, the core of the injury to the self around which radiated both the regression and the later lack of structure was the transition from mother to father. The trauma occurred as the grandiose self turned for confirmation to the idealized, omnipotent father. He wielded added impact because of the disillusionment with the mother, both because of the birth of the brother and mother's fears of the patient's narcissistic rage. But the father crushed the tender, prized, and quite grandiose little-girl self. As the little girl presented herself for adoration to her powerful father, she experienced the chill of clinical detachment and cold disdain. In the experiences of family nudity, the exhibitionistic wish was both stimulated and denied, but the brutal disdain of spontaneous self-pleasure or the invitation to admire was communicated in all her father's interactions. Her friends had observed that the father radiated an aura of depreciating disdain. Children were inferior beings who were to be made into proper people, surely not to be warmly enjoyed.

The patient quickly renounced her exhibitionistic and narcissistic strivings and allied herself with her father. She experienced a reinforcement of her more infantile grandiosity by a kind of identification with his disdainful absoluteness, though there was no lack of internal source for the reactive tyranny she would need to impose on all potential admirers.

Her adult sexual life was a perpetual quest for the man who would be the suitable admirer of her infantile splendors, the man who would lavish all on her. As each candidate failed and she tyrannically tried to coerce his admiration, she was incredulous and affronted by his withdrawal; she would try further coercion and scathingly castrate her would-be suitor with reminders of his inadequacy. She would become further disillusioned because of an awareness that the suitor's reactions were not spontaneous, or that he was then too weak to be of value.

It was not difficult to project the bind in which her husband had found himself. Even before the divorce, he had periodically tried to extricate himself from the marriage. When he did so, he was faced, of course, with her uncomprehending rage and bottomless depression, followed by frantic coercive promises. It was his final abandonment that precipitated her wish for treatment.

As the treatment unfolded, I, too, was presented with urgent demands for help. For actually, her wish to be really admired was usually not experienced consciously. As it emerged preconsciously, she became more tense and edgy, threatening to break into narcissistic rage at any moment. She became much more coercive and demanding at such times, needing a variety of narcissistic homeostatic functions. Although these intense, specific needs were preconscious, she could tolerate no delay in their understanding and subsequent amelioration. They were both a defense against the traumatic state anticipated with the experiences of the wish, and symptomatic of the traumatic state itself. I always attended to those homeostatic functions with inevitable failure, and she reacted with rage and imminent fragmentation. As the analysis went on and the homeostatic capacity improved, we could get nearer to the wishes and their attendant responses.

This sequence was encapsulated in a theme often repeated in dreams. In the early stages of the analysis, she would be admiring a landscape, often from a height, and then become aware of a dangerously rising sea. Later, she would catch the attention of a much admired man who indicated that she was, indeed, special, after which she would become aware of a storm gathering in the distance.

Yet, as she discovered, for example, that she actually found herself wearing a dress she hoped I would like, she was intensely ashamed and furious with me. The trauma of the intense overexposure of her own and father's body was worked through repeatedly in such contexts. Most of all, though, the intensity and cruelty of her father's utter contempt for such wishes for admiration of her body were gradually connected with her own shame and real feeling of intense vulnerability. At such times she could movingly weep for herself and experience me as genuinely understanding. Thus, with great delicacy, the gentle tendrils of the vulnerable self were extended to me for gentle understanding. She could then evoke compassion, and she was satisfied by it.

As the tenderer central portions of the self engaged more in the analysis, she became more involved with her lifelong interest in fine art. She brought in reproductions of Ingres paintings as they symbolized her own ideals of beauty. And she became especially preoccupied with the work of the French classisist, Jacques Louis David, whose the Oath of the Horatii, a picture very popular in Revolutionary France, depicts the legendary Horatii—three brothers about to battle another three brothers, Curratii, for the glory of Rome. They are pridefully raising their arms in patriotic purpose, indifferent to the mournful, suffering women depicted in the background. Mrs. R. was quite conscious of being identified with those hapless women. In thinking of these women who were victimized by the heroic men, she suddenly thought of Brunhild. Brunhild was surrounded by a magic fire, placed there by her father. It could only be penetrated by a fearless and pure man—Siegfried. How similar to the plight of Mrs. R. The fire of her narcissistic rage had indeed been placed around her by her damaging encounter with her father. She, like the sad women of the Horatii, had given her heart to him, only to be hurt by his own grandiose conceptions of himself. In turning passivity into activity and in protecting her vulnerability under the armor of a split-off, imperious grandiosity, she, like Brunhild, turned away any man who would touch her.

The rage had been proportionate to the injury. The injury was to the grandiose self — the perfect, beautiful, adorable child. The father was expected to confirm the child's beauty and perfection. The lack of such a response threatened fragmentation of the self, of the organization that was a whole self. In part, that organization might have been already exaggerated because of the mother's "excessive" response to the child — one could only be whole if one were adorable. In any case, average, realistic confirmation was not available; instead, the father's scathing, moralistic demeanor inflicted active injury to the self. The energy needed to coerce such a recalcitrant and damaging portion of the world was very great — and hence the rage.

Discussion

This patient's injury to the self was severe and crippling.[1] The restless search to heal her wound and continue her development dominated her life. She failed to develop either ego ideal or superego. It was remarkable how justified she felt in her rages at me and at others. She experienced no guilt. She frequently feared retaliation, but even that fear was minimal. Her primary anxiety with respect to me was that I would cease to do what I was "supposed" to do for her. The prospect of retaliation evoked injured self-righteousness more often than fear. But as she became more stable, and as there were both more enduring cohesion and better integration of the grandiose self, her capacity to perceive the needs of others and feel a corresponding concern for them began to evolve spontaneously. Her

[1] The nucleus of her pathology was at the earliest oedipal level, which suggests that the need for the self-object's function had not disappeared with the advent of the oedipal period. Indeed, the possibility for serious failure in function of the parental response is an area that can cause considerable future pathology. Kohut, of course, has described the traumatic disillusionment in the parent during this period and its consequences for the later weakness in the idealization of the superego. This patient shows the nucleus of severe pathology in a very traumatic *mirroring*. And, in fact, one might look at much of the parental role during the oedipal period as a mirroring function — not of the whole child, but of the more valued masculine or feminine editions the child is trying to create. The parents' primary function and value to the child is still essentially a narcissistic one, though more narrowly defined. The parent must be the model to idealize and the mirror to reflect the child's growing gendered self.

intense idealization—and fear—of me was gradually replaced with a friendly affection. She found that she had more energy for work, and she began to feel the need for more meaningful internal goals. She recognized that her effort to coerce a blissful recognition of her adorableness from the world was both impossible and inappropriate, and she confined herself more and more to the task of working it through in the analysis.

The "wrong" to which the patient reacted with rage was an inevitable misunderstanding of an imperfection in either my response or my character: in other words, in her view I had failed to comply with an archaic narcissistic need. The urgent need to right the wrong of the nonempathic connection was uppermost. The capacity to experience the analyst in this way and to work through the experience resulted in many favorable transformations of the primitive, brittle narcissistic structures into capacities for empathy and reliable self-esteem. The rages, as noted, decreased in frequency and intensity, with corresponding increases in understanding of both the past determinants of the vulnerabilities and the analyst's real position in the matrix of their re-experience.

Several authorities have related pathological aggressiveness in children to defects in ego organization. Anna Freud (1949) believed that the "appropriate therapy was to be directed to the neglected, defective side, i.e., the emotional libidinal development" (p. 497). According to Beata Rank (1948), "By providing an emotional climate favorable to the development of an ego which has the capacity to organize and to control drives, we may be able to modify or even eliminate the destructive element of aggression" (p. 48). These formulations may be more specifically understood in the light of the psychology of the self. The "favorable emotional climate" is the good parenting that provides the required self-object. Availability, optimal mediation of tension—including protection against overstimulation—the capacity to enjoy the child and have proper appreciation of his emerging capacities are among those crucial parental functions. The cases these authors cited exhibited gross deficiencies in these very areas.

Balint's (1965) description of the transference vicissitudes of adult patients suffering from a "basic fault" corresponds with some of the narcissistic transferences delineated by Kohut. Although Balint conceptualizes the regressive analytic relation of these patients in terms of object love—"primary love," in his terms—the phenomena are strikingly similar: "The object [analyst] is indeed only an object and must be treated as such, i.e., no consideration or regard can be paid to its interests, sensitivities or well being; it must be, and in fact is, simply taken for granted" (p. 124). When the analyst is unable to fit in easily with such needs,

Balint writes, hate is generated. He describes the necessity for the analyst to understand the patient's need to use him in this way as he relives early deficiencies in parental care in order to make "a new beginning."

However, if one considers that these attacks and impossible demands on the analyst stem from the need to repeat earlier experiences of frustration because of guilt over underlying aggression, one approaches them differently. The analyst then calls the patient's attention to the facts of his aggression, his misuse (in adult reality terms) of the analyst, the impossibility of satisfying his demands, or to some possible violation of his standards. But narcissistic patients only experience such confrontations and interpretations as rebukes against their need to use the analyst as their self-object. The analyst is then in the undesirable position of reduplicating the past and denying to the patient the opportunity to distinguish it from the present. An interruption in the analysis may then result.

Viewing the problem developmentally, in terms of the hierarchy of the models of the mind proposed by Gedo and Goldberg (1973), one cannot appropriately use the construct of guilt to explain the phenomena. Guilt belongs to a later stage of development — it follows the internalization of the superego, i.e., the resolution of the Oedipus complex. The patient I have described here clearly demonstrated an absence of guilt. After considerable working-through, she could begin to consider herself wrong in areas touching her vulnerability. But by the time she was able to do that, narcissistic rage was no longer a salient problem. The resolution of the self-vulnerability made the rage unnecessary and then permitted the growth of the capacity for guilt. Such an understanding of the patient's experience of the analyst as a reproduction of an earlier infantile state that antedated significant structural accretions, permits the systematic working-through of the damage.

Aggression and Narcissistic Rage

Kohut's formulations regarding the nature and genesis of narcissistic rage in the context of the cohesion of the self greatly facilitate the systematic and empathic treatment of narcissistic problems. They also offer clarification and separation of properties heretofore attributed to the concept of the aggressive drive, and help delineate a developmental line of aggression. It is beyond the scope of this paper to give a detailed review of the concept of the aggressive drive or to spell out that line entirely, but a

251

few comments may be helpful in indicating the direction of continuing theoretical expansion.

Freud's first formulations of what he later called aggression were closer to our current concepts of narcissistic rage. In 1915, he wrote, regarding hate, that "the true prototypes of the relation of hate are not from sexual life, but from the ego's struggle to preserve and maintain itself" (p. 138). At that time, he regarded hate as a derivative of "ego instincts" concerned with self-preservation and opposed to libidinal drives.

When, in 1920, he postulated the death instinct and the aggressive drive deriving from it, he reformulated ego instincts as libidinal cathexes of the ego and hence no longer in conflict with libido. He warned of the speculative nature of the death instinct. He later added (1923) that the "distinction between the two classes of instincts does not seem sufficiently assured and it is possible that facts of clinical analysis may be found which will do away with its pretension" (p. 42).

Hartmann et al. (1948) subsequently tried to make a more explicit parallel between the properties of an aggressive drive and the sexual drive. They characterized aggression as having an "impetus" that required discharge. The degree of intensity varied, but the aim of total discharge was destruction. Brenner (1971) agreed with the conceptualization of aggression as a drive, but he saw the aims of aggression as varying from one stage of life to another. He pointed out that death is a meaningless word before a certain age and "The recognition that others feel as we do is likewise absent in the very young" (p. 141). He added that "aggressive aims vary with mental development and experience " They seem to be related to what hurts or frightens a child. Stone (1971), in his extended review of psychoanalytic thought on the subject, went further. He questioned the usefulness of retaining the concept of "primary or essential aggression." He stated, "The murderous thrust originally awakened in the earliest experiences of helplessness may provide *Anlage* of hostility, rage, and aggression resembling 'drive.' However, this cannot be drive in the inborn, constant, autochthonous sense of psychoanalytic usage" (p. 220). He added that "Whereas pain, death, and destruction can be, and too often are, the results of aggression, there is little reason to assume the existence of a primary drive to bring them about for their own sake" (p. 239).

I suggest that Kohut's concept of narcissistic rage accounts for the nature of aggression during the consolidation of the self as both "drive" and "reactive." It may well be that the locus of driven aggression is in the process of the cohesion of the self and its converse, the threatened fragmentation of the self. Whereas parental participation is required for the

252

cohesion of the self, the failure of such participation results in a variety of vulnerabilities in the self. The failure is experienced as a hurt. Hence, the self-vulnerability is both reactive — to the parental failure — and internal, a continuing intrapsychic state. It is the violation of important infantile narcissistic needs that "hurt or frighten the child" or leave him feeling helpless. The internal experience of the external event of hurt or helplessness is the interference with the self. Kohut's concept of narcissism may delineate an important aspect of all infantile aggression — that is, aggression that occurs until the internalization of the superego at the resolution of the Oedipus.

Sibling rivalry is a most exquisite example of narcissistic vulnerability in action. The issues are in sharp focus: who got more, the conviction that the other sibling did, the need to "even" a score that is never easily evened. In normal households this does not lead to murder, but it is a most frequent cause of minor mayhem, and there is usually little empathy for the sibling offender.

Internally and in fantasy, however, narcissistic rage — or narcissistic tensions — may also be an important source of oedipal aggression. The degree of resolution of the latter depends not only on conflict with other structures, but also on the degree of interference or facilitation of phallic self-expansion. The limitation of the area of narcissistic concern to that of phallic and gender-related self-expansion reduces the area of narcissistic vulnerability and hence the rage. But it is the involvement of the phallic grandiose self that contributes an element of the characteristic coloring of infantile oedipal rivalry — there can be only one big penis, the father's, and it must be erased and destroyed. Indeed, the driving quality of infantile object-directed aggression may be precisely due to the vulnerability of the restricted, but yet grandiose, phallic self whose injury is the cause of the child's wish to blot out the offender.

It is the gradual limitation of those aims and their transformation into workable, realizable goals and the subsequent involvement with more discrete acts that changes the pattern of aggression further and then aids in its internalization. In its dynamic interaction with the experience of the responding parent, it becomes transformed into guilt.

The more boundless violent forms of aggression usually occur in the disruption of earlier phases of self-cohesion (e.g., mergers) or at the points of transition between phases of self-development. The variety and intensity of parental participation is also a factor in the intensity of the aggressive response, for during these phases the parental response is part of the structure. As Kohut has shown, the self-vulnerabilities during the phase of whole self-cohesion, before the restriction to gender- and

253

phallic-related narcissism, may be split off and/or repressed with the development of postoedipal structures, but these vulnerabilities are the source of later spiteful, tyrannical, outwardly directed aggression, or, as he suggests, the psychosomatic disturbances of inwardly directed narcissistic rage.

Kohut has further called attention to the difference between narcissistic rage and mature aggression, emphasizing the boundlessness and inexorability of the former, and the limited, realistic, goal-oriented, and deeper empathic awareness of the latter. Threats to the integrity of the mature self still summon a protective, aggressive response that may be of considerable intensity. These threats, however, constitute real dangers to life and limb, or real challenges to the existence or integrity of groups or institutions with which one has enlarged one's ideals. The response is sufficient to protect rather than to erase. The limitations of the means and ends noted above determine the response. With greater flexibility and independence, with the expansion of the self and the relative emancipation from obligatory dependence on archaic self-objects, there is need to explore and deepen experience. This we understand to be creativity, and its motivation at this level is self-expansion.

However, when aggression has these limited properties so much at the service of specific aims of the broader organization, it merits neither the appellation "drive," in the sense Stone has noted, nor the description "destructive."

Following Gedo and Goldberg's (1973) hierarchical schema of models of the mind, we may best understand aggression as a function of different organizational phases. The nature of the structure determines the properties of aggression. Before self-cohesion, aggression can be thought of as a pattern of diffuse discharge. With self-cohesion, aggression acquires the characteristic noted in narcissistic rage. It acquires its driving properties from the importance of self-cohesion. Restriction of narcissistic aims to phallic- and gender-related expansion restricts acute narcissistic vulnerability to those aims and conflicts, but also helps to give the characteristic coloring to infantile oedipal aggression. Later mature forms of aggression may be employed for realistic defense and for real responses to real and specific threats. The intensity may be very great as these aggressive responses connect with the central experience of vulnerability of the nuclear cohesive self. As aggression is used in the service of self-elaboration and creativity, its forms change further and it further acquires the properties of refinement, precision, and flexibility.

None of these forms of aggression necessitates the hypothesis of a separate continuous driving force. The driving qualities of aggression in the phase of consolidation of the self derive from the imperatives of the self's cohesion. Perhaps the generalized statement can be made that the organization of the apparatus as a whole helps to determine a direction of growth and in general is a "driving force" using aggression in its many forms as one of its tools for both its maintenance and its growth.

REFERENCES

Balint, M. (1965), *Primary Love and Psychoanalytic Technique*. New York: Liveright Publishing Corp.

Beres, D. (1952), Clinical notes on aggression in children. *The Psychoanalytic Study of the Child*, 7:241-263. New York: International Universities Press.

Brenner, C. (1971), The psychoanalytic concept of aggression. *Inter. J. Psychoanal.*, 52:137-144.

Freud, A. (1949), Aggression in relation to emotional development: normal and pathological. *The Writings of Anna Freud*, 4:489-497. New York: International Universities Press, 1968.

Freud, S. (1915), Instincts and their vicissitudes. *Standard Edition*, 14:111-140. London: Hogarth Press.

——— (1916), Some character types met with in psychoanalytic work. *Standard Edition*, 14:309-331. London: Hogarth Press, 1957.

——— (1920), Beyond the pleasure principle. *Standard Edition*, 18:7-66. London: Hogarth Press, 1955.

——— (1923), The ego and the id. *Standard Edition*, 19:3-66. London: Hogarth Press, 1961.

Gedo, J. & Goldberg, A. (1973), *Models of the Mind*. Chicago: University of Chicago Press.

Hartmann, H., Kris, E., & Loewenstein, R. (1948), Notes on the theory of aggression. *The Psychoanalytic Study of the Child*, 3/4:9-34. New York: International Universities Press.

Kohut, H. (1966), Forms and transformations of narcissism. *J. Amer. Psychoanal. Assn.*, 14:243-272.

——— (1971), *The Analysis of the Self*. New York: International Universities Press.

——— (1972), Thoughts on narcissism and narcissistic rage. *The Psychoanalytic Study of the Child*, 27:360-400. New York: International Universities Press.

Rank, B. (1948), Aggression. *The Psychoanalytic Study of the Child*, 3/4:43-48. New York: International Universities Press.

Stone, L. (1971), Reflections on the psychoanalytic concept of aggression. *Psychoanal. Quart.*, 40:195-244.

April, 1974

III

PSYCHOANALYTIC EDUCATION

The Problem of the
Training Analysis

H. A. VAN DER STERREN, M.D. (*Amsterdam*)

with a Preface by

HENRY SEIDENBERG, M.D. (*Chicago*)

Faced with reconciling irreconcilables, training analysts have for many years been studying the problem of the training analysis and its relation to the psychoanalyic education of their professional analysands. The issue centers around the ways and means of synthesizing the analyst's role as therapist, administrator, and educator.

Dr. van der Sterren's paper makes a timely contribution to the continuing attempt to resolve this dilemma. Other papers dealing with the issue have appeared in recent journals. The *Journal of the American Psychoanalytic Association* presented two papers promulgating opposing views: McLaughlin (1973) challenges the active contribution of the training analyst to the administrative deliberations and decisions of his institute regarding the progression in training of his own analysand. Calef and Weinshel (1973), on the other hand, make the point that the training analyst is in a position to assess his candidate-patient's capacity to be analyzed and to analyze. Under certain circumstances, such assessments may be reported to the administration of the institute. In past years many other authors have represented differing views of resolving this dilemma. Recently, Fleming (1973) sees four problems in training analysis that are not present in the usual therapeutic situation: "I hope to show that the exigencies of training when imbricated with educational realities have a bearing on both the therapeutic transference-counter-transference interactions and on the development of self-analytic skills. These ... problems appear, first, in the candidate's experience of being a patient; second, his experience in also being an analyst; third, his integration of the simultaneous experience of being a patient and a student analyst with both a training analyst and supervisor; and fourth, his experience in terminating his training analysis" (p. 24). "It is not important

---

Dr. H. A. van der Sterren died suddenly on April 27, 1974. This paper was originally written in honor of Dr. Richard Sterba, on the occasion of his 75th birthday.

Dr. Henry Seidenberg is Dean of Education at the Chicago Institute for Psychoanalysis.

whether the training analyst writes a letter to the Education Committee; the important thing is the way he handles reality while simultaneously keeping the analytic process moving ahead" (p. 31). Kairys (1964) advocated that the training analysis be separated from the rest of analytic training as a way of managing the incompatibility of combining the role of teacher-judge and therapist in the training analyst.

Because Dr. van der Sterren ends his paper with a request for information from other institutes as to how they have solved the above problem, I wish to conclude this preface by describing the method in use at the Institute for Psychoanalysis in Chicago. The selection of candidates has always been a two-step procedure. Acceptance of the applicant was made after several interviews. If the applicant was in analysis, his analyst's opinion and advice were sought; if he was not in analysis, he was referred to a training analyst. Following a period of analysis, the candidate would, on his own initiative, apply for matriculation (seminars and supervised analysis). Again he was interviewed and his analyst asked for an assessment. The analyst reported at his own option. Throughout the course of the training the analyst was asked for assessments.

In 1973 this procedure underwent a modification. The training analyst, who had heretofore been asked whether he wished to contribute to selection and progression decisions involving his training analysand, is no longer officially informed of a selection or progression issue, nor are his advice and assessment solicited. The other steps in selection and progression remain the same.

At the Chicago Institute we look upon confidentiality as an important consideration in maintaining the integrity of the psychoanalytic process. Even more vital is the need to protect the analyst and his patient from the anxieties that would inevitably be generated by breaching the design of the psychoanalytic situation. It is for this reason that the training analyst is no longer solicited for assessments of his analysand. We are observing our new stance and hope to report our findings at a later time.

We are grateful to Dr. van der Sterren for bringing us the approach of the Dutch Psychoanalytic Society to the problem of the training analysis.

Problems of psychoanalytic training and, in particular, problems pertaining to the training analysis have long been a subject of interest. I have the impression that there exists a widespread measure of dissatisfaction with the present state of affairs. Usually one finds that the drawbacks of the prevailing system are pointed out, while changes that might ameliorate its faults are seldom proposed. In the process of reading the numerous publications and discussions on this subject, especially certain detailed expositions of relatively trivial points, I have not been able to escape the feeling that all of this somehow was intended to obscure one single difficult, but very special, problem that overshadows all others.

In my opinion, this cardinal and preponderant problem is inherent in the rule prevailing in most of the analytic societies requiring the training analyst sooner or later to convey his opinion and evaluation of the candidate to the training committee. This creates a situation, as many other writers have also pointed out, in which the training analyst must simultaneously assume two functions that are in essence mutually exclusive. Specifically, he must be a therapist, with the attendant attitude of benevolent neutrality, and—at the same time—he must pass judgment. Nor does this judgment remain within the confines of the consultation room; it is imparted to others who must make decisions affecting the future career of the candidate. The progress and continuation of the analysis, and sometimes also the recognition of the candidate as an analyst, depend on this judgment.

Such an arrangement is very wrong. For in this fashion the candidate becomes *realistically* dependent on the analyst with regard to his future training, career, and work. This fact is so completely contradictory to a cardinal principle of analytic work—i.e., the benevolent neutrality of the analyst—that I cannot overcome my astonishment that, despite the recognized incorrectness of such a method, it continues to be practiced. The fact of this *real* dependency affects the course of the analysis *always*—and sometimes to a severe degree—from the first to the very last day.

After all, the aim of the analysis is to enable the analysand to gain disposal as fully as possible of the talents and capabilities that have been compromised or inhibited by the neurotic process. The analysis should aim at the analysand's becoming, as far as possible, a genuinely independent human being. We know the essential importance—especially in the transference—of the analysis of needs and feelings of dependency, protection, and submission, of wishes for praise and approval, and of the fears of punishment and disapproval; and of the persistent defenses against these passive needs, or of stubborn resistance against a reasonable degree of acquiescence. But when the analyst has the power, and even the duty to decide on the fate of his analysand, then analysis of the aforementioned essential features is rendered impossible. For a *real* dependency is a given fact, and not susceptible to analysis. An additional difficulty is that it becomes impossible to distinguish between the neurotic dependency—or the defenses against this—and the real dependency, so that the neurotic dependency-feelings often become harder to deal with. Other writers, too, have pointed out the incompatibility of preserving an attitude of "benevolent neutrality" toward the analysand on the one hand, while being required on the other hand to report to a committee that will make decisions, in large part based on this opinion, affecting an important sector of the analysand's life. Yet it would seem as if the realization has failed to strike home that in this way the very essence and core of the analytic process is being attacked, and in many quarters the same old method nonetheless continues to be followed with seeming equanimity—or perhaps, even so, with trepidation.

A further consideration underlying my criticism is the *objective* difficulty — at least in my opinion — of trying to evaluate the current state of affairs in an analysis, and the even greater difficulty of trying to estimate future developments. I sometimes say, knowing that in so doing I exaggerate, that the two people least able to estimate the progress of an analysis are the analyst and analysand themselves, and that the people best qualified to judge this are an uncle and aunt whom the patient visits once a year.

Furthermore — and this is even more important — there are powerful *subjective* factors influencing the opinion of the analyst regarding the candidate. Unconscious libidinal and aggressive feelings of the analyst toward the candidate are commonly recognized as potential pitfalls — *but* the unconscious narcissism of the analyst is a far more important and serious source of potential trouble. There are colleagues who are so convinced of the excellence of their own work that they deem every candidate they have in analysis suitable to become an analyst; and there are others who cannot conceive that one of their candidate-patients might ever hope to attain a level as high as their own. I myself have seen the results of the former orientation: many candidates whose aptitude had been praised by their analysts turned out to be abject failures in the course of several years.

When in 1959 I was elected chairman of the Dutch Psychoanalytic Society — which at that time meant that I was automatically also chairman of the Training Committee — we discussed this problem, and the Society accepted our proposal that henceforth the training analyst be forbidden to communicate information regarding his candidate to the Training Committee, or (for that matter) to anyone else. Although this proposal met with quite fierce opposition, it was ultimately adopted by a considerable majority.

Once this decision had been made, the remainder of the training program was modified to suit the new conditions. The person who wishes to enter training addresses himself to the Training Committee which has been chosen — elected — by the Society. The Committee appoints three training analysts, each of whom separately interviews the potential candidate, and each of whom independently submits his own opinion regarding the suitability of the applicant. Of course, the applicant is fully aware of this procedure. It is noteworthy that in general the opinions of the three interviewers prove to have a high degree of congruence. If the applicant is accepted for analytic training, he chooses from the available list the training analyst with whom he wishes to do his analysis. His analysis thus becomes in every sense a regular therapeutic analysis, which need be in no way inferior to a normal therapeutic analysis. It is my opinion that the training analysis need not be carried any further or "deeper" than an ordinary therapeutic analysis, as is sometimes averred. As long as a reasonable therapeutic result is achieved, I am generally satisfied. When the analysis has been under way for at least a year, the candidate may participate in the theoretical courses, but he is not required to do so. After one more year, he may participate in the technical seminars (once again, he does not have to), after which he is expected to commence with his first control analysis without too much delay; in fact, some candidates postpone this step for quite some time. This analysis is supervised by a training analyst, but not by the same one the candidate has been in analysis with—or with whom he is still in analysis (as frequently occurs). Twice a year the supervisor submits a brief evaluation of the candidate's work to the Training Committee. The candidate is required to treat at least three cases under supervision, but many exceed this number.

The decision whether or not to admit the candidate to membership in the Society, which signifies his recognition as an analyst, is based on the opinions of the three colleagues who interviewed him prior to his acceptance for training, and on the opinions of his supervisors.

The objection has often been made that under the present system the controls safeguarding the quality of the candidates have been so attenuated, that nowadays many unsuitable candidates are nevertheless able to become analysts. In my opinion, one should not underestimate the value of the opinions of the supervisors. Moreover, a certain measure of control exists while the candidate's own analysis is still going on. If I notice that a patient—and thus also a candidate in training—communicates in a very confused way, this confusion then becomes a topic in the analysis. And should I notice that a candidate manifests psychotic traits, I would also bring this into discussion in the analysis, and pose the question whether the candidate's wish to become an analyst is a wise one. I have never had to deal with such a situation, but in any case these points of discussion and the ensuing results would remain completely within the framework of the analysis and within the confines of the consulting room.

I have been impressed by the fact that many of those who write on the subject of training analysis find encounters with their candidates at courses and seminars a serious problem. I readily admit that such encounters can influence the course of an analysis, can complicate transference and countertransference relations, but in my opinion when the significance of such incidents for the analysand is thoroughly discussed, the result is often ultimately beneficial to the entire analysis. Some writers find it hard to decide whether they think that the supervisor should limit his role to that of helper and teacher, or whether he should also analyze the candidate. In my opinion, the latter practice should most decidedly be avoided: I find it confusing, impossible, and improper.

The essence of the system as it now functions in the Netherlands is that, although the entire training program is followed under the tutelage of the Training Committee, the training analysis proper has been so detached from the system that it can take the course of a regular therapeutic analysis. I myself have a great sense of well-being from this system, and I even have the impression that candidates nowadays, when they come for supervision, work better than they did formerly. And when this question was once again brought to discussion in the Society a couple of years ago, the great majority of members once again proved to favor the present system.

I have surveyed the literature on this subject, and I wish to give a brief — and therefore probably incomplete — report of my findings:

1. A great many writers agree with me that the way in which the training analysis is conducted in most of the societies is incorrect: that when one functions both as analyst and judge of the candidate, a situation of real dependency results. But, it is alleged by some, meticulous technique will suffice to solve this pressing problem. The concrete elements that make up such a special technique are not reported, and this I understand — for there *is* no technique other than the one we strive to apply as well as we can in our ordinary therapeutic analyses: namely, the correct one. Or, in Kairys' (1964) words: "Taken as a group, the papers that make technical recommendations for dealing with the transference problems of the training analysis seem to me to fall far short of what is needed. . . . These small prescriptions for an enormous problem are like advising aspirin for encephalitis" (p. 498).

At the London Congress in 1953, many colleagues were of the opinion that the problem should be dealt with by the application of this "better" technique. Of these, I shall mention only Grete Bibring (1954), Paula Heimann (1954), Jeanne Lampl-de Groot (1954), Nils Nielsen (1954), and Martin Grotjahn (1954), but one finds this suggestion repeated over and over again in the literature. Anna Freud (1970), too, defends this position; but she at least furnishes a number of examples of her conception of this modified technique. This has not persuaded me, however, to change my opinion: the situation in which the analyst must also be a judge of the candidate is wrong and cannot be solved by a matter of technique.

2. Another small group also voices objection against the training analysis in this form and setting, but includes this point in a sweeping

criticism of the total system prevailing in training institutes. Some of these colleagues do not explicitly name the situation that I myself view as the principle drawback, i.e., the *real* dependence of the candidate on his analyst and on the analyst's judgment. In this group, I include Michael Balint (1948, 1954), who, however, fails to make clear to me exactly which changes he would like to see made, and Siegfried Bernfeld (1962), who would do away with the entire systematic organization of analytic training, and would, in my view, replace it with something even worse. Szasz (1958) is a kindred spirit who considers the whole training set-up far too authoritarian and who opposes its continuation on the present compulsory basis.

3. The Swiss Psychoanalytical Society follows its own unique method. Fritz Morgenthaler and Jacques Berna (1967) describe the situation in Switzerland, where no organized institute and no formal theoretical courses or supervision exist. This state of affairs is in part a result of a lack of geographical concentration; the analysts are spread out at considerable distance from one another. Frequently, applicants for admission to analytic training have already been in analysis for some time, and are advised by the training committee of the society concerning further training and study. Morgenthaler and Berna's report is not clear about whether or not the opinion of the colleagues with whom the candidate is, or has been, in analysis is sought, and what role, if any, this plays. This point would be crucial in determining my acceptance or rejection of the system.

4. In the entire literature I found only two colleagues who shared my own view of where the main difficulty lies, and who advocate or have designed a similar solution: Nacht and his co-workers, and Kairys. As early as 1953, at the London Congress, Nacht (1954) stated:

It seems to me that other modifications, this time outside the work of the analysis and concerned especially with the rules which govern the training of the future analyst, might profitably be considered. They would tend amongst other things to improve the conditions for a training analysis and to make them more nearly those of a purely therapeutic analysis, and also to change the situation of the analyst in relation to the candidate, to neutralize it in some way so that the career of the future psychoanalyst should not depend on his own analyst's opinion of him. Only the supervisors, for example, would decide on the abilities and capacities of the candidate, who would thus be judged by his work and not by the course of his analysis [p. 253].

And in 1961, Nacht et al. wrote: "Here in Paris we have been much occupied with cutting down the various inconveniences or dangers, and we have developed means for diminishing the candidate's state of dependence in respect to his analyst. The method adopted by the great majority of the training committee handling the didactic analyses in Paris, consists of practically removing from the analyst charged with handling the didactic analysis all personal initiative in other aspects of the student's training, and all direct influence in appreciating the results obtained" (p. 113).

From this, I conclude that in Paris and in the Netherlands, at about the same time — yet completely independently — decisions were made to apply approximately the same remedy. Kairys' article appeared in 1964. He gives a rather complete summary of the various opinions, examines them critically, quite honestly sets forth and considers the difficulties in this area, and gives a lucid review of the various means that have been advocated toward improving the situation. At the end of his article, he presents the following conclusion:

> The most serious problem of all lies in the fact that the training analyst must play two incompatible roles in relation to his student-analysand: he must analyze and simultaneously be a teacher and judge. There is general agreement in the literature that the dual function of the training analyst may seriously hamper the training analysis. Various suggestions for avoiding this difficulty have been made. The author of this paper advocates that the dilemma be resolved by separating the training analysis from the rest of the analytic training [p. 511].

It should be clear that I fully agree with Kairys' position. And I will be very glad to learn how other institutes have solved this problem.

REFERENCES

Balint, M., (1948), On the psychoanalytic training system. *Internat. J. Psycho-Anal.,* 29:163-173.
_____ (1954), Analytic training and training analysis. *Internat. J. Psycho-Anal.,* 35:157-162.
Bernfeld, S. (1962), On psychoanalytic training. *Psychoanal. Quart.,* 31:453-482.
Bibring, G. (1954), The training analysis and its place in psychoanalytic training. *Internat. J. Psycho-Anal.,* 35:169-173.
Calef, V. & Weinshel, E. M. (1973), Reporting, nonreporting, and assessment in the training analysis. *J. Amer. Psychoanal. Assn.,* 21:714-726.
Fleming, J. (1973), The training analyst as an educator. In: *Second Conference of the Chicago, Pittsburgh, and Topeka Institutes;* I. Ramzy, Co-ordinator, pp. 11-38.
Freud, A. (1970), Probleme der Lehranalyse. *Psyche,* 24:
Grotjahn, M. (1954), About the relationship between psycho-analytic training and psycho-analytic therapy. *Internat. J. Psycho-Anal.,* 35:254-262.
Heimann, P. (1954), Problems of the training analysis. *Internat. J. Psycho-Anal.,* 35:163-168.
Kairys, D. (1964), The training analysis. *Psychoanal. Quart.,* 33:485-512.
Lampl-de Groot, J. (1954). Problems of psychoanalytic training. *Internat. J. Psycho-Anal.,* 35:184-187.
McLaughlin, J. T. (1973), The nonreporting training analyst, the analysis, and the institute. *J. Amer. Psychoanal. Assn.,* 21:697-726.
Morgenthaler, F., & Berna, J. (1967), Psychoanalytische Ausbildung. *Bull. Schweiz. Gesellschaft Ps-A.,* no. 5.

Nacht, S. (1954), The difficulties of didactic psycho-analysis in relation to therapeutic psycho-analysis. *Internat. J. Psycho-Anal.*, 35:250-253.

_____, Lebovici, S. & Diatkine, R. (1961), Training for psychoanalysis. *Internat. J. Psycho-Anal.*, 42:110-115.

Nielsen, N. (1954), The dynamics of training analysis. *Internat. J. Psycho-Anal.*, 35:246-249.

Szasz, T. S. (1958), Psycho-analytic training. *Internat. J. Psycho-Anal.*, 39:598-613.

March, 1973

IV

PSYCHOANALYTIC
HISTORY

A Commentary on Freud's Treatment of the Rat Man

JEROME S. BEIGLER, M.D. (*Chicago*)

The purpose of this paper is to demonstrate the specific impact on the patient of Freud's having fed the Rat Man. I view the feeding as a causal facet of Freud's evolving pioneering technique, which in 1907 still retained many parameters, but was brilliantly successful (Jones, 1955, p. 263) because of the force of his personality and his therapeutic genius.

Stimulated by the publication of the "Original Record of the Case" (Freud, 1909, pp. 251-318) containing "the actual notes 'made on the evening of the day of treatment'" (Strachey, 1955, p. 253), the literature on the case of the Rat Man has by now become extensive. Areas for fruitful research nevertheless remain.

Clinical Vignette

Because of an experience with a postpsychotic patient I had treated some years previously, I was struck by the note Freud wrote on December, 1907: "He was hungry and was fed" (1909, p. 303). My patient was a 30-year-old man who had been hospitalized many months for the treatment of a recurrent paranoid schizophrenia. He was in remission, and I was seeing him supportively as an outpatient twice a week. His appointment was the last of the day, and on this particular day I knew I required coffee to manage his session. I also knew that if I had coffee, it would be wise if he did too — though I knew that if he did, there would be repercussions. So we had coffee, and in a few minutes he was raging psychotically, barely able to remain seated. But, with perseverance, by the end of the hour he had reconstituted his self and seemed to have gained something in the experience. I understood the sequence as being due to an unavoidable breach in the therapeutic barrier ordinarily existing between patient and therapist.

The therapeutic barrier is established by the implicit understanding that the analysand's productions will be viewed by the analyst only as material to be analyzed, thus serving to control the dread of omnipotent fantasies and providing the ambience for the whole psychoanalytic process. The analysand is thereby encouraged to externalize his self-monitoring functions to the analyst and is helped to tolerate anxieties engendered when derivatives of unconscious fantasies are confronted (Beigler, 1972). When I offered my patient coffee, I became a startlingly out-of-context "real" person, which to him meant that both he and I might react to his fantasies as though they were real. Thus, I could temporarily not function for him as an auxiliary ego, superego, and self (Beigler, 1972). His fantasies of narcissistic merger (Kohut, 1971) and oral aggression became accentuated, more anxiety than he could tolerate was mobilized, and he fragmented. My unexpected and independent action ruptured his view of me as a self-object, and, perhaps because he understood the human frailty that necessitated the coffee, he raged in narcissistic fury over the disappointment that he could not fuse with an omnipotent, idealized parent imago (Kohut, 1972). Evidently because I had anticipated some of this, I was able to remain ostensibly calm, and, as he witnessed my survival of his onslaught, he again became able to use me as auxiliary structure and by the end of the hour he had regained "self"-control.

When, some time after this incident occurred, I read Freud's original notes that he had fed his patient, I was alerted to search for evidence of a similar, albeit attenuated, reaction in the Rat Man (Boyer & Giovacchini, 1967, pp. 322-323). Careful reading of Freud's daily notes does seem to confirm my expectation, but, before examining the evidence, it might be of interest to view Freud's feeding of his patient in its historical context.

Jones (1955) tells us that in 1907 "Freud permitted a more familiar attitude towards his patients than he did later, or has been the method since used by analysts. He no longer, it is true, invited them to meals with his family, as he had done in the eighteen-nineties, but he would still occasionally have refreshments brought in during the session for both himself and the patient" (p. 230). Anna Freud, in a personal communication, explains "If the patient came from a long distance and/or had missed a meal, he might have asked for something. Any reaction would be analyzed" (1973).

All this, when combined with Freud's own subsequent remark: "When I brought him something to eat ..." (1909, p. 311), suggests that the feeding was a casual incident, probably a snack, brought into the hour by Freud himself, and not intended in a therapeutic mode per se.

The "Original Record"

We turn now to a detailed examination of the "Original Record" (pp. 252-318). By December 28, 1907, the patient had been in analysis almost three months and the work was progressing rapidly, with the achievement of many insights. In the immediately preceding sessions, they had been working on "Paul's" distress over his intense identification with his mother and a resurgence of his guilt over his omnipotent loving and hating fantasies about his father which were triggered by the illness of Dr. Pr., who was a close friend of his late father's and was suffering from the same illness, emphysema. Freud comments to himself about the excellence of the patient's insight (p. 300). Further associations follow, which refer to oedipal-complex fantasies: guilt over the father's death and fury related to the women in his life (sister, mother, and Gisela). These were given on the patient's own initiative and were therefore very much under his control. "This consecutive account of events swallowed up any reference to current happenings" (p. 303).

In sharp contrast to the self-control conveyed in the above hour, the atmosphere of the analysis conveyed by the associations changed immediately after the patient was fed in the next hour. He continued his story from the previous day about events at Unterach, describing his many compulsions associated with Gisela (pp. 188-190). "It suddenly occurred to him that he must make himself slimmer," (p. 303). A series of associations referring to intense loss of control then followed:

> He began to get up from the table—of course he left his pudding—and to run about in the sun till he dropped with perspiration ... further bouts of running. He dashed up mountains ... On the edge of a steep precipice he had the idea of jumping over ... mountain climbing ... spur himself on ... the top of the mountain ... fallen out ... father collapse ... horsewhip ... a great deal of rage ... challenging him to a duel ... compulsion to talk ... forced himself ... to talk incessantly ... talked a lot of nonsense ... obsession for counting ... obsession for protecting ... obsession for understanding ... fear of death ... his running about in the sun had something suicidal about it ... "one of these days you'll have a stroke" ... wished his cousin dead in his rage [pp. 303-307].

The patient then told of protecting Gisela from the stone in the road at Unterach.

273

In contrast to the feeling of control conveyed in the hours immediately preceding, this hour conveys agitation, suggestive of an attenuated version of my patient's temporary disintegration following my having given him coffee. It is perhaps not irrelevant that Freud's notes for December 28 take up three and a half printed pages, which (except for the record of Jan. 2) is much longer than any other entry, reflecting the quantity and intensity of the patient's associations.

The very first of these associations—to make himself slimmer—led to the uncovering of suicidal impulses, both of which arose, says Freud (p. 189) as "reactions to a tremendous feeling of rage ... directed against some one who had cropped up as an interference with the course of his love." The immediate association to being fed, that of making himself slimmer, leads via the meaning of the German *dick* to cousin Dick, the oedipal rival.

It seems that the breach of the analytic barrier (ordinarily fostered by abstinence) between analysand and analyst, which enables the whole process of free association, was a source of overstimulation (Shengold, 1965, 1967) and provided an increment of credibility to the patient of his omnipotent fantasies. That omnipotence, was a problem to the Rat Man, as it is with other obsessive-compulsive patients, is readily documented (Freud, 1909, pp. 233-234, 235n., 298-300, *et passim*). If his cannibalistic wishes could be gratified in "reality," then presumably so could others, the most pressing ones proving to be the oedipal fantasies on which he had been working in the immediately preceding hours. One can conjecture about fantasies of oral-impregnation, the negative Oedipus, and homosexuality, but the immediate evidence indicates the oedipal problem as uppermost. With such fantasies seemingly on the verge of realization, the patient's agitation is understandable.

The repercussions of the feeding episode continued for several hours.[1] The second postprandial hour deals with further oedipal fantasies of rage against Dr. Pr. (perhaps accentuated by an unconscious fantasy of omnipotently having caused his death), identifications with his mother, followed by two primal-scene equivalents. There follows an association to a herring stretched between two women (Freud's wife and mother) "extending from the anus of one to that of the other. A girl cut it in two, upon which the two pieces fall away (as though peeled off)" (pp.

---

[1] It is of parenthetic interest that the next entry is dated *"Dec. 2—*Interruption owing to Dr. Pr.'s illness and death" (p. 307). Strachey wonders whether it should not have been *"Jan. 2,"* but that is the apparently correct date on the next entry after this one. In 1907, December 28 was on a Saturday. The next scheduled hour would have been Monday, December 30, but Freud notes an "interruption," so the most likely date is December 31.

307-308). Associations led to his not having eaten the herring provided in the food Freud had given him the previous hour. He believed the girl who cut it was Freud's daughter. Some weeks previously, the patient had fantasied copulating on top of this daughter via a stool hanging from his anus while lying on his back (p. 287), further evidence that feeding the patient stimulated his oedipal fantasies. During the first postprandial hour the oedipal fantasies were accompanied by considerable agitation, in this second hour they were presented in a more reconstituted and defended anal-regressive style. It is the prominence of relatively healthy anal defenses that leads Greenson (1966, p. 150) to refer to this patient as "regressed hysteric" rather than borderline.

The next hour, January 2, 1908, he "apparently had only trivialities to report and I was able to say a great deal to him today" (Freud, 1909, p. 308). Freud then became therapeutically aggressive, asking many questions and making conjectural interpretations. As a result, they established via associations to worms in stools that a rat had the important unconscious significance of being an anal-penis. The patient then associated to what seems a screen memory: "the greatest fright of his life," the illusioned movement of the wings of a stuffed bird belonging to his mother with which he had been running. He thought "it had come to life again and threw it down" in terror. Freud interpreted the resurrection of the dead sister and father, but one must also consider Grunberger's interpretation of the boy's anal-sadistic wish to castrate the phallic mother's penis, behind which may be the wish to castrate the father. This latter interpretation is given further support by the next series of associations dealing with voyeuristic fantasies, which also point to a search for the hidden female phallus (Grunberger, pp. 160-161).

Toward the end of this highly productive hour, the associations again led to the herring. Fishes have no hair because "scales interfere with the growth of hair ... This is what determined the appearance of the herring in the transference phantasy. Once when he had told me that his girl had lain on her stomach and her genital hairs were visible from behind, I had said to him that it was a pity that women nowadays gave no care to them and spoke of them as unlovely; and for that reason he was careful that the two women [in the phantasy] should be without hair.... When I brought him something to eat he thought at once that it had been prepared by two women" (p. 311). So again the evidence seems to indicate that the patient was still coping with the repercussions from the meal. The specific fantasies were of oedipal ambitions dealt with via anal regression. Part of Freud's genius for such intense analytic work seems to have been his own candor, which in the setting of his then current technique would set an encouraging example for the patient, even though Freud's residual masculine uneasiness over the appearance of the female genital is apparent.

In the next hour, January 3, Freud consolidated the important discovery of the rat-worm-penis and the fantasies of anal intercourse. He also solved another element in the fantasy of the herring stretched between the two women, which evidently had tormented the patient: "A girl cut it [the herring] in half, upon which the two pieces fell away (as though peeled off).... The girl was one he had ... taken to be ... my daughter" (pp. 307-308). In the notes to the hour of Jan. 2, Freud adds: "the girl who performed the difficult task [of cutting the herring in half] with *'easy virtuosity'* " (p. 310; my italics). The next day, Freud goes on: "he told me, in high spirits, the solution of the last phantasy. It was my science that was the child which solved the problem with the gay superiority of 'smiling virtuosity', peeled off the disguises from his ideas and so liberated the two women from his herring-wishes" (p. 311). Thus the element of the girl cutting the herring in the original fantasy was an allusion to a wish to be relieved of his torment by Freud's brain child, psychoanalysis. The "high spirits" of the patient, the "gay superiority" of the "smiling" or "easy virtuosity," the obvious pleasure in Freud's proud acknowledgement — "It was my science that was the child which solved the problem" — all indicate an element of enthusiasm in the ambience in which the analysis was conducted. Despite all the anal, depressive, and masochistic torment, Freud and the patient evidently enjoyed a mutual fascination. The notes contain many references to the patient's cheerfulness and several approving references to his "excellence." This analytic pair consisted of a 30-year-old highly intelligent patient in the throes of being helped out of a tormenting disability and a 51-year-old charismatic genius-analyst, at the height of his power, who reveled in the opportunity to solve obscure scientific problems while fashioning a cure for the previously incurable. To have had so brilliant a result with so difficult a patient in only eleven months was no small achievement, and one can begin to understand how it happened.

But let us return to the hour of Jan. 3. After solving the facet of the herring fantasy described above, Freud and his patient went on to the formula rat = worm = penis and the infantile sexual theory of anal intercourse. Strachey (1959) in his introductory note to Freud's paper "Character and Anal Erotism" (1908) reminds us that the theme of anal eroticism, which has since become so familiar to us, aroused tremendous indignation when it first was published, and was undoubtedly partly stimulated by the analysis of the Rat Man. Jones's comment on the same paper is also relevant:

It certainly produced an effect, chiefly undesirable. The very idea of connecting the erotic excitability of one particular part of the body, and that such a lowly one as the anus, with spiritual qualities such as character traits seemed to be the most outrageous thing Freud had yet done.... I well remember the jeers with which the psychiatric staff [of Kraepelin's Psychiatric Clinic in Munich] ... greeted it, vying with each other in ribald remarks ... Since then the correlation Freud then established has become almost a commonplace of general knowledge ... But at the time there is no doubt that the paper in question much increased the odium with which his name was becoming associated [pp. 295-296].

Although Freud referred to the anal-erotic qualities of feces as early as December 22, 1897 in a letter to Fliess, (Freud, 1887-1902, pp. 239-240) and wrote on the erotism of fecal retention in 1905 (p. 186) and also in 1908 (p. 171), the material revealed in these hours with the Rat Man concerning anal intercourse was new. There is evidence that Freud himself was uncomfortable about his discoveries. He refers to the patient's fantasies as "especially revolting to him [the patient] when brought into connection with his father and the women he loved. And when we consider that the same situation was reproduced in the compulsive threat [a rat sanction] which had been formed in his mind after the captain had made his request [to pay Lieutenant A.], we shall be *forcibly* reminded of certain curses in use among the Southern Slavs" (Freud, 1909, pp. 214-215; my italics). Similarly, Freud seems judgmental when he states that "This libidinal urge [anal intercourse] is as *double-sided* as the Southern Slav curse[2] of arse-fucking" (p. 311; my italics).

[2] For the details of these curses, Freud refers us (p. 215n) to the periodical *Anthropophyteia* edited by F. S. Krauss (1905), who published annual folkloric compendia of obscene jokes and anecdotes, which Freud praised (1910, pp. 233-234). Since the reference is sufficiently inaccessible, when I found a cardiologist friend, D. M. Obradovic, who was able and graciously willing to provide a translation from the Slavic, it seemed worthwhile to make it more readily available. The Slavic in which these particular curses were spoken turns out to be an obsolete dialect from the Dalmatian coast. The excerpt consists of raillery between two lusty affectionate peasants, Sime and Pavle, enjoying "poking fun at each other" at a bucolic gathering. The relevant banter is as follows:

Sime: Where are you going to travel?
Pavle: To Novi Pazar, may Lazar fuck you; to bring a load of straw, may your ass-hole burst from a cock; to bring another load of straw, may your ass stand on a cock!
Sime: You are dear to me and I would give myself to you!
Pavle: If I ate shit, I would give you some too!
Sime: I am like your brothers!
Pavle: May the dog fuck you!
Sime: May the lead in your cock get sick!
Pavle: May you stay healthy, and may you swing on your cock!

There are many references to anal material for several weeks prior to the hours under discussion, but now, evidently prompted by a regression in response to the oedipal fantasies stimulated at this stage of the analysis by the feeding, the anal erotism came into sharp focus. After Freud told him that a rat was a penis, he had a flood of associations, most of which were more directly oedipal in nature. That the patient had achieved significant insight is evidenced by this flood of associations and also by the fact that he came the next hour, Jan. 4, in a cheerful mood. But then he became provocative: "This transference was the latest of his deliria about behaving badly and he brought it out in a very complicated form. . . . He thought that I made a profit out of the meal I had given him; for he had lost time through it and the treatment would last longer" (p. 314). The fantasy of paying Freud 70 kronen for undertaking the first night with his bride also occurred to him. He rejected his pleasure over Freud's praise in previous hours with "I shit on it" (p. 315). I believe this is further evidence that a significant piece of insight had been achieved, in that the patient reacted as though Freud had made an anal penetration that had to be rejected. Greenson (1965) has described a similar mechanism in a patient of his. From this present vantage point, it seems that the fantasy of a herring stretched between the two women indicates the patient's strong feminine identification, wishes for anal penetration by the idealized father-Freud, a pregnancy fantasy ("he must make himself slimmer"), and a wish for the resolution of this seemingly

---

Sime: How long is the walk from the cunt to the ass-hole?
Pavle: If you start from the cunt in the morning, you will reach the ass-hole for lunch!

Pavle: How much would you ask to blow my balls through my cock?
Sime: Two yellow lemons!
Pavle: And if I drive my cock and balls into your ass?
Sime: That I would do cheaper — for two small fish!
Pavle: I would break the jaws of your ass!
Sime: You have a nice moustache; if you had it on your ass, it would be softer to sit on!

Sime: One guy lost his cock in you!
Pavle: Another found it and the first asked: "Give me back my cock"!
Sime: Would you like it more to spend summer on the cock or to spend winter in the ass-hole?
Pavle: When you start to eat shit, order some for me!

Pavle: Did you see bronze on my cock?
Sime: I got rid of it by fucking you!

Pavle: What would you give your brother-in-law for lunch?
Sime: Shit! (all burst out laughing).
Pavle: (to the serving girl): May you be filled with cocks like a match-box is filled with matches! You are dear to me!

impossible problem (the cutting of the herring by Freud's science-child). It is possible that one of the unconscious reasons the treatment worked so well is that Freud and the patient loved[3] one another, and the patient *did* participate importantly in fashioning Freud's new science. Both participants may have been adaptively living out an intense interlocking of unconscious wishes under the realistic guidance of Freud's unusual therapeutic and scientific skills.

In assessing Freud's genius, Paul Kramer (1973), in a personal communication stresses his capacity to perceive the unconscious, to organize and synthesize his perceptions, his incredible memory, fund of energy, his love of truth and capacity for self-confrontation; similarly Eissler (1971, p. 295; 1973) stresses Freud's ability to accept his own passivity, femininity, and motherliness. In addition, I believe, judging from the evidence in his analysis of the Rat Man, that Freud's genius expressed itself in his drive to inseminate and generate. As Riviere (1958) has said, Freud engaged in "an act of creation in which his hearers and readers were his medium, his vehicle in the process, as well as both the source and the abode of his creation. It was a deeper impulse in him—a capacity to construct and create something, a living body, to build up outside himself a body of knowledge that comprehends the single facts of which it is formed and yet transcends them, thus becoming an independent whole in itself.... There was a marriage in him of the seeker after existing truth and the creator giving the world a new living truth in the scientist and the artist in one" (pp. 146-147).

Further presumptive evidence of the tenability of this surmise concerning Freud's generativity is furnished by the work in the next two hours, which deal with the patient's dream of going to the dentist to have a bad tooth pulled out (Freud, 1909, p. 315). His associations led to a failure of emission during intercourse, a childhood theory that human reproduction was effected by the man "piddling" into the woman, and his forgetting a condom. He also "had an addendum to the dream. The tooth did not look at all like one, but like a tulip bulb" (p. 317). Freud emphasized the castrative significance of the dream, but in later writings he also realized the relevance of tooth-extraction dreams to childbirth (cf. Freud, 1900, p. 387, n. 3).

---

[3] Freud (1921) defines "love" as sexual love and sexual union, but also: "self-love ... love for parents and children, friendship and love for humanity in general, and also devotion to concrete objects and to abstract ideas (p. 90).... love alone acts as the civilizing factor ... that ... brings a change from egoism to altruism ... this is true both of sexual love for women ... and also of desexualized, sublimated homosexual love for other men, which springs from work in common" (p. 103).

From the patient's spontaneous associations, the significance of child-birth seems uppermost; and in my view it is a confirmatory sequel to the work of the previous hours, which unconsciously signified to the patient a successful anal penetration, insemination, and pregnancy with a new self, all triggered by the timely feeding of the meal and carried through constructively through Freud's vigorous and skillful psychoanalytic inter-ventions.

The agitation in the hour of December 28 is in marked contrast to the relative calm of these last few hours and serves further to highlight the impact of the feeding. The feeding neither caused his agitation to subside (Kestenberg, 1966, p. 156) nor "impeded the progress of this patient's behavior" (Zetzel, 1966, p. 227), but seems to have stimulated much material via an emotional storm that Freud was strong enough to turn to the patient's considerable advantage.

Freud's Technique

The case history of the Rat Man reports, for the first time, an analysis carried out with the help of free association (Nunberg and Federn, 1962). Jones (1955) tells us that "the discovery of the 'free association' method . . . evolved very gradually between 1892 and 1893,[4] becoming steadily refined and purified from the adjuvants—hypnosis, suggestion, pressing, and questioning—that accompanied it at its inception" (p. 242). Erikson (1955, p. 8) understands the evolution of technique as a direct function of progress in Freud's self-analysis, particularly his own resistances against passivity.

Freud (1925) reconstructs the history of his change of technique:

The means which I first adopted for overcoming the patient's resistance, by insistence and encouragement, had been indispensable for the purpose of giving me a first general survey of what was to be expected. But in the long run it proved to be too much of a strain on both sides, and further, it seemed open to certain obvious criticisms. It therefore gave place to another method which was in one sense its opposite. Instead of urging the patient to say something upon some particular subject, I now asked him to abandon himself to a process of *free association*—that is, to say whatever came into his head, while ceasing to give any conscious direction to his thoughts [p. 40].

Kris (1951) assesses Freud's technique in 1907 as follows: "If we reread Freud's older case histories, we find, for example, that the conspicuous

---

[4] Cf. Freud, 1898, p. 282; Jones, 1953, p. 244.

intellectual indoctrination of the Rat Man was soon replaced by a greater emphasis on reliving in the transference . . . [B]etter understanding and management of transference was probably not initially connected with any new theoretical insight. It was a process of increasing skill, of improved ability, in which Freud and his early collaborators shared . . ." (pp. 17-18).

The original record of the case of the Rat Man shows that Freud in 1907 was still insistent, encouraging, therapeutically aggressive, and "intellectually indoctrinating," but free association had become an important mode. Other elements in the setting in which the analysis was conducted are Freud's interest in and enthusiasm for the patient. These feelings are apparent in the daily notes themselves, which contain approving comments about the patient, and also in the fact that Freud presented the case history and its progress at five different meetings of the Vienna Society between October 30, 1907, and April 8, 1908 (P. Federn, 1947; Nunberg and Federn, 1962), and that he selected this case to present to the first international congress in Salzburg, where on April 27, 1908 he held his audience in rapt attention for five hours. As illustrated in previous sections of this paper it is not difficult to assess the impact on the patient of Freud's vigorous personality and interest.

Jones (1955) comments:

the day-to-day notes . . . written every evening . . . [are] invaluable as affording a unique opportunity for watching Freud at his daily work so to speak: his timing of interpretations, his characteristic use of analogies to illustrate a point he was making, the preliminary guesses he would make privately which might subsequently be either confirmed or disproved, and altogether the tentative manner in which such piecemeal work proceeded. . . . He gave his patients . . . fuller expositions of the theory of psychoanalysis than he did later on . . . not in the least to induce any conviction in the patient, but simply to provoke him to produce more relevant material [p. 230].

Freud's analytic powers showed at their best in his unraveling of this case. His delicate and ingenious interpretation and elucidation of the most tortuous mental processes, with their subtle play on words and thoughts, must evoke admiration and were hardly surpassed in any other of his writings. . . . [Freud] added a general theoretical chapter which is a contribution of the utmost value to our understanding of this baffling neurosis. When one compares it with the previous knowledge of the subject, which had been cast in purely intellectual terms, it can fairly be called a revolutionary progress [pp. 263-264].

Anna Freud (1966) cogently points out: "In 1909 when Freud published his 'Notes Upon a Case of Obsessional Neurosis', it was a pioneering achievement to look behind the apparent pathogenic importance of recent events, such as the father's death, difficulties in love affairs, etc., and to unearth the upsetting events of the *anal-sadistic stage* as preceding them" (p. 119, my italics; see also Loewenstein, 1969, p. 59).

Kanzer (1952) believes the patient seduced Freud into a symbolic anal penetration by his anxious helplessness (p. 183). "Nevertheless, in retrospect, it may be seen with what skill and intuition Freud's theoretical explanations took cognizance of and dealt with the transference" (p. 189). Schur (1955) conjectures that Freud's therapeutic result was related to the patient's ego stimulating activity of intellectual understanding, which, especially in the initial phase, may constitute progress, as compared to a deep preverbal regression (pp. 160-161).

By contrast, Major (1971) provides an amusing sidelight by having presented an excerpt from the case to his class of candidates without identifying its source. The students criticized it vigorously as an example of poor technique!

Van der Leeuw (1966) thinks the case is a "result of experiences gained by the use of the psychoanalytical situation and the basic rule" (p. 133).

Zetzel (1966) conjectures that the patient's "positive identification with a father surrogate, Freud, may have been the central factor which impelled him towards greater mastery of unresolved intrapsychic conflict" (p. 238). Myerson (1966), too, emphasizes the patient's looking to the father to provide structure with which to control "his frightening inner and outer world" (p. 141), thereby predisposing him to a passive homosexual attachment.

Morgenthaler (1966) emphasizes the influence of Freud's personality: Freud "approached his patient with the firm conviction that despite the reigning confusion he would win through to a clear understanding of him . . . The Rat Man was privileged to encounter in the person of Freud an exceptionally gifted analyst who carried conviction by the mere fact of his personality" (p. 206).

Giving more credit to Freud's technical ability, Simon (1973) describes "the complexity, richness, and *imagination* involved in his thinking. Reasoning by analogy, inspired guesses, creative use of the ideas of other thinkers, knowing what to look for . . ." (p. 456); and Grunberger (1966) attributes the success to "Freud's active and gratifying technique" (p. 163).

We know Freud was a charismatic genius-analyst who, with a combination of technical knowledge and force of personality was able to achieve a brilliant result in a patient with what Deutsch (Payne, 1966), in agreement with Freud, called a "moderately severe" and Zetzel (1966) considered a "severe" obsessive-compulsive neurosis. Nowadays, we are accustomed to less spectacular results achieved over much longer periods of time. Freud (1925) changed his style because "in the long run it proved too much of a strain on both sides, and further, it seemed open to certain obvious criticisms" (p. 40). Perhaps Kohut (1971), who recently has highlighted the developmental aspects of narcissism and of the self in personality disorders (including the obsessive-compulsive), puts it best: "But just as the surgeon in the heroic era of surgery was a charismatically gifted man who performed great feats of individual courage and heroic skill while the modern surgeon tends to be a calm, well-trained crafts-man, so also with the analyst. As our knowledge . . . increases, the formerly so personally demanding treatment procedures . . . gradually become the skilled work of insightful and understanding analysts who do not employ any special charisma of their personalities but restrict themselves to the use of the only tools that provide rational success: interpretations and reconstructions" (pp. 222-223).

In summary, then, I have tried to demonstrate the therapeutic impact of Freud's having fed the Rat Man. I believe the feeding provoked an emotional storm by its breach of the patient-psychoanalyst therapeutic barrier. The primarily oedipal material then induced an anal regression through which Freud was able to make important discoveries concerning anal passivity. Freud's ability to use the material so successfully to the patient's interest is evidence of his therapeutic genius, the strength of his personality, and the intensity of his generative impulse.

REFERENCES *

Beigler, J. S. (1972), The restitution of adaptive defenses during the termination phase. Unpub-lished.

Boyer, L. B., & Giovacchini, P. L. (1967), *Psychoanalytic Treatment of Schizophrenic and Char-acterological Disorders.* New York: Science House.

_____ (1973), Personal communication.

Eissler, K. R. (1971), *Talent and Genius.* New York: Quadrangle Books.

Erikson, E. H. (1955), Freud's "The Origins of Psychoanalysis." *Internat. J. Psycho-Anal.,* 36:1-15.

Federn, P. (1947), Professor Freud: The beginning of a case history. In: *The Yearbook of Psycho-Analysis,* ed. S. Lorand. International Universities Press, 1948, pp. 14-20.

Freud, A. (1966), Obsessional neurosis: A summary of psychoanalytic views as presented to the Congress. *Internat. J. Psycho-Anal.,* 47:116-122.

Freud, S. (1887-1902), *The Origins of Psychoanalysis.* New York: Basic Books, 1954.

_____ (1898), Sexuality in the aetiology of the neuroses. *Standard Edition,* 3:261-295. London: Hogarth Press, 1962.

_____ (1900), The interpretation of dreams. *Standard Edition,* 5:339-625. London: Hogarth Press, 1953.

_____ (1905), Three essays on the theory of sexuality. *Standard Edition,* 7:125-293. London: Hogarth Press, 1953.

_____ (1908), Character and anal erotism. *Standard Edition,* 9:167-175. London: Hogarth Press, 1959.

* A more complete bibliography is available from the author.

283

_____ (1909), Notes upon a case of obsessional neurosis. *Standard Edition,* 10:153-320. London: Hogarth Press, 1955.

_____ (1910), Letter to Dr. Friedrich S. Krauss on *Anthropophyteia. Standard Edition,* 11:233-235. London: Hogarth Press, 1957.

_____ (1921), Group psychology and the analysis of the ego. *Standard Edition,* 18:67-143. London: Hogarth Press, 1955.

_____ (1925), An autobiographical study. *Standard Edition,* 20:3-74. London: Hogarth Press, 1959.

Greenson, R. R. (1965), The problem of working through. In: *Drives, Affects, Behavior,* ed. M. Schur. Vol. II. New York: International Universities Press, pp. 277-314.

_____ (1966), Comments on Dr. Ritvo's paper. *Internat. J. Psycho-Anal.,* 47:149-150.

Grunberger, B. (1966), Some reflections on the Rat Man. *Internat. J. Psycho-Anal.,* 47:160-168.

Jones, E. (1916), The theory of symbolism. In: *Psychoanalytic Papers* (5th Edition). Baltimore: Williams & Wilkins, 1949.

_____ (1953), *The Life and Work of Sigmund Freud.* Vol. I: *The Formative Years and the Great Discoveries.* New York: Basic Books.

_____ (1955), *The Life and Work of Sigmund Freud.* Vol. II: *Years of Maturity 1901-1919.* New York: Basic Books.

Kanzer, M. (1952), The transference neurosis of the Rat Man. *Psychoanal. Quart.,* 21:181-189.

Kestenberg, J. S. (1966), Rhythm and organization in obsessive-compulsive development. *Internat. J. Psycho-Anal.,* 47:151-159.

Kohut, H. (1971), *The Analysis of the Self.* New York: International Universities Press.

_____ (1972), Thoughts on narcissism and narcissistic rage. *The Psychoanalytic Study of the Child,* 27:360-400. New York: International Universities Press.

Krauss, F. S. (1905), 457. Poklisti se [To Poke Fun at Each Other]. *Anthropophyteia,* 2:420-426. Translated by D. M. Obradovic.

Kris, E. (1951), Ego psychology and interpretation in psychoanalytic theory. *Psychoanal. Quart.,* 20:15-30.

Lipton, S. D. (1971), Freud's Analysis of the Rat Man Considered as a Technical Paradigm. Presented to the Chicago Psychoanalytic Society, May, 1970. Abstracted by M. Berger in: *Bull. Philadelphia Assn. Psycho-Anal.,* 21:179-183.

Loewenstein, R. (1969), An historical review of the theory of psychoanalytic technique. Abstracted by J. S. Beigler in: *Bull. Philadelphia Assn. Psycho-Anal.,* 19:58-60.

Major, R. (1971), Interpretation 1907: Contribution a l'etude de la technique analytique. *Rev. Franc. Psychoanal.,* 35:527-542. Translated by J. Palombo.

Morgenthaler, R. (1966), Psychodynamic aspects of defence with comments on technique in the treatment of obsessional neurosis. *Internat. J. Psycho-Anal.,* 47:203-209.

Myerson, P. G. (1966), Comments on Dr. Zetzel's paper. *Internat. J. Psycho-Anal.,* 47:139-142.

Nunberg, H., & Federn, E. (1962), *Minutes of the Vienna Psychoanalytic Society.* Vol. I. New York: International Universities Press.

Payne, E. C., Jr., reporter (1966), Summary and discussion of E. R. Zetzel's "Additional Notes Upon a Case of Obsessional Neurosis" (see Zetzel, 1966). *Bull. Phila. Psychoanal. Assn.,* 16:44-47.

Riviere, J. (1958), A character trait of Freud's. In: *Psychoanalysis and Contemporary Thought,* ed. J. D. Sutherland. London: Hogarth Press, pp. 144-149.

Schur, M. (1955), Comments on the metapsychology of somatization. *The Psychoanalytic Study of the Child,* 10:119-164. New York: International Universities Press.

Shengold, L. (1965), The rat and the tooth: A study of the central clinical significance of over-stimulation. Abstracted by J. S. Silverman in: *Psychoanal. Quart.,* 34:471-479.

_____ (1967), The effects of overstimulation: Rat people. *Internat. J. Psycho-Anal.,* 48:403-415.

Sherwood, M. (1969), *The Logic of Explanation in Psychoanalysis.* New York: Academic Press.

Simon, S. (1973), Review of: *Freud: Living and Dying,* by Max Schur. *Psychoanal. Quart.,* 42:451-457.

Strachey, J. (1955), Editorial Note. S. Freud, Notes upon a case of obsessional neurosis (1909). *Standard Edition,* 10:253. London: Hogarth Press.

_____ (1959), Editorial Note. S. Freud, character and anal erotism (1908), *Standard Edition,* 9:168. London: Hogarth Press.

van der Leeuw, P. J. (1966), Comment on Dr. Ritvo's Paper. *Internat. J. Psycho-Anal.,* 47:132-135.

Zetzel, E. R. (1966), An obsessional neurotic: Freud's Rat Man. In: *The Capacity for Emotional Growth.* New York: International Universities Press, 1970, pp. 216-228.

January, 1974

On Freud's Psychotherapy of Bruno Walter

GEORGE H. POLLOCK, M.D., Ph.D. (*Chicago*)

Bruno Walter, world-renowned conductor, was a patient of Freud's for a very brief period sometime in 1904, when Walter was 28 years old. A view of Freud's technique as reported by a patient may be of interest — and is the *raison d'être* for this short essay.

Bruno Walter, originally Schlesinger, was born in a tenement section of Berlin on September 15, 1876. Very early in his career, he became an admirer of Gustav Mahler, who was instrumental in obtaining an early conducting post for Walter by writing to Dr. Theodor Loewe, the director of the Breslau Stadt theater, where there was a vacancy for a young conductor. Walter received the contract, but Loewe suggested that the young conductor change his family name of Schlesinger (literally, Silesian) because of its frequent occurrence in the capital of Silesia. Bruno chose Walter as his stage name, "thinking of Walter von Stolzing, Walther von der Vogelweide, and of Siegmund in Die Walküre, who would have liked to be Frohwalt but who was compelled to call himself Wehwalt" (Walter, 1946, p. 89).[1] In 1911, when Walter became an Austrian citizen, the name was legalized.[2]

Director, Chicago Institute for Psychoanalysis; Fellow, Center for Psychosocial Studies, Chicago; Professor, Department of Psychiatry, Northwestern University.

This research was supported by the Anne Pollock Lederer Research Fund and the Fred M. Hellman Research Fund of the Chicago Institute for Psychoanalysis.

[1] Excerpts from *Theme and Variations,* by Bruno Walter, translated by James A. Galston. Copyright 1946 and renewed 1974 by Alfred A. Knopf, Inc. Reprinted by permission of the publisher.

[2] Walter chose his last name from musical and culture heroes he idealized and with whom he may have wished to be identified. Walther von der Vogelweide (1170-1230), a Middle High German lyric poet and minnesinger of noble birth, in his earlier years wandered about as a court singer and finally received a fief from Frederick II in 1215. His works include love songs, political songs, and religious songs.

Walter, like Mahler before him, had longed for a post in Vienna, which he had visited in 1897. "Only Vienna attracted me. Vienna — where Mozart, Schubert, Beethoven, and Brahms had lived, where music flourished, and which was the home of the world's most magnificent opera — was identified in my mind with music itself" (p. 99). Enchanted by Mahler, his sisters, and the opera, Walter continued to visit Mahler in Vienna and obtained "strength and vitality" from these contacts. At age 22, he was appointed chief director at Riga and was very successful in his efforts at revitalizing the orchestra of the Opera there. In October 1898, Mahler offered Walter the position he had dreamed of — conductor of the Vienna Court Opera, to begin in 1900 at the expiration of his two-year contract with the Riga Opera. Feeling that by then Walter would have gained the maturity necessary for such a position in Vienna, Mahler said that he counted on Walter to help him. "My heart urged me to go to Vienna, but careful consideration counseled against such a move. I felt that it was necessary to become firmly rooted within myself before exposing myself ... to the powerful influence of Mahler.... So it seemed advisable to wait until my ego had firmly crystallized. My reply to Mahler's letter was frankly to that effect, but he would not admit the justification of my standpoint, felt disappointed in me and forsaken by one on whom he had relied. Thus came about the first and only discord in our relations. While it lay heavy on my heart, it could not move me from my decision" (p. 144).

Walter married Elsa Korneck in the spring of 1901, and in the fall of that year, Mahler repeated his offer, and this time he accepted the post of Director of the Vienna Opera. In his autobiography, *Theme and*

Siegmund, Wotan's mortal son, is the father of Siegfried, the hero of Wagner's operas. Siegfried forges a great sword from the broken one of Siegmund, kills a dragon with this powerful weapon, and becomes invincible in battle.

The mention of Walter von Stolzing, the hero in Wagner's *Die Meistersinger von Nürnberg,* probably comes closest to informing us about Bruno Walter's hopes and expectations of Gustav Mahler, his mentor and teacher. His disappointment with Mahler, as will be seen, possibly contributed to the difficulty that finally brought him to Freud. This opera is Wagner's only work dealing with real people and comedy situations. The theme in the opera that seems to tie the three idealized figures together and may have indicated Bruno Walter's anticipation of help from Mahler is the relation between the older and wiser Hans Sachs and the younger, passionate Walter von Stolzing. Through Sachs's help, Walter's Prize Song wins the acclaim of all, as well as the love of the beautiful Eva. The prize offered by Eva's father includes her hand in marriage, all his money, as well as general acclaim for the composer of the song. Although Sachs himself is eligible to enter the competition, he renounces this option and instead assists Walter in attaining his goals — marrying Eva, winning the musical contest and becoming a master of the singer's guild.

The theme of receiving help, acclaim, and admiration from the older, powerful patron, god, or mastersinger in order to attain success may have been of psychological significance in the new surname Bruno Walter selected.

Variations, Walter describes how Mahler and his sisters cordially be-friended the young couple and how Mahler introduced Walter to the various officials and department heads at the Opera, where both men conducted. Work went well, but

my hopeful mood was soon to vanish under the influence of a severe shock. Mahler assigned to me some of the operas he had prepared, confident that I would maintain the artistic level and spirit of his performances. In addition, a considerable number of other works were entrusted to me. Among them was Tannhäuser. I felt that the performance, not counting one role that was woefully miscast, was not lacking in dramatic and musical vitality. How surprised, nay shocked I was when I read on the following morning a furious attack on me in one of Vienna's leading papers, the Neues Wiener Tagblatt. It was more than adverse criticism, more even than a personal insult. What I read was a loud protest against my activity in so prominent a place, a summons to fight against my very existence. It was the first time in my life that I had been so violently abused. The expressions used were so extravagantly uncomplimentary—one of them was that "I would not do as the leader even of a riflemen's band"—that the obvious malice should have weakened the general effect. I was nevertheless deeply dismayed, and my bewilderment increased when a number of similar voices were raised against me in quick succession. Mahler told me at once—and I found out later how right he had been—that these attacks were nothing but the first bugle call of a campaign directed against him [p. 157].

Walter goes on to indicate how Mahler himself helped to swell the ranks of his own enemies, his peremptory manner in questions of art, his summary engagements and dismissals, and his fight against tradition and custom. Mahler's exceptional creativity also contributed to the violent oppositional current.

So, instead of attacking Mahler directly and thus running the risk of mobilizing his many supporters, Mahler's critics chastized him for appointing a young and inexperienced conductor to so prominent a post in Vienna's musical life.

One can understand Walter's shock and concern when the Vienna papers began to attack him; the fulfillment of his ideals—to conduct in Vienna and to work with Mahler—was severely threatened.

The acts of hostility increased, and Walter detected opposition from the ranks of the artists as well. A number of small but widely read newspapers joined the attack, and both Mahler and Walter were jointly criticized—Mahler because he had engaged Walter. Nobody took Walter's part, and Mahler could do nothing to help his protégé.

To make matters worse, [Mahler] was personally preoccupied..He had become ac-quainted with Alma Schindler, "the most beautiful girl in Vienna," and had fallen in love with her. As might have been expected, the spiritual storm unleashed rather late in his life—he was then forty-one years old—eclipsed everything else. He seemed to be unaware of my position, or at least of its dangers, and felt disinclined to take my worries quite seriously. As for myself, the more clearly I recognized the perilous aspect of my situation, the less I felt inclined to bother my friends or those who were well disposed toward me with my affairs. I was astonished beyond expression and wholly perplexed.

My work surely did not merit reckless insults, but my nature made me wonder if it did not deserve serious censure. It would have been unlike me not to have tried to become conscious of my every possible weakness and mistake. It seemed to me that I was wanting in critical watchfulness while at work; I found that my modifications of tempi were immoderate; I discovered unreliability and even awkwardness in my technique of conducting; and so, hardly had a few weeks passed, when I was actually unable to conduct and became convinced that there was more than a drop of truth in the flood of malicious criticisms.

The foundation of my professional existence had been shaken. I began to be doubtful, if not of my musicianship, of my mission as a conductor. All my previous successes did not seem to count. Here in Vienna, the city of music and the home of my choice, I had been weighed and found wanting. It happened that at that very time the Cologne Opera offered me the post of chief conductor under exceptionally favorable conditions. Great was the temptation to forsake the unbearable Vienna atmosphere at the end of the season and to regain my self-assurance in more sympathetic surroundings.

My wife and I had almost made up our minds to accept the Cologne offer, when she decided to hear Mahler's opinion first. I suggested to her that she save him the embarrassment of having to take sides. Were he to counsel against Cologne, he would add to his responsibility for my fate in Vienna, while in the other case it would seem as if he wished to offer me as a sacrifice to his enemies. My wife disapproved of what she considered my exaggerated considerateness and decided to consult Mahler without my knowledge. Then she confessed having called on him and reported to my surprise that in his opinion I had, through no fault or weakness of mine, "lost the game" in Vienna: he who had once lost in Vienna could never again be victorious. Mahler would, of course, be willing to abide by the terms of my contract, but in my own interest he would advise accepting the Cologne offer. This report had a rather unexpected effect on me. I suddenly felt strong, was conscious of my responsibilities to myself, and quite certain of my decision: I had been done a wrong, and it would be cowardly to take it lying down. "Let me be victorious here first, and then I'll go," I said to my wife. She bravely consented, we stayed, and I was victorious.

But my road was a long and arduous one. It was most arduous at the beginning, when, as I said before, I had come to the conclusion that I did not know how to conduct. With what evil forebodings did I look forward to every *pizzicato* chord of the strings and to every freely entering upbeat in any orchestral group. No matter how I beat, both the chord and the upbeat would lack precision. How terrible that slow 6/8 measures became inexact when I beat them in two and stiff when I beat in six. And not only did I, in these and similar instances, feel insidiously inhibited in my conducting technique, but I also began to droop musically. My excessive watchfulness of details interfered when I had to anticipate a longer phrase or tried to satisfy the demands of synthetic interpretation. I felt as if I had happened into a bog and was sinking lower and lower. And there was no one in sight to come to my aid.

There was nothing for me to do but help myself. Like the fantastic Baron Münchhausen, I pulled myself out of the bog by my own bootstraps. I increased my watchfulness, self-criticism, and technical experimenting at rehearsals. On the other hand, I vetoed every bit of self-observation during performances, forcing myself to concentrate exclusively upon the music as a whole and to subordinate details. Above all, however, I tried to become conscious again of my own strength of mind and to re-establish contact with my former firm ego. The method proved successful. My technical studies at orchestra rehearsals bore fruit, and my reproachful appeal to my own strength of mind produced a reinvigoration of my musical work. Gradually I felt at my performances that I could afford to make conscious use of my growing technical accomplishments, that I was able to insert a certain amount of critical listening and observation without jeopardizing the flow and continuity of the music. I knew then that the most important part of my fight, that against my own uncertainty, had been won.

I had never again spoken to Mahler about myself. I was under the impression that he was too thoroughly absorbed in his personal affairs to be greatly interested in my musical activities. What was my surprise, therefore, when, after a performance of Gluck's *Orfeo*, Hassinger, Mahler's factotum, handed me a folded piece of paper on which were words in this effect: "Bravo! Very fine. Noble in expression, moderate in the tempi. Greatly pleased. M." These were the first encouraging words from him during that critical period. They had upon me almost the effect of a draft from that fairy-tale bottle of medicine that causes every wound to heal.

It had in the meantime become clear to me that the sham insurrection against me would have to subside before I could think of bringing about my rehabilitation in the sphere in which I had almost been wrecked. I therefore decided first to prove my musicianship in another field. It was a fortunate coincidence that Arnold Rosé, with whom I had had many a private musical session, invited me to be the assisting pianist at one of his chamber music recitals at Bösendorfer Hall. The distinguished audience that frequented the Rosé recitals, and the press received me with a most gratifying warmth. It was both significant and fortunate that the praise bestowed on me on that occasion as well as on following ones came from what might have been called Vienna's musical conscience. From that time, my connection with Arnold Rosé became ever closer, and we joined later in giving classic sonata recitals, beyond his regular evenings of chamber music. Our recitals were continued regularly through fifteen years and became a fixed institution in Vienna's musical life [pp. 158-160].

Arnold Rosé, the husband of Gustav Mahler's sister Justine, had been the leading first violinist of the famous orchestra of the Vienna Court Opera and the Philharmonic Concerts.

At last, in 1902, I was able to score the operatic success I had longed for and that was to make up for the many disappointments I had suffered. Mahler entrusted to me the revival of Verdi's *Un Ballo in Maschera*, to which the Opera assigned its finest young voices. On that evening I made a conquest of the Opera, and even my enemies succumbed to an attack of nervous aphonia. Although they recovered later, their voices never regained their original metallic resonance. My critical adversaries finally confined themselves to the part of the professional faultfinder, less effective, but greatly in vogue in Vienna. When, soon thereafter, Angelo Neumann, the head of the Prague Theater, invited us all to come to Prague, so that his audiences, too, might enjoy the much-praised Vienna production, I understood that a new and more pleasant epoch had set in for me [pp. 161-162].

Thus, on the basis of his own talent, perseverance, and will, Walter had triumphed, even in the absence of support from his hero, Mahler.

Now Walter felt more secure and, since his wife was pregnant, they moved into larger quarters. Walter enjoyed his "comfortable middle-class existence," feeling gay and contented.

To prevent my being too thoroughly coddled by a friendly fate, the guardian angel to whom my education and chastisement were entrusted had felt it proper to insert into that period of peaceful contemplation an illness that caused me a great deal of anxiety during the year after the birth of our first child [this illness appeared in 1904[3]]. I was attacked by an arm ailment. Medical science called it a professional cramp, but it looked deucedly like incipient paralysis. The rheumatic-neuralgic pain became so violent that I could no longer use my right arm for conducting or piano playing. I went from one prominent doctor to another. Each one confirmed the presence of psychogenic elements in my malady. I submitted to any number of treatments, from mudbaths to magnetism, and finally decided to call on Professor Sigmund Freud, resigned to submit to months of soul searching. The consultation took a course I had not foreseen. Instead of questioning me about sexual aberrations in infancy, as my layman's ignorance had led me to expect, Freud examined my arm briefly. I told him my story, feeling certain that he would be professionally interested in a possible connection between my actual physical affliction and a wrong I had suffered more than a year before. Instead he asked me if I had ever been to Sicily. When I replied that I had not, he said that it was very beautiful and interesting, and more Greek than Greece itself. In short, I was to leave that very evening, forget all about my arm and the Opera, and do nothing for a few weeks but use my eyes.

Walter did as he was told, proceeding to Sicily by way of Genoa and Naples. "Mindful of Freud's instruction," he was determined not to think of his affliction, and in this he was aided by the stimulus of his unfamiliar surroundings. "In the end, my soul and mind were greatly benefited by the additional knowledge I had gained of Hellenism, but not my arm." He was rejoined by his wife in Genoa, and they went on to Monaco, where he hoped the warmth would improve his arm.

Every day I climbed a rock in order to expose my ailing arm to the sun, but in vain. When I got back to Vienna, I poured out my troubles to Freud. His advice was—to conduct. "But I can't move my arm." "Try it, at any rate." "And what if I should have to stop?" "You won't have to stop." "Can I take upon myself the responsibility of possibly upsetting a performance?" "I'll take the responsibility." And so I did a little conducting with my right arm, then with my left, and occasionally with my head. There were times when I forgot my arm over the music. I noticed at my next session with Freud that he attached particular importance to my forgetting. I tried once more to conduct, but with the same discouraging result. It was at that time that I discovered Feuchtersleben's *Contributions to the Dietetics of the Soul.* I read and studied, trying assiduously to find my way into the lines of thought expressed in the brilliant book, in which a physician, who at the same time was a poet, wisely tried to point out to suffering humanity a way that has since been made practicable. I also tried to familiarize myself with Freud's ideas and to learn from

[3] Bruno Walter's daughters were: Lotte Schlesinger Walter, born in Vienna, October 4, 1903; and Grete Schlesinger Walter, born in Vienna, September 21, 1906.

292

him. I endeavored to adapt my conducting technique to the weakness of my arm without impairing the musical effect. So, by dint of much effort and confidence, by learning and forgetting, I finally succeeded in finding my way back to my profession. Only then did I become aware that in my thoughts I had already abandoned it during the preceding weeks [pp. 164-168].[4]

Intrigued by this account of Freud's treatment of Walter, I began to search for possible additional information about their relationship, but found no reference to Bruno Walter in Freud's correspondence or in his biographies. I was rewarded, however, when I located a short paper written by Richard Sterba (1951), "A Case of Brief Pyschotherapy by Sigmund Freud." In an interview with Sterba, Walter gave an account of his encounter with Freud: "it was Freud's sincerity and decisiveness in his advice which made him take the evening train to Genoa, the same day that he had his first interview. He had never met Freud before. He felt confident immediately that he had put himself in the hands of someone who was trustworthy in every respect and who knew about human nature" (p. 79). What Walter told Sterba corroborates the account he gives in his autobiography. The whole treatment consisted of five to six interviews. Sterba postulates that Freud's suggestive support of Walter allowed him "to regain control over the muscular functions of which an unconscious inhibition had taken possession" (p. 79).

Some confirmation of what Sterba presents as an explanation of the "therapeutic success" achieved by Freud can be found in Freud's (1905) paper on "Psychical (or Mental) Treatment," in which he describes the possible therapeutic effects of travel, the importance of diverting attention from symptoms, the determination to recover as a significant effective agent in outcome, the importance of winning the patient's confidence, the significance of the physician's personality in "bringing the patient into a state of mind favourable for his recovery" (p. 292), the role and importance of suggestion in therapy—especially in hypnosis, where the physician is endowed "with an authority such as was probably

[4] Freiherr Ernst von Feuchtersleben, 1806-1849, was an Austrian physician, poet, and philosopher. He was appointed dean of the faculty of medicine at the University of Vienna in 1844. He wrote medical works, poetry (one of his poems was set to music by Mendelssohn), and philosophical essays. One of his best-known philosophical collections is *The Dietetics of the Soul* (1854).
I obtained a copy of the seventh edition of *The Dietetics of the Soul* and found it to be a work dealing with self-cure, self-meditation, and self-control. "Dietetics" refers to mental ethics and mental dietetics. Feuchtersleben attempts to philosophically and morally demonstrate the power of faith and will to cure mental diseases. For example, "Bodily infirmity may be relieved or even gradually and permanently removed, by a powerful impulse; and we may reasonably expect the same beneficial results from strong volition, the deepest and most special of all mental impulses" (p. 70). One might speculate that Walter perceived Freud's handling of him as corresponding to Feuchtersleben's philosophy and that the book was the "successor" to Freud.

never possessed by the priest, or the miracle man, since it concentrates the subject's whole interest upon the figure of the physician; it does away with the autocratic power of the patient's mind which ... interferes so capriciously with the influences of the mind over the body" (p. 298). When Freud wrote this paper, he was in a transitional phase in his development of therapeutic technique; his treatment of Walter seems to fit his 1905 description of the therapeutic process.

Although the available data do not constitute bona fide analytic material, one might tentatively suggest, speculate, or conjecture about the psychological significance of the Freud-Walter therapeutic relationship. Walter came to Vienna, like Mahler, his mentor, and like Freud who, as did Mahler, came from Bohemia to fulfill his life's ambitions. Finally achieving his ideal goal of working with Mahler in prestigious Vienna, he finds himself under attack, not for his own shortcomings, although his self-esteem and self-confidence were shaken, but because of Mahler's difficulties with the musical critics. Mahler does not come to his support and defense, but instead suggests he leave Vienna and abandon his career there. This mobilizes repressed rage in the mild Walter, but catalyzes an aggressive surge of activity, which was aided by the support of Mahler's brother-in-law, Arnold Rosé. During the course of this struggle Walter had no symptoms. Only after the unpleasant situation had been resolved and at a time when he was relatively comfortable did his "conductor's cramp" appear. Walter himself connects this delayed disorder with "wrong I had suffered more than a year before." What seems suggested is the delayed effect of a traumatic state which only later, as is seen in some traumatic situations, became manifest when the external danger no longer existed. Unlike Mahler, who disappointed Walter and probably evoked suppressed and repressed rage in him, Freud gave him emotional support. He reassured him and assumed a responsibility for his professional work that Mahler had abrogated. The loss of Mahler's love was shattering to Walter; later, when Mahler did praise him, he became ecstatic and filled with narcissistic self-love. Walter's symptoms did not all disappear in a short time, but the internal significance of his relation with Freud permitted him to overcome the disability that presumably never returned to affect his later stellar conducting career, in which his role as the leading interpreter and conductor of Mahler after the composer's death played so important a part.

Two works that Mahler composed when he was ill but did not conduct were *Das Lied von der Erde* and his Ninth Symphony. Alma Mahler handed the scores to Bruno Walter for final revision before printing, and in November, 1911, six months after the composer's death, Walter conducted the first performance of *Das Lied*; early in 1912, he presented the Ninth. Walter wrote in 1958, "It was a heavy responsibility to take my great friend's place and introduce his work to the world. Here was the fulfillment of the sense of dedication which, when I had been shaken by his First Symphony in Hamburg [Walter was only eighteen at the time, June, 1894], had made me see my future as one of service to his work (Walter, 1958, p. x). Walter closes his Preface to his biography of Mahler with these words: "I am, despite — or, perhaps, because of — the distance of time, conscious of closer contact with a man of genius, to whom I owe much in my life, a man who was, in decisive years, my model, a man whose deep humanity will always remain with me" (p. xv).

Once again, we can speculate, without too much conjecture, that even supportive-suggestive brief therapies have their intrapsychic significance, determinants, and consequences.

REFERENCES

Feuchtersleben, E. (1854), *The Dietetics of the Soul.* 7th ed. New York: C. S. Francis.

Freud, S. (1905), Psychical (or mental) treatment. *Standard Edition,* 7:283-302. London: Hogarth Press, 1953.

Sterba, R. (1951), A case of brief psychotherapy by Sigmund Freud. *Psychoanal. Rev.,* 38:75-80.

Walter, B. (1946), *Theme and Variations: An Autobiography.* Translated by James A. Galston. New York: Knopf.

_____ (1958), *Gustav Mahler.* New York: Knopf.

February, 1974

The Last Introspective Psychologist Before Freud: Michel de Montaigne

ERNEST S. WOLF, M.D.
AND JOHN E. GEDO, M.D. (*Chicago*)

Three hundred years before Freud, Michel de Montaigne embarked on "a thorny undertaking, and more so than it seems, to follow a movement so wandering as that of our mind, to penetrate the opaque depths of its innermost folds, to pick out and immobilize the innumerable flutterings that agitate it" (II:6,273).[1] He was successful to an astonishing degree. To be sure, Montaigne was no systematizer: "I, who cannot see beyond what I have learned from experience, without any system, present my ideas in a general way, and tentatively ... I speak my meaning in disjointed parts, as something that cannot be said all at once and in a lump" (III:13,824). Nevertheless, the "disjointed parts" of his obser-

---

This paper was originally written in honor of Dr. Richard Sterba, on the occasion of his 75th birthday.

[1] Montaigne's contribution to psychology has been largely overlooked or misunderstood. Today he is often thought of as a literary figure; this judgment, however, is quite erroneous. Montaigne did not write for publication, nor did he regard his *Essays* as artistic endeavors, although, eventually, he did become interested in publishing and probably also took pleasure in his artistry. He was the outstanding representative in his age of the tradition of moral philosophy (the closest parallel to his work can be found in that of the Roman stoic Seneca). It is only the generation of Montaigne's immediate successors, such as Descartes, that psychology developed as an independent discipline, abandoning the humanist introspective tradition which was then continued only in the realm of the arts (Gedo & Wolf, 1975). The full emergence of a scientific introspection had to await Freud's genius. "From the point of view of scientific method, one can say that Montaigne, in 1580, was three hundred years ahead of his time and that among his contemporaries only some physicians could have had an inkling of his attainment" (Telle, 1968, p. 228; our translation).

All references to the *Essays* are to the Frame translation (1965) and cite book (II), chapter (6), and page (273).

vations can be extracted from his *Essays* and assembled to make explicit, if not a system, at least a consistent point of view with regard to psychological phenomena. The image of Man's psyche that emerges is a remarkably modern one. The surprise engendered by the congruence between Montaigne's man and Freud's needs to be tempered, however, by several considerations. The antihumanist bias of nineteenth- and twentieth-century scientism has infused the cultural ambience with such powerful and generally unconscious disregard for human strivings that we react to any contrary scientific opinion with surprise, regarding it as unique and original. Such surprise is unjustified. Rather, one might expect that a man of Montaigne's intelligence and integrity who commits himself totally to honest self-exploration, using techniques of free association similar to Freud's, would make similar discoveries. Moreover, the decline of classical education over the last hundred years has clouded the importance of Montaigne's and Freud's familiarity with Greek and Latin sources. L. Whyte (1960) has demonstrated at some length that the genius and originality of Montaigne and Freud lie not in the discovery of the unconscious, as one so often hears, but in making the "irrational" accessible to scientific study.

I

"My style and my mind alike go roaming" (III:9,761), Montaigne says about his quest for self-knowledge. "I cannot keep my subject still. It goes along befuddled and staggering, with a natural drunkenness. I take it in this condition, just as it is at the moment I give my attention to it (III:2,610-611).

"No one is exempt from saying silly things.... Mine escape me as nonchalantly as they deserve.... I speak to my paper as I speak to the first man I meet. That this is true, here is proof" (III:1,599). The style and composition of Montaigne's *Essays*[2] reflect this free-associational roaming of Montaigne's mind. In the prologue to "Of repentance" (III:2,610-621), he summarizes his method and his aim to present himself: "Each man bears the entire form of man's estate. Authors communicate ... in some special and peculiar capacity.... I am the first ... with my whole being" (III:2,611). He lets his mind wander freely and reports it truthfully: "Musical fancies are guided by art, mine by

[2] The word "essay" was first used by Montaigne in 1580. It is best translated as "try-outs," "experiments," "trials." It was a fitting designation for Montaigne's intent. It is the invention of this novel literary form that has caused him to remain so well known to the intellectual community.

chance. . . . To accomplish it I need only bring it to fidelity . . . I speak the truth . . . as much as I dare."

He dared so much that, until recently, only bowdlerized versions were easily accessible.[3] He reveals the intimacies of his amours, not omitting references to occasional impotence or premature ejaculations. All the details of his daily life are laid bare. Though he knows that "few men have been admired by their own households, the reader gets to know him as well as does his valet.

Having allowed his mind the freedom to roam, Montaigne cannot fail to notice that now the direction of his thought is guided by unconscious forces. "My will and my reasoning are moved now in one way, now in another, and there are many of these movements that are directed without me" (III:8,713). The unconscious is experienced like an outside influence: "for there are many movements of ours that do not come from our will" (II:6,271). Not only thinking, but also the body is subject to forces not subject to the conscious will. "For I ask you to think whether there is a single one of the parts of our body that does not often refuse its function to our will and exercise it against our will" (I:1,72). Frequently implicit is the concept of conflict: "How many times do the forced movements of our face bear witness to the thoughts we were holding secret, and betray us to those present.'" Montaigne enumerates a long list of organs and bodily functions that act "without our knowledge . . . without the consent, not only of our will, but even of our thoughts." The strength of psychosomatic connections was well known to him: "The mind . . . has such a tight brotherly bond with the body that it abandons me at every turn to follow the body in its need" (III:5,641). He describes placebo effects (I:21,74) and suggests that a healthy mind may keep the body healthy: "The soul in which philosophy dwells should by its health make even the body healthy" (I:26,119). He inveighs against artificial mind-body dichotomizing: "Those who want to split up our two principal parts and sequester them from each other are wrong. On the contrary, we must couple and join them together again . . . so that their actions may appear not different and contrary, but harmonious and uniform" (II:17,484-485).[4] Postures and "gestures can arise in us unperceived."

[3] Sayce (1972) comments on Montaigne's audacious approach to sex and notes that for a couple of centuries what he had to say on the subject lay hidden in a realm of secret knowledge and veiled references.

[4] It is interesting to note that, despite Montaigne's warning, Western thought, following Descartes, abandoned the holistic view of man. Cartesian philosophy facilitated the rapid progress of physical science and technology, albeit at the cost of neglecting basic human needs and strivings. It is only with Freud that one can detect a beginning return from this detour and a renewed aim toward a humanistic science; the philosophical basis for his work began with Kant's correction of both materialistic and idealistic aberrations and was developed mainly by Schopenhauer and Nietzsche. For a fuller discussion of these historical developments, see Gedo & Wolf (1975).

Montaigne remembered from his "tenderest childhood" ... "some indefinable carriage of the body ... characteristics and propensities so much our own and so incorporated into us that we have no way of sensing or recognizing them" (II:17, 479).

Montaigne anticipated the genetic point of view in psychoanalysis: "I find that our greatest vices take shape from our tenderest childhood, and that our most important training is in the hands of nurses ... these are the true seeds and roots of cruelty, tyranny, and treason; they sprout there, and afterward shoot up lustily, and flourish mightily in the hands of habit ..." (I:23,78). But it is not only nurture that Montaigne recognizes: "In the first place, it is a nature speaking, whose voice then is all the purer and stronger because it is more tenuous" (I:23,78). Parents should not excuse their children's sadism, dishonesty, and deceit on "the grounds of their tender age and the triviality of the subject." They "must be carefully taught to hate vices for their own sake" (I:23,79). Childhood sexuality was not excluded from Montaigne's insight, and to illustrate, he quotes a poem by Horace:

> The ripened maid delights to learn
> In wanton Ionic dance to turn,
>   And fondly dreams, when still a child,
>   Of loves incestuous and wild [III:5,651].

Indeed, Montaigne anticipates play therapy: "It must be noted that children's games are not games, and must be judged in children like their more serious actions" (I:23,79). He would seem to have also come close to recognizing the never-ending role that infantile sexuality plays in adult love relationships. He liked the fashion of having marriages arranged "rather by a third hand than by our own, and by the sense of others rather than by our own." For "it is a kind of incest to employ in this venerable and sacred alliance the efforts and extravagances of amorous license" (III:5,646). Discussing sexuality in another context, he stated: "The whole movement of the world resolves itself into and leads to this coupling. It is a matter infused throughout, it is the center to which all things look" (III(5,652). It would be difficult to state more clearly and forcefully what is one of the basic tenets of a Freudian view of man.

In thus letting his mind explore itself freely, Montaigne discovered the power of unconscious forces opposing themselves to his will. Having noticed that these forces, which act "without our knowledge," also affect bodily functions as well as posture, he could then easily see them as equally effective in determining behavior. Though Montaigne is often thought of as one of the philosophical thinkers of the premodern era and rarely as one of the great psychologists, it must become clear, even upon a cursory reading, that his interest was not in abstract philosophical propositions but in the hard facts of everyday life as observed by a man with a sharp reporter's eye. During his early career as a lawyer and then as a judge in the courtrooms of Bordeaux, Montaigne had been widely exposed to the actualities of human foibles and failings. The practice of jurisprudence, like that of journalism and medicine, is a sobering experience that anchors the mind to reality and tempers intoxicating flights of the imagination.[5] Actions are likely to be judged in moral terms. Montaigne was one of the great moralists of all time, albeit with increasing understanding he became more tolerant of the transgressions of his fellow men — but hardly of his own. Inevitably driven by his insights into viewing mental life as an arena for conflict, he did not become an easy apologist for victims of circumstance, but insisted on the importance of man's self-generated and self-directed participation in his fate. He took issue with the Stoics, who saw choice between apparently equal and indifferent things — for example, picking a coin out of a number of like ones — as issuing from external, accidental, and fortuitous impulses. Not so Montaigne: "... nothing presents itself to us in which there is not some difference, however slight ... there is always something extra that attracts us, though it be imperceptibly" (II:14,463). To him, choice is always an active process, and the obstacles to be overcome, whether external or internal, are the measure of man. Virtue, Montaigne says, "demands a rough and thorny road; it wants to have either external difficulties to struggle with ... or internal difficulties created by the disordered appetites and imperfections of our nature" (II:11,308). But how can choices be made when both the vicissitudes of external circumstances and the weakness of man's nature have to be overcome? Paraphrasing from Epicharmus, Montaigne states it very clearly: "It is the understanding ... that sees and hears; it is the understanding that makes profit of everything, that arranges everything, that acts, dominates, and reigns; all other things are blind, deaf, and soulless" (I:26,112). Psychoanalysis knows no better definition of the ego.

[5] We find here another interesting parallel with Freud, who considered jurisprudence before deciding on a scientific, and eventually medical, career. Montaigne's subsequent career as a counselor to kings and as a real power in the making of royal policy through the exercise of wisdom and psychological expertise is the optimal outcome we may imagine for the kind of career Freud wished to pursue at one period in his adolescence. Freud may well have sensed the need to anchor himself in the rigorous discipline of law, whether man's or nature's, to safeguard himself against the soaring power of his imagination. (Cf. Montaigne: "Unless you keep them busy with some definite subject that will bridle and control them, they throw themselves in disorder hither and yon in the vague field of imagination" (I:9,21).

Montaigne knows that the path to virtue is guided by understanding and that the understanding can be deepened and strengthened in its struggles. The passions are unavoidable, as even the Stoics were forced to admit, but they can be ruled by reason. In the uneducated man, the impression of the passions does not remain superficial but penetrates right to the seat of reason, infecting and corrupting it (I:12,31). Like Freud, to whom what is moral was self-evident, Montaigne takes the desirability of virtue for granted, and, like Freud, he is not a preaching moralist. He knows that virtue is not its own reward, but only a desirable by-product of the reasonable life. What moves men, what is the aim even of reason, is pleasure. "In truth, either reason is a mockery, or it must aim solely at our contentment.... All the opinions in the world agree on this — that pleasure is our goal — though they choose different means to it ..." (I:20,56). Yes, even "in virtue itself the ultimate goal we aim at is voluptuousness." Unmistakably, Montaigne has recognized a force that fuels man's activities and imposes its aims. This is true even of man's highest achievements in the arts. "Whoever takes away from the Muses their amorous fancies will rob them of the best subject they have and the noblest matter of their work" (III:5,644). Pleasure is sought and pain is avoided. "For who would listen to a man who would set up our pain and discomfort as his goal?" (I:20,56). Pain is bad, but the worst pain is the anxious anticipation of it. Montaigne quotes Ovid: "Death holds less pain than does the wait for death" (I:14,37). As for himself, Montaigne fears nothing more than fear itself (I:18,53). Fear of fear, that is, anxiety, can drive out all wisdom from his mind, he quotes from Cicero (I:18,53). Anxiety thus becomes the supreme evil.

The damage done by anxiety may not be reparable. "If I were once conquered and thrown by [the passion of fear], I would never get up again quite intact" (III:6,686). Montaigne seems to have observed and understood traumatic states, because he continues the above passage: "I have no secondary defense: no matter where the torrent should break my dike, I would be helpless and be drowned for good." Montaigne's metaphor cannot be distinguished from Freud's scientific conceptualization of the economics of traumatic neurosis (Freud, 1915-1917, p. 273; 1920, p. 31). The economic point of view is also in evidence when Montaigne discusses the painful accumulation as well as the relieving discharge of libidinal tension: "The appetite that sweeps us away into intercourse with women seeks only to drive out the pain that ardent and furious desire brings us" (II:12,364). Montaigne knows that other dangers threaten to overwhelm man. He notes depressive depletion, by quoting Ovid concerning the fate of Niobe: "Petrified by her woes"

(I:2,7). He illustrates narcissistic mortification with an anecdote: ". . . Diodorus the dialectian died on the spot, seized with an extreme passion of shame, for not having been able to shake loose, in his own school and in public, from an argument that had been put to him" (I:2,8).

Some activities of the soul, however, can resist the torrent that floods into helplessness: "To consider and judge the danger is in a way the opposite of being stunned by it" (III:6,686). Insightful reason protects against being traumatized.

Montaigne also observed a variety of defensive maneuvers. A selected list of examples illustrating his awareness of defense mechanisms might include the following quotations. *Displacement:* "The soul in its passions will sooner deceive itself by setting up a false and fantastical object, even contrary to its own belief, than not act against something" (I:4,14); and ". . . people . . . push in indiscriminately wherever there is business and involvement, and are without life when they are without tumultuous agitation. . . . It is not that they want to be on the go, so much as that they cannot keep still . . ." (III:10,767). *Negation:* ". . . those who have denied [pain] in word have admitted it in practice" (I:14,37). *Projection:* "Every day and every hour we say things about another that we would more properly say about ourselves, if we knew how to turn our attention inward as well as extend it outward" (II:8,287). *Repression:* "A man must see his vice and study it to tell about it. Those who hide it from others ordinarily hide it from themselves. . . . they withdraw and disguise it from their own conscience" (III:5,642). *Reaction Formation:* "Those who flee Venus too much sin no less / Than those who do pursue her to excess" (III:5,644; from Plutrarch). *Transference:* "Those who prolong their anger and hatred beyond the affairs in question, as most men do, show that it comes from another part of them and from a personal cause" (III:10,774).

Like all introspective psychologists, Montaigne warns against easy remedies: "Let us not look for our disease outside of ourselves; it is within us, it is planted in our entrails. And the very fact that we do not realize that we are sick makes our cure more difficult" (II:25,522). Insight, though desirable, is not for everybody. ". . . We must probe the inside and discover what springs set men in motion. But since this is an arduous and hazardous undertaking, I wish fewer people would meddle with it" (II:1,244). Clearly, Montaigne is no advocate of wild analysis.

We would not be justified were we to infer from these selected insights that Montaigne had a clear and complete image of mental functioning by our present standards. Nevertheless he does organize his observations sufficiently to come to some basic conclusions. Having discovered the importance of the very earliest experiences in forming human character, he can then formulate something akin to a genetic point of view: "All things are weak and tender at birth. Therefore we must have our eyes open to the beginnings" (III:10,780). Similarly, one can discern an attempt to deal with basic drives: "Impetuous desire instantly casts the mind and limbs into thoughtlessness and disorder," and he distinguishes subtly between the desires that come from nature and those that come from the disorder of our imagination (III:10,771). "Let us also call the habits and condition of each of us *nature*," he says somewhat speculatively (III10,772). Not only sexual passion but the power of aggression is familiar to him: "Among other vices," he says, I cruelly hate cruelty, both by nature and by judgment, as the extreme of all vices" (II:11,313). This seems more than a play on words; rather, it suggests Montaigne's awareness of using his "cruel nature" in a judgmental process of reaction formation to control itself. And, finally, he knows these drives combine into a grandiose fantasy that holds away over all of mental life. His discussion of man's concern for reputation and glory, which he calls the most irrational of humors, deserves to be quoted at length:

It is the most contrary and stubborn of all, *because it does not cease to tempt even souls that are making good progress.* There is hardly any other illusion whose vanity reason condemns so clearly; but it has such live roots in us that I do not know whether anyone yet has ever been able to get clean rid of it. After you have said everything and believed everything to disown it, it produces such an ingrained inclination against your arguments that you have little power to withstand it. For, as Cicero says, even those who combat it still want the books that they write about it to bear their name on the title page, and want to become glorious for having despised glory [I:41,187].

The foregoing quotations represent only a small sample to illustrate the depth of Montaigne's insight, and they are not intended to convey a comprehensive account of his psychology.[6] Montaigne had a coherent theory about man's psychic life. It may be useful here briefly to compare his "system" with that of psychoanalysis. In so doing we are quite aware that Montaigne himself was strongly opposed to any kind of systematization and never took this additional step to organize his findings. Nevertheless, a consistent pattern does emerge from a careful scrutiny of his stated views. This psychology had developed through the use of systematic introspective methods, essentially indistinguishable from that of free association. These methods were aimed at illuminating man's inner life and the subjective meaning of his behavior, rather than focusing on

[6] For a comprehensive treatment of Montaigne's psychology, see our chapter "From the History of Introspective Psychology: The Humanist Strain" (Gedo & Wolf, 1975).

the outward behaviors accessible to an observer. Careful distinctions between thoughts and words, between consciousness and mentation, and between volition and the sum total of motivations bring this psychological system into close proximity to the topographic and structural theories of psychoanalysis. Montaigne explicitly understood a number of the other key concepts to be formulated by Freud and his followers. To mention only the most significant of these, he discussed psychosomatic correlations, autonomous functions, traumatization and working through, defenses, the signal function of affects, intrapsychic conflicts, internalized morality and ideals, characterology, the meaningfulness of dreams, narcissism and the cohesiveness of the self, psychopathology as a consequence of regression to archaic modes of function, and therapeutic change by means of insight. Montaigne recognized the fundamental position of the pleasure-unpleasure principle, and he looked at phenomena from dynamic, genetic, economic, and adaptive points of view.

As a matter of fact, it may be easier to grasp the comparison between Montaigne's "system" and that of psychoanalysis by listing their differences rather than their points of agreement. In this regard, the most significant findings may well be the fact that nothing in Montaigne's *Essays* is in disagreement with psychoanalysis with the single exception of his unempathic condemnation of neurotic irrationality in phobias. The differences between the introspective psychology of the sixteenth century and that of our age are attributable entirely to the fact that Freud succeeded in penetrating *further* into the opaque depths than Montaigne, or anyone else before him, had done. Thus, Freud added to the accumulated knowledge of the Renaissance the psychoanalytic understanding of transference across a repression barrier, the compromise formation in dreams, parapraxes and neurotic symptoms, the distinction between primary and secondary processes (in other words, the decipherment of the language of the unconscious), as well as the import of infantile sexuality for neurosogenesis.

These are omissions of enormous significance, and they probably condemned Montaigne's contribution to its ultimate fate: that of making its principal impact on the community of humanists in the generation immediately succeeding his own—figures such as Cervantes and Shakespeare, and later, Goethe, Flaubert, or Nietzsche (Jones, 1937; Boullier, 1921; Frame, 1955). Montaigne's self-analytic efforts were apparently successful, to judge by the testimony of the *Essays,* but they were suitable for emulation only by men of rare intelligence and courage who could, moreover, afford to devote themselves totally to the life of the mind. Mankind has seldom produced more than one or two such figures in any

305

century. Montaigne's psychology has relatively little to say about just those matters that proved to be central in enabling Freud to apply his psychological discoveries to the treatment of other people. Some people—indeed, some of the most eminent personages of his age—did turn to Montaigne for psychological assistance, but what he encountered clinically were generally the most intractable of psychiatric disturbances, and he was unable to develop any systematic therapeutic approach. The application of an introspective psychology to therapeutics was destined to await an opportunity that would make those with manageable, delimited neurotic symptomatology present themselves for assistance to a psychologist of Freud's genius. Such an opportunity was to be made possible in the eighteen-nineties by Charcot's delimitation of hysteria as a syndrome worthy of study and treatment.

II

Who was this great man whose perceptive and probing spirit carried the introspective psychology of the Renaissance to its culmination?[7]

Michel de Montaigne was born on the last day of February, 1533, in his father's chateau not far from Bordeaux. He died there almost sixty years later on September 13, 1592. His life, quite aside from the *Essays,* is of unusual interest.

In France, the unfolding spirit of the Renaissance had reached a peak of intellectual efflorescence during the first half of the sixteenth century. Nearly simultaneously, the Reformation and the civil strife engendered by it had begun to claim their first victims. In his lifetime, Montaigne became acquainted with the noblest ideas of man while intimately witnessing the horrors and dangers of religious civil wars. The former shaped his life, whereas the terror of the times and of painful illness racked him without really touching him.

On his father's side, Montaigne was descended from the Eyquem family, who for several generations had been prosperous wine merchants and had recently purchased both the chateau and the title of nobility. Montaigne's mother, born Antoinette de Louppes (Lopez), was the daughter of a Marrano from Aragon; her father's family had left Spain in 1492 because of the expulsion of the Jews. Her mother came of a

[7] We do not intend to produce a psychobiography of the author in this paper. We add this historical sketch in order to place Montaigne's psychological work within its proper context and to illustrate the personal and cultural matrix out of which an introspective psychology may develop.

prosperous family from Toulouse, business associates of the Eyquems. Montaigne's mother lived under the same roof with him all his life and survived him by a number of years; it must remain a matter of intriguing speculation that this most open and loquacious of autobiographers never mentions her, nor does he favor the reader with even the most cursory glance at either his wife or his only surviving daughter. Yet, the society of beautiful and well-bred women was always dear to him; perhaps, as he hints, he used lovemaking as a diversion during his days of youth and wantonness. His closest friend chided him on these escapades with women. Montaigne and Etienne de la Boétie were drawn to each other by an inexplicable and fateful force when both were already grown men. Montaigne preferred their lovingly harmonious friendship to the more ardent and scorching companionship of women. About La Boétie he could say: he is myself. His friend's sudden death precipitated another round of riotous lovemaking, which was followed by a proper and correct marriage, apparently happy if not passionate. Of his six children, only one daughter survived infancy.

In sharp contrast to the utter disregard of his mother, Montaigne writes tenderly about "the best and most indulgent father" that ever was. Pierre Eyquem de Montaigne was of small stature with a mild and pleasant mien. In his youth he had been a soldier, and even in his sixties, when he was mayor of Bordeaux, he maintained his physical vigor with regular bodily exercises. Michel loved and admired his father, who, though not a learned man himself, opened his house to the scholars and men of letters of his time. The older Montaigne revered these savants like holy persons and collected their sayings and discourses like oracles. In spite of his disclaimer of worship, his son's *Essays* testify to similar proclivities. Perhaps the most striking expression of the humanistic spirit in the Montaigne household is to be found in the carefully planned educational experiments that so profoundly influenced the future essayist. Having made all the inquiries a man can make among men of learning and understanding, Pierre hit upon the expedient of placing the young Michel into the hands of tutors who were wholly ignorant of French but well versed in Latin. No one spoke anything but Latin to the youngster, and he was over six before French became more than an alien tongue to him. One catches a glimpse of the gentleness of this rearing upon reading that, in order to protect him from too brutal a jolt, young Michel was awakened by music. Only when a novel kind of game failed to teach his son Greek did Pierre, being extremely afraid of failing in a thing so close to his heart, at last let himself be carried away by conventional practice. He sent the six-year-old to the Collège de Guyenne, which was then flourishing and the best school in France. Andreas Goveanus was one of its greatest principals; he and a number of other teachers at Guyenne were of the same Jewish origin as Montaigne's maternal grandfather. Another of his tutors was the Scottish poet and humanist George Buchanan, afterward the teacher of James I, who completed the dramas *Jepthes* and *Baptistes* at Guyenne. During his student days, Montaigne played leading parts in Buchanan's Latin tragedies. Muret, the great humanist, was also on the faculty and became a friend. In later life, Montaigne continued to associate with eminent men. Henry of Navarre, Amyot, Jacques Peletier du Mans, Monluc, Turnebus, and Justus Lipsius were included among his friendships. Through these worthy preceptors, he learned to love the noble ancients. The ideas of Socrates and the Stoics, the poetry of Horace, Virgil, and Catullus, the writings of Cicero and Seneca, and Plutarch especially, became his admired models.

Little is known about the young Montaigne's whereabouts from his thirteenth to his twenty-first year. Probably he studied law at Toulouse and spent some time in Paris. He then began a legal career, first at a law court at Perigueux, later as a counselor in the Bordeaux Parlement. It is here that he met his friend La Boétie and married the daughter of a colleague three years before his father died in 1568. Having inherited his father's possessions, he retired to his château in 1571, one year after resigning from the magistracy. He devoted most of the rest of his life to study, contemplation, and writing his *Essays*. However, this retreat was interrupted by many trips to the royal court, by lengthy travel through Germany, Switzerland, and Italy, as well as by twice serving as mayor of Bordeaux. Montaigne was a firm Catholic and loyal to the ruling monarchy. At the same time, his reasoned moderation in religious and political matters made him a trusted friend and counselor to the leader of the Protestant party, Henry of Navarre. When the latter, after many years of civil war, finally acceded to the throne as Henry IV, he invited Montaigne to join him at court. By that time, Montaigne was a sick man and unable to follow his king. He died in September, 1592, of acute quinsy, after many years of suffering from renal stones.

For the present, we must restrict ourselves to this sketchy outline of Montaigne's biography. Nevertheless, as psychoanalysts, we wish to offer some impressions. On the whole, Montaigne appears to have been free of the manifestations of neurotic conflicts. On the other hand, there is some evidence of early narcissistic fixations. Various documents suggest that Montaigne's mother was more than usually attached to the dowry she brought into the marriage and that she resented becoming a mere guest in the house that for over 30 years had been hers. In her old age she bitterly complained about having been victimized by both her husband and her son. One surmises that she was a woman who was less than motherly in warmth and affection. Montaigne's rather detached view of mankind, especially its feminine half, bespeaks a basically narcissistic orientation that may have been the result of his mother's self-centeredness. Perhaps this may also account for his seemingly excessive idealization of his father. He was cautious in his relationships and, in general, designated ordinary friendships as nothing but acquaintances and familiarity. The great exception was his passionate and tender love for La Boétie, about which he said, "Our souls mingle and blend with each other so completely that they efface the seam that joined them" (I:28,139). This beautiful description of total union between self and other appears to have been an alter-ego relationship analogous to the mirror transference described by Kohut (1971).

La Boétie was also his admired moral mentor. For the first ten years after his friend's sudden death, Montaigne's identification with his lost love object was so strong that in the early *Essays* we hear La Boétie speaking through the writings and ideas of Montaigne. A similar identification with the revered father is also plausible, particularly when it is recalled that Pierre de Montaigne, in his day, kept a journal of his soldierly travels and thus had also provided a model for the future writer. In Kohut's terms we would say that Montaigne needed La Boétie, and perhaps the father he overvalued as well, as idealized self-objects in order to overcome the deficiency in his own psychic structure that had resulted from traumatic disappointments in his relations with his unempathic mother.

During the years of self-analysis and work on the *Essays,* Montaigne may gradually have worked through his narcissistic vulnerability. The tone of the *Essays* became warmer and more personal as the depth of his insights led to a broader human outlook. Montaigne became more and more himself, original and unique, unquestionably a genius. Perhaps he had exchanged the archaic personalized idealization of La Boétie, who failed him by dying, for the idealization of the ancients who would not disppoint him. In that sense, the La Boétie affair may well have been the delayed adolescence of a genius. During his last years, a deep friendship with Marie de Gourney testified to a new freedom that included even women within the boundaries of his expanded self.

REFERENCES

Bouiller, V. (1921), *La Renommée de Montaigne en Allemagne.* Paris.

Frame, D. (1955), *Montaigne's Discovery of Man.* New York: Columbia University Press.

_____ (1965), *Montaigne: A Biography.* New York: Harcourt, Brace & World.

Freud, S. (1915-1917), Introductory lectures on psycho-analysis. *Standard Edition,* 15/16. London: Hogarth Press, 1963.

_____ (1920), Beyond the pleasure principle. *Standard Edition,* 18:7-64. London: Hogarth Press, 1955.

Gedo, J., & Wolf, E. (1975), From the history of introspective psychology: The humanist strain. In: *Freud: The Fusion of Science and Humanism* [*Psychological Issues, Monog. 34*], ed. J. Gedo & G. Pollock. New York: International Universities Press.

Jones, P. (1937), *French Introspectives from Montaigne to Gide.* Cambridge: Cambridge University Press.

Kohut, H. (1971), *The Analysis of the Self.* New York: International Universities Press.

Montaigne, M. de (1580), *Complete Essays.* Translated by D. Frame. Stanford, Calif.: Stanford University Press, 1965.

Sayce, R. (1972), *The Essays of Montaigne: A Critical Exploration.* London: Weidenfeld & Nicolson.

Telle, E. (1968), A propos du mot "Essai" chez Montaigne. *Bibliothèque d'humanisme et Renaissance,* 30:228.

Whyte, L. (1960), *The Unconscious before Freud.* New York: Basic Books.

March, 1974

V

A TRIBUTE

To Heinz Kohut:
On His 60th Birthday

JOHN E. GEDO, M.D. (*Chicago*)

It was shortly after Heinz Kohut's graduation from the Chicago Institute in 1950 that I stumbled upon the psychoanalytic scene in that city; and I matriculated as a candidate at the Institute just as he was assuming the major teaching responsibility of his career, a survey of the historical development of psychoanalytic psychology—an assignment he continued to carry out for over a decade. I witnessed the occasion that, for many of us, seemed to mark his rise to the intellectual leadership of the local analytic community: his presentation of the paper containing his most fundamental ideas—the essay on introspection and empathy—at the celebration of the 25th anniversary of the Chicago Institute. I learned further about his work through some glimpses into the organizational activities he devotedly carried out in behalf of psychoanalysis in his roles as President of the Chicago Society and later as President of the American Psychoanalytic Association. Still later, when he chaired the Committee on Scientific Activities on which I served with him, I was able to observe directly the manner in which he devoted himself to a complex organizational task. I saw the infinite patience that leads to getting things just right, the courtesy and tact that induce varied personalities to lend themselves to the common task, and the scientific judgment and tactical skill that blend into the elusive quality of leadership. Finally, in the course of the past six years, in a curious variety of circumstances, as an editor, colleague, and friend, I have had privileged access to much of Heinz Kohut's scientific production at some pre-publication stage.

Actually, a fair number of people who participated in celebrating his

A modified version of an address delivered on June 2, 1973, to friends, students, colleagues, and other intellectual collaborators of Heinz Kohut's on the occasion of his 60th birthday.

313

60th birthday have known him both longer, and in some respects more intimately, than I. Nonetheless, I suspect that I was not asked to commemorate the occasion because I am in possession of some special talent for framing appropriately sentimental expressions about the passing of the years. In any case, on the subject of age there is nothing to add to Petrarch's pithy comment: the olive dries up. I trust that the bent of my own scientific preoccupations may justify my selection, as it should enable me to examine the significance of this anniversary within a wide frame of reference. In this attempt, I will focus my discussion on two interrelated themes: first, a review of Kohut's scientific contributions, particularly in terms of their significance within the general development of psychoanalytic thought; second, biographical reflections, with specific emphasis on certain questions concerning the problem of creativity—questions that are raised by the individual life curve of Kohut's achievement.

In choosing such a focus, I am suggesting that Kohut has succeeded in opening new territories for psychoanalytic psychology, that his work constitutes a decisive advance in psychoanalytic thought, that he has brought about a major extension of the boundaries of the psychological universe bequeathed by Freud to his successors. And I would like to add at this point that the significance of such an achievement is not dependent on its specific details, i.e., on the clarity and power of Kohut's delineation of these previously insufficiently explored human depths.

Therefore, in my view, we are celebrating today not primarily a scientific observer and theorist—however accurate Kohut's descriptions may be and however cogent his explanations—but a man who has courageously stepped into hitherto unexplored and unknown regions. And it is not the fact of his having reached the specific age of 60 that we are commemorating—we simply celebrated this birthday because it happened to be the nearest notable anniversary since the publication of *The Analysis of the Self,* the book in which he has acquainted us with the most substantial harvest of his intellectual daring.

It is easy to overlook the courage that had to sustain Kohut when he embarked on the intellectual course of his recent work, which, as he knew, was bound to disturb the peace of the psychoanalytic world. For myself, however, I am inclined to agree with the judgment of Niccoló Machiavelli, one of the greatest practitioners of psychology applied to the social realm, who saw the hazards of such a course when he said: " . . . the envious nature of men, so prompt to blame and so slow to praise, makes the discovery and introduction of any new principles and systems as dangerous almost as the exploration of unknown seas and continents."

314

The quality of intellectual courage was already evident in Kohut's first major psychoanalytic contribution, his paper on "Introspection, Empathy and Psychoanalysis." Nearly two decades after its initial presentation, it is difficult for most of us to imagine how radical and unacceptable the ideas put forth in this paper were in the climate of analytic opinion that prevailed in 1957. In this succinct methodological study (and in its complementary discussion of applied psychoanalysis, the 1960 review "Beyond the Bounds of the Basic Rule"), Kohut called into question the comfortable assumption that Freud's investigations had on the whole illuminated the depths of human mental life, insofar as it is accessible by the psychoanalytic method, and that analysts could now devote themselves principally to efforts at validation, refinement, and correlation with neighboring disciplines. The ego-psychological school of thought in particular, which was committed to these assumptions, was quick to suspect the danger implicit in Kohut's ideas. They were especially disquieted by Kohut's skepticism about the relevance of data obtained by methods other than that of free association—so much so, indeed, that without the personal influence of Maxwell Gitelson, Kohut's advocacy of a return to self-analytic introspection as the royal road to new depth-psychological discoveries might well not have been published in the official journal of American psychoanalysis.

I believe that "Introspection, Empathy and Psychoanalysis" is Kohut's single most important work because it signified the end of the leading paradigm of ego psychology. Like the subject of Thurber's cartoon, "Touché!," however, the decapitated at first hardly noticed their demise. Nor did Kohut's work of the next several years give any outward hint that he would take his own methodological prescription seriously as a call to action and attempt to match the results of Freud's self-analysis and early clinical work with a fresh harvest of introspective-empathic insights. He was seemingly involved with problems of psychoanalytic education, as shown by his 1962 paper on "The Psychoanalytic Curriculum," and with professional organizational issues, as exemplified by the two presidential messages he delivered during his term of office as President of the American Psychoanalytic Association. In 1965, well within the sixth decade of his life, when he had completed his distinguished administrative services, he seemed to be the unlikeliest of candidates to blow down the walls of Jericho with trumpet blasts about man's archaic depths.

As one of Kohut's former students and as a colleague whose creative work had flowed as a result of his priceless encouragement and detailed criticism, I was firmly convinced that he would now become one of Hartmann's successors, developing elegant explanatory theories about the clinical findings of psychoanalysis. My erroneous prediction was based on widely shared and long-continued observations of Kohut as an expositor of metapsychology, as a discussant of scientific papers, as a most incisive thinker who seemed always able to remain in sharp focus, even when dealing with concepts at the highest levels of abstraction. In this regard, perhaps only those who attended his two-year sequence of lectures on psychoanalytic psychology can fully appreciate his ability. A personal anecdote will illustrate the impact he had upon his students. One of his requirements was that students keep a set of notes about his course. Feeling offended by this request, which seemed to imply that I could not digest the material without memoranda, I decided to square the account by proving that I could put down on a single sheet everything of worth he would tell us in the two-year course. True, I was able to stick to my resolve. To my chagrin, however, the stained and dog-eared paper to which I committed my microscopic scribblings gradually became so valuable that it acquired the status of a talisman. By the end of the course, I felt as if I carried in my pocket a key to the secrets of depth psychology. But I finally decided to throw the paper away; I had discovered that its contents had become a part of me. Those who are interested in acquiring a taste of Kohut's skill as a teacher might want to read the chapter he prepared in collaboration with Philip Seitz for Wepman and Heine's book *Concepts of Personality,* which appeared in 1963. There you will find the heir of Heinz Hartmann I had expected. I like to imagine that Kohut chose to bury this aspect of his self in a book that was not meant for psychoanalysts because he knew that he was destined to undertake a different voyage — a voyage for which his metapsychological mastery would be no more than preparation and equipment.

There was another good reason for expecting Kohut to invest himself in the elaboration of theoretical subtleties: one of the most important facets of his character is his profound traditionalism, in the sense of a commitment to continuity, i.e., to past history, by means of a continual renewal of its enduring values. In this regard, the intensity of his devotion to the cause of psychoanalysis in the German-speaking countries comes to mind. I do not know how often he has crossed the ocean with the primary purpose of teaching, but we have several notable records: his address at the celebration of the 50th anniversary of the psychoanalytic institute in Berlin and his "Laudation" for Alexander Mitscherlich when the latter received the Peace Prize in Frankfurt. And recently he has undertaken a psychoanalytic study of certain martyrs of the German resistance against national socialism that may bring psychoanalysis to the attention of the German people in an inspiring and memorable way.

In stressing this attachment to his origins, I do not wish to imply that Kohut's cultural roots are narrowly Austrian; on the contrary, they are broadly European — witness the many summers of his childhood and youth which he spent in France, the year as a medical student in Paris, his residence in England during the early stages of the war. His adherence to these origins is matched by his intense loyalty to his psychoanalytic forebears.

Kohut's analytic career has tirelessly repeated a pattern of homage to Freud as a source of fresh inspiration. The great new clinical discoveries he has made public since 1966 have been couched in the traditional language of psychoanalysis — conservative enough to satisfy Hartmann, who read *The Analysis of the Self* and approved its publication as a monograph of *The Psychoanalytic Study of the Child*. Indeed, many readers may have read Kohut's recent work without becoming aware of the fact that it transcends the paradigm of psychoanalysis as we have known it. On the other hand, some who have realized the full implications of his psychology of the self have tended to be impatient with the conservatism of his theoretical concepts. When confronted by such impatience, he has been known to respond with the quip that it was up to his critics to start the metapsychological revolution, or, in more serious moments, with the sobering thought that a scientific community cannot maintain its cohesion if it is deprived of its traditional boundaries too abruptly.

As a matter of fact, the announcement of Kohut's innovative conclusions in the 1966 paper "Forms and Transformations of Narcissism" took the form of a simple amendment of the libido theory — namely, the correction of Freud's original hypothesis that, in the course of development, narcissistic libido is transformed into object libido (and, conversely, that under certain circumstances object love is regressively changed back into narcissism). Kohut's new paradigm was stated in terms of postulating independent lines of development for narcissism and object love. Several way-stations of the maturation of narcissism were then described, including certain optimal transformations, which, in the language of 1905, might be thought of as sublimations of narcissistic libido. This apparently minor realignment of an old hypothesis in a neglected area of psychoanalytic psychology brought clarity and order to a wide array of phenomena that had previously been left unexplained or had been fitted into existing schemata with considerable strain. Most strikingly, it illuminated the preservation of object love in severe narcissistic regressions, a finding amply documented by analysts who had dealt with schizophrenic patients. It put the humorlessness and lack of empathy displayed by narcissistically fixated individuals into a coherent developmental framework, and it clarified those impairments of creativity that are not caused by neurotic inhibitions. A long period of intensive study was required for most of us to grasp that these important but seemingly scattered insights constituted the camouflaged vanguard of a scientific discovery of major proportions.

The dimensions of the discovery began to emerge with greater definition in the 1968 paper outlining a synthetic psychoanalytic approach to the treatment of narcissistic personality disorders. First of all, Kohut was proposing that, since narcissism has an independent line of development, related maturational disturbances are bound to result in a different set of syndromes from the ones produced by sexual conflicts involving incestuous objects, i.e., the etiological source of neurotic problems. The phenomenology of this new nosological grouping was described in *The Analysis of the Self* and has been supplemented in each of Kohut's subsequent papers. Without quite abandoning his previous mode of discussing these disorders within the framework of the libido theory, Kohut has gradually shifted his emphasis to a definition of the crux of these problems in terms of a successful but insecure achievement of self-cohesion, subject to temporary fragmentation under the impact of certain specific types of frustration. He firmly differentiated these disorders from the psychoses, in which, according to his schema, self-cohesion is never completely achieved. Kohut's nosology thus eliminates the wastebasket category of borderline conditions.

The second major proposal of this work was the technical suggestion that a truly classical analytic approach to narcissistic problems should be feasible. If the analysand's commitment of his diseased self to the analytic process is not prematurely interfered with, either through moral education or incorrect interpretations of its alleged defensive purpose, one can observe the development of stable transference-like conditions in which one can eventually discern an intense object relation with the analyst, who is subjectively experienced as part of the patient's self. Correct interpretation of the disturbances of these archaic bonds to the analyst permits genetic insight and gradual mastery of fixations at immature levels of object relations. Through these formulations, a broadening of the range of applicability of classical analysis has been achieved; a road to the analytic treatment of many patients with problems of delinquency, addiction, and perversion, and of certain previously intractable characterological disorders of depressive, masochistic, obsessional, and paranoid types had been opened.

This expansion of the effectiveness of analytic treatment is in itself a substantial achievement. In view of the practical limits on the number of patients who can receive adequate analytic assistance, however, we must not allow ourselves to measure analytic progress primarily on the basis of its therapeutic efficacy. In any event, Kohut's contribution is likely to have even more profound effects on psychoanalysis as a scientific discipline than it has had on clinical practice. He himself has largely refrained from spelling out the improvements in psychoanalytic psychology made possible by his new clinical findings. One exception to his restraint in this direction was the new solution to the problem of aggression that he presented in his 1971 Brill Lecture, "Thoughts on Narcissism and Narcissistic Rage." Here, he offers a conceptualization that does not invalidate previous hypotheses, but demonstrates their irrelevance. In every area of psychoanalysis there are similar possibilities for posing the questions of our psychology in a more fruitful manner as a consequence of Kohut's discoveries, but, in the present context, it would be neither appropriate nor feasible to cite specific examples.

Kohut's discoveries have significantly sharpened our focus and extended the boundaries of the field we are able to survey under the aegis of the basic rule of free association. The insights thus far gained through the exploration of these new territories have invalidated little of significance in our previous clinical theories; they have nonetheless revealed that much of what we have known did not have the universality we had attributed to it, but simply constituted a special case that now needs to be fitted into the new, larger schema.

Whenever I have asked Kohut whether he intended to work out the implications of his clinical theories for metapsychology, he has responded, with a mixture of impatience and wistfulness, that this is a task for the next generation of analysts. I suspect that he feels some regret about the metamorphosis that has deflected him from becoming the successor to Hartmann, whom he so greatly admired. What has come to the fore in him instead is perhaps (to use his own latest conceptual refinement) a more nuclear aspect of his self—i.e., a combination of his deepest ambitions and his most firmly anchored ideals. His recent creations have been entirely psychoanalytic—yet, at the same time, they strike me as novel, not only in substance but also in form. It is my impression that in the last year he has also been more prolific than ever. The glimpses I have had of his new work still reveal certain clinical preoccupations—with such problems as thought disorders or messianic personality types, for example—but his interest seems to have shifted to issues that transcend the therapeutic arena.

The application of the psychology of the self to the study of man in his social setting has led Kohut to the borders of general history: his new efforts may lead to exciting new collaborative intellectual work among varied disciplines. The questions that have engaged him most passionately in recent times are the deepest concerns of the human condition: tragedy and martyrdom, creative conflict and the potential for greatness, leadership and mass enthusiasm, lapses into barbarism and despair.

These are difficult subjects, and, indeed, up to now, have hardly been touched upon by psychoanalysis. Can they be successfully approached by science? I will not try to answer this question—in particular, it would be presumptuous for me to assess the ultimate value of Kohut's unpublished contributions in this area on the basis of my fragmentary acquaintance with them. But I will comment on one of their attributes. With the Brill Lecture in 1971, Kohut began to cast his thoughts into a new mold. Instead of attempting to describe his new formal departure in detail, I shall try to make my point by means of an analogy.

Standard psychoanalytic communication might be described metaphorically as a short story, i.e., however significant and rich in overtones it may be, it is essentially topical in its organization and makes its point in a straightforward way. By contrast, Kohut's recent work is polythematic; it has the complex structure of musical composition. He argues, not in linear fashion, but from multiple perspectives. Consequently, not all readers will be able to grasp the total gestalt of his work after a first reading and some will react with angry bewilderment and confusion to the great number of seemingly incoherent details, while others, led astray in a different direction, will respond with enthusiasm to the charismatic gestalt of the work, but fail to grasp the important concrete details that he has supplied in support of his over-all thesis. Could it be that he has absorbed his father's musicianship in this new, transmuted form? I believe that my view of his thinking processes will seem less surprising if we recall that in two of his earliest psychoanalytic publications he succeeded in shedding light on the mysterious relationship between musical form and the psychology of musical experience.

I turn now to my second task: the examination of the specific kind of creativity that Kohut represents: an unusual and distinguished scientific career in which the greatest contributions are being made after the middle of the sixth decade of life.

Analytic studies of creativity have not yet taken the measure of such a career. For the most part, they have dealt with supremely creative people whose work is more or less evenly distributed throughout the life span; the one exception has been our preoccupation with the career of Freud, which exemplifies a pattern that might be called the creativity of maturity. It has covertly been assumed that this is the normal timetable for a psychoanalyst. Hence it is not expected that analytic contributions will be made before the age of 40; serious scientific work is supposed to be produced in the fifth decade, and perhaps through the sixth, gradually tapering off in the seventh. This creative profile is often contrasted with one allegedly typical for mathematicians, lyric poets, and certain natural scientists whose glory years are those immediately following adolescence.

I am quite aware of the fact that the simplistic contrast between the creativity of youth and that of maturity does violence to the complexities of real life: many distinguished contributors do their best work between the ages of 25 and 50, for example. Nonetheless, I shall risk further over-simplification by asserting that Heinz Kohut represents still another specific type, that of a mind that has flowered in its later years. It seems that he has long had a presentiment that the most important crisis of his life would occur in middle age and that he would come out of it with enhanced creative powers. At least, this is how I interpret his only effort in the application of analysis to a specific work of art, his paper on Thomas Mann's *Death in Venice*. Analytic interpretations of literature can often be understood as externalizations of pieces of incomplete self-analytic work. Mann wrote his novella in his mid-thirties, and Kohut attained his insight into the significance of this story of the waning of creative powers at the same age. I think the achievement immunized both men against the fate of Gustave Aschenbach.

Thus, we are celebrating not merely Heinz Kohut's past but also his future, a future that should bring to psychoanalysis a further expansion into hitherto untouched areas — a harvest made possible only for men in later life. A few weeks ago I told Kohut that I had been trying to find an example of a writer whose major work, produced late in life, had thematic similarities to his own. And when I mentioned that I had finally discovered one, namely, Euripides, he replied, with a touch of amused embarrassment, that the major intellectual achievement of his adolescence had been a study of one of Euripides' plays. Of course, I should not go so far as to venture my private expectation that we will yet receive from him a series of works that will compare with the output of Euripides' great final years. We realize how fallible our judgment is, how influenced by our emotions — and how cautious we should be, therefore, in making predictions. But in our affectionate wishes and hopes we need not exert a similar restraint. Thus, as Heinz Kohut enters the zenith of his creative

life, we ask fate to grant him what he himself most desires. In the words
of Friedrich Hölderlin:

> Nur *einen* Sommer gönnt, ihr Gewaltigen!
> Und einen Herbst, zu reifem Gesange mir . . .
>
> A *single* summer grant me, great powers,
> and a single autumn for fully ripened song.

January, 1974

322

VI

PSYCHOANALYSIS
AS SCIENCE

The Future of Psychoanalysis

HEINZ KOHUT, M.D. (*Chicago*)

I have spoken on many festive occasions but never on one that focused on
me. It is a strange experience. I feel that I cannot do wrong, since you are
willing today to forgive me my shortcomings; nor can I do right, since,
measured by what I can achieve in reality, your expectations are undoubtedly too high. But I will not worry and will let my thoughts flow—
not unchecked, of course, but also, as befits the hour, without the rigor
and caution I would usually be inclined to apply.

I shall begin with two personal stories. The first is no more than an
anecdote with easily graspable meaning. The second, however, although
the account of a real event, has taken on the coloring of a private myth. It
has become interwoven with those elements in me that transcend the
personal: the goals and ideals—*our* goals and ideals—to which I have
increasingly devoted my life.

Here is the anecdote, and you will have no trouble understanding how
it relates to the present moment. Sixteen years ago I returned for the first
time to Vienna, the city where I was born and raised, and which I had
left nearly two decades before. I was with my wife and my then seven-
year-old son. Among the people there whom I had not seen for all those
years was an old uncle who was a man of considerable influence. On the
day before we were to leave again, this uncle suddenly expressed the wish,
probably in anticipation of his death, which indeed occurred not long
after our departure, to make a gift to my son. That evening we joined
him for dinner, after which he took us to the largest toy store in town,
Muehlhauser's—the F. A. O. Schwartz of Vienna—a large establishment
with several floors of toys. It was 9 P.M.; the store—as do all stores in
Vienna—had closed at 6, but because of my uncle's political influence,

Address given in Chicago on June 2, 1973, at the banquet following the Symposium on "Psychoanalysis and History."

I suppose, a phone call had summoned the management. Somebody was waiting, let us in, locked the doors behind us, and turned on the lights; and we were there all by ourselves. My uncle looked at my son, who gazed at his surroundings with big eyes, and said: "You may have anything here you like." At first my son was speechless and paralyzed. But some prompting from the attending manager of the store loosened him up, and we found ourselves upstairs in the section where the electric trains were soon circling around their various complex tracks. And then the balance began to shift. "Can I really have everything?" my son asked. "Yes, everything!" So, hesitatingly at first, but in ever quickening succession, he began to point at various items in the display. This?! he asked. Yes, of course! And this? and this? Of course. Then give me this! he ordered. Yes. And this! he commanded. The clerk who accompanied the manager took his orders and, one by one, put things away into boxes — engines, cars, stop signs; bridges, houses, mountains — just as fast as my son's demands were expressed. I saw my son's face becoming flushed with excitement; a dream was coming true, the world of limitations and reality was giving way. The old uncle, the manager, the clerk, all watched — for different reasons — the spectacle with glee. But I became more and more uncomfortable, and finally I said, softly but firmly: I think that we have now enough.

This evening, here, on the occasion of the meeting, conceived by Dr. Ernest Wolf, with which you are honoring me, receiving a beautiful gift from the candidates at the Institute, learning about the fact that a great university is bestowing an honorary degree on me, hearing John Gedo's review and generous evaluation of my work, seeing and enjoying the presence of this gathering, which includes some of the finest minds of modern psychoanalysis, I feel that it is *I* who need a father to tap me on the shoulder and tell me: Wake up! Enough!

I do not have such a father anymore and, for a lifetime, have had to be, as all of us must be, my own father when I am in danger of over-stimulation; I have to set my own limits and curb the onrush of painful excitement by my own devices. The father that I have set up in myself, that internal ally who helps me maintain the integrity of myself under psychologically trying circumstances, has taught me, from way back in my life, to turn to reflection, to the search for meanings and explanations. And I have learned that the enjoyment of these mental activities must often take the place of the direct gratifications that are hard to keep in bounds. And, increasingly, and with changing emphasis in the course of my life, these thoughts and reflections have become attempts to understand myself, to understand other individuals, and, most recently, also, though tentatively and with great caution, to understand man as he feels, reacts, behaves in the arena of history.

And here comes the second memory, to which I referred earlier as a personal myth. It is the memory of the only time I saw Freud—that symbol of the father, that personified allegory of the curbing and explaining efforts of which I spoke. It was a moment that was the low-point of my life, yet also, in its propelling power, a high-point—the wellspring of the most important commitments of my future. It was in 1938 when, on a sunny day in Vienna, I went to the railroad station because I had learned that Freud was going to leave our city. I cannot tell you the story, because there is no story to be told. I was a young man; the world that I had known, the culture in which I had grown up, had crumbled—there was nothing to hold on to. Yet, here was the symbolic event: an old man was leaving the city of my parents, and I, a young man, was tipping my hat as the train took him away.

I will not dwell any longer on the personal. Just as that moment at the railroad station became the germinal point for my professional and scientific future, just as it turned me, over the years, from efforts concerning myself to the attempt to help others and to make contributions to science, so will I now, having touched on this pivotal moment in my life, turn toward general reflections, in particular concerning that great content of my life, of the lives of so many of us here: the science of psychoanalysis, the psychology of the depths of the human soul. The question to which I will address myself this evening, however, concerns not the value or the validity of the contributions made so far by individual psychoanalysts, not even the significance of the immense oeuvre of Freud, but the *vitality* of psychoanalysis—in other words, I will address myself to the question of its future.

Festive occasions frequently engender a cheap optimism, when imper-manence and insignificance are denied and a prosperous future is cheerily predicted. Or such occasions may provide a forum for cheap pessimism, for the Jeremian outcry of the aged who proclaim the inevit-able decline and fall of everything—a forum for those, in other words, who predict that the younger generation, and all who will follow them, will fail. I will avoid both of these positions as I evaluate the future of psychoanalysis.

Let me begin by stating a conclusion first. Contrary to the opinion of a number of thoughtful colleagues, I have become convinced that, judging by *intrinsic* factors, analysis has great potentialities, that this science, this new and pioneering foray into the hitherto unexplored, not only has a future but also is still quite young, that our present analytic investigations do not yet penetrate very far beneath the surface. Yet I must add to this seemingly overoptimistic credo that I believe that psychoanalysis, will, before long, be exposed to the potentially most significant moment of its early internal development: the moment when there will be no more analysts who have come under the direct influence of Freud and his charisma—even in a brief glance at a railroad station.

What I am speaking about is the moment when Freud who, as an archaic image is still living on concretely in those who serve as substitutes for him, will die a second time, i.e., will finally die. I am speaking of the moment when the community of analysts will realize that they have not inherited an identification, goal-setting as well as curbing, but have been given the legacy of an opened door, allowing entry into the vast unexplored area into which the first explorers could make only a few halting steps.

The realization of the death of the father, of the disappearance of an idealized figure, can have two results. It can bring about rebellious destruction: after discarding the father's values and goals, the new generation then turns away from the labors that were imposed by the idealized figure's goal-setting demands. Or it can bring about a surge of independent initiative: after the integration of the father's values and goals has been accomplished, the youthful minds of the new generation penetrate further into the regions that the ancestral efforts had made accessible.

It is my prediction, then, that psychoanalysis is not far from an important point in its development. At that point, it will be decided whether a critical developmental task will be avoided or whether it will be engaged. In the first case, analysis will enter a period in which it will restrict itself to continuing its careful codification and systematization of the already explored, and will then die. In the second case, it will enter a more or less prolonged period of questioning its past, of struggling against the temptation of rebelliously discarding its inheritance, followed by the examination of daring new paths into new territories. This will be a period of great danger, of excited battles and debates—but analysis will have a chance to emerge from it, to go on to live and to thrive.

The future generation of psychoanalysts will have to accomplish two specific tasks before it can mobilize that creative initiative and, secondarily, those resources of talent which will enable it to move more deeply into the territory of man's psychological experiences. I have already mentioned the first of these two tasks. It is the full integration of the inherited value system that now guides us. This task includes not only those comparatively minor though by no means insignificant modifications achieved through the separation of the wheat from the chaff, of the essential from the unessential, but also the correlated undoing of certain regressive changes in the ideals that have brought about compliance which is not based on the comprehension of the meaning of the inner demand — ritualistic obedience to the letter rather than to the spirit of the inner command. The second task is the re-evaluation of the inherited value system itself and even, if necessary, its substantial transformation, in order to bring it into harmony with the character of the new generation and to make it relevant to the specific problems and tasks with which the new generation will be confronted by the surroundings in which it will live. About the first task I can speak with assurance; about the second, however, only tentatively, because the validity of my statements depends here on the validity of certain specific predictions about the nature of the future environment, specifically about the nature of the psychological environment in which the man of tomorrow will live.

What is the essence of the present value system of the psychoanalyst? Does it require further integration? Has it undergone regressive changes that need to be reversed?

The highest ideal of the psychoanalyst is his commitment to truth. Specifically, he strives to see psychological reality clearly and realistically, to unmask and discard the illusions and falsifications that arise in consequence of wish-fulfilling tendencies in himself and in those he wants to help. These tasks are the essence. The rest are instrumentalities in the service of the search for unembellished and unmitigated psychological truth. The uncovering of the repressed, with the aid of free associations and dream analysis; the use of the couch, of daily interviews, on the one hand; the tolerance, for tactical reasons, for the temporary maintenance of illusions, on the other hand — all are, despite their importance, tools in the service of the principal ideal: to expand the realm of awareness, to establish what is fact and what is fancy with regard to man's psychological life.

What are the obstacles in the path that leads to this ideal? I will here not take up those extensively studied dynamics of psychic life — the defenses and resistances — that stand in the way of living up to the ideal, but will address myself to the problem of the integration of the ideal itself.

For a number of reasons, I have, on this occasion, avoided technicalities, in particular the use of technical terms. But it is clear to those who are familiar with my work that I am speaking here of the process that in the treatment situation I call "transmuting internalization." Certain patients who as children were deprived of the opportunity to merge

329

themselves psychologically into a powerful figure in their environment, who were deprived of the security of feeling themselves a part of such a person, will during analysis attempt to accomplish a psychological task that was not completed in childhood. Although such a patient will begin by identifying himself with the gross and manifest features of the admired therapist, he will go on, if the process is not interfered with, to discover, little by little, the therapist's realistic shortcomings. In so doing, however, as he is discarding the relationship to an illusionary idealized person, he is strengthening certain structures in his own personality that had been laid down insufficiently, particularly in the area of his guiding values and ideals. The ultimate result of this process is not the incorporation of the *analyst's* values and ideals, but the idealization of standards that are in harmony with the *analysand's* personality and relevant to the tasks with which *he* is confronted in his *own* life.

The coming generation of psychoanalysts will similarly have the opportunity to divest its image of Freud of certain specific features that have remained concrete, and thus to achieve a genuine integration and strengthening of its ideals. The replacement of a concretely experienced archaic object by a strong set of ideals and values, furthermore, is likely to be followed by a surge of independent initiative, which in the case of the scientist may lead to renewed scientific advances.

What are the features that are likely to prove genuine in the analyst's ideals, and what will be discarded as bound to Freud's personality (his idiosyncrasies, as it were); to the atmosphere that surrounds a period of pioneering discoveries; and to the historicocultural environment in which Freud and his collaborators lived and worked?

Although I am here envisaging features that a future generation of analysts might not retain in their then firmly integrated ideal, the consideration of this possibility does not mean that my admiration for Freud's personality and genius has lessened.

If I conclude, for example, that Freud's (1912) advice that analysts should "model themselves during psycho-analytic treatment on the surgeon, who puts aside all his feelings, even his human sympathy" (p. 115) dealt with a time-bound necessity for the early practitioner but is not part of the essence of the value system of the analyst, this opinion does not diminish my admiration for Freud. He gave this advice at a time when the effect on the analyst's psyche of the prolonged exposure to the childhood passions of their analysands had not yet been tested and when the danger of overinvolvement and irrational response must have required emotional detachment as a protective shield. And, despite the fact that Freud's actual behavior toward his patients could indeed be full of human warmth, I have little doubt that the emotional reserve expressed in the quoted statement was an integral part of his particular personality. I see no reason, therefore, why the analyst of today or tomorrow must continue to idealize an attitude that may not be in harmony with *his* personality, especially in view of the fact that the growing familiarity with our subject matter enables us to be indeed much more relaxed than was possible for the analyst of the early days.

Or, to give another example, let us assume that Freud—perhaps in reaction to having been duped in childhood, or in reaction to being exposed to humiliations from the very society that claimed to be guided by the ideal of love for the fellow man—let us assume that such experiences prompted him to demonstrate that man's religion-building capacity was deleterious and that its creations had to be rejected as nursemaids' tales (1927). Or consider the following statement, which is in a similar vein: "If I had another life of work ahead of me," he wrote (concerning what he called "such distinguished guests as religion, art, and others"), "I would dare to offer even those high-born people a home in my lowly hut" (1936, p. 115). If it could be established that there was a genetic connection between, on the one hand, Freud's capacity to dissect the great values of man and to determine their derivation from the primitive and archaic in the human soul and, on the other hand, his growing up as a member of a minority group surrounded by the values of a majority which, despite professing high beliefs of kindness and love, humiliated and persecuted him and those with whom he identified, such a discovery would neither diminish Freud's human or scientific stature nor could it be used as an argument against the validity of his conclusions. Yet, if the analyst of the future, or if this or that analyst now, does not share Freud's emphasis on the unmasking of, let us say, religious values, I see no reason why he should feel either disloyal to Freud or unfaithful to the scientific tenets of psychoanalysis.

Or, as a final example, take Freud's touching admission concerning his attitude toward the insane ". . . that I do not care for these patients, that they annoy me, and that I find them alien to me and to everything human" (1928, p. 21). What exemplary openness he showed here about this trait in his personality, especially when it is viewed against the background of the profound explanations of serious mental disorders that he had given to the world, in spite—or perhaps even because?—of his need to keep an emotional distance from the psychotic mind (cf. Eissler, 1971, pp. 318-320). And yet, I have no hesitations in adding that this specific attitude does not belong to the intrinsic value system of the analyst, and that even its current remote derivatives—such as the occasionally encountered insistence that therapeutic techniques involving empathic responsiveness toward archaic mental states must not be called psycho-analysis—may well be discarded by the analyst of the future, who will not be afraid that every move into new territory exposes him to the danger of the irretrievable loss of his professional identity.

As I mentioned earlier, the task of integrating an ideal and our attitude toward it not only requires the discarding of those concrete features of the ideal that belong to its precursor, the idealized person, and to our relationship with him, it also involves the undoing of certain regressive changes—the reversal of the regressive development from idealized value to archaic command, from living according to the spirit of the ideal to the ritualistic and often fanatically pursued observation of accessory formalities.

The regression of values is a historicopsychological fact that can be easily observed. And I believe, by the way, that here is one of the many areas to which only the historian trained in depth psychology and the depth psychologist trained in history, if they have achieved a synthesis of the points of view and of the operations of the two disciplines, can address themselves with the hope of achieving a thorough grasp of the phenome-non. Values, like people, are subject to specific developmental changes. They are most attractive in their early prime—not perhaps when they have just been created, but not long thereafter. They are youthful then, carried with enthusiasm, and, while already purified of the excited intolerance that, at the beginning, accompanied the overcoming of the former oppressors in the heated battles of the revolutionaries, they are imbued with the glow of a meaning that is still in contact with the pressing task of reform to which they are related. The liberators of yester-day, however, may become the oppressors of tomorrow. And their values, too, may undergo a change. The content of the values remains the same, but instead of being beacons of progress they now become the code of the narrow-minded and, finally, the rationalizations of a new tyranny.

These considerations apply not only to the historical development from national, social, and political liberation to a renewed tyranny, but also to the development of a science. Indeed, I believe that the exhaustion of the vitality of some sciences is related more to such psychological factors, manifested in a curve from excited discovery over status-preserving professionalism to extinction, than to such abstract cognitive issues as the obsolescence of a paradigm (Kuhn, 1962) and the like. Or, in still different terms, one might say that a science grows older in proportion to the shift of its emphasis from the *field* it investigates to the specific *tools* it employs in investigating it.

Why is it, for example, that so few members of the faculties of the history departments of our great universities are here today? Why have they not come to find out what the psychology of the depths of the human soul may have to offer to them? I believe that I can discern one strand at least in the complex weave of their reasons for staying away. It is related to the pride of the historian in a specific brand of vision and, in the obverse, to the contempt for the different tools employed by the psychoanalyst's perception. Professor Schorske, who understands me well, responded to my outlook by stating this view in a fine formulation. "I am sure you must know," he told me, "that the problem of a confining idealization applies in any intellectual discipline, surely in the field of history." Yes, I do know. And I am grateful for the fact that I can here quote him rather than be required to talk about my own field, where I would have no trouble in demonstrating the presence of similar trends.

But having discussed the fact that the next generation will have to integrate its ideals and free them from impurities, I shall now focus my attention on the examination of a specific creative endeavor that the next generation will be able to undertake once the consolidation and purification of its value system has been accomplished: the re-evaluation of the basic values themselves, not just their integration and modification.

To change one's values is a staggering psychological task. And to advocate such a change, perhaps even to predict that such a change might come about, is likely to expose the advocate, perhaps even the cautious predictor, to the anger of those whose values seem to be under attack.

Why should it be so hard to change one's values? Although I cannot speak at length about my own views on the psychology of values and ideals this evening, a few general remarks are indispensable before I can turn to my specific prediction.

Our values and ideals occupy the position in our psyche that in the beginning of our lives was held by the idealized omnipotent adult who, on the one hand, towered above us but into whom we, on the other hand, merged ourselves and whose power we then experienced as our own. Our values and ideals have retained the quality of absoluteness, unmodifiability, and supremacy that characterized the idealized self-object; and questioning them, suggesting that they can be changed, appears to deprive us of this all-powerful part of ourselves—a threat to which we react with indignation and with the tendency to fight. Still, values do change, and the ability to change them is surely compatible with mental health. On the other hand, however, it is one of the characteristic features of average mental health that *some* values exist at any given point in time that we *experience* as being absolute and unchangeable.

I should like to emphasize another rule concerning the general psychology of values. What we identify as our values and ideals relates to psychological patterns that are not yet established with complete firmness — despite the paradoxical fact that we experience the content of these values and ideals as absolute and unchangeable. Values and ideals, in other words, are psychological structures that guide us toward certain goals despite the fact that we still harbor some reluctance to do their bidding. Values can, therefore, have two fates. Their content can change, i.e., they can be replaced by new values; or they can disappear. They disappear if our reluctance to live in accordance with them ceases. They have then become ego functions, a content of the ego. It is in this sense that we should understand one of Freud's favorite quotations, F. T. Vischer's saying, "Das Moralische versteht sich von selbst": what is moral goes without saying, requires no effort, or, with Jones (1955, p. 416), "is self-evident."

And now a final general remark. It is instructive to observe the emotions that accompany the change and the disappearance of our values and ideals. A change in values and ideals, especially when they begin to give way under the pressure of a different set of values of greater vitality, is first reacted to with rage, with the furious resolve to preserve the prized internalized self-object at all costs. But, once the old ideal has been replaced by the new one, the new one is now held to be as perfect and absolute as had been its predecessor. (In the historical arena, analogous phenomena can be observed in wars of religion and other ideological clashes.) In the second case, however, i.e., when values disappear and become ego functions, there is no rage but rather a subtle sadness — a melancholy at the loss of a long-term protector and leader.

But now I must leave generalities behind and reveal the specific change in the hierarchy of values that will, I believe, occur in psychoanalysis. The full integration of his ideals may allow the analyst of the coming generation to become the pacesetter for a change in the hierarchy of values of all the branches of science concerned with man, through a shift of emphasis from a truth-and-reality morality toward the idealization of empathy, from pride in clear vision and uncompromising rationality to pride in the scientifically controlled expansion of the self.

I will admit to feeling almost defenseless when I now imagine the reactions that my prediction will evoke from two sides. Defenseless *vis-à-vis* those who will immediately reject it on the grounds that I am advocating or welcoming a regressive development from science to kindly sentimentality, and even more defenseless *vis-à-vis* those who will immediately tend to accept it with enthusiasm on the basis of the mistaken notion that the pious injunction "love thy neighbor as thyself" will again come in the ascendancy, although now in a scientific guise.

In addition, since I can foresee that my hypothesis will quickly be drawn into the ingrained emotional dialectic of maleness versus femaleness, of paternal versus maternal attitudes, I hasten to stress my conviction that empathy is not a sex-linked capacity. It is a broad, autonomous mental function, present in all human beings, present at every level of development — from the baby's first instinctive enmeshment with his human surroundings to those rigorously controlled mental processes that supply the primary data of observation to any science of complex psychological states.

My prediction, as I will try to demonstrate, is based on careful observation and sober reflection. The facts on which my conclusion rests were not only obtained during decades of clinical work with adults, but were also derived from observing the young, specifically the questioning attitude taken by many of the young people of today toward our value system, toward that seemingly absolute and unchangeable value system that was implanted in us as the quintessence of the scientific ideal of the nineteenth and twentieth centuries — in our case transmitted to us via beliefs held by Freud. And lastly I also took into account my impression that the psychological tasks the coming generations will have to face will be different from ours because the sociocultural milieu in which they will live will be different.

I have already mentioned the deleterious *intra*professional effect of tool-and-method pride: it de-emphasizes discovery, it emphasizes formal refinement and conservatism. And I have also spoken of the deleterious *inter*professional effect of tool-and-method snobbishness: the wasteful isolation of the various branches of science from one another. These two losses, however, seem to me to be of lesser importance and more easily opposed or remedied than yet another one. Scientists in general have, on the one hand, isolated themselves from the community at large by their pride in the perfection of their operations and in the exactness of their conceptual and technological framework, while, on the other hand, despite their achievements, their activities are increasingly experienced as irrelevant by some of the most committed and searching minds of the younger generation. And indeed, if we survey the grave, the ominous events that have been shaping man's historical destiny during this century, the scientist can hardly see himself as having been more than a dehumanized technician, *internally* helpless, with his ingrained tool-and-method pride, to relate in depth to the crucial issues of our times. Will it

335

be the psychoanalyst who will here lead the way? Will it be the example of psychoanalysis that will demonstrate to the other branches of science that the use of tools and methods involves no more than the employment of ego functions? The analyst, as does every man of science, has, of course, the right to enjoy the exercise of his abilities and skills to the fullest, but there is no need for the idealization of these functions. I believe that once we relinquish the idealization of our tools and methods, the exhilarating expansion of the self, a new kind of humanitarianism in the form of a scientific empathy, will gain ascendancy.

Empathy is, I am convinced, not just a poor relation of those other forms of cognition that we hold in high esteem because we consider them functions of our prized intellect. Empathic modes of perceiving ourselves and our surroundings exist from the beginning of our lives side by side with other, nonempathic modes of perception. And empathy, as holds true for nonempathic cognition, has its own line of development, can be trained, refined, and employed with scientific rigor. Psychoanalysis is par excellence the science of empathy, of that "mechanism," as Freud (1921) said, "by means of which we are enabled to take up any attitude at all towards another mental life" (p. 110n). As a newcomer to nineteenth-century science, however, psychoanalysis has always felt methodologically insecure in comparison with the established sciences. And we have underplayed or hidden our reliance on empathy, have been ashamed of it as not scientific. I believe that the psychoanalyst of the future, if he can become unashamedly proud of his stance of scientific empathy, will be able to provide all the sciences of man with that common ideal—an organizing principle of their various specialized activities—for which they will have an increasing need in the world of tomorrow.

What was the world of yesterday in which psychoanalysis was born? What will be the world of tomorrow to which psychoanalysis may yet make its weightiest contributions?

The world of yesterday (which seems to those of us who are of middle age and beyond to be the world of today) was still the world of the individual—a world descended from the Renaissance. It was the world of the independent mind—of the proud scientist: standing tall, clear-sighted. And it was also the world of intense interrelationships between clearly defined people. It was a world that exposed the child to over-stimulation by involving him in the emotions and conflicts of the adults who surrounded him, exposing him to a degree of participating excitation and temptation that his psyche was not yet ready to handle. This was the time when psychoanalysis was born. It gathered its data through the activities of the nineteenth-century scientist, proud of his intellectual clarity, eager to distance himself from a demimonde of sentimental fuzziness, of tenderhearted perception. And it set about investigating the personalities and the lives—whether in the terms of psychopathology or in the terms of normal variation—that had been formed in consequence of the exposure to the clashes of clearly delimited individuals and of families and groups made up of clearly delimited, of strongly—perhaps overly strongly—interrelated people. This is the matrix of analysis as we know it from our literature and as we still tend to view it today.

The world of tomorrow, however, is not likely to be the same. Changes are not abrupt, of course, and just as the older generation sees only the yesterday in the today, so may the younger generation see only the tomorrow as significant and overlook the potent remnant of a past whose influence is still felt everywhere. What will be the sociopsychological essence of the world of tomorrow? Will it remain a world of individuals as was the world of yesterday? Will the children and grownups of tomorrow's world continue to confront the problems of overinvolvement and overstimulation—of traumatic interpersonal conflicts that have become endopsychic? For the answer to these questions I turn to the prophets of all psychocultural tomorrows, the great artists, poets, and writers. They are no longer dealing with the problems of psychological man as we have known him; indeed, they seem strangely unpsychological to us so long as we remain walled off from the problems of tomorrow's world. I will not call as my witnesses the most profound prophets of this tomorrow—the musicians of atonal sound, the sculptors of disjointed form, the painters of disintegrated line and color, the poets of the language-decomposed— who, in their work, are demonstrating the breakup of the unresponded self and its artistic reassemblage. I will instead turn to a writer whose message, perhaps because his genius was not quite of the order of the greatest in those other fields, may therefore speak more clearly to our average minds. I ask you to think of the writings of Franz Kafka, in particular of *Metamorphosis, The Trial,* and *The Castle.*

Mr. K. is Everyman, the Everyman of a tomorrow that, I believe, is already discernible today. He is the Everyman who had been exposed to the unempathic indifference of his family and who has therefore remained grotesquely grandiose and thus estranged from the world. And he is the Everyman who feels that society, too, that latter-day extension of the family, is indifferent to him and who, therefore, wanders through the world, empty, flat, yearning for something he cannot understand any longer because the part of himself that once was eager to demand welcoming empathy and empathic response has long been buried and has ceased to be available to him. The cold voices of the family speak of him as the cockroach, in the impersonal third pronoun, and to the unreachable judges of the trial and to the unreachable rulers high up in the castle he has become a number, rejected without even an attempt to justify his rejection in individual terms.

Is this truly the world of tomorrow? Yes and no. "No," if we understand this question in a literal sense, but "yes" if we attempt to focus with predictive empathy on the leading psychological problems the man of tomorrow will have to face — indeed is already today increasingly facing.

Most analysts will, I believe, agree with me that the forms of the psychic illnesses we are treating are changing, that, even though they might still be in the majority, we are seeing fewer people whose disorder is the result of unsolvable inner conflicts, and increasingly more who suffer from having been deprived of that give and take with a close and interested environment, which would have enabled them to shed the asocial grandiosity of infancy and thus become self-confident and secure participants in a meaningful world of adults. But I do not have to evoke the specialized professional experiences of the analyst to make my point. Who has not felt a whiff of the cold anonymity of the Trial when he was caught as a patient in the wheels of a big impersonal hospital? Who has not stood anxiously in line somewhere, while somebody, behind a desk, was delaying his response to him, and was thus demonstrating his impersonal power over him, for one terrible fraction of a second? I believe these indignities — although they have undoubtedly always existed — have now taken on an ominous symbolic flavor. They point to a future to which only a few of the greatest artists have begun to respond in depth.

But I must hurry on in my argument, tempting though it is to broaden the base of my assertions. What I am saying is that in a world of stabilized populations, of increasing uniformity, of lessened space to roam in, of mass movements and efficient totalitarianism, the individual will be confronted by new problems of psychological survival. A shift from the joys of action to the enriching potentialities of his inner life may well be one of his avenues of escape, as I have suggested in another context (Kohut, 1973). The expansion of the self, its increasing capacity to embrace a greater number and a greater variety of others through a consciously renewed and cultivated deepened empathy may be a second one. And psychoanalysis appears to have emerged just at this crucial time to be man's scientific leader in both of these directions.

From the beginning of life, it is empathy, the psychological extension of an understanding human environment, that protects the infant from the encroachment of the inorganic world. And it is human empathy, as we mirror and confirm the other and as the other confirms and mirrors

338

us, that buttresses an enclave of human meaning—of hate, love, triumph, and defeat—within a universe of senseless spaces and crazily racing stars. And, finally, it is with our last glance that we can yet retain, in the reflected melancholy of our parting, a sense of continuing life, of the survival of essential human sameness, and thus protection against the fallacy of pairing finiteness and death with meaninglessness and despair. This is an axiomatic belief, no more provable than the Hitlerian dogma that only eternal war and destruction are reality. And if I say that in the hierarchy of the values of science in general and of psychoanalysis in particular the primacy of empathy will be established, I cannot prove the validity of this future pre-eminence any more than one could prove that tool-pride, the pride in clear vision and in the undistorted perception of reality, deserve the crown.

Only one detail will I stress once more at the end. Our unashamed commitment to the survival of human life, the commitment to contribute our share to the preservation of the vitality of a fulfilling human life, is not only compatible with scientific rigor; scientific rigor is indeed indispensable. True, a patient who, on the one hand, had been overstimulated as a child will, despite his noisy love-demands, experience a calm, objective therapeutic atmosphere as basically wholesome and, in the long run, as a support during the task of raising his conflicts into awareness and solving them. And the emotionally undernourished patient, on the other hand, will, despite his overt self-centered coldness, experience a positively toned atmosphere of nonrejecting empathy as being in the long run the appropriate medium for the performance of *his* therapeutic work. But these considerations concern only the emotional climate in which the therapeutic interactions take place, not the details of analytic technique and the dynamics of the cure. Analysts do not hold the simplistic view, for example, that people who suffer from early deprivations must now have them made up for by a belated therapeutic compensation. The image of the aging Ferenczi, allowing his patients to sit on his knees, trying to provide them with the love of which they had been deprived in their childhood, does not represent our ideal (cf. Freud, 1931). We are aware of the complexity of the results of early deprivation; but we do not encourage the therapeutic re-emergence of childhood demands in order to give now what had been missing in the past so that their curbing and transformation can finally be achieved. The position of primacy in our hierarchy of values that will be attained by the ideal of achieving an ever-broadening and deepening scientific empathy for the varieties and nuances of human experience relates, in other words, to a broad motivational context, not to a set of rules concerning methods and operations. Or, to express the same thought in still another way, our leading ideal will not be passionate truth-finding softened by humanitarian considerations, but the empathic expansion of the self with the aid of scientifically trained cognition.

But I must come to a close. Despite the apparent complexity of my presentation, my argument was simple. I believe that psychoanalysis will in the not too distant future examine itself afresh, will reorganize its basic stance, will transmute its inheritance into new, creative initiative. And, because it is the science that reaches farthest into the breadth and depth of the human soul, I suggest that it will be the leader in the revolutionary undertaking of shifting the hierarchy of the values of the scientist of the future. Pride in clear vision and realism will turn into the nonconflictual enjoyment of *ego functions*. But scientific empathy, the broadening and strengthening of this bridge toward the other human being, will be the highest *ideal*. If the analyst will lead the sciences of tomorrow into this direction, he will most significantly have entered the decisive battle of the future: the struggle between the human world, a world in which the varieties of psychological experience are cherished, and a nonhuman world, the world foreseen by Kafka, whose regimentations and regularities resemble the inexorable laws that establish the organization of inorganic matter. We cannot predict how this battle will end or where the victory will ultimately lie. But we do know on which side the psychoanalyst must fight, upon which side psychoanalysis, this new sun among the sciences of man, will shed its understanding warmth and its explaining light.

REFERENCES

Eissler, K. R. (1971), *Talent and Genius*. New York: Quadrangle Books.

Freud, S. (1912), Recommendations to physicians practising psycho-analysis. *Standard Edition*, 12:109-120. London: Hogarth Press, 1958.

———— (1921), Group psychology and the analysis of the ego. *Standard Edition*, 18:65-143. London: . Hogarth Press, 1955.

———— (1927), The future of an illusion. *Standard Edition*, 21:1-56. London: Hogarth Press, 1961.

———— (1928), Letter to Istvan Hollos of October 4, 1928. In: Schur, M., *The Id and the Regulatory Principles of Mental Functioning*. New York: International Universities Press, 1966.

———— (1931), Letter to S. Ferenczi of 13 December 1931. In: Jones, E., *The Life and Work of Sigmund Freud*, Vol. 3. New York: Basic Books, 1957, pp. 163-165.

———— (1936), Letter to Ludwig Binswanger of 8 October 1936. In: Binswanger, L., *Erinnerungen an Sigmund Freud*. Bern: Francke Verlag, 1956.

Jones, E. (1955), *The Life and Work of Sigmund Freud*, Vol. 2. New York: Basic Books.

Kohut, H. (1973), Psychoanalysis in a troubled world. *This Annual*, 1:3-25.

Kuhn, T. (1962), The Structure of Scientific Revolutions. *International Encyclopedia of Unified Science*, Vol. 2, no. 2. Chicago: University of Chicago Press.

October, 1973

The Psychoanalyst in the Community of Scholars

HEINZ KOHUT, M.D. *(Chicago)*

As a psychoanalyst, I am accustomed to seeing the world and its events as they are reflected in the experiences of the individual. I am thus tempted to react to the honor bestowed upon my work and myself by speaking in personal terms of what the support of a great institution such as this University has meant to the thinking, working, and creating self. The moral support that institutions can provide for the lonesome worker is indeed important. I feel, however, that the significance of the occasion is not definable within the framework of individual psychology, and I have accordingly decided on a subject for my talk more in keeping with the deeper meaning of this day. The title of my essay, The Psychoanalyst in the Community of Scholars, is, therefore, meant to indicate that I have set my sights on a broad topic: I will examine the relationship of psychoanalysis to the university; or, stated in more general terms, I will discuss some problems of the integration of a specific new system of thought, psychoanalysis, into the established body of the intellectual life of our time as it is represented by our universities.

As all of us know, and as we seem to have accepted with some resignation and without too many questions — although we should be deeply disturbed and puzzled by the fact — psychoanalysis and the universities have on the whole not been on good terms. It remains illustrative of the lack of integration of analysis within the university that, when Freud received finally, after many delays, his professor's title from the University of Vienna, it was given to him not for having made some of

Address given at the University of Cincinnati on November 16, 1973, in response to receiving the honorary degree of Doctor of Science.

341

the most daring steps in the intellectual history of modern times,[1] but for his solid, yet by no means world-shaking, contributions to neurology and neuropathology.

It would be a worthy challenge for a skilled and unbiased historian to investigate the relationship between psychoanalysis and the universities and — how could he resist the temptation? — to assign the share of blame for the fact that the doubtlessly still prevalent attitudes of mutual suspiciousness and mutual contempt have not been overcome.

I am not a historian — unfortunately. If I had another life to live, I think I would try to become one, because I am convinced that a new and revolutionary science of history is the logical next step, the natural development that ought to follow the revolutionary step Freud took with regard to the psychology of the individual. Being neither a trained historian of the traditional type, nor, of course, yet that revolutionary historian of whom I like to dream, I must restrict myself here to a few comments. What is the explanation for the lack of integration of psychoanalysis within the mainstream of modern science?

It is frequently thought that common prejudice has played a role in blocking the way to the acceptance of Freud's work. "Rest assured," Freud wrote to a friend in 1908, "that, if my name were Oberhuber, . . . my innovations would have met with far less resistance" (Abraham & Freud, 1965, p. 46). Perhaps so — but I do not think that this sociological explanation is satisfactory. Prejudice may well have contributed to the delay in Freud's obtaining his professorship at the University of Vienna. But even had Freud been a member of the ethnic and religious majority in Austria, I believe that psychoanalysis as a body of science would still not have been accepted by his great alma mater. No, the narcissistic tensions aroused by differences in ancestry were not the essential difficulty. The contributions to the traditional branches of science made by numerous other scholars and scientists of Freud's religious extraction, whatever personal rejections they may have had to suffer, were after all accepted by the University of Vienna and became fully integrated into the body of knowledge that was recognized as valid science by its faculty. And if anyone still doubts the essential correctness of this view, I recommend that he read (in Rosenbaum, 1954) the touching correspondence

---

[1] As I have stated in earlier communications and as will become apparent again in the course of the present one, I believe that the crucial significance of Freud's contribution lies neither in his invention of the enormously fruitful methodology of psychoanalysis nor even in the vast number of psychological discoveries he was able to make with the aid of hiw new methods, but rather in his having created a science that allowed empirical and conceptual access to a field which heretofore had been open only to the nonscientific responses of artists and writers, i.e., a science of the human soul in all its complexity.

between Freud and Hebrew University, that young representative of traditional scientific thought. Freud begins the correspondence hopefully—he speaks of "our university" in his first letter of October 16, 1933—but in his final letter of December 5, 1933, he is referring coldly to "the University of Jerusalem"—with the same disappointment concerning the acceptance of psychoanalysis to which he had felt exposed throughout his life by almost all the institutions of higher learning.

Another well-known explanation for the nonacceptance of psychoanalysis is derived from the analyst's experiences in individual psychotherapy; it is the claim that the rejection of analysis is due to "resistance." As you know, the term "resistance" refers to the fact that the confrontation with unconscious mental contents increases the repressive forces. Analysis confronts man—layman and scientist alike—with all those strivings within himself which he has painfully learned not to know; no wonder, then, that people in general and scientists in particular will reject a science that threatens the maintenance of the established repressions.

This is simple and persuasive reasoning; but I think it is no more adequate than the explanations that are based on social considerations. It would require a paper of its own to defend this assertion against the objections that could be raised at this point. Suffice it to say that the mechanism in question is undoubtedly frequently in evidence when people are for the first time confronted with specific psychoanalytic findings. And it would also not be difficult to point out certain individuals in whose case the loudly voiced and angry rejection of psychoanalysis does clearly rest on personal psychological dynamisms that are indeed akin to resistance. But I do not believe that the lack of integration of the body of knowledge accumulated by psychoanalysis into the scientific sectors of our civilization can be explained in this way. Psychoanalysis was, after all, created by man and is deeply understood by many people. Various aspects of analysis, furthermore—albeit highly selective ones—have found increasing acceptance inside and outside of science. Why, then, does the gap between analysis and the sciences still persist? Why is the bestowal of an honorary doctor-of-science degree upon an analyst *for his psychoanalytic work* still an event of some significance in 1973, more than 70 years after the publication of *The Interpretation of Dreams* (1900), more than 90 years after the first analytic observations (the case of Anna O.) were recorded (Breuer & Freud, 1893-1895, pp. 21-47)? No! Scientists with their (on the whole) greater than average ability to accept facts, whatever their emotional connotations, should be expected to have learned by now to make the necessary psychological adjustments and, within their strongly walled-off autonomous egos, to have furthered the work of the integration between psychoanalysis and the established scientific disciplines.

One of the profoundest explanations of the psychological forces that oppose the acceptance of analysis was given by Freud nearly 60 years ago. Put briefly, Freud (1917) said that analysis — in particular its central claim of the existence of unconscious mental processes — tended to be rejected because it had made a discovery which offended man's delusional but tenaciously held conviction that he was master in his own psychological household. To paraphrase Freud's reasoning succinctly: his findings — like those of Copernicus and Darwin before him — constituted a narcissistic blow to people and they reacted with narcissistic anger in the form of attacks on psychoanalysis.

I have always had the greatest admiration for this deceptively simple essay by Freud, and I continue to hold his formulation in high regard. It is, however, my conviction that it refers to a factor that is, in the long run, no more decisive than the social and psychological forces of which I spoke earlier. All these explanations — and yet another one to which I will turn shortly — neglect the presence of counterforces, the creation of countercurrents if you will, which enable man through the use of a variety of psychological means to accept the seemingly unacceptable. It may be an unpleasant blow to our pride to realize that we don't live in the center of the world, that our earth is a negligible speck of dust in the universe — still, we all have managed to accept this fact without suffering from lowered self-esteem. It may be unpleasant to realize that we were not separately and uniquely created by God as the ultimate product of his creative ability, that mankind is, at best, a small link in the developmental chain of living matter. Still — disregarding the Monkey Trial — we all have managed to accept this aspect of reality as well and don't seem to be unduly depressed about it. Indeed, I believe that most people experience a distinct pride after having acknowledged the explanatory power of these theories: an enhanced feeling of well-being, a narcissistic increment, which is based on their having been able to rise above themselves through the action of their mind, to participate in a surpassing reality through the acceptance of a truth that has validity beyond the limits of their individual existence.

But I must turn to yet another psychological impediment which, in my opinion, accounts at least as much for the isolation of psychoanalysis among the sciences as do social bias, resistance against the repressed, and the rejection of the notion of an unconscious mind. It is a psychological constellation that is not only responsible for the gap separating psychoanalysis from the other sciences, but tends also to divide other branches of science from one another. I have called this divisive force tool-and-method pride, or tool-and-method snobbishness (cf. Kohut, 1975, p. 335).

I deliberately chose this descriptive term in the hope that it would be easily understood. It refers to the increasing esteem in which the specific methods that each branch of science develops in the pursuit of its goals tend to be held, to the awe, even, with which the devoted specialist does ultimately look up to the idealized methodology of his field. The characteristic mixture of pride in his technical and conceptual methodology and contempt toward the uninitiated which the specialist tends to develop leads not only to the isolation of the various branches of science from one another, but also to the internal rigidification of each branch of science and thus to its lessened vitality as it shifts its emphasis from the field being investigated to the specific means it has developed in order to explore it.

Although my remarks about this point must be brief, I do not want them to be simplistic. I know that sometimes means and ends cannot be neatly separated, that—as was certainly true for depth psychology—the discovery of a pioneering method can be the decisive step which opens a new field. I am not speaking against the importance of method, nor am I belittling methodology and specialized skills; I am only saying that they should not be idealized, that, in psychoanalytic terms, they should remain ego functions. The ability to master them to perfection should be enjoyed by the practitioner. If the attainment of technological mastery becomes the supreme ideal of any branch of science, however, then its creative spirit will be stifled and its survival will be in doubt.

This is a broad topic and one that I cannot pursue very far today. Let me call to mind, however, the moving and beautiful portrayal in Richard Wagner's opera *Die Meistersinger* not only of the problems posed in this conflict but also of the balanced human attitude that their solution requires. The Meistersinger were a guild that stifled the free expression of art by more and more rigidly applied rules. Yet, the greatest among them, Hans Sachs, not only retained his receptivity for a beautiful song, even though it transcended the narrow rules, but also could simultaneously maintain the realization of the value of a conservative methodology. "Verachtet mir die Meister nicht, und ehrt mir ihre Kunst!" ("Do not hold the masters in contempt, but do revere their art!") he tells the creative rebel who feels that the tool-and-method pride of the established profession has left no room for his originality.

But I will now return to my main line of thought and express again my

345

conviction that there is little question about the fact that one of the barriers which has isolated psychoanalysis from the established branches of science has been tool-and-method pride; and that there is little question, furthermore, that the responsibility for the existence of this barrier is shared by both sides. I would also suggest that the increasing rapprochement between psychoanalysis and the established sciences is due to the fact that this particular wall is gradually being lowered through mutual adjustments. It is being lowered through the efforts made by some workers in the established sciences; by experimental psychologists, for example, who are beginning to treat the data collected by psychoanalysis with respect and who are enriching their own research by focusing their attention on topics that have been made accessible to them by analysis. And the barrier is also being lowered through the effort of some psychoanalysts; by those, for example, who are attempting to prove the correctness of some of the empirical findings of psychoanalysis with the aid of the traditional methods of science, specifically through the methods of statistical evidence.

I have now reached a turning point in my reflections. Having examined a number of factors that might explain the lack of a full integration of psychoanalysis with the established sciences, and having come to the conclusion that none of them, alone or in combination with the others, can account for the relative exclusion of the psychoanalyst from the community of scholars, I must now turn to those features of psychoanalysis that are indeed responsible for its continuing isolation. I will not, however, approach this crucial issue directly but will first consider an important question that might be raised at this point.

Is it really true that analysis is not accepted by our modern Western culture? Has it not, on the contrary, become one of the pillars on which the modern world rests—like dialectic materialism, relativity and quantum physics, and the visual world of Picasso? And is it really true that analysis is not accepted by our universities? Has is not, on the contrary, exerted a strong influence upon certain activities carried out within the universities? We need think only of many departments of pyschiatry and schools of social service, of some departments of psychology, of social and political science, history, theology, anthropology, and even jurisprudence, to realize that psychoanalysis has achieved a solid foothold in the universities. And in other important areas of modern Western civilization—consider for example, the psychological novel, the psychological play and movie—the influence of analysis is often so great that it appears at times to interfere with the unfolding of the genuine virtues of the creations in these fields, by bringing in psychological understanding from

346

the outside, as it were, instead of letting it emerge from the depth of the creative writer's soul. Yet, despite the scholarly eclecticism at universities which extends its tolerance toward analysis, and despite the enthusiasm with which some of the insights of psychoanalysis are employed by certain groups of artists, I remain unconvinced of the acceptance of analysis by our culture.

Let me give you a concrete illustration of the puzzling nature of the serious difficulties faced by the attempt to bring about a valid integration of psychoanalysis with other scientific disciplines. An increasing number of professional people from various fields—from psychology, anthropology, jurisprudence, for example—are nowadays undertaking psychoanalytic training. I do not deny the desirability of this enterprise—indeed, I have been its staunch supporter for many years. But I have also been disconcerted about a specific paradoxical result of such training. Having undergone the training, the trainee will not infrequently move into one of two directions: he may, after a while, emotionally and intellectually return to his original discipline with little obvious enrichment from the psychoanalytic experience—or he may become a psychoanalyst, more or less dropping the knowledge and skills of his primary profession. And even where an unusually gifted person is indeed able to achieve an apparent integration—such as a skilled historian's now greater ability to write pathographies of historical personages—it strikes me that he is now (in essence) using two separate skills side by side, that the essentials of the two branches of science have not achieved a new synthesis through the emotional and intellectual work of an individual who was trained in both of them. One is reminded of the mode of perception in the figure-ground experiments: one sees either one configuration or the other; but it is impossible to see both of them at the same time.

We are thus still left with a puzzling question concerning the relationship between psychoanalysis and the other sciences, i.e., we must still define the nature of the obstacle that stands in the way of the true acceptance of the central area of the methods and findings of psychoanalysis by the other sciences.

There is, indeed, no lack of evidence for my assertion that the solid integration of psychoanalysis with the other sciences has not yet taken place. Not only does the acceptance of psychoanalysis always seem to be only temporary and to remain precarious—witness the repeated assertions that analysis has become old-fashioned, that it has been superseded by more modern developments—and not only is it usually accompanied by loudly voiced expressions of uneasiness and caution, but also, and most importantly, I believe that the acceptance of analysis always concerns only its peripheral areas. Indeed, I cannot shake off the uncanny impression that analysis is losing its essence in the process of being accepted, that, in particular, it is in danger of drifting toward the repudiation of its proudest achievements when it tries to become acceptable to the other branches of science. The feeling of uneasiness that I experience under these circumstances is not due to any particular- istic professional snobbishness on my part, is not related to any feeling of superiority about the analyst's proficiency in the use of the psychoanalytic situation; it is akin to the dismay that is evoked in me when I see how the profoundest insights obtained by analysis about the tragic condition of man are being put to use in cleverly concocted movies, plays, and novels. In either case, when analysis presents itself through the medium of art or when analysis becomes, as it were, all science, when it is no more than subtle phenomenology or when it tries to become all dry, quantifying formulation — in either case do I recognize incompleteness, in either case do I know that an integral part of this great new edifice of human thought is now missing.

It may seem that the object of all these complicated reflections is simply to observe — as is often said with reference to the profession of medicine — that psychoanalysis is partly art and partly science, and that I do not like it when it becomes completely one or the other. One could put it that way; but I don't think that one would have done justice to the problems involved. It is true that it is my wish to demonstrate that psychoanalysis in its very essence consists of two seemingly antithetical constituents, of which one may be especially attractive to the artistic temperament while the other will be more in tune with the sober intellect of the scientist's personality. It is, however, not my primary aim here to describe the emotional responses of different people to the different facets of analysis: I wish to define, if ever so briefly, that two-layered substance of analysis which I believe accounts for its revolutionary nature, which in fact sets it apart from the established sciences, which explains its singular position in modern culture, and which is, in particular, the most important cause of the fact that it is not fully integrated with the other branches of science and thus with the universities.

The aim of science is to provide explanations of the phenomena observed by man, ultimately in order to increase his mastery over nature. As far as the interests of science itself are concerned, this mastery is confined to the realm of cognition, although intellectual progress may lead secondarily to increased technological control. In order to achieve cognitive mastery over the world he observed, scientific man had to rid

348

his thought processes of certain archaic or infantile qualities: he had to give up subjectivity (i.e., he had to learn to observe external phenomena and to explain them in their interactions as, in essence, unrelated to himself); he had to relinquish the animistic conception of nature (i.e., he had to realize that natural phenomena are not to be explained in analogy to self-experience: as volition or emotion, for example); and he had to learn to move in his explanations increasingly away from his sensory impressions. To give a simple illustration: a flash of lightning is not to be understood as a god's angry attack on man; it is to be formulated in mathematical and physical terms as a discharge process between different levels of electrical tension.

I believe it is the incompleteness of man's cognitive development — his unacknowledged, still persisting temptation to return to animistic thought and to anthropomorphic concepts — that has created a defensive hypersensitivity to psychoanalysis, a science that seems to be unscientifically animistic and anthropomorphic because it deals with the inner life of man. Psychoanalysis is the science of complex mental states, the science of man's experiences. It thus poses the ultimate challenge to scientific thought: to be objective and (in its explanations) phenomenon-distant in the area of the subject, the human soul, the human experience itself. It is the emotional hardship of meeting this challenge, not the complexity of the intellectual work, that accounts for the fact that psychoanalysis was of necessity a very late development in science. And the full integration of analysis with the established sciences will, therefore, be the manifestation of a decisive progress in man's acceptance of scientific thinking.

The difficulty of making this step toward the integration of analysis with the body of the established sciences is great, and more than good will and the overcoming of the usual tool-and-method pride is required to achieve it. The emotional attitude needed if this task is to be truly faced is not a tolerant welcome to a feeble straggler, but open confrontation with a trailblazing pioneer. The completion of the task is, as I see it, in jeopardy from both sides: from the side of the traditional scientist who walls himself off against analysis out of fear that the acceptance of its methodology will undermine the constructed edifice of scientific thought; and, even more importantly, from the side of the analyst who, in his wish not to appear unscientific, tries to adopt not only the formal style of the theories of the established sciences but even their methods of observation.

This uneasiness among analysts is not new. Freud expressed it as early as 1895, in the *Studies on Hysteria*, when he acknowledged that his case histories sounded "like short stories and ... lack the serious stamp of science"; this appearance, he added apologetically, was due to the nature of the subject matter and not, he said, to "any preference of my own" (Breuer & Freud, 1893-1895, p. 160).

Is the suspicion of the other sciences justified that psychoanalysis is unscientific? Is the analyst's uneasiness that his activities may "lack the serious stamp of science" warranted? I do not believe the answers to these questions are difficult to find.

Each empirical science begins with observations, with single items, or with sets and combinations of them; these are then brought into an explanatory (causal) relationship with other single items in the field of observation, or with sets of them, in order to explain their behavior. We have the mass of a stone, the mass of the earth, and the speed of the stone's fall; and by correlating these three observable items we are led to an explanatory assumption, to the hypothesis, let us say, of a gravitational pull of masses. Or we observe the fact that a person's ideation is leading him to a certain wish, see then that he reacts with anxiety to this wish, and, finally, we witness the disappearance from consciousness of the ideation concerning the wish; and by correlating these three observable items we are again led to an explanatory assumption, let us say in this case to the hypothesis of a mechanism of repression. It is thus not any unusual quality of its explanations that make psychoanalysis different from the other sciences but rather the great complexity of the elements of its primary observations. Psychoanalysis does not deal with psychological phenomena of the order of simplicity that would, for example, be given if we measured the time that elapses between the occurrence of a sudden loud noise and the startle reaction. Should an analyst, who observes a person's response to an experience in his current life which resembles that of a specific traumatic experience in his childhood, attempt to break up these two experiences—that of yesterday and that of his childhood—into minutiae, he could not go very far in this direction without losing the grasp of the essence of the events, without dealing with irrelevancies.

In this context it is of interest to ponder Goethe's famous refusal to accept Newton's theory of color, in particular Newton's claim that the summation of all the colors of the spectrum would give white or, in the reverse, that white light could be dissolved into the colors of the spectrum (by being refracted via a prism). There is no doubt that although Goethe was wrong as far as the physics of light is concerned, his position was valid within the context of a psychological theory of colors. (Cf. Heisenberg, 1952, pp. 60-76, esp. p. 64, where he says: "It is clear to all who have worked ... on Goethe's and Newton's theories, that nothing can be gained from an investigation of their separate rights and wrongs.... basically the two theories simply deal with different things.") From the point of view of the observer's experience, white is a phenomenon that cannot be meaningfully understood as the summation of the colors of the spectrum.

It is not easy for the mind of modern man, steeped from childhood in the outlook of the physical and biological sciences, to accept the fact that a scientific attitude toward a world of subjective experiences is no less valid (and in certain contexts vastly more relevant) than the scientific attitude toward a world of objective sensory data. The following reflections, however, will demonstrate that each of the two approaches is valid within its own (operationally defined) sphere. For the physicist, the essential nature of the phenomena perceived by man's senses as heat and color is identical. He conceives of them in the analogizing imagery of waves and differentiates them only by the different frequency of these waves along the time axis. The energic constellations experienced by man as the sensation of heat and as the perception of redness thus form an unbroken continuum for the physicist, notwithstanding the fact that one kind of receptor in man's biological equipment (certain sensory-end organs in the skin) is attuned to heat, while another one (certain sensory end-organs in the retina of the eye) is attuned to the color red. From the point of view of the psychologist who deals with man's experiences, however, warmth and redness may have vastly different connotations — as evaluated by the psychologist, warmth and redness may be clearly disparate experiences that do not form a continuum.

It may be objected here that it is the very hallmark of science that it is able to go beyond the perception of the senses, and that it is, therefore, a characteristic achievement of science to discern unity (a continuum) behind phenomena which to mere sensory perception appear to be diverse (discontinuous). Such an objection, however, is based on an antipsychological bias and thus on circular reasoning. True enough, the investigations of science will at times lead to results that may appear bizarrely at variance with the impressions of everyday life. Science will indeed sometimes discover alikeness, relatedness, continuity, when the common-sense approach can only see dissimilarity, lack of relatedness, and discontinuity. And, by contrast, science will also sometimes discover diversity, essential unrelatedness, or lack of continuity, where the unscientific observer obtains the impression of unity, relatedness, or continuity. But such discoveries, which are at variance with common-sense perception and judgment, are not restricted to observations within the sphere of the physical and biological sciences; they occur also in scientific psychology and, par excellence, in depth psychology, i.e., within the sphere of the psychology of complex mental states. The claim, for example, of the essential psychological unity of the triad of orderliness, penuriousness, and obstinacy (Freud, 1908) may strike the common-sense observer as preposterous — yet to the depth-psychological scientist the genetic-dynamic interrelatedness of these psychological features is as obvious as is the fact for the physicist that heat and redness occupy neighboring positions in the spectrum of energic constellations. Or, to end these reflections on a less technical note, temperatures of various ranges are conceptualized by the physicist as only quantitatively different, whereas, for the psychologist, it is obvious that coldness, warmth, and heat may be qualitatively divergent experiences, symbolizing (e.g., in dreams) cold emotional indifference, warmly empathic (maternal) care, and scaldingly destructive criticism.

But if the psychoanalyst will not abandon the position that his subject matter is man's inner experience, how can he prove that he is able to discern with any degree of certainty the experiential configurations with which he deals? Just as the observer in the other empirical sciences must rely ultimately on his sensory impressions, however refined they might have become through instrumentation, so must the psychoanalytic observer ultimately rely on introspection and, especially, on vicarious introspection, i.e., on empathy, for the gathering of the meaningful and relevant data in the field of his observations (see Kohut, 1959). He uses his sensory impressions, of course, as he hears the analysand's words and sees his gestures and movements — but these sensory data would remain meaningless were it not for his ability to recognize complex psychological configurations that only empathy, the human echo to a human experience, can provide. An unreliable instrument! some might say. Yes and no. The answer is yes, if the instrument is handled without care and training, if intuition is relied upon instead of persevering waiting, checking, and comparison. The answer is no, however, if we recognize the need for the continuous study of safeguards against error, for watchful alertness to the possibility that our bias might lead us to erroneous perception, and for arduous practice in the use of the instrument. It may well be, furthermore, that training in empathy requires the overcoming of specific obstacles. In some individuals, at any rate, the access to the empathic capacity seems to have been blocked by the development of the nonempathic mode of cognition — perhaps analogous to the relation between the phylogenetic stunting of man's olfactory sense and the evolutionary ascendancy of his vision. But, unlike smell, empathy — i.e., cognition via the narcissistic investment of the other—is still a powerful, potentially reliable, and at any rate irreplaceable instrument of observation. And training in its use imposes tasks upon the analyst that are in essence the same as those that are confronted by all the other empirical sciences, i.e., by those empirical sciences where the observed is essentially dissimilar to the observer—by the biologist, for example, who examines stained tissue sections through the microscope—by those sciences, in other words, where empathy must not be employed.

I trust that I have now made clear why I must object when psychoanalysis is welcomed among the fashions of the day on the basis of the erroneous notion that it is no more than a specific, sophisticated art—an art of understanding people via the resonance of empathy. And I trust I have also succeeded in demonstrating why I must reject the acceptance of psychoanalysis among the sciences of our times when this acceptance rests on the restrictive approval of its explanatory formulations and on the rejection of the empathic mode of its data-gathering processes, which is looked upon as an undesirable shortcoming, to be superseded, the sooner the better, by traditional methods of scientific observation. Both of these positions disregard the very nature of psychoanalysis—of this important advance along man's road toward the increasing ascendancy of his intellect. Both of these positions disregard the fact that the decisive step analysis has taken in the development of scientific thought is that it has combined empathy and traditional scientific method, that it has introduced scientific truth-finding with regard to processes that can become accessible only through the scrutiny of the inner experiences of man.

Let me pause here for a moment and clarify the purpose of the preceding reflections. As I have already intimated: I think that the present occasion transcends the personal, that it represents a step toward the integration of analysis into the community of scholars. My preceding effort to define those qualities of analysis that I believe contain its essence were, therefore, intended to deepen that channel of communication between psychoanalysis and the other sciences, which, I feel, has been opened today. But I do not wish to leave it at that. Feeling accepted, I will not only acknowledge a gift but will offer something in return.

But what can analysis, this newcomer to modern science, contribute to the more established fields? What can analysis give to the other sciences, from whom it has received—or with whom it shares—the striving for scientific objectivity and for experience-distant explanations? The answer is: the introduction of empathy into the field of science.

I know that, while you may be taken aback by this statement, you will, after all I have said, not be afraid that I am calling here for a return to sentimentalizing anthropomorphism, to an animistic perception of the world. No, what I have in mind is something else. I am thinking of the introduction of empathy into the university in two specific, interconnected ways: firstly, its employment as a tool of observation, a move that will increase the depth and breadth of the investigations conducted by a number of traditional scientific disciplines; and, secondly, its employment as the matrix into which all scientific activities must be embedded if they are not to become increasingly isolated from human life, if they are not to be our inhuman masters instead of our servants and tools.

You may well wonder at this point whether I am not exaggerating the importance of the role of empathy—in human life in general, and as a potential ingredient of science. Was it not enough that I argued its case as a legitimate and valuable instrument of scientific observation in the service of the science of complex mental states? Am I not going too far when I now also claim that with its aid the formulation of new research aims of other sciences can be facilitated, that—to state it concretely—the psychoanalyst, because of his training in empathy, may be able to help other researchers to gain access to new areas of investigation, to outline problems that the workers in the established fields have failed to recognize and to pose questions that have not yet been raised by them? Are these assertions not extravagant? you will ask. Yet, I am crowning it all by proclaiming that empathy should become the guiding ideal of all the sciences, that the scientist's commitment to it should take the place of the pride in his methodological and technological expertness which he has felt up to now.

I must admit that these statements may well seem fanciful and idiosyncratic—or worse: that they may seem to constitute simply another instance of the idealization of a specific tool, and of the conceited conviction that a position of superiority is bestowed upon those who have become experts in its use.

But such is not my view. Skill in the use of empathy as a tool of observation no more bestows a position of superiority on the depth-psychologist than skill in the use of the telescope on the astronomer, or skill with the electromicroscope on the virologist. I do not even claim that the psychoanalyst's knowledge of the deeper reaches of man, his familiarity with man's most profound strivings and conflicts, gives him the right to assume a position of leadership with regard to the evaluation of the hierarchy of human activities and thus of the significance of the goals and aspirations of the scientist and scholar within the social fabric of the university. No, while in certain respects the psychoanalyst may explore the human soul more deeply and broadly and in greater detail than do other observers of man, his vision of man tends to be restricted by the fact that he observes people in a specific therapeutic context, and in a specific setting, the psychoanalytic situation. The analyst is indeed able to learn a great deal that is applicable to the grasp of man's general behavior; still, I would consider it to be the expression of the conceit of the specialist if the analyst were to claim that he knows of necessity more about man than, let us say, the anthropologist, the historian, the sociologist, or the political scientist. What is needed in this realm is the co-operation of specialists, and thus their mutual enrichment, but not the ascendancy of one branch of the sciences of man over the others.

The situation is different, however, with regard to the full appreciation of the significance of the important role empathy plays in human life, a significance which vastly transcends that of its usefulness as a tool of scientific observation. Here, at least at this point in the history of human thought, it is indeed the psychoanalyst who has the broadest access to the relevant data. He knows that, despite its essentially narcissistic nature, empathy is a fundamental mode of human relatedness; that it is not only a powerful basic psychological bond between individuals, but that indeed it constitutes the very matrix of man's psychological survival. And since today's occasion has assigned to me the role of addressing the community of scholars as the representative of psychoanalysis, I feel justified in pursuing the task of demonstrating to you the enrichment that the appropriately tempered acceptance of the empathic outlook would provide for the sciences.

Before undertaking the task of demonstrating the potential fruitfulness of the employment of empathy in science, however, I will first summarize my opinions about the importance of empathy in human life in general. I have compressed my views into three propositions: (1) Empathy, the recognition of the self in the other, is an indispensable tool of observation, without which vast areas of human life, including man's behavior in the social field, remain unintelligible. (2) Empathy, the expansion of the self to include the other, constitutes a powerful psychological bond between individuals which—more perhaps even than love, the expression and sublimation of the sexual drive—counteracts man's destructiveness against his fellows. And (3), empathy, the accepting, confirming, and understanding human echo evoked by the self, is a psychological nutriment without which human life as we know it and cherish it could not be sustained.

As viewed from the vantage point of the present-day problems of science, no further explanation of the foregoing definitions should be necessary here.[2] The fact, however, that a whole older generation of scientific psychotherapeutic depth-psychologists had to fight the primary battle of their lives against unscientific "cure through love" (Freud, 1907, p. 90), had to take up militant positions as defenders of a scientific "explaining" psychology against a merely "understanding," i.e., an unscientific, psychology (cf. Hartmann, 1927), makes it advisable to expand my previous statements at this juncture. Specifically, I will now discuss briefly the relationship between the first of my propositions (that empathy, correctly employed, is an indispensable tool of scientific observation) and the other two (that empathy constitutes a psychological bond between individuals and groups which diminishes their aggression; and that empathy is an important source of psychological nutriment without which psychological life as we know it could not be sustained).

Those who feel that our primary battle must still be against mysticism, occultism, and sentimentalizing obfuscation will not only continue to stress the purely cognitive aspects of empathy as a data-gathering instrument, operating via "vicarious introspection" (as I did in my essay of 1959), but will also shy away from emphasizing the importance of the valuable effects of empathy in the social field (as I am now doing in propositions [2] and [3]). I have no doubt that the battle against mysticism has not yet been won and that the fight against unscientific sentimental psychology must be continued. I am convinced, however, that, taking a broader view, this issue should now be seen as a subsidiary one, and that the task of integrating tool-and-method science into a larger matrix of human values is now becoming paramount.

Looked upon solely as a tool of observation, as a specific cognitive process—one might indeed call this aspect of empathy "the empathic process" as Dr. Warren Bennis (1974) has suggested—empathy is value-neutral. It can only be correct or incorrect in its perception of the actualities of the inner life of another individual. And it may also be rightly asserted, in opposition to my propositions (2) and (3), that empathy (even correct empathy) can serve inimical ends, is often used for destructive and asocial purposes.[3]

---

[2] I can make this statement especially in view of the fact that I have extensively discussed scientific empathy in previous publications. (See, for example, Kohut, 1959; Kohut, 1971, esp. pp. 300-307; and Kohut, 1973, esp. p. 14.)

[3] In this context we need to think only of the psychological means, empathically attuned to the psychological state of an opponent, employed in war propaganda, to make an enemy lose courage and give up the fight; or of the skills of the salesman who, empathically assessing the victim's readiness to be persuaded, will use these empathic data in order to sell inferior merchandise, etc.

356

There can be no doubt, however, that, under normal circumstances, empathic modes of perception are, from the beginning of life, amalgamated to feeling states that are characterized by an intermingling of two experiences (see Kohut, 1971): (a) that the child is able to understand the self-object via empathy, and (b) that, simultaneously, he feels empathically understood by it. And it is this set of experiences which par excellence reassures the child that he is not losing control over the self-object and thus assuages his destructive narcissistic rage (see Kohut, 1972). There can also be no doubt that the beginnings of empathic cognition occur within a specific matrix which sustains the healthy narcissism of the individual by providing psychological nutriment to the self (for example, through "mirroring" [see Kohut, 1971]). As with the maturing of the individual, furthermore, the cognitive aspect of empathy will be employed with increasingly appropriate discretion (e.g., in science, in general, in the investigation of man but not in the investigation of man's nonhuman environment), so also with the aggression-reducing and with the self-esteem-nourishing and humanness-sustaining aspects of empathy. The empathic bridge to the inner life of the other, to his experiences, and the empathic bridge of others to us, to our experiences, continue to assuage our rage and destructiveness and continue to sustain our human essence. But we are now also able to maintain control over the noncognitive dimensions of empathy: restrain them where they interfere with our objectivity, but give them free rein where they serve our larger goals. Within the area of the present inquiry, our ideal as scientists can be condensed into a single evocative phrase: we must strive not only for scientific empathy but also for an empathic science.

I am eager to turn to the task of providing concrete illustrations of that interaction between the empathic process as a mode of cognition, on the one hand, and the wholesome social effects of empathy, on the other hand, in order to illuminate the potential role empathy can play for science. Before doing so, however, I will again present my reasoning — but now in the form of a brief summarizing statement. Yesterday's depth psychology had the obligation of defining its borders as clearly as it could — it had to emphasize that it did not employ the nonscientific methods of a cure through love, which characterize so many therapeutic cults. This obligation has not ceased, of course; but our priorities have changed. I believe that present-day depth psychology — employing scientific empathy — no longer needs to see the struggle to establish itself as a science as its major task. On the contrary, it is my conviction that, having secured its own position as a science, it is now able, indeed it is now obligated, to assist the other sciences, in particular as organized in the universities, in their task of determining a matrix of meaning—empathic science—for their activities. It must offer its help, as the community of scholars attempts to re-examine the hierarchy of its values, in order to chart its course in today's—and tomorrow's—world.

But enough of generalities and abstractions! I know that they do not convince and I shall therefore turn again to the specific and concrete. I shall begin by giving you two examples which will illustrate my claim that empathy, as an instrument of observation, has important, and in certain fields irreplaceable, perceptive powers—in particular, that, with its aid, certain aspects of human life can be understood and therefore recognized, which, without it, would not be understood and would therefore remain unseen. Specifically, I shall describe two instructive instances which indicate the existence of as yet largely untapped potentialities of this psychological function, demonstrating that people with unusual gifts for empathy, or people whose empathic function has had the benefit of special training, will remain open-minded, and thus able to see reality in a new light, where others, with lesser gifts or lesser training, can react only with stereotyped indignation or with hate.

Allow me, then, to describe two such instances in which empathy transcended the boundaries that are usually imposed on it. The first is an example of untrained, naive empathy; the second is more mundane: it occurred in the course of my professional work.

My first illustration concerns an episode in the life of the folk singer Bob Dylan (Hentoff, 1964) which took place years ago, shortly after the assassination of President Kennedy, at a time when our grief and horror about this event were still fresh and intense. Dylan was to receive an award from a civil-liberties group. Aware of the profound difference between himself and the conventional, middle-class gathering at which the honor was being bestowed on him, he wanted to demonstrate something of his own essence, which he felt in danger of deserting by accepting the award. Thus, instead of giving voice to his appreciation and pledging support for the causes of the civil-rights movement as was expected of him, he shocked his audience by talking about Lee Oswald. This is what he said: "I told them I'd read a lot of his [i.e., Oswald's] feelings in the papers, and I knew he was up-tight. [I] said I'd been up-tight, too, so I'd got a lot of his feelings. I saw a lot of myself in Oswald, I said, and I saw in him a lot of the times we're all living in. And, you know," Dylan continued, "they started booing. They looked at me like I was an animal."

Dylan's responsiveness to human isolation, to the despair that motivates the perpetrator of a crazy deed, has a touch of the genius that allowed Dostoyevsky to grasp the humanness of the sinner, to extend his ability to recognize essential human alikeness to the farthest reaches of depravity—it was a feat of empathy. Whatever the admixture of nose-thumbing rebellion in Dylan's provocative act, he yet demonstrated that a self may expand its borders to comprehend another human experience, even when this empathic resonance leads to social ostracism, to rejection, even when the temptation to join in the prevailing mood, and thus to reap the rewards for not upsetting an established psychological equilibrium, seems irresistible.

The second example, too, concerns the recognition of human suffering in human depravity. But it is not naive, it does not have the flavor of that mixture of rebellion and saintliness that characterizes Dylan's stance; it illustrates the sober scientific or professional use of empathy by a trained observer. It occurred in my function as supervisor of an analyst in training whose patient was a lonely man who suffered from the feeling that he was different from the rest of humanity, and that he was thus unacceptable. We had made some progress in understanding his experiences, present and past, and the analyst had begun to transmit to the patient our understanding of how the rejection of his maleness, of the boyish core of his personality, by his bizarre and unpredictable, yet powerful, mother had affected him, and how deprived he had felt by the withdrawal of his more humanly predictable, but weak and retiring, father. In response to feeling understood by the analyst, the patient had become less suspicious and thus less cautious in his communications. It was at this point, however, that he began to give accounts of his unspeakable cruelty to animals, which strained our empathic capacity, our tolerance, to the utmost. In his childhood he had had pets to whom he was kind much of the time, but whom he would occasionally beat unmercifully, often without any provocation, to the point of injury or even death. Hard as it was to maintain our empathic intention in the light of these stories from his childhood, our task became even harder with regard to the accounts of his present activities, particularly his behavior to his cats, whom he usually pampered but whom he would suddenly pick up and smash against the wall, again often to the point of injury or death.

I do not wish to burden you with the most appalling details of the patient's actions; even without hearing about them you will surely understand that we were upset and indignant. Indeed, we felt close to abandoning the analyst's tolerant attitude of readiness for empathic comprehension. We felt close, in other words, to following the example of those therapists who have reported wholesome consequences when, in analogous circumstances, they openly expressed their indignation and, as they saw it, reacted honestly and appropriately to a patient's wrong-doings. We did not take this road, but gritted our teeth and continued to attempt to understand the meaning of the patient's activities. Was he trying to frighten the therapist? Was he trying to make himself un-acceptable out of fear of the increasing affection he might have felt for the therapist? Was he expressing hatred for somebody in a symbolic way, or was he giving beatings in order to revenge himself for beatings he had received? None of these interpretations and attempted reconstructions[4] hit the mark — although the last was indeed not far off target. The empathic insight leading us to the correct understanding of the patient's behavior to animals came, not surprisingly, not from the student analyst but from me. It came from me — or it came from me first — not because I possess any extraordinary powers in the area of scientific empathy, but mainly, I believe, because — unlike my student — I was not directly exposed to the impact of the patient's upsetting accounts.[5] I understood that this patient's behavior to animals was a wordless description of how he had felt when he was a child. At that time he had felt cruelly tossed about and smashed — just as the animals felt now when he tossed them about and smashed them, i.e., when he repeated the bizarre behavior of his mother, who seemed to understand him and thus led him to expect sensible empathic responses to his needs and aspirations, but who then, unpredictably, would ridicule and reject him, and would bitingly and sarcastically belittle the very attributes that he had just proudly exhibited to her. Indeed, at such moments he was exposed to tortures and injuries equivalent to those he inflicted on his pets. No saying, in my view, is more

---

[4] I am presenting the various psychological configurations obtained through trial empathy in order to demonstrate one aspect of *scientific* empathy. The use of empathy in depth psychology is not based on the not-further-to-be-defined intuition of the observer — it is a specific, disciplined cognitive process. The trained analyst learns to resist being convinced by the Aha! experience of empathic pseudoclosures. He patiently defines the greatest variety of possible configurations and then evaluates the emerging material — including the patient's reaction to trial interpretations — as evidence for or against the correctness, the exactness, and the relevance of the meaning he had attempted to define.

[5] The relatively shielded position enjoyed by the supervisor (or consultant) deserves serious attention as a methodological factor in psychoanalytic research. The benefits resulting from the protection of the consultant's cognitive processes (including the greater relaxation with which he can extend his empathy toward the data) have to be weighed against the detrimental effect resulting from the possible distortion of the material through the passage via the analyst and through the artifacts introduced by the supervisory situation. On balance, however, I believe that the advantages may often be greater than the disadvantages — especially where the investigation concerns emotion-ally trying, regressive forms of psychopathology. And I believe, therefore, that the situation we have traditionally used as a teaching device is also a promising instrument of research.

erroneous than the one about the sticks and stones that break your bones and the words that never hurt you.

I will forego, here, the attempt to marshal the evidence to support the reconstruction I presented and restrict myself to expressing the hope that it will be taken on trust that the analytic interpretations based on that reconstruction had a wholesome effect on the patient and on his subsequent behavior. I cite this case as an example of humanizing, of healing empathy, of empathy as a bridge between human beings — as a demonstration of the type of empathy that is capable not only of safeguarding humanness within our increasingly inhuman world, but also of reclaiming psychological territory that seems already to have become irretrievably dehumanized and of returning it to the domain of living, feeling man.

With the preceding examples of empathy, I have attempted to demonstrate the power of this psychological function both as an instrument of cognition and as a civilizing force. In these two broad realms, empathy seems to me to be irreplaceable. I believe, therefore, that the importance of the empathic mode of man's relationship to his human environment, that the importance of that "mechanism by means of which we are enabled to take up any attitude at all towards another mental life," as Freud put it (1921, p. 110n), can hardly be overestimated. If I had sufficient time at my disposal, I would be able to demonstrate that empathy, the resonance of essential human alikeness, is indeed — from birth to death — the power that counteracts man's tendency toward seeing meaninglessness and feeling despair; that the widespread existential malaise of our times rests not so much on a philosophical but rather on a concrete experiential basis; that our propensity for it is due to the insufficient or faulty empathic responsiveness which we encountered during the crucial period when the nucleus of our self was formed. And I could show how the intense needs of those whose self has thus been undernourished make them the easy prey of any seducer who promises to relieve their sense of emptiness, of any make-believe which will, even if only temporarily, give them that feeling of being empathically valued and accepted which they should have internalized as children and which they should now possess as their unquestioned psychological property. But if this feeling is lacking, then any relief is welcome — whether it is provided by drugs and wordless touching in encounter groups or by nationalistic ecstasy and merger into mystical experience.

But do I then suggest that science, that the universities, should supply the emotional substance that fulfills these needs? Am I suggesting that the universities should embrace a quasi-religious mystique of empathy, a

361

religion of empathy which is to take the place of the religion of love? Of course not! Neither do I expect—or even want—our professors to be saints nor do I believe that any of the current sainthood fads—think of the Jesus freaks and of the pseudo-Buddhists among the young—will carry us toward a solution of our problems.

But there exists, among the best perhaps of our young people, a new attitude that deserves our attention. It is an attitude of naive un-wordliness coupled with a disinterest in and often contempt for the traditional values of our culture. On first sight, it might seem to be nothing more than the attitude we have learned to expect from adol-escents. But it is part of the stable outlook of these young people, often persisting long into adulthood, and, while it is unworldly, it is by no means unrelated to the world. These young people show us that the ideals we are offering them—specifically, the ideals of scholarship and of truth-finding research which reached the peak of their power at the end of the nineteenth century—that these ideals no longer sustain and lead them. Clear-vision and tool-and-method pride, the ideal of the search for truth, sustained our learned communities well into the beginning of our century. But we have also seen the isolating effects of scientific pride; we have seen how easily the tool-and-method-oriented scientist submitted, with undiminished pridefulness, to the totalitarian regimes of this century and hence to some of the most inhuman goals the world has ever known.

Science cannot prove, of course, that man should be guided by humanitarian ideals—just as it cannot prove, as it tried to do on the basis of a vulgarized Darwinism when it allied itself to the fascist regimes of the early part of the century, that *in*human ideals, the gospel of the survival of the fittest, are justified. Still, while our scientific insights concerning the importance of the empathic bond between people do not lead us to a proof of the validity of humanitarian ideals, they go a long way toward increasing our awareness of how much of the human essence we abandon when our overriding pride imbues the specific ego functions involved in truth-finding, rather than the expansion of our selves that we undertake in order to sustain the fellow human being.

What I support, then, is the infusion of our specialized activities with a new kind of humanitarianism—not with the humanitarianism of the Age of Reason, which accompanied the formation of our universities as we now know them and which has grown old, uninspiring, and ineffectual, but with the new and scientifically buttressed recognition that man cannot fulfill his essential self in any better way than by giving emotion-ally nourishing support to man, i.e., to himself and to his like.

No governmental system of regulations, no social apparatus providing for reasonable economic equality, no international union of nations maintaining world peace, however noble their aims and however efficient their technology, can, on the basis of their technological perfection alone, give the fundamental emotional sustenance to man that he needs for his psychological survival. Even if the aims of these institutions are chosen in harmony with the results of the best scientific studies undertaken by experts trained at our universities in the traditional fields of knowledge, even if their methods have been refined on the basis of experiments carried out by our most advanced academic researchers, institutions alone cannot sustain man any better than sufficient calories, optimal temperature, and bacteria-free cleanliness can sustain the psychological and biological survival of our babies. Food, warmth, and cleanliness are of course indispensable; and so are the great social institutions of man. But unless the food, the warmth, the cleanliness, are provided with empathic human responsiveness, and unless the child's growing body and forming personality are responded to with empathic acceptance, the baby's growth and survival will not be sustained.

We must, of course, not caricature a principle by its exaggerated application to details. I want the physicist to probe the secrets of the atom, I want the surgeon to refine his skills, and I believe that the historian must continue to devote himself to the objective discovery of facts and documents. But if, in particular, the university is nothing more than an organization that provides laboratories for its researchers, libraries for its scholars, and salaries for its employees, if it is no more than an aggregate of specialized technicians, each trying to explain a sector of reality with his own tools, then it will continue to lose its relevance for a younger generation that is already deeply disenchanted. The preaching of the old values of scholarship and of Nobel Prize-seeking research will not do, nor will the expansion of divinity schools and of departments of philosophy, where all too often lines of thought are being pursued uneasily, whose irrelevance the best of the faculty have themselves long recognized within the silence of their souls. And, much as I love the subject matter of the humanities, I do not believe that the emphasis on this branch of learning to the detriment of the hard sciences will give to our great centers of scholarship the vitality they need.

But how can the universities, how can the sciences amalgamate their knowledge to life-sustaining goals and thus become once more the intellectual leaders, the pioneers of our society, become once more the embodiment of ideals that are acceptable to our young?

Freud (1925) once defined thought in the following beautiful way.

363

Thought, he said, is "an experimental action" carried out with "small expenditure" of psychic energy (p. 238). I believe that an analogous definition can be applied to the activities of the university. Just as it is the function of thought to rehearse various courses of possible action before the whole personality decides to which particular one it will commit its energies, so it is the function of our universities to undertake experiments that should determine the direction of man's commitments in the larger arena of civilization. Our universities should be the proving ground where scholars test alternative means of support for the survival of human life in its physical, biological, and psychological dimensions.

Will the university again be a community of scholars rather than just a place where separate, technique-defined specialities are held together by administrative convenience? Can universities, can *one* university, undertake the daring step of becoming a microsociety, an enclave within the framework of society at large, which in trial actions undertakes the self-examination of social processes that cannot be performed outside its walls?

This is not the place to spell out the details of specific "experimental actions," of—I am using the hallowed term with some reluctance—specific research projects that a university might undertake in order to make a contribution to the definition and solution of some of the crucial problems of our age. Still, I have to present at least some concrete, illustrative examples of questions which scholars might ask who have recognized that the employment of empathy can indeed enrich their work.

Take, for instance, even the maxim of the life-sustaining, civilizing, curative power of empathy itself. It is obvious that, as soon as we turn from the assessment of the role it plays in the relationship of two individuals—be it mother and child, or psychotherapist and patient—and begin to examine its potentialities in the social arena, the psychoanalyst's knowledge alone will not carry much weight. Clearly, it would be suicidal to apply the two-step procedure of empathic understanding and scientific explanation directly to some of the sources of evil in our world. It is one thing to grasp the human suffering hidden behind a patient's cruelty to animals, it is another thing to be tolerant and understanding toward the antihumanitarian activities of a dangerous fascist politician and the appeal he exerts upon the multitudes. Even if we acquire increasing understanding of the psychology of the charismatic or messianic leader, even if we grasp the psychological needs of those who follow him, our tolerant communication will not set up the move toward health in the political arena that we are able to achieve in the therapeutic situation. It is here, however, where the university, through the co-operation of scholars from a variety of fields, can devise a framework of experimental actions within its own microcosm, can formulate answerable questions and thus throw light on the limitations as well as on the possible extension of the effectiveness of empathy in the social field.

Although outside the scope of conventional research, the goals to be reached through those investigations that require the employment of empathy (in addition to the use of the traditional tools of scientific cognition) are not chimerical. Neither would it be impractical to pursue them. True enough courage would be required if a university were to make a serious attempt to implement the kind of program I have in mind. But we should take it for granted that every decisive step in the history of science, every pioneering move forward in man's grasp of his world, requires the overcoming of prejudice, requires courage, requires the ability to survive despite ostracism and ridicule. The move, furthermore, toward a redefinition of the guiding philosophy of the university does not have to occur with revolutionary speed; it may proceed via small testing steps, let us say in the form of a limited number of investigations which, in their aim and methodology, are influenced by the analyst's knowledge of man's problems and man's personality.

I suggested some time ago, for example, that a university hospital would be a splendid testing ground for the investigation of the dehumanizing effect of the large institution, of the specific fear of losing his self to which the individual is exposed when he finds himself caught within the machinery of an impersonal process—even when the goal of the process is beneficial to him. Would not such an investigation provide a fine opportunity for the co-operation of scientists of various disciplines? The literary scholar could study the meaning of Kafka's insights concerning the man who finds himself in nonresponsive surroundings, from *Metamorphosis* to *The Trial* and *The Castle*; and he could cull the essential lessons to be learned from the keen observations provided by Solzhenitsyn in his *Cancer Ward*. The psychoanalyst could examine the reactions of those of his analysands who were exposed to the process of diagnosis and treatment in a big medical institution. Observers, trained in empathy, could interview individual patients at various stages of processing and could attempt to determine how one could best relieve their loneliness and fright; or how one could tap the emotional resources of those who face the last step of human existence.

The application of the results of such a research project would be of great value in transforming the hospital—the place where at one time or another most of us have to live through hours of gravest concern; the

365

place where most of us were born and where most of us will die—
from a factory that houses diagnostic and therapeutic machines into a
dwelling place for human beings. Nevertheless, my proposal to study the
hospital was not made primarily in order to bring about humanitarian
improvements in a specific setting, great as the need for these specific
improvements might be, but with a much broader aim in mind. This
study, and others like it, would, I believe, increase our understanding of
some of the central psychological problems of modern man: the understanding of man's problems in a world—the world of tomorrow—where
the individual will be increasingly pitted against surroundings that
reduce him to painful anonymity, that deprive him of his most precious
possession, his self.

Let me give you one final example of an area in which the insights of
the psychoanalyst might stimulate and enrich scholarly investigations
within the broader social field. The observation of certain specifically
vulnerable individuals has taught us that they may react to the loss of
empathic responses from others by experiencing themselves as dead,
inanimate, nonhuman—in particular, as machines (cf. Tausk, 1919).
And I have reached the additional conclusion that the not-infrequent
delusion, harbored by certain mentally ill patients, that they are being
watched, that they are being penetrated electrically by someone who
reads the secrets of their thoughts, expresses their perception of a world
that to them has become devoid of empathy. Such patients demonstrate
via their delusions that they experience their surroundings not as warmly
empathic, not as reflecting their presence with pleasure and as responding to their needs, but as cold, indifferent, mechanical, nonhuman,
machinelike, and thus as hostile to their survival. These are manifestations of individual personal deprivation, the revival of a person's tragic
early childhood—a childhood, for example, in which he had been confronted by bizarrely unempathic parents.[6] But there exist specific social

[6] The significance of certain psychopathological phenomena can often be grasped more easily
when they are the manifestations of a minor deviation from normal mental functioning (i.e., when
they occur fleetingly and have not overwhelmed the patient's personality) rather than the symptoms
of a major disturbance (i.e., when they have established themselves for protracted periods and have
overwhelmed the healthy sectors of the patient's personality). These considerations apply also
with regard to the recognition that the delusion of being observed by rays and other electrical
devices is the expression of the patient's experience that a deterioration of empathy from the
side of his environment has taken place. My own first lead to this insight, for example, came to
me as I was listening to the report (see Palombo, 1972) of the treatment of a seven-year-old boy who
was in general in good touch with reality and, although beset by fears and inclined to be suspicious
and provocative, was clearly not psychotic. At a time when the therapist had aroused the hope in the
boy that he would be empathically responsive to his needs (and thus be different from his parents),
the therapist responded to a communication of the child in a way that the child experienced as

analogies to these experiences. Think of the ill-defined anxiety that reports about the use of electronic bugging and wiretapping by governmental agencies arouse in most of us. I do not believe it is mainly guilt—realistic and conscious or even unrealistic and unconscious—that is responsible for the discomfort we feel. I think, rather, that the ominous quality of the use of these devices stems from the fact that they constitute a replica, in the social field, of that dehumanized corruption of empathy which plagues the psychotic patient who suffers from the delusion of being observed. The delusion portrays the transformation of empathy into a force that coldly and inimically intrudes into the patient's self instead of modulating its responses to his needs. Similarly, through the use of bugging and wiretapping, the social environment appears to have undergone a pernicious change: instead of being benevolently responsive to the individual, it has become a hostile force trying to penetrate into the individual's most private communications and thus into his thoughts.

Would not insights such as these, obtained with the aid of the trained empathic perception of the depth psychologist, be of great value to the historian, the political scientist, the sociologist, the anthropologist? Would not the synthesis of these insights with those obtained via the traditional nonempathic methods of investigation lead the way to the definition of new problem areas and to the formulation of significant new testable hypotheses? Would we not via this route illuminate the workings of certain important forces that are active in the society in which we live? And would we not perhaps, with the aid of our increased understanding, be also enabled to increase our control over these forces?

But enough! I am in danger of burying my message, my assertion, under the mass of evidence adduced in its support. Let me repeat my claim, therefore. It is the claim that psychoanalysis, as a system of thought, can make a contribution to our universities which no other

---

unempathic. The child, who had been looking forward eagerly to the more intensive schedule of psychotherapy now being introduced by the therapist, had discovered a dispenser of orange juice in one of the clinic offices and had asked the therapist to give him some of the juice. Instead of reacting to the child on the basis of the understanding that the child's wish expressed his eager and hopeful attitude toward what he trusted he would now obtain in the therapeutic relationship, the therapist thought he had to curb the child's wish for direct oral gratification. The child responded by developing the conviction that the pens the therapist carried in his shirt pocket were microphones which transmitted his confidences to a tape recorder and thence ultimately to the child's parents. I think the child's temporary paranoid delusion is to be understood as a message to the therapist: "You are just as coldly unempathic as my parents!" Although this clinical vignette can be no more than an illustration, since I neither treated the child nor followed the ongoing process of therapy as a consultant, I have since observed similar instances in my analytic practice in which an analysand's association temporarily took on a paranoid flavor after I had been unempathic and was thus experienced by the patient as the traumatically unempathic parent of his childhood.

science is able to make at this time: not only by adding its specific tools and methods and its specific findings to the armamentarium of methods employed by the sciences and to the fund of knowledge gathered by them, but also by helping the university to redefine its goals, by helping the individual scholar to reassess the hierarchy of his ideals.

Psychoanalysis is neither starry-eyed and sentimental about the human personality nor out of touch with the basic psychological needs of man. It neither preaches the inhuman gospel of the conception of man as a Darwinian animal who, uninfluenced by altruistic values, submits to the law of the jungle, nor dispenses armchair ideals of boundless humanitarianism, nor proclaims a gospel of suprahuman love. Yet, when in the search for meanings and ideals we arrive at the axiomatic conclusion that it is man's ultimate purpose to support the survival of man, then psychoanalysis should be able to supply those empirical data of observation that allow us to define realizable goals for our society by taking into account the deepest insights science has so far achieved about the nature of the human soul.

There are critical periods of transition in the developmental history not only of the individual but also of the group — periods when an established equilibrium has to be abandoned, when a new self has to be formed. The outcome of the struggle during such periods decides whether man will move toward health or illness, toward forward-moving new solutions, or whether he will decline. Our civilization appears to be faced with the challenge of finding new ways for human survival in a mass society. The university as we have known it — as it grew from its humanistic beginnings in the Renaissance to its modern culmination: its imposing achievements in biology and physics — expressed the aspirations of the thinking, searching individual who had emerged from medieval anonymity. But as social surroundings have changed and have themselves become the greatest danger to man's survival, the universities have not sufficiently responded. They have carried on business as usual in the pursuit of their old purposes and, simultaneously, have tended to adapt to the new surroundings without attempting to redefine their role and to reassess the structure of their goals. And in particular — and here lies, I believe, the gravest consequence of their inertia — they have not mobilized their resources in the service of that shift of aims from the conquest of nature toward the control of human destiny that the changing pattern of civilization demands.

A significant number of scientists have already begun to realize these facts. They have not yet acknowledged that they, and thus the universities, have become increasingly less relevant to modern man, but they have clearly grasped that they are often used by forces with whose aims they do not agree. The example of the technological exploitation in war of basic scientific findings—from physics to psychology—is the most obvious one; but there are many others. The reaction of science, of the universities, to these evils has been more or less makeshift and on the whole ineffective. I do not wish to belittle personal courage in this respect, and I do not deny that instances of individual resistance to the exploitation of scientific thought have made their historically significant mark. But individual courage is not enough. What is needed is a transformation of the guiding system of ideals within the scientific community.

Man used to take for granted that he was helpless *vis-à-vis* the powers of nature, the helpless victim of storm and plague; that he could do no more about these forces than to resign himself and pray. Science has changed this sense of resignation. Physics and biology have provided us with explanations which have become the basis for a technology that has given man mastery over forces which—so he had believed—would remain forever beyond his control.

But having gone some distance toward the conquest of nature, man still considers himself to be helplessly carried along by the currents of history and by the tidal waves of cultural change. Although there is less prayer now, there is resignation and, at times, even a snobbishly aristocratic pessimism that rejects the supposedly hollow optimism of the attempt to influence the course of history and to control the speed and direction of cultural change. Taking the long view, however, we may well be less helpless than we think. With the advent of depth psychology, man is beginning to have instruments and concepts that give him greater access than ever before to the forces that motivate him. The attainment of a broader understanding of his own aims and purposes can bring him, in turn, closer to an effective control over his own actions.

It is here that the courageous scholar and scientist must again become the intellectual leader of man, must supply man with the reasoned blueprints for mastery in hitherto unconquered realms.

To put the matter in a nutshell, the university's failure has been to carry on its traditional labors in the pursuit of specialized endeavors while closing its eyes to the tragedy of man, who suffocates in an increasingly inhuman environment that he, himself, continues to create. The present isolation of psychoanalysis from the universities should thus be taken as a sign that an unhealthy cultural stalemate has not been fully broken; its beginning integration, however, is not only a step toward the full mobilization of a creative struggle for new meanings and ideals and new

369

scientific goals, but also indicates the presence of a movement toward renewed cultural health.

REFERENCES

Abraham, H. C., & Freud, E. L., eds. (1965), *A Psychoanalytic Dialogue: The Letters of Sigmund Freud and Karl Abraham.* New York: Basic Books.

Bennis, W. (1974), Discussion remarks at Round-Table Conference: "Empathy and the Scientific Method," University of Cincinnati, April 20, 1974.

Breuer, J. & Freud, S. (1893-1895), Studies on hysteria. *Standard Edition*, 2. London: Hogarth Press, 1955.

Freud, S. (1900), The interpretation of dreams. *Standard Edition*, 4 & 5. London: Hogarth Press, 1953.

–––––– (1907), Delusions and dreams in Jensen's *Gradiva. Standard Edition*, 9:7-95. London: Hogarth Press, 1959.

–––––– (1908), Character and anal eroticism. *Standard Edition*, 9:167-175. London: Hogarth Press, 1959.

–––––– (1917), A difficulty in the path of psycho-analysis. *Standard Edition*, 17:135-144. London: Hogarth Press, 1955.

–––––– (1921), Group psychology and the analysis of the ego. *Standard Edition*, 18:67-143. London: Hogarth Press, 1955.

–––––– (1925), Negation. *Standard Edition*, 19:233-239. London: Hogarth Press.

Hartmann, H. (1927), Understanding and explanation. In: *Essays on Ego-Psychology.* New York: International Universities Press, 1964, pp. 369-403.

Heisenberg, W. (1952), *Philosophical Problems of Nuclear Science.* New York: Pantheon.

Hentoff, N. (1964), The crackin', shakin', breakin' sounds. *The New Yorker*, 40:64-90, October 4, 1964.

Kohut, H. (1959), Introspection, empathy, and psychoanalysis. *J. Amer. Psychoanal. Assn.*, 7:459-483.

–––––– (1971), *The Analysis of the Self.* New York: International Universities Press.

–––––– (1972), Thoughts on narcissism and narcissistic rage. *The Psychoanalytic Study of the Child*, 27:360-400. New York: International Universities Press.

–––––– (1973), Psychoanalysis in a troubled world. *This Annual*, 1:3-25.

–––––– (1975), The future of psychoanalysis. *This Annual*, 3:325-340.

Palombo, J. (1972), Psychic trauma: The adventitious organizer. Paper presented to the Panel on Trauma, Amer. Assn. of Psychiatric Services for Children, Washington, D.C., November, 1972.

Rosenbaum, M. (1954), Psychoanalysis at the Hebrew University: The Freud-Eitingon-Magnes correspondence. *J. Amer. Psychoanal. Assn.*, 2:311-317.

Tausk, V. (1919), On the origin of the "influencing machine" in schizophrenia. *Psychoanal. Quart.*, 2:519-556, 1933.

January, 1974

Is Psychoanalysis a Social Science?

PAUL PARIN, M.D. (*Zurich*)

with discussion by ROBERT A. LeVINE, Ph.D. (*Chicago*)

AND LAWRENCE FRIEDMAN, M.D. (*New York*)

From its very beginnings, psychoanalytic theory has been applied to the phenomena of human society and cultural life. One of its basic discoveries, the Oedipus complex, used Sophocles' drama as an allegory to be subjected to psychological interpretation as work of art and myth at the same time. With the exploration of the unconscious, the relation of the examined object to "other individuals" appeared in a specific way: "In the individual's mental life someone else is invariably involved, as a model, as an object, as a helper, as an opponent; and so from the very first individual psychology in this extended but entirely justifiable sense of the words, is at the same time social psychology as well" (Freud, 1921, p. 69). The application of psychoanalysis to all areas of society proved so fruitful that Freud (1933) could write: "Strictly speaking there are only two sciences: psychology, pure and applied, and natural science" (p. 179).

The answers found by applied psychoanalysis are psychological explanations. This is more than a result of its method; the underlying assumption is that all social behavior derives from the conscious and unconscious mental life of the human beings who form society. Thus, the study of society is an applied psychology.

Of course, we do not deny that psychology is applicable to the study of social groups or that every past, present, and future society is made up of

---

This paper and the discussion that follows were originally given in Chicago at the Symposium on Psychoanalysis and History held on the occasion of Dr. Heinz Kohut's 60th birthday, June 2, 1973.

individuals. But we shall try to show that psychoanalysis is not merely applicable to the study of society but is a social science in its own right.

In this paper we take social science to be not the purely functional systems of modern sociology that have partly absorbed psychological explanations for social behavior but those theories that form part of a general anthropology and contribute to a diachronic theory of the evolution of mankind. Our model, like that of LeVine (1973), "differs from the functionalist framework in putting less emphasis on the need to maintain equilibrium and more on the variety of stable and unstable adaptations that exist at one point in time" (p. 138). In our view, society, as studied by social science, is not the sum total of individuals but the expression of the sum total of the relations and correlations of these individuals with each other (Marx, 1857-1858). These "relations and correlations" cannot be submitted to psychoanalytic investigation. As LeVine (1973) puts it: "Individuals, and only individuals, can be psychoanalyzed. Customs, institutions and organizations cannot be, and any attempt to do so involves dispensing with those elements in the clinical method that give psychoanalytic assessments their validity" (p. 209).

According to our model, therefore, psychoanalysis no longer leads to causal explanations of social conditions. Emphatically, it remains a psychology. However, it makes for a broader understanding of those "relations and correlations" that cannot be explained by the action of psychical energies but are caused by other forces studied by history, anthropology, etc. In comparison with Freud's (1930) views as expressed in *Civilization and its Discontents*, causality is inverted. The historical process is put in motion by ecological factors, technical innovations, and economic urges. Psychoanalysis explains how the historical process is shaped under given conditions, why it takes a specific course and way and timing.

There can be no doubt that social processes "are influenced" by their carriers. It is the mode of action and the impact of such influence that needs discussion. In every known society, a child is specifically socialized after the dissolution of the oedipal conflict. Within the framework of the material potential and the biologic *Anlage,* society has produced lasting psychic structures that exercise effective functions. LeVine speaks of intrapsychic dispositions and a network of dispositions stressing the social function of acquired psychic structures. The members of a people, a tribe, a class, a caste, are never what one might call a blank. The differences among them are so great that some have compared them with the differences among the species in the animal kingdom and have said that mankind is subdivided into numerous pseudospecies (cf. Erikson,

1968, p. 487). On the basis of this, the theory of "natural man" as opposed to society must be abandoned. We cannot give a description of natural man because he does not exist. Or, as the anthropologist Walter Goldschmidt (1966) says: "There is no nature versus nurture, no biology versus culture, there is only the hyphenated man-in-society" (p. 4).

Psychoanalysis, as well as social science, has to do with man's second nature, which is dynamically effective and specifically social, and which may be traced back to psychic development. The theory of history is not invalidated by taking psychoanalysis as a social science. Men make history without knowing it. Psychoanalysis has to accept that this is so; it cannot explain why, and from its results alone one cannot make any forecast as to the future course or set any guidelines. On the other hand, it can explain how history is translated into social behavior, how men of a society go about making history.

For the last three decades, a renewed confrontation with biology has initiated a shift in psychoanalytical conceptualization and has, surprisingly, changed the course of psychoanalysis, leading it away from natural science. The question "inborn or acquired?," as put in clinical examinations, and the second, related, question of how far man's natural *Anlage* and his adjustment to civilization determine his mental life have lost their heuristic value. The "complemental series" (Freud, 1905) of constitutional (or inborn) and accidental factors (acquired in the course of life and by interaction with the environment) is no longer of help in explaining the social activities of men. The observations of infants made by Rene A. Spitz, the tracing of a child's development, the observation of identical twins in their earliest infancy have brought about new notions. Even in a one-year-old, the respective share of either component is impossible to determine. The *Anlage* as a variable with possibly known limits is integrated into the complemental series; its effect has long acquired a novel quality by the time it is examined. The *Anlage* cannot be determined or assessed even by means of the most profound analysis of an individual, and it cannot serve to explain man's behavior in society or in any group. The more we learn about the effect of the elements discernible from the viewpoint of natural science, the more we understand the relevancy of psychosocial processes and the more clearly we see that man's development as a social being shaped by his environment obeys its own laws.

The development of ego psychology has long proven that the human ego, equipped with instinctual energies, among others, has the function that instinctual behavior performs in animals. Man's instinctual equipment, his genetic inheritance, acquired in phylogenesis, is biologically

373

determined. It covers a large vector of adaptability. The psychical apparatus, with the capacity to adapt to reality that develops out of it, must be ascribed to the influence of man's environment, to that of the developmental process studied in analytic therapy, and, lastly, to the influence of socialization. The biological extension of psychoanalytic theory has thus led to better understanding of the autonomy of psycho-social processes and to the realization that there is little to learn about behavior patterns from the theory of instincts.

Ever since Freud (1887-1902) was forced to recognize that his patients could not distinguish between fantasy and reality, that "there is no 'indication of reality' in the unconscious" (p. 216), psychoanalysis has understood that "psychical reality requires to be taken into account alongside practical reality" (Freud, 1914, pp. 17-18). To investigate psychical reality is the major interest of analytical practice, which "is based on a love of truth—that is, on a recognition of reality—and that it precludes any kind of sham or deceit" (Freud, 1937, p. 248). Practical or objective reality, as Freud usually termed it in later years, was meant to play a different role. By adapting to its demands, the individual develops his ego. Objective reality is perceived in a more or less distorted way. Within the process of socialization, however, the individual has to adapt to a social reality that can be perceived in a distorted way, but is not changed in its objective impact. In adaptation the laws governing social forces, as well as those studied by psychology, are effective. Psycho-analytic concepts relate to the process and to the result of adaptation. Whenever these facts have not found due consideration, psychoanalytic theory has focused on "reality testing," not only as an important tool, but as the origin and reason for adaptation. Rapaport (1959), assessing Freud's position in 1915, concludes that reality in psychoanalytic theory designates the external source of stimuli, including the subject's body, but excepting the somatic sources of drives and affects. Had practical reality remained nothing but a "source of stimuli" for psychoanalysis, one could hardly speak of social science.

In 1950 Hartmann wrote: "In contrast to some other schools of psychology, psychoanalysis includes within its scope of interest the structure of reality [especially] the structure of society" (pp. 92-93).

Does it really? We would say that to date this is only rudimentarily so, that Freud's conception of objective reality was basically phenomeno-logical and that Hartmann's ego psychology too, has remained so; at least, his "average expectable stimulations" and the degree of adaptive-ness with reference to environmental situations (average expectable— i.e., typical—situations, or on the average not expectable—i.e., a-typical — situations) (Hartmann, 1950) are based on a phenomenological concept. Freud (1927) examined the function of various institutions of civilization, religion in particular. However, his convincing interpretations come to a dead end wherever psychological explanation alone will not do. The "struggle between the individual and society" (Freud, 1930, p. 141) cannot be fully understood as long as "creating a unity out of the individual human beings" (Freud, 1930, p. 140) is viewed as the aim of the process of civilization. It probably is not the *aim*, but one *aspect* of every process of civilization.

By the end of the fifties, analysts became far more aware of the psychological limits of the perception of reality. They have come to understand that "The criteria chiefly used by Freud [for objective reality] are those of science, or more correctly, those that find their clearest expression in science" (Hartmann, 1956, p. 257). Perception of objective reality is not only hampered by magical thinking. "The child learns his approach to reality in constant relation to the adult's approach to it. It adjusts to a world which is not only to a considerable extent man-made, but also man-thought. As a consequence, two different criteria of reality develop, and in the world of every individual both play a role" (p. 257). Even "The scientific conception of knowledge of reality" is to a great extent "of the socially accepted kind" (p. 258). This knowledge is not only a content of our mind but in many respects serves as the basis for our actions and, just like the capacity to perceive objective reality, is part of the ego's adjustment to its environment. "At any rate," Hartmann states, the psychoanalyst "can, strictly speaking, be an analyst only in so far as he is able, in the thinking and acting which constitute his work, to detach himself from the socialized knowledge of man and to move on the level of what Freud calls reality" (p. 259). We would add: in order to see our way in social reality, we must study, not only society in its historic evolution, but also the forces acting in it, especially the "correlations and relations" that may be part of a general science of man. Actually, in the course of the past fifteen years, numerous papers have appeared that try to confront unmodified psychoanalysis with objective social reality; of course, due consideration must be given to the legitimate autonomy of both.

Ethnopsychoanalysis tries to apply psychoanalytic investigation to members of cultures other than the one where psychoanalysis originated. The advantages of this procedure are obvious. The analyst is forced constantly to re-examine and reconsider all social factors from the technical and economic foundations of the society to the patterns of child rearing. In so doing, he is less biased by his attitudes and sentiments than

375

when working within his own culture, where he more or less shares with his patient his own experiences with the environment. A twofold result may be expected: psychological knowledge about human beings who have grown up differently, and an extension of psychoanalytic theory.

Our own experience in this field was gained in former French West Africa, where, owing to the existence of primary schools even in areas remote from the centers of Western political and economic influence, the people speak French. The first main research was done with the Dogon, a people of millet planters living in an arid savannah mountain in the Mali Republic. Their extended families follow a patrilinear descent and live in close-knit village communities (Parin et al., 1963). The second investigation was made with the Agni in the fertile rainwoods of the Republic of Ivory Coast. This people, cousins of the famous Ashanti, has a matrilinear kin-organization and developed from a hunter-and-gatherers subsistence to proud guerriers and slave traders who finally became coffee planters (Parin et al., 1971). Basing our work on the study of a rich anthropological literature further elucidated by some sociological investigations, Rorschach test series, etc., we tried to focus on a psychoanalytic approach. Reconstructions were facilitated by the intensive direct observation of infancy and child-rearing practices. The principal part of our procedure consisted of a series of daily one-hour sessions with normal adult people (more men than women).

In our work with the Dogon and the Agni who volunteered for the psychoanalytically oriented interviews, we proceeded by using psychoanalytic theory, primarily with as little modification as possible, to explain the psychological phenomena observed. Since the beginning of our investigations seventeen years ago, we have modified our technique to adapt it more and more to the usual technique of psychoanalytic exploration and treatment. Thus, we arrived at a "cultural-specific psychoanalytic model." In other words, we had to modify or even extend the analytic theory to fit with the specific development of each social (cultural) group (people, class, etc.). By such broadening of the observational bases, we gained more leeway in modifying analytic theory to accommodate the culture-specific psychoanalytic models we had developed. Obviously, it is essential to assess, as far as possible, all social factors and processes in terms of their underlying nonpsychological forces before examining the relevance of psychological principles for them.

Our procedure for such a re-examination of theory can be outlined by using the example of the Oedipus complex. We must admit, however, that we are not able to contribute very much to finding an answer regarding the universality of the Oedipus complex, since we examined thoroughly only three cultures, including European patients in whom general occurrence of the Oedipus complex had not been disputed.

The first modification we had to make was to speak of the oedipal *conflict* (instead of *complex*). For our theory, this more general term implies that we could find neither the same tendency to repression nor the same coherence of its components in the unconscious as with European patients. For boys and girls of all three cultures, we found that, during the unavoidable phallic phase of development of the libido and of the ego, the libidinal wishes center entirely on the person who cared for the child up until then. In this phase, any person or group of persons who lays claim on the "mother" is considered to be an intruder. While the child's wishes are sexual, other than sexual claims on the fostering person may also be felt as an intrusion by the child. This conflict generates strong affects. Even in cases where rivalry with the intruder is seen, the wish to eliminate the intruder and the fear of being castrated or killed by the "father" in retaliation are not always called forth. Fears of mutilation, however, always appear with boys and girls alike, but they are relatively independent of the intruding object. Dogon boys, who are often nursed up to the phallic phase, frequently fear as a result of this conflict that they will be deserted by their mother. The focusing of aggression in the form of anal-sadistic strivings and the expectancy of retaliation seem to depend on that course of the anal phase which is typical for our environment. However, with the Dogon and the Agni — not only during the oedipal conflict, but even in a later stage — libidinal cathexis and aggression may be directed simultaneously toward the same persons without necessitating repression of one of the two ambivalent strivings. The ambivalence may be strong; yet the ambivalence *tension* remains low. Ultimately, the affects force the child to acquiesce in some way in a triad or, in other words, to abandon the object-related libidinal interests in favor of its narcissistic ones. With this resignation, the forceful development of the instinctual drives during infancy and early childhood is temporarily suspended in the latency phase. Thus, an important and often decisive step toward socialization is accomplished. This step may be made without a determining introjection in the final phase of the oedipal conflict. Since, in both cultures, formation of the superego is not characterized by a major, singular introjective process, development of the superego appears to be far more loosely connected with the oedipal conflict than with us.

In any case, the child's choice of the love object at the beginning of the phallic phase is potentially incestuous. However, the child's environment, usually structured as a family, is the place where collective interests take precedence over individual instinctual interests. The society on which the child depends gives its "egotistical" wishes a direction that allows for the physical and emotional survival of the individual *and* of the group. It accepts the oedipal conflict as inevitable and among other regulations contributes rules of exogamy and taboos on incest to its outcome. We do not consider the later emotional impact of these rules to be genuine horror of incest; it is merely a *consequence* of the inevitable psychosocial conflict in the oedipal stage.

The most important point is that the Oedipus conflict takes place between the individual and society and not between the various psychological structures of the individual psyche. Therefore, in the oedipal conflict, narcissistic interests of the child conflict with the social interests (of its environment), the outcome being that the development of the ego and of the superego of necessity leads to a permanent remolding of the psychic structure. In the course of reconstruction in psychoanalytic therapy, it might appear as if the Oedipus complex emerged independently of the social context, because any human environment requires a certain amount of internalized adaptation to reality (ego formation). Only when such internalization is attained should we speak of the Oedipus complex. Now, only the wishes from the id and the defenses erected against them in the ego are provided with instinctual energy.

To confront persons molded by hitherto unfamiliar social factors with analysis necessitates no change in the principles of metapsychological thought. The closer we have applied psychoanalytic theory, the better we have been able to understand psychological findings with people of those exotic cultures.

For instance, we can confirm that the developmental phases of the libido follow exactly the course established so far. Different practices of child rearing have their greatest influence on the vicissitudes of the drives and on ego-formation, rather than on the maturation of the instinctual drives. Nor is any change in the genetic viewpoint necessary.

Our studies of the Dogon and the Agni point to some typical features of the superego and the ego that shed light on the question of whether psychoanalysis is a social science. Differentiated from the ego, a superego was found in each culture to be the successor to earlier object relations and the carrier of idealized representations. However, it seems to originate out of very diversified phases and developmental steps, and in its functions it appears to be far more dependent on the actual environment than heretofore believed. This form of superego we call "clan conscience." In characterizing the ego of normal persons in these cultures, we speak of "group ego." This is our term for a special molding of the ego. The adult ego is largely dependent on the typical psycho-logical makeup of the individuals in the environment and on specific behavior patterns in the social setting that warrant ego autonomy, as Rapaport conceived of this term. What seems to be a close dependence of the individual on figures and institutions within the social network enriches the ego with mechanisms contributing to its proper functioning. These results of the ethnoanalytic confrontation suggest that we should review some psychoanalytical concepts established in our culture in the light of social factors. Above all, we should study the extent to which the impact of macrosocial environment sets limits to the autonomy and to the functioning of even a mature psychic structure, a well-established super-ego, and an ego oriented to the reality principle.

In his recent book, LeVine (1973) takes great care to convince the reader that human psychology follows its own laws, that social actions are not exclusively the result of social pressures. He warns against confound-ing in observable social behavior the sequels "of enduring disposition and response to environmental pressure" (p. 286). In psychoanalytic theory, this central problem found only a moderate elaboration. It was expected that the mature ego oriented to the reality principle would warrant adaptation and would deal with social pressures in a rational way. An exception was made with war neurosis and similar conditions, which were explained by the pressure of environment (called "traumatic situation") upon acquired psychic structure.

However, in analytic therapy the immediate perception of objective reality to be attained by the patient through establishment of the reality principle is not enough to deal in a rational way with social pressures. The reality principle implies that the instinctual strivings of the id are adequately adjusted to the requirements of the immediate environment. We think that the analyst should perceive the *extended* social environ-ment "beyond the reality principle." The power and production situa-tions, with all the institutions, regulations, and value systems they involve, call for investigation comparable to the psychoanalytic explora-tion of the unconscious. For society affects the psyche of the adult without his having to be conscious of it. One can say of a mature ego, fully oriented to the reality principle that, the greater its flexibility in adapting to its immediate tasks, the less inclined it is to perceive the transforming influence of the extended environment.

Psychoanalytic research has given due consideration to the social environment during early childhood, but we know far less about the social phenomena constituting the content of the parent's and educator's ego ideal. In practice, the extended society — the people, class, or cast to which the patient belongs and his participation in social groups — may have been sufficiently taken into account. In psychoanalytic theory, however, such factors have only recently been accepted for investigation with adolescents. Yet, in every analysis one can see that social performance — professional activity, for instance — may deeply affect the psyche of the person in action, that it causes internal conflicts or helps to overcome them, and that it has an essential influence on the cathexis of the self, and of the objects, and on the relation of the superego to the ego. Such observations, however, will lead to success only if one takes into consideration that a good official not only fulfills useful organizational functions but also exerts his power by pressure on his fellow men; that an entrepreneur not only has an interesting profession requiring initiative but also is an exploiter; that a factory worker not only has a tedious manual job but thereby serves interests that are opposed to his own.

Establishment of the reality principle presupposes reality testing. This is an indispensable function of the ego, whether the principle is wholly established or not. Only where this function is still more or less intact can the ego retain its relative autonomy.

From experience with hospitalized mental cases, we know that even severely confused patients with an exceptionally troubled and reduced self-perception are able to test outer reality to a certain degree. One will hardly find a mental patient who does not react with protest against his internment, however kindly and considerately he may be treated. It is all the more astonishing that normal, intelligent persons do not react to the influence of a society which leads to a lasting or transitory adjustment of the ego and superego — such influence seems to be beyond their perception.

Structurally, this situation is easy to explain. The modified ego is no longer able easily to perceive the social factors to which it has adjusted its structure. Only potential consequences such as dwindling satisfactions, the decline of self-esteem (perceived as a depressive feeling), and sometimes the recollection of earlier conditions or of no longer effective but not fully invalidated demands of the ego ideal, are consciously felt.

In analytic investigation, these adjusive processes are suggested primarily by the quality of the relation to the object. In place of object-related transference, one finds wishes of narcissistic gratification. The more alienated the social situation, the less a libidinal response is expected or accepted. The object representations are cathected mainly with narcissistic energy. The patient no longer expects response from the analyst, but hopes for repair of his functions. However, the achievement of narcissistic gratifications offers but temporary recovery of self-esteem.

The originally cathected object-related aims cannot be abandoned. They take effect out of repression: in other words, they cause frustrations, which in the narcissistic realm are compensated by outward success, by gratification of aggressive claims for power and other aggressive strivings, and which contribute to the enhancement of the libidinal cathexis of the self only to the point at which frustration again takes the upper hand.

The empathic analyst who works from the psychic reality of his patients, as well as the socially conscious one who has investigated the structure and underlying conflicts and forces of social reality, treat the same patient and, in the ideal case, will call forth the same analytic process.

The situation of the socially conscious analyst is comparable to the case in which an analyst has to work with patients who have remained in a pathological dependence on the narcissistic wishes of their parents, described (by Richter, 1960, p. 62) as "narcissistic projections of the parents upon the child." From childhood, such persons have had to adjust to an unusual degree. For them, interpretations do not become acceptable until they have learned to distinguish their own ego interests from those of their parents. First of all, mechanisms of projective identification and of participative projection with attitudes and claims of the parents must be made conscious and must be corrected so that the patient can perceive the reality of his parents. This could not be achieved if the analyst were no more able to perceive the reality of the parent's pathological behavior than is his patient. In the same way, we believe that the analyst must see clearly the influence that the macrosociety (culture) of a people, a class, a social stratum has on his patient. Then only can the analysis tackle those portions of the ego that have been formed or deformed by the adjustment.

Typical processes and mechanisms that facilitate practical analytic work have been established. We know about the narcissistic gratification in aggressive or masochistic acting out of the status or class interest, and about the distorted heterosexual relations that follow from the social debasement of women, conforming to the standards of bourgeois society. The superego can unconsciously undergo major modification in its content and mode of action. Studies made during the war showed that soldiers in training, by identification with the aggressor, arrive, not only at a new content of their ego ideal, but also at very different demands of the superego on the ego. Identification with the leader or with ideal systems, fractioning of the superego, and revival of long-relinquished, preautonomous nuclei of the superego were used to explain pathological behavior in unusual social situations. Similar processes seem to have a

381

major, as yet unexplored, importance in everyday life as well. Establishment of an identity in the final stage of adolescence, as described by Erikson, is probably but one of many very different processes where the outside world effects cathexis of the self and the interrelation of the psychic structures. Although this is not effected independently of earlier development, the potential result is largely modified.

One mechanism that has proved very usful in practical work is that of identification with a social role. Such identifications can be permanent, yet sometimes they appear only temporarily or as emergency mechanisms. Identification with a social role can affect the superego like a manic mechanism, insofar as the ego dispenses with otherwise valid demands of the superego. At the same time, intrastructural conflicts in the ego can be bridged. The mechanism serves as orientation to the outside world and, therefore, sometimes functions like a defense mechanism against demands of the id, and against affects. When compared with a complex defense mechanism — retrenchment of the ego, for instance — the major difference lies in the immediate libidinal and often aggressive gratification of the instinctual drives, which gives the mechanism somewhat the character of a labile symptom formation. Contrary to a symptom, identification with a social role usually goes hand in hand with narcissistic gratification, which is, however, often only temporary.

In analytic technique we have a special tool for making conflicts visible. The psychoanalytic situation, of necessity, involves the revival of conflicts experienced earlier and subsequently internalized. They yearn to be acted out with the person of the analyst. This is the phenomenon we call "transference."

Anna Freud (1969) suggested that as analysts we transfer our predilection for the observation of conflict and contradiction from the individual patient to our relation with our environment. Should we do so, we will certainly be in good company. Freud himself was of the early opinion that neuroses are the consequence of conflicts that society has failed to settle for its members. Modern anthropology, on which ethnopsychoanalysis is founded, as well as Marxist doctrine, are based on the contradictions existent in society and that lead to conflicts between groups of people and classes. One can well view the life of human societies and their development as a sequence of conflicts, respective solutions, and subsequent new conflicts.

Conflicts in the social structure and internal conflicts in the acquired psychic structure of its members are interrelated. This interrelation, however, is not of such a simple nature that all conflicts apparent in society must be borne out by the individual. Inner conflicts and social conflicts do not abide by the same laws. With inner conflicts, biological forces assume the quality of social effectiveness. The mutual influence of both systems, society and inner life, may be described as a process that does not come to an end with the years of psychic development. The culture-specific, socialized man of whom we have a metapsychological conceptualization has an actual social environment that influences him. Thus, man appears as a social being shaped by a society rich in conflicts, the influences of which determine his development, his social situation, as well as his mental life. Social science, however, must understand that psychoanalysis, when exploring the conscious and unconscious life of the psyche, engages in the study of an agent that, by its own laws and with its own conflict-born forces, shapes the course of history and takes an active part in cultural and social processes. The more comprehensive and well founded the results of psychoanalysis are, the more important is its role as social science.

October, 1973

Discussion

PROFESSOR LEVINE:

Dr. Parin and his colleague Dr. Morgenthaler impose monumental challenges on themselves when they leave their clinical practice in Switzerland to undertake psychoanalytic research in West Africa. The complications involved in attempting psychoanalytic work under such unusual conditions are enough to deter most clinicians from it; but Drs. Parin and Morgenthaler apparently experience these complications as fascinating aspects of the frontier they came to explore, rather than irritating barriers to their standard work. We need more such psychoanalytic pioneers on this anthropological frontier.

Dr. Parin's paper raises many issues worthy of discussion, but I can choose only two for these brief comments. On the whole, I agree with him that psychoanalysis *is* a social science and that it has far from realized its potential development within the social sciences. I also agree with his conclusion, if I understand him correctly, that the major cross-cultural differences are to be found less in the *content* of underlying conflicts than in the choice of defenses and their symbolic elaboration.

But I shall address myself to other issues of a more preliminary and pressing importance.

383

First, I should like to offer my own interpretation of Dr. Parin's emphasis on understanding the social and cultural context of the individual in itself before proceeding to the intrapsychic level of analysis. This requirement can be seen in terms of the empathy the psychoanalyst uses as his tool of investigation. As Kohut (1959) has made it clear in his well-known paper on the subject, empathy has its cultural basis in the patterns of experience shared by patient and analyst. In a drastically different culture, however, the psychoanalytic investigator cannot presume that these similarities exist. He does not know the African pattern of experience and how closely it matches his own. While at home he may take shared experience for granted; in the field it is not only questioned, but must become an object of inquiry in and of itself. Thus does the psychoanalyst in another culture necessarily become an anthropologist, learning the indigenous points of view in detail before he can legitimately delve into the depths of intrapsychic structure. Cultural phenomenology must precede personal phenomenology in his field work.

My own current research, for example, is on embarrassment in certain African groups. To study this phenomenon empathically, I must be able to put myself in the place of an African who becomes embarrassed when a taboo is likely to be breached. In order to do this, I must know the entire system of taboos as he knows it, and that means understanding the social structure in which he operates. I am in a still more favorable position if my understanding of the social structure goes beyond his views to include the social pressures acting upon him of which he is unaware. I must, in short, do an anthropological study before raising the psychoanalytic questions that motivate my research. Similarly, the psychohistorian must do extensive historical research to provide the cultural basis for his own empathy with historical figures. Having investigated an exotic social and cultural environment as never before, the psychoanalyst is likely to come away with an increased appreciation of the impact of social environment on individual behavior. I gather from Dr. Parin's paper that this was the case with him. This suggests that *doing* ethnopsychoanalysis can affect one's theoretical views, in the way that Freud's clinical experience affected the development of psychoanalysis. I believe that significant contributions from psychoanalytic anthropology and psychohistory similarly require the acitve and prolonged involvement of psychoanalysts whose theoretical views are evolving in response to the data they collect.

The second point in Dr. Parin's paper to which I shall call attention is his description of group ego and clan conscience among Africans. While

I have always been uneasy with these concepts, I have become convinced that the phenomenon they refer to is not only a real one but very widespread among pre-industrial peoples and that it has important implications for psychoanalytic ego psychology. My conviction is based not only on my own research among Africans but on that of colleagues working in other parts of the world. For example, two of our most sophisticated investigators in the field of psychoanalytically oriented anthropology— Dorothy Eggan, whose dream research among the Hopi Indians is well known, and William Caudill, who conducted extensive investigations of child development and psychiatric disorders in Japan—found it necessary to emphasize the positive value set on emotional and moral interdependence in the cultures in which they were working and the way in which it contrasts with Western values of autonomy. In their work and in that of Dr. Parin, it seems clear that these values have their intrapsychic counterparts, in less internalization and the greater involvement of social structure for aspects of personal functioning regarded as purely individual in our culture. If this is true, psychoanalytic anthropology gives us access to persons of less moral and emotional autonomy, less sharp boundaries between self and other, less individuated self-representations, who are nevertheless well adapted to their cultural environments. Such persons should be able to teach us a great deal about the diversity possible in relations between psychic structure and social structure. The comparative study of the self, building on the work of Kohut, would represent one promising way of approaching this still largely unknown territory in research. If we become able to listen as well and as clearly to these people in foreign cultures—and in other historical epochs—as psychoanalysts listen to their patients, advances in psychoanalytic knowledge and social-science knowledge will follow.

DR. FRIEDMAN:

Dr. Parin's purpose is to make the human sciences continuous with each other—to go beyond formal relationships and *ad hoc* efforts at cooperation to achieve a real, substantive integration.

To call psychoanalysis a social science merely because it deals with families which are units of society does not suit Dr. Parin's rigorous approach. His question is: *How* does psychoanalysis deal with the individual in society? Does it see him as a piece of nature coming up against a man-made environment? If so, psychoanalysis is no more a social science than plant physiology is a landscaping science, or metallurgy an architectural science. In such a view natural science and social

385

science would be separate, interdigitating fields, drawing on each other in the random fashion that we see in psychohistory, psychobiography, psychoesthetics, etc.

Dr. Parin's answer is that current psychoanalysis does *not* regard man as a piece of raw nature. It regards him as a biological creature, yes, but one who is always and inevitably shaped by society. We can never outline man's natural nucleus; any given behavior is a socially conditioned derivative.

Dr Parin's own research adds compelling force to his argument. The metapsychology so "natural" to us at home is not the metapsychology of all humanity. Dr. Parin shakes us out of our provincial complacency. Why, indeed, should we ever have expected these patterns to be immutable? There is no reason to suppose that anything in the mind (or in the body) is immune from development, modification, evolution. Certainly, Freud believed in the evolution of psychic structure.

Assuming that culture is the agent of change, we must conclude that *mental structures are reflections of social structures.* We may argue about which structures are more quickly influenced and which lag behind, how subtle or direct the influencing is, and which times in a person's life cycle he is most influenced. But, overall, Dr. Parin shows that, in a manner of speaking, variable, historically specific social forces become frozen into the mind as psychic structure.

Does *that* make psychoanalysis a social science? True to his purpose, Dr. Parin will not accept even that accommodation. Even if psychoanalysis and the social sciences are merely describing the same social forces from diverse viewpoints, the disciplines themselves might be disparate.

It is this strictness that makes Dr. Parin's project so valuable for pinpointing the issue. We will not have integrated the sciences of man until the *laws and descriptions* of the historical sciences are themselves a part of the laws and descriptions that relate to the individual (or vice versa, as others have proposed).

Once social forces have left their imprint on psychic structure, they can be—and have been—dealt with in purely psychological terms. But Dr. Parin suggests that the perception of reality is also a function of the mind: if reality includes the laws and forces of social history, psychoanalysis will inevitably have incorporated social science into its own *descriptions.* Theoretically, it would be as impossible to make an accurate psychoanalytic description without referring to social *forces* as it would be to omit reference to a mothering figure.

This is the crux of the argument. But a difficulty arises from the very

386

problems of describing reality. Any kind of reality, intrapsychic or social, even ultimately physical, allows an infinite variety of descriptions. When we describe something, we are choosing from many possible abstractions Some of these abstractions or scientific laws may be true or false. In that sense, they are objective. But the *type* of abstraction we choose is not true or false; it is chosen because it answers our needs. In that sense, most of our descriptions are arbitrary.

For instance, there are many ways to conceptualize the mind: we can take an esthetic approach, the philosophical view of the existentialists, the point of view of ethical analysis, or a social-science approach such as that suggested by Dr. Parin.

What, then, is *special* about psychoanalysis as a description of the mind? The psychoanalytic view of the mind results from a treatment situation. Though its *purpose* is understanding and its *uses* are manifold, psychoanalysis is a type of description designed to describe what happens in treatment. (The origin and development of psychoanalytic concepts amply demonstrate this.) That does not make psychoanalysis more pragmatic than any other theory. It simply specifies the perspective from which the mind is discussed; it establishes the categories of dissection that the theory will employ.

Consequently, in order to understand what kind of description psycho-analysis is, we have to know what kind of treatment psychoanalysis is. I think it is not inaccurate to say that fundamentally psychoanalytic treat-ment is the clarification of opportunities. The reality that a patient is confronted with is one that is relevant to his purposes. The reality that an analyst confronts is one relevant to the fate of a variety of purposes belonging to a variety of patients.

Psychoanalysis is a drive theory. Even when it speaks of conflict-free and neutralized areas, its mission is to be aware of the relation of perceptions to drives. Psychoanalysis always asks: What imprint do wishes place on reality? By looking at the way the *patient* organizes reality, the psychoanalyst is provided with two principles for organizing his *own* concepts: (1) the patient's wish structure itself, including conflict and the wish to be free of conflict and pain; (2) an image, presumably shared by the patient, of an optimum, over-all gratification permitted and fostered by the culture — an image of maturity (Hartmann, 1939).

The evaluation of reality — the affective coloring, the highlighting, the discriminating, the selecting — is the *patient's*. That is why Freud con-fined himself to what Dr. Parin calls phenomenology, leaving the evalua-tion and meaning of experience to the patient (Hartmann, 1956, p. 265).

In other words, psychoanalysis is a system of descriptions relevant to

387

the *individual's* principles of abstraction, whatever they may be. In this respect psychoanalysis is unique. Its approach is unlike the approach of any other discipline: the social sciences, the philosophy of history, or aesthetics. The laws that Dr. Parin sees and the abstractions he makes concerning the alienation of the worker from his product, the exploitation of one class by another, the bureaucratization of life roles, the debasement of women, the loss of craft satisfactions — are all relevant to particular kinds of questions only. We could choose to look at the same matters quite differently. The notion of ego distortion illustrates the differences between the conventional psychoanalytic approach and Dr. Parin's.

In psychoanalysis, "a distorted ego" does not mean an ego that rejects some particular, authoritative formulation of events. It is shorthand for a patient's rigid way of wishing, which rules out perspectives that require a different approach. The analyst's freedom from social reality is not an X-ray ability to strip events of their conventional significance and see through to the skeleton; events don't have a skeleton. The analyst's clear ego represents his flexibility in surveying the interplay of human desires with events.

But I think Dr. Parin takes a very different position when he suggests that the patient's ego has been deformed by the general structure of society and should be repaired. He is not simply maintaining a degree of flexibility that is greater than the patient's; he is introducing what, from the patient's standpoint, is an arbitrary analysis.

By arbitrary I do not mean untrue or irrelevant. I am not saying that there can be no social science. If the patient were concerned about the laws of society, if he were also an anthropologist or a historian, Dr. Parin's interpretation of social reality *would* reply to a corresponding set of questions. But for a patient *qua* patient, Dr. Parin's social critique would probably answer only questions about what attitudes Dr. Parin himself endorses.

What would distinguish this from suggestion? Psychoanalysis tries to minimize suggestion by dealing exclusively with the patient's *own* analyses, so to speak, plus a view of maturity or optimal growth — which has little suggestion in it, but presumably also has roots within the patient. (Without such roots, as in the case of a classic psychopath, or someone from another culture, we would have to speak of conversion or indoctrination.)

By adhering to its own terms, psychoanalysis is protected from being an arbitrary way of categorizing the world, since its principles are, in effect, those of whomever it is dealing with. Any *other* system would be organized around the particular interests of the investigator.

Even the small objective social reality that the psychoanalyst cannot escape—his relationship with the patient—is already hard to define neutrally. Even the analyst's disciplined purposes, tied though they are to the patient's interests, still manage to color his perspectives. Surely one of the revelations of Dr. Kohut's work is, by contrast, the awareness of how close to sin the concept of narcissism had previously crept, and partly because it seemed to be a frustrating limit in treatment.

Similar coloring of other concepts, defense and resistance, for example, have often been described. These shadings are arbitrary perspectives because they arise from the *analyst's* purposes, not the patient's.

But these arbitrary perspectives are as nothing compared with what we must accept as we approach the sciences of history. Not only are we always involved in history as we are not in a patient's life, but we are also immensely handicapped by never having the opportunity to see its fruition.

I like Dr. Parin's description of human societies as "a sequence of conflicts, respective solutions, and subsequent new conflicts." In that respect we must grant that the life of societies is like the life of individuals. But individuals are mortal: they mature and decay. There is a final outcome. Their opportunities are limited—so limited that those opportunities can define a science like psychoanalysis. The individual himself, with his circumscribed interests and finite potential, can show us what his conflicts are and what constitute solutions. Therefore, psychoanalysis can objectively reveal his problems. History, on the other hand, knows no maturity or conclusions. Only the next phase of history can *objectively* define historical problems and solutions out of the welter of today's happenings. Whatever historic truths we discover in the present will include an arbitrary perspective.

Mixing a science having substantive values with another that requires that we attach our own holds great danger for both sides. To be objective in the historical sciences is to be always aware that we filter complex events through the grid of what is important to us. No temptation should blur our recognition that moral considerations are never far from our thoughts nor easily disentangled from our terms. If the sciences were joined, the natural self-selection of problems that psychoanalysis provides and which leads to categories of health and maturity, could camouflage our historical bias. We might award psychological credits and debits to social phenomena that we like and dislike. We might speak about objective forces that deform the ego when we should be talking of patterns in which people are imbedded in which we judge to be bad. As Hartmann (1939) reminds us, a term like *narcissism* could disguise judgments like *alienation* or *anti-progressivism.* As a being who can be "distorted" by society, "natural man" would re-emerge to do battle with—or be defeated by—bad societies. The door Dr. Parin had sealed would open again, admitting psychoanalytic romanticism—the myth of an uninhibited human nature—and its political counterpart, psycho-analytic Utopianism.

Psychoanalysis would also suffer. We would take a theory that is justi-fied by its bearing on *anyone's* needs, and tether it to views arising from the choice of particular theorists. (What is oppression to one man is complementarity or coordination to another.)

With these dangers in mind, I raise the following question: Must psychoanalysis relinquish all special privileges outside of its own domain in order to safeguard its privileged perspective—its descriptive para-mountcy—in matters of motives and valuation? If the answer is yes, then psychoanalysis can offer the subject of society only what every other human science does: one more arbitrary slice of the world, one more thread in the fabric, one more set of variables, one more collection of structures and forces, a useful and necessary service to the overall product.

I do not find that a happy conclusion. If we *could* connect the human sciences, either by introducing social science into psychoanalysis, or the reverse, our knowledge of society and our power to deal with the awful problems before us would expand immeasurably. For psychoanalysis sharply illuminates how individuals form and organize their values. And the evaluation of the individual that psychoanalysis undertakes feeds off of the meanings, forms, and structures that social science studies.

The trouble is that we have no way of knowing these surrounding structures, which are composed of social and ecological forces, save by observing what people make of them. It is as though we could tell the grain of the wood only by the sculptor's respect for it. Or as though we could watch the decision-making process, but could only guess the issues presented to it.

Even a technological innovation, which seems to be such a plainly evident opportunity, is actually an unknown matrix of possibilities and irrelevancies, unless seen through the eyes of a given people. Dr. Eissler (1965) reminds us of this in his statements on the Roman attitude toward inventions. A modern axe to the Tasaday, a new agriculture in India, movable type or gunpowder to the ancient Chinese—the invention itself is a cipher, or more accurately, the invention is our own technologically biased nominee for the role of Important Factor. If that is true of so discrete a factor as an invention, less tangible forces must be enigmatic indeed.

In such a morass, perhaps our best hope is to accumulate as many different kinds of patterns as possible. Perhaps we should interweave as many specialized, heterogeneous sciences as we can. (I think of Erikson's approach.) Perhaps the wish we all have to conquer everything with a connected chain of theories is a snare, distracting us from the clumsier but surer course of piling theory upon theory, of countering perspective with perspective, of interdisciplinary borrowing and lending, of conversation between untranslatable languages. It is, after all, a very dense reality that we are trying to understand.

I don't know what the answer is. But I am grateful to Dr. Parin for bringing it closer by focusing the issue so sharply.

DR. ·PARIN:

Dr. Friedman raises many questions that really require a broad discussion of our diverse views on the theory of science as well as the exposition of clinical material. Instead of this, I shall briefly discuss two points, the most critical ones he has made.

First, he thinks that my analysis of society would necessarily be an arbitrary one, that in analytic theory this would lead to suggestion, or to the conversion or indoctrination of the patient. Second, he says that after having sealed the door to the utopia of good, old natural man, I would open it again for psychoanalytic utopianism, a notion of ideal society, or at least to the possibility of assessing the laws of history.

I do *not* believe that he raised these two major objections only because my view is very close to Marxist thought, or more exactly to the method of dialectic materialism. (I think it is — though many Marxist scholars would not admit it.)

The first objection may rest upon a kind of agnosticism about "objective reality." Dr. Friedman thinks that objective social reality is even "hard to define neutrally" in psychoanalytic therapy. The observation of transference, of resistance, of change in transference, of the transference neurosis — to mention only the most familiar items — enables the analyst to assess the objective social reality in psychoanalytic therapy. The evaluation of these processes allows for a far better understanding of the analytic process than "a view of maturity or optimal growth," which is static, not congruent with psychic life, which is characterized by conflicting forces and the interaction of structures.

391

I think, furthermore, that history is not more and not less arbitrary than any science of man, though it includes theories about the present period that will be checked by the future. I have chosen, of course, a theory of culture very close to that which underlies psychoanalysis: I speak of conflicts, solutions or results, and new conflicts. About 40 years ago, Otto Fenichel proved, that this view is the common denominator of dialectic materialism and psychoanalytic theory. But I think that one cannot say that this and other existent descriptions of social reality are abstractions taken from an infinite variety of descriptions chosen at random.

Certainly, social and historical events have no skeleton. But they do have a physiology and a genetic growth. Evolution is an accumulative and selective process; the forces acting in it are abstractions that are put under scrutiny in the light of their tangible effects. The notion of ecological, economic, and similar forces is not less or more arbitrary than the notion of instinctual drives. Both notions are abstractions corresponding to a network of facts which lend probability to them and enable them to be close descriptions of real forces. Both are understandable by human logic and underly the process of scientific investigation. They may be modified or changed whenever new facts or better explanations arise. I do not think that they are any more difficult for our patients to understand, accept, or reject, or of any less interest to them, than the interpretations we used to give of unconscious wishes.

The second critical point of a utopian view would be easy to discard: the model of a conflict-born psychological apparatus in a conflict-born and conflict-producing society should eliminate any thought of a simplistic optimism. I have no other utopia than that of all people studying human affairs: to come closer to the laws and principles governing complex processes, which underlie a continual change and in which we are involved ourselves.

I accept Dr. Friedman's warnings that one could easily be biased in this matter. But I do not agree with his warning that we should rather pile theory upon theory. I think we should try to organize our work and thoughts as far as possible. But this is a problem leading too far off the mark into the theory of science.

REFERENCES

Eissler, K. (1965), *Medical Orthodoxy and the Future of Psychoanalysis*. New York: International Universities Press.

Erikson, E. H. (1968), Die Ontogenese der Ritualisierung. *Psyche*, 22:481-502.

Freud, A. (1969), *Difficulties in the Path of Psychoanalysis: A Confrontation of Past with Present Viewpoints. The Writings of Anna Freud*, vol. 7. New York: International Universities Press, pp. 124-156.

Freud, S. (1887-1902), *The Origins of Psychoanalysis: Letters, Drafts and Notes to Wilhelm Fliess (1887-1902)*. New York: Basic Books, 1954.

_____ (1905), Three essays on the theory of sexuality. *Standard Edition*, 7:125-243. London: Hogarth Press, 1953.

_____ (1914), On the history of the psychoanalytic movement. *Standard Edition*, 14:3-66. London: Hogarth Press, 1957.

_____ (1921), Group psychology and the analysis of the ego. *Standard Edition*, 18:67-143. London: Hogarth Press, 1955.

_____ (1927), The future of an illusion. *Standard Edition*, 21:3-56. London: Hogarth Press, 1961.

_____ (1930), Civilization and its discontents. *Standard Edition*, 21:59-145. London: Hogarth Press, 1964.

_____ (1933), New introductory lectures on psycho-analysis. *Standard Edition*, 22:3-182. London: Hogarth Press, 1964.

_____ (1937), Analysis terminable and interminable. *Standard Edition*, 23:211-253. London: Hogarth Press, 1964.

Goldschmidt, W. (1966), *Comparative Functionalism: An Essay in Anthropological Theory*. Berkeley: University of California Press.

Hartmann, H. (1939), Psychoanalysis and the concept of health. In: *Essays on Ego Psychology*. New York: International Universities Press, 1964, pp. 3-18.

_____ (1950), The application of psychoanalytic concept to social science. In: *Essays on Ego Psychology: Selected Problems in Psychoanalytic Theory*. New York: International Universities Press, 1964, pp. 90-98.

_____ (1956), Notes on the reality principle. *Ibid.*, pp. 241-267.

Kohut, H. (1959), Introspection, empathy and psychoanalysis. *J. Amer. Psychoanal. Assn.*, 7:459-483.

LeVine, R. (1973), *Culture, Behavior, and Personality*. Chicago: Aldine.

Marx, K. (1857-1858), Grundrisse der Kritik der politischen Oekonomie. In: *Marx und Freud: Ueber Aggression*, ed. W. Lepenies & H. Nolte. Munich: Hanser, 1971.

Parin, P., Morgenthaler, F., & Parin-Matthèy, G. (1963), *Die Weissen denken zuviel: Psychoanalytische Untersuchungen in Westafrika*. Zurich: Atlantis, 1972, Munich: Kinder.

_____ (1971), *Fürchte deinen Nächsten wie dich selbst: Psychoanalyse und Gesellschaft am Modell der Agni in Westafrika*. Frankfurt a.M.: Suhrkamp.

Rapaport, D. (1951), The autonomy of the ego. In: *Collected Papers*. New York: Basic Books, 1967, pp. 357-367.

Richter, H. E. (1960), Die narzisstischen Projektionen der Eltern auf das Kind. In: *Jahrbuch der Psychoanalyse*, Vol. 1. Cologne: Westdeutscher Verlag.

October, 1973

VII

APPLIED PSYCHOANALYSIS

Oscar Wilde's Narcissism

JEROME KAVKA, M.D. (*Chicago*)

> To love oneself is the beginning of a life-long romance.
> Oscar Wilde, *Epigrams*

Most of us have been touched by the literary giant, Oscar Wilde: by his novel *The Picture of Dorian Gray*, by his plays, or, more commonly, by his many witty and often profound epigrams, which have crept into our daily speech.

Psychoanalysts, in their applied analytic work, have often been accused of that state of cynicism which, in Wilde's words, "knows the price of everything and the value of nothing" (1890, p. 47). We should remember, however, that Wilde welcomed criticism, engaged in it, and was interested in it as a serious art form (Ellmann, 1968; Weintraub, 1968). With characteristic humor, he said, "To give an accurate description of what has never occurred is not merely the proper occupation of the historian, but the inalienable privilege of any man of parts and culture" (1894, p. 197). With this warning from the subject himself about the limitations of pathography, I venture on this Wild[e] analysis.

Biographies of Wilde tend to be passionate and partisan, often revolving around accusations or disavowals of his homosexuality. He was a colorful personality, and his life is in many ways as interesting as his literary work. Wilde's obvious characterological pathology, his flamboyant behavioral paradoxes, beg psychological investigation.

Grinstein's (1973) psychodynamic study of Oscar Wilde notes certain parallels between the artist's life and repetitive themes in his creative

---

Based on a discussion of "On Oscar Wilde," by Alexander Grinstein, M.D., presented before the Chicago Psychoanalytic Society, September 23, 1969, and published in *This Annual*, 1:345-362.

works. Both Wilde and the fictional Dorian Gray felt responsible for the death of a female three years younger, considered themselves guilty beyond redemption, and ultimately had to destroy themselves. Dorian Gray repressed his grief and deep longings for the lost actress, a loss that had rekindled the loss of his mother in infancy. In the vain attempt to reunite with the lost object, Dorian Gray, through a series of heterosexual, homosexual, and narcissistic attachments, deteriorates to the point of homicide and suicide. Similarly, Wilde, following the loss of an important heterosexual object, his sister, grieved inconsolably and regressed into homosexuality and narcissism.

In essence, Grinstein not only notes similar characterologic responses to traumatic losses by the creative artist in his own life and by the fictional hero in the novel, he also attempts — too valiantly, I believe — to force his psychological explanations into the framework of structuralized oedipal conflicts. Grinstein seems to have proposed capacities for object love on the part of the author that are belied by the knowledge we have of his personality. Grinstein's analysis would more nearly apply to a neurotic individual and does not do justice to the complex richness of Wilde's character.

Wilde was victimized by unbearable narcissistic tensions, related in part to unneutralized exhibitionistic drives. His life style, as well as that of his fictional hero Dorian, reveal developmental fixations and maturational failures which clearly characterize a narcissistic personality disorder. In the face of these pregenital symbiotic attachments and their reenactments in homosexual behavior, the vicissitudes of Wilde's narcissistic development are of more than casual importance.

My own predilection is to attend to the disharmonies in Wilde's defensive structure and capacities for ego integration in the face of enormous narcissistic tensions. Not only can the creative product then be seen as a form of self-revelation of underlying intrapsychic struggles, but the creative process itself can be understood as a step in the direction of self-cure through the re-establishment of self-cohesion.[1]

Temporary creative spells, and even the more extensive creative commitments that characterize the professional artist, can now be understood as narcissistic transformations when viewed from the standpoint of Kohut's limpid metapsychological theories of the self (1971). Kohut's detailed metapsychology of narcissism goes beyond content analysis and allows for subtler analyses of form and style as well as more determinant explanations of the creative process itself in the life of the artist.

[1] For a similar approach to the meaning of the creative process, see Rose (1971, 1972, 1973).

It may be of interest that the entire Wilde family showed strong creative dispositions. Lady Wilde, a descendant of the Irish Gothic novelist Charles Robert Maturin, wrote extensive prose and poetry under the pen name of Speranza; Sir William, the father, was not only a skilled surgeon of the highest rank, but he wrote extensively on a variety of topics; brother Willie, perhaps the least creative of all, was a journalist. Biographical histories of these family members suggest that intense narcissism paralleled the degree of their creativity.

"The Maladie of Reverie"

Grinstein (1973) recognizes that Wilde's "writings and speeches were so filled with deliberate deception, that his real self was often obscured by a 'mist of words'" (p. 345), and I feel that the basis of this suppressive style can be detected in biographic data about the mother. It was she who encouraged suppression in her own writings and in her direct encouragement for the use of theater as a means of avoiding the painful realities of life (Wyndham, 1951, p. 178). This observation deserves emphasis, inasmuch as her son, the writer, appears to have complied. In the preface to his novel, he sets the tone for a major theme, concealment: "To reveal art and conceal the artist is art's aim. . . . Those who go beneath the surface do so at their peril. . . . Those who read the symbol do so at their peril" (1890, pp. 9, 10).

Early in *Dorian Gray*, the artist says, "I have grown to love secrecy" (p. 13). Wilde makes a virtue of a necessity. Distortion and inaccuracy were consciously encouraged in his family (White, 1967). One of the most urgent distortions involved suppression of feelings about the death of his sister. Concealment has gone so far that in the numerous family biographies one gets only meager information about her death and the attendant circumstances and hardly anything of her flesh-and-blood quality. This is remarkable inasmuch as she lived to the age of ten years! I suspect Wilde's mother vigorously suppressed discussion about her child. Her furious social activities, her interest in spiritualism, her habit of sitting in the shadows in candlelight, and her emphasis on staying young seem to indicate depression and unresolved mourning (White, 1967).

Wilde's compulsively repetitive preoccupation with the theme of suppression is probably based on an identification with his mother's avowals of the importance of forgetting. Lord Henry's encouragement of various methods for intensifying the stimulus barrier by means of sensual indulgences is a fictional representation of Lady Wilde's exhortations. However, the compelling pressure for abreaction of losses of self-esteem is un-successfully inhibited. Wilde was able neither to forget nor remember effectively, with the result that the necessary abreaction of his grief remained unresolved, despite the acceptable form of self-revelation by means of dramatic fictionalizing that ultimately determined his writing career.

Concerning Wilde's feelings for his sister, his own son writes:

About three years after my father's birth, Speranza's dearest wish was fulfilled in the arrival of a daughter, who was given the names of Isola Francesca. Isola was, from the moment of her birth, the pivot around which the family affection of the Wildes revolved. Speranza, with the calm aloofness affected by Victorian parents, may have pretended to be indifferent, but my grandfather and the boys frankly worshipped Isola, and when she died, after a short illness, at the age of ten, the family was inconsolable [Holland, 1954, p. 21]

This statement about aloofness and indifference underlines Speranza's ambivalence to the child and possibly refers to her conduct after the child's death. Wilde wrote of the "maladie of reverie" and in the novel describes a number of violent deaths, but the death of his sister was not to be discussed.

The silence about Isola is in sharp contrast to the general amount and quality of talking among the Wildes. Yeats was to say: "When one listens to her [Speranza] and remembers that Sir William Wilde was in his day a famous raconteur, one finds it in no way wonderful that Oscar Wilde should be the most finished talker of our time" (Wyndham, 1951, p. 181).

In addition to their volubility and eloquence, the Wilde family were flagrant exaggerators. Vyvyan Holland's biography (1954) is pathetic in its extensive disavowals of his father's homosexuality. Lady Wilde lied about her age, and Oscar lied about his age. His son Vyvyan (who was also expected to be a girl and would have been named Isola) is not certain of his own birth-date because each of his parents assumed the other had registered it — an evidence of casualness bordering on irresponsibility.

Lady Wilde, Speranza, who claimed to be descended from Dante (wishful thinking based upon an idealization), was a humorless woman who "put opinions first — facts second" (Wyndham, 1951, p. 163). When she wrote about her child Oscar, her correspondent could not tell the child's gender. To the bitter end, she believed in her son's innocence. Wilde himself lied to his counsel; his paramour, Lord Douglas, was a known liar; and Frank Harris (1959), an important biographer, was regarded as a flagrant liar. In the face of all this apparent lying, Wilde biographers certainly face a challenge!

Statements by Speranza encourage fictionalizing: there would appear to be a relationship between his interest in becoming a playwright and the following editorial she wrote:

All civilization is going the same path, for the whole science of happiness now is to forget; and at the theatre alone can weary humanity hope to find "the waters of forgetfulness." Life is becoming such a tangled mess of claims and duties, such a feverish flush of evanescent excitement, such a desolating flood of small observances that kill all great thoughts, such a poisonous growth of weeds that choke the good seed till no soil is left for a serious purpose or a deep passion to take root in, that we all long to fling off the whole burden at times; to forget the weary treadmill of social customs and usages; to end the vain strivings between desires high as heaven and the iron limitations of a cruel fate strong as the gates of hell; and peace comes to us best at the theatre. Therefore, the weary, overworked, exhausted slaves of society throng the theatres everywhere seeking rest without dullness and excitement without effort [Wyndham, 1951, p. 178].

Another statement by his mother closely resembles Wilde's avowed promulgation of sensual indulgence, a form of acting out designed to suppress unavowed grief and mourning. Wyndham notes, "She once addressed a bashful youth: "When you are as old as I am, young man, you will know that there is only one thing in the world worth living for, and that is sin" (1951, p. 169). Lady Wilde's biographer implies that she even encouraged the very style that Wilde mastered:[2] "Epigram is always better than argument in conversation, and paradox is the very essense of social wit and brilliancy. The unexpected, the strange combination of opposites, the daring subversion of some ancient platitude, are all keen social weapons" (Wyndham, 1951, p. 80).

Apparently, the boy Oscar listened to his mother! Keep quiet about your sister, write plays, use epigrams and paradox. Did she tell him this directly? It is doubtful. In *The Picture of Dorian Gray,* he writes: "I can sympathize with everything except suffering. I cannot sympathize with that. It is too ugly, too horrible, too distressing. . . . The less said about life's sores, the better" (1890, p. 42). At another point, the artist in the novel says, "I always hear Harry's views from his friends. It is the only way I get to know of them" (p. 47). Speranza was always surrounded by people, and I suspect Wilde got to know many of her opinions from them.

Not only was Oscar influenced to write by his writing mother, his brother Willie also wrote poetry. Like his father, Oscar, too, was unfaithful to his wife, and like his brother Willie, he became divorced.

Identifications with his father also play an important role in the disavowal of grief. Grinstein emphasizes the importance of Wilde's knowl-

---

[2]An identification with his mother may account for Wilde's mastery of irony, perceptively described by San Juan (1967).

edge of his father's sexual exploits over a ten-year period. He suggests: ". . . out of his unconscious need to repeat his father's experience Oscar Wilde provoked the trial of Alfred Douglas's father (a man also involved in flaunting his extramarital affairs), thus creating a situation in which his own personal and sexual life was brought before the public eye. Like his father, Oscar Wilde himself became the object of scandal and fulfilled the prediction of notoriety that he had made years before. The results of the trial brought about a deterioration of his personality" (1973, pp. 356-357).

That the father's character contributed significantly to Oscar Wilde's narcissistic fixations is suggested by the father's continuous unresolved problems with women, a form of Don Juanism. By the time of his marriage, at the age of 36, to Oscar's mother, aged 25, he already had three illegitimate children. Within a year of their marriage, their first child, Willie, was born. Oscar was born two years later. Sometime during the year of Oscar's birth, 1854, a nineteen-year-old girl, Mary Travers, consulted Dr. Wilde, and he began an affair with her that lasted for ten years and terminated in the sordid trial that practically forced his retirement. The timing of these events has implications which, to my mind, are more potent psychologically than any possible overt identification on Oscar's part with his father's legal difficulties.

Only two biographers have noted that Dr. Wilde's affair with Mary Travers began when Oscar was in utero or shortly thereafter.[3] Thus, the father's regressive reaction to his wife's pregnancy must have had a decisive influence on the boy's ultimate gender confusion. Combined with Oscar's strong feminine disposition, which was encouraged by the mother's wish for a girl, it is even likely that Oscar was unconsciously rivalrous with his father's young paramour. The notable affair had gone on, sometimes quite openly, during Oscar's entire childhood. Grinstein's reconstruction contending that Wilde turned to homosexuality after his son, Vyvyan was born should be related to a probable increase in homosexual, narcissistic tensions in the father when Oscar was about to be born. It seems likely, however, as suggested by a number of biographers, that overt homosexual acting-out had already taken place when Oscar was at Oxford, which he entered in 1871.

[3]"Mary Travers, aged 19, consulted Dr. Wilde in the summer of 1854" (Pearson, 1946, p. 10). ". . . He met her [Mary Travers] in the year in which Oscar was born, when Speranza spent a great deal of time with the two boys in the nursery" (White, 1967, p. 154).

Wilde's Struggle Against Self-Fragmentation

Grinstein, in attributing Wilde's homosexuality to a failure to resolve an oedipal conflict that resulted from his attachment to his sister and her subsequent death, fails to distinguish between object-love and object relations of a narcissistic type. Whereas Grinstein casually refers to narcissism, he does not explore the importance of symbiosis in the nature of Wilde's object relations. I see Wilde's life style as a long series of futile adaptations following on the failure of oedipal maturation. Biographies of Wilde do not describe any kind of relationship to his wife that can be characterized as object love. The wife resembled the sister in some ways, and Wilde's comments on her hair and ivory hands have pregenital fetishistic overtones (Hart-Davis, 1962).[4]

Wilde demonstrates some warmth toward men and boys who appear to be projected self-objects and idealized parent imagos. His affection toward his own children, likewise, is on the basis of a narcissistic identification. Vyvyan Holland (1954), his son, confirms his father's childlike qualities.

Whereas Grinstein views the sister as an incestuous object whose death aroused guilt on an oedipal basis, I am inclined to view Wilde's reaction to his sister's life and death in terms of narcissistic mortification and in response to his mother's grief. Thus, Isola's death may be seen as a screen for an early narcissistic loss of self that occurred after the birth of this same girl when he was three years of age. We recall that early in life he was raised as a girl;[5] a traumatic degree of castration anxiety would preclude any solid consolidation of the oedipal position in this vulnerable boy, so that pregenital determinants are more significant than genital

---

[4] Wolf (1969) emphasizes the fetishistic precursors as an explanation for the focus on clothes as transitional objects:

> The birth of Isola when he was three must have been more than usually disrupting and traumatic for Oscar. Not only did he lose his special relationship to his mother of being "the baby"; apparently he also had to suddenly change the aspect of his self-image that is concerned with gender identity. I believe Oscar reacted to the loss of his dresses almost as if they had been love objects and tried to resurrect the lost object by mutation and identification. I think it is this experience that gives Wilde's feminine identification so much the flavor of an identification with his own archaic female self, when he was the beautiful one (ms. p. 4, unpublished).

[5] While it was not uncommon in that period for boys to be dressed in female-type garments, a number of factors, especially the mother's expectations, inclined Wilde toward a feminine identification.

ones, and narcissistic object relations and mortifications more characteristic than object love.

Wilde's contact-seeking was in the service of restoring his self-cohesion,
and his erotomania reflects a fleeting contact with reality during periods
of self-fragmentation. The young girl who dies before maturation is not
only his sister, but himself as self-object, at age three and again at age
thirteen. E. Wolf (personal communication), also intrigued by the
problem of identifications in Wilde's character, takes a position similar to
mine: "The birth of the sister was a loss of self doubly because of the
diminished availability of the mother as a self-object *and* because of the
loss of the self that was represented by the clothes (girl's clothes) as a
self-object. Through an alter-ego relationship with the sister's becoming
a self-object, Wilde was then later able to reconstitute a cohesive self,
only to lose it again, forever, with her death."

When Wilde writes, "What the paradox was to me in the sphere of
thought, perversity became to me in the sphere of passion" (1905, p. 81),
he demonstrates precise self-scrutiny, but not yet insight; and this
characterizes all of Wilde's work—a remarkable capacity for observing
people (especially as behavior is ordered in the gender framework,
male/female), but no genuine capacity for synthesis. He distorts reality
because he has a poorly synthesized sense of self, especially as a male. One
wonders whether he in any way genuinely regarded himself as male.
Although it is known that he defended himself against bullies, in essence
he was not a typical, vigorous boy, and, as Pearson (1946) notes, he did
not play boy's games.

Wilde's Creative Thrust Toward Self-Cohesion

If, as Kohut (1971) suggests, the artist has difficulty in neutralizing
narcissistic cathexes and his exhibitionistic libido shifts frequently between himself and the narcissistically invested product with which he
remains most closely identified, it should be possible, by a close study of
the thematic content of the creative product to clarify the author's self-
representations and narcissistic transformations.

Wyndham tells us (p. 173) that whenever Oscar visited his mother he
shed his posing and became very nearly natural; the opportunity for
merger with the mother apparently made the poseur defenses unnecessary. In the novel *Dorian Gray*, by contrast, genuine love on the part of
Sibyl mitigated against merger and therefore obliged the hero to aban-

don her. The incapacity to cathect Sibyl with object love because she can only represent a narcissistic self-object is the underlying tragic theme of the novel. The hero's fixation to narcissistic self-objects is dramatically elaborated in the symbolic painting-mirror, a concrete representation of a narcissistic mirror transference.[6]

Some of Wilde's early references to Dorian in the novel are suggestive of Wilde's later relation to Lord Alfred Douglas, his paramour—an instance of nature eventually imitating art:

When our eyes met, I felt I was growing pale. A curious sensation of terror came over me. I knew I had come face to face with someone whose mere personality was so fascinating that, if I allowed it to do so, would absorb my whole nature, my whole soul, my very art itself [p. 15].

I couldn't be happy if I didn't see him every day. He is absolutely necessary to me [p. 17].

Don't take away from me the one person who gives my art whatever charm it possesses: my life as an artist depends on him [p. 21].

Kohut (1971) has noted how "certain creative personalities appear to require a specific relationship (as in a narcissistic transference) during periods of intense creativity" (p. 316). Such a symbiotic need on Wilde's part, which was earlier expressed in the novel, was later objectified with Douglas, who wrote: ". . . from the time he met me till the day of his death the only thing he wrote when I was not with him (generally sitting in the same room) was precisely this De Profundis screed which is a letter to me! . . . and from the day when we were separated till the hour of his death he never wrote another line" (1940, pp. 116-117).

In the analysis of narcissistic personalities, Kohut (1971) was able to discover in retrospect "that the narcissistic forces which are now directed toward a new self-object, the creative work, had been active much earlier but had then been bound up in the noncreative elaboration of narcissistic tension states" (p. 321). He sees creativeness as "related to the mobilization of formerly frozen narcissistic cathexes, in the area of both the grandiose self and the idealized parent imago" (p. 308). He feels that "in certain artists, notably in some poets" one can see "the intimate connection between frustrated contact needs and a persistent wish for merger, which, however, gradually changes into a broad, sublimated empathic merger with the surroundings, and finally brings about the

---

[6]Earlier students of the phenomenon of "the double" in literature allude to the struggle against self-fragmentation and for self-cohesion in *Dorian Gray* and Wilde's exquisite description of unsuccessful defenses against narcissistic fixation. Both Rank (1914) and Tymms (1949) relate the theme of thanatophobia in the novel to fears of destruction of the self.

405

development of a keenly sensitive attitude toward the world" (p. 315).

Wolf (personal communication) sees Wilde's adult life as an "attempt to reconstitute a cohesive self through alter-ego relationships or through the creation of self-objects (the artistic products)."

I believe that the structure and thematic content of the novel *The Picture of Dorian Gray* illustrates the struggle for the restoration of self-cohesion and the maintenance of narcissistic balance. The form, in some ways, even resembles a therapeutic process. For example, there appears to be a therapeutic alliance between Dorian and Lord Henry in the novel, and it is difficult to distinguish at times whether Lord Henry is encouraging a form of expression through free association or is encouraging acting out:

"You could not have helped telling me, Dorian. All through your life you will tell me everything you do."

"Yes, Harry, I believe that is true. I cannot help telling you things. You have a curious influence over me. If I ever did a crime, I would come and confess it to you. You would understand me."

"People like you—the wilful sunbeams of life—don't commit crimes, Dorian" (1890, p. 51).

Lord Henry is practically telling Dorian that fantasies are troubling him, not deeds.

After a long, detailed description of his ventures into perfumes, jewels, clothes—narcissistic pleasures—Dorian admits that these helped him forget his fears. Again, near-insight by Wilde: "For these treasures and everything that he collected in his lovely house, were to him means of forgetfulness, modes by which he could escape, for a season, from the fear that seemed to him at times to be almost too great to be borne" (p. 124). There is material indicating the reciprocation between homosexual acting-out and other narcissistic preoccupations.

Wilde even formulates an abreactive theory of therapy with overtones of free-association technique, yet it all seems to end in mockery and becomes a rationalization for acting out:

I believe that if one man were to live out his life fully and completely, were to give form to every feeling, expression to every thought, reality to every dream—I believe that the world would gain such a fresh impulse of joy that we would forget all the maladies of mediaevalism, and return to the Hellenic ideal—to something finer, richer than the Hellenic ideal, it may be. But the honest man amongst us is afraid of himself. The mutilation of the savage has its tragic survival in the self-denial that mars our lives. We are punished for our refusals. Every impulse that we strive to strangle broods in the mind and poisons us. The body sins once, and has done with its sin, for action is a mode of purification. Nothing remains then but the recollection of a pleasure, or the luxury of regret. The only way to get rid of temptation is to yield to it [1890, p. 24].

Acting out, suggests Wilde, is not a solution to developmental failures, but rather an inevitable consequence of unsuccessful narcissistic trans-formations. In his own case, his successful artistic product seems to give evidence of the narcissistic transformation that we customarily call sub-limation.[7]

Summary

In a traditional psychoanalytic study of Oscar Wilde, Grinstein (1973) fills a significant gap in the biography of a great and paradoxical writer. He explains Wilde's ultimate personality deterioration largely as a conse-quence of the tragic loss of his ten-year-old sister when Wilde was not quite thirteen years old. This is interpreted as the loss of an oedipally cathected object, followed by inevitable guilt and retribution.

My examination of Wilde's personality and writings suggests that he was suffering from a narcissistic personality disorder. His life was a long series of complaints supervening on the failure of oedipal maturation; his capacities for object love and genital maturity were minimally developed, if at all. Failures of developmental consolidation are evi-denced by symbiotic fixations and thwarted genital achievements which indicate that the loss of the sister was more important as the loss of a self-object — thus, as a narcissistic mortification — than as the focus of a genitally cathected object love.

The urgency to abreact a narcissistic loss was countered by avowed suppression on the part of the mother, who thus interfered with mourning resolution. She did, however, encourage narcissistic trans-formations through writing and was responsible, to some extent, for Wilde's becoming a playwright. *The Picture of Dorian Gray* can be viewed as a protoanalytic document demonstrating near-insight and frus-trated attempts at self-cure. As a successful artistic product, it gives evidence of that narcissistic transformation characterized as sublimation.

Future studies of Wilde might elaborate his self-concepts and narcis-sistic transformations.

---

[7]The success of Wilde's effort is underlined in a study of the revisions of the novel he made in order to "emphasize psychological, dramatic, and aesthetic effects over ethical, didactic and moral precepts" (Lawler, 1969, p. 2).

407

REFERENCES

Douglas, Lord A. (1940), *Oscar Wilde: A Summing Up.* London: Duckworth.

Ellmann, R., ed. (1968), *The Artist as Critic: Critical Writings of Oscar Wilde.* New York: Random House.

Grinstein, A. (1973), On Oscar Wilde. *This Annual,* 1:345-362.

Harris, F. (1959), *Oscar Wilde.* Lansing, Mich.: Michigan State University Press.

Hart-Davis, R., ed. (1962), *The Letters of Oscar Wilde.* New York: Harcourt, Brace & World.

Holland, V. (1954), *Son of Oscar Wilde.* London: Rupert Hart-Davis.

Kohut, H. (1971), *The Analysis of the Self.* New York: International Universities Press.

Lawler, D. L. (1969), *An Enquiry into Oscar Wilde's Revisions of The Picture of Dorian Gray.* Ph.D. diss., University of Chicago.

Pearson, H. (1946), *Oscar Wilde, His Life and Wit.* New York/London: Harper.

Rank, O. (1914), *The Double.* Chapel Hill: The University of North Carolina Press, 1971.

Rose, G. J. (1971), Narcissistic fusion states and creativity. In: *The Unconscious Today,* ed. Mark Kanzer. New York: International Universities Press, pp. 495-505.

———— (1972), *The French Lieutenant's Woman:* the unconscious significance of a novel to its author. *Amer. Imago,* 29.

———— (1973), On the shores of self: Samuel Beckett's "Molloy" — irredentism and the creative impulse. *Psychoanal. Rev.,* 60:588-604.

San Juan, E., Jr. (1967), *The Art of Oscar Wilde.* Princeton, N. J.: Princeton University Press.

Tymms, R. (1949), *Doubles in Literary Psychology.* Cambridge: Bowes & Bowes.

Weintraub, S. (1968), *Literary Criticism of Oscar Wilde.* Lincoln: University of Nebraska Press.

White, T. D. V. (1967), *The Parents of Oscar Wilde, Sir William and Lady Wilde.* London: Hodder & Stoughton.

Wilde, O. (1894), Phrases and philosophies for the use of the young. The Chameleon, December, taken from *The Epigrams of Oscar Wilde, An Anthology,* ed. A. Redman. New York: John Day, 1954, p. 10.

———— (1890), *The Picture of Dorian Gray.* New York: Airmont, 1964.

———— (1905), *De Profundis.* New York: Vintage Books, 1964.

Wolf, E. S. (1969), Discussion of "On Oscar Wilde," presentation by Alexander Grinstein to the Chicago Psychoanalytic Society, September 23, 1969. Unpublished.

Wyndham, H. (1951), *Speranza, A Biography of Lady Wilde.* London and New York: T. V. Boardman.

November, 1973

Notes on Benvenuto Cellini

CHARLES KLIGERMAN, M.D. (*Chicago*)

The celebrated Benvenuto Cellini (1500-1571) has long been considered a prototype not only of the Renaissance bravo, but also of the temperamental artist who lacks inhibition and disdains the conventions of the ordinary world. Cellini has, in addition, been termed psychopathic, delinquent, morally insane, or, at best, narcissistic. Popular legend credits him with brawling, whoring, murdering, and creating beautiful works of art, all with equal insouciance. Even his great translator, John Addington Symonds (1887), who on the whole regards his subject with sympathetic understanding, states in his Introduction to the autobiography, ". . . when I come to speak about his homicides, it will be obvious that he enjoyed killing live men quite as much as casting bronze statues" (p. 6). Much of Cellini's reputation derives from his own statements in the famous work, which he dictated in the vigorous Tuscan vernacular at the age of 58, and which stands as one of the great autobiographies of all time. But a careful examination of this book will convince the reader that Cellini never killed any man lightly (except perhaps during his service as bombardier in battle defending the pope). Indeed, Symonds himself later softens his statement considerably. The three or four men Cellini killed were all murdered either in the heat of passion or in self-defense, with the exception of his brother's slayer, whom he waylaid in cold blood, as we shall describe more fully later.

But it was not homicide, not too unusual in his violent age, but arrogance, quick temper, and a sharp tongue that got Cellini into trouble. Vasari described him as "in all his doings of high spirit, proud,

---

This paper was originally written in honor of Dr. Richard Sterba, on the occasion of his 75th birthday.

lively, very quick to act, and formidably vehement; a person who knew only too well how to speak his mind to princes" (see Symonds, 1887, p. 13). Others referred to his "habit of excessive frankness, his harsh manners, readiness to take affront, and implacable hatreds" (p. 14). This *terribilita*, however, was counterbalanced by kindness, generosity, a nobility of spirit and an essential honesty.

It is clear that Cellini was a narcissist who valued himself very highly and who became infuriated at any real or fancied slight, or at what he felt to be unfair treatment. His grandiosity and feeling of specialness are confirmed by his full concurrence with what Pope Paul III said to certain critics when he pardoned Cellini for killing his enemy Pompeo in an altercation: "Know then that men like Benvenuto, unique in their profession, stand above the law;[1] and how far more he, then, who received the provocation I have heard of." It should be noted, however, that in regard to his "profession," Cellini showed little of the temperament and instability that characterized his personal relations; he worked assiduously, seriously, and with great dedication, never satisfied with anything less than perfection, severely critical of shoddiness, and humbly reverential toward his art and toward certain idealized figures like Michelangelo.

It would be impossible to encompass the richness of Cellini's personality in the scope of this brief essay, but I should like to examine two childhood memories described in his autobiography and trace their relation to certain recurrent patterns that played a decisive role in the artist's life.

Cellini was born in Florence on All Souls' Day (November 2), 1500, the son of Giovanni Cellini and Elisabetta Granacci. The parents had been married eighteen years before producing any children (two boys were miscarried), but finally in 1499 a daughter, Niccolosa, was born. The Cellinis expected their next child also to be a girl (to be called Reparata), and when the surprised and joyous father beheld a boy, he raised his eyes to God and thanked him for the precious gift, saying, "Let him be welcome — Benvenuto." Thus, from the very beginning, Cellini was marked as one of those darlings of fortune who, because of unique circumstance of birth, are especially valued and adored. In addition, his extraordinary artistic gifts soon became obvious to an ambitious father, and the stage was set for what Greenacre (1957) has called the artist's "love affair with the world" (p. 490). Throughout Cellini's life, the expectation of a positive response from father surrogates was crucial to his psychic equilibrium.

[1] Cf. the similar position of Raskolnikov in Dostoevski's *Crime and Punishment*.

410

In his autobiography, following his account of the details of his birth, Cellini (1730) reports the following:

Andrea Cellini was yet alive when I was about three years old, and he had passed his hundredth. One day they had been altering a certain conduit pertaining to a cistern, and there issued from it a great scorpion unperceived by them, which crept down from the cistern to the ground, and slank away beneath a bench. I saw it, and ran up to it, and laid my hands upon it. It was so big that when I had it in my little hands, it put out its tail on one side, and on the other thrust forth both its mouths. [The word is *bocche*, so I have translated it by *mouths*. But Cellini clearly meant the gaping claws of the scorpion— Symonds.] They relate that I ran in high joy to my grandfather, crying out: "Look, grandpapa, at my pretty little crab." When he recognised that the creature was a scorpion, he was on the point of falling dead for the great fear he had and anxiety about me. He coaxed and entreated me to give it to him; but the more he begged, the tighter I clasped it, crying and saying I would not give it to any one. My father, who was also in the house, ran up when he heard my screams, and in his stupefaction could not think how to prevent the venomous animal from killing me. Just then his eye chanced to fall upon a pair of scissors; and so, while soothing and caressing me, he cut its tail and mouths off. Afterwards, when the great peril had been thus averted, he took the occurrence for a good augury.

When I was about five years old my father happened to be in a basement-chamber of our house, where they had been washing, and where a good fire of oak-logs was still burning; he had a viol in his hand, and was playing and singing alone beside the fire. The weather was very cold. Happening to look into the fire, he spied in the middle of those most burning flames a little creature like a lizard, which was sporting in the core of the intensest coals. Becoming instantly aware of what the thing was, he had my sister and me called, and pointing it out to us children, gave me a great box on the ears, which caused me to howl and weep with all my might. Then he pacified me good-humouredly, and spoke as follows: "My dear little boy, I am not striking you for any wrong that you have done, but only to make you remember that the lizard which you see in the fire is a sala-mander, a creature which has never been seen before by any one of whom we have credible information." So saying, he kissed me and gave me some pieces of money [pp. 56-57].

Notwithstanding all the dangers of interpreting manifest content, even the sophisticated layman will perceive the meaning of the first memory. It is a fantasy of castration or castration threat as punishment for the crime of persistent masturbation in defiance of paternal authority. Benvenuto refuses to drop his pretty little crab. Coupled with our knowl-edge of his life, certain inferences can be drawn from this passage: (1) the tendency toward (phallic) exhibitionism; (2) the extreme wil-fulness and stubbornness that characterized Cellini all his life, particu-larly in response to any attempt to take something away from him; (3) the benign, protecting aspect of the paternal superego that existed alongside the castrating, threatening part. In this sense, the declawing resembles the rite of circumcision, in which the sacrifice of a token part preserves the whole. (4) Finally, there is the element of miraculous

411

escape and good augury—the prediction of a charmed life. And, indeed, the many instances of Cellini's survival in the face of the most desperate situations seem almost incredible. He survived involvement in wars, the plague, syphilis, imprisonment, poisoning, armed clashes against great odds, and the malevolent machinations of popes and princes. Perhaps the most remarkable fact of his life is that he died in his bed at the ripe age of 71.

The castration theme is also portrayed dramatically in Cellini's heroic statue of Perseus holding the head of Medusa in the Loggia dei Lanzi in Florence. Although the theme of this statue was actually suggested by Duke Cosimo de'Medici, that of another major project was entirely Cellini's own conception. Designed for Francis I but never completed, it was a colossal statue of a nude Mars rising 54 feet from the middle of a fountain, with a broken lance raised on high in the right hand—truly a cry of defiance and triumph. This statue would seem to be a representation of Cellini's idealized grandiose self (cf. Kohut, 1971), which had been organized reparatively around whatever traumatic disappointment was contained in that first screen memory. The fact that Cellini's flattering identification of this statue with the king himself pleased the king enormously does not detract from this view. For Benvenuto genuinely admired this great and generous prince, who not only stood as an idealized self-object, but seems to have returned much of Cellini's feeling. "He [the king] laid his hand upon my shoulder saying, 'Mon Ami, I know not whether the pleasure be greater for the prince who finds a man after his own heart, or for the artist who finds a prince willing to furnish him with means for carrying out his great ideas.' I answered that, if I was really the man his Majesty described, my good fortune was by far the greater. He answered laughingly: 'Let us agree then, that our luck is equal' " (1730, p. 350).

The second memory—referring to an incident that took place when Benvenuto was five years old—deals with a very different set of childhood conflicts, although it also contains elements of ambivalent violence on the part of the father[2] and an augury of magical specialness. The early image of his father playing the viol was of deep significance to Benvenuto. Giovanni Cellini was both a gifted musician and a highly skilled engineer and designer-craftsman. But his passion for music was by far the

---

[2]The blow of love-hate delivered by the father on a special occasion is reminiscent of a practice found among some Orthodox Jewish mothers of slapping the daughter's face when informed of the first menstrual period. Ostensibly this is for good luck—the rush of blood to the cheeks should persist as a beautiful complexion.

412

stronger, and he strove mightily to superimpose this interest on his rebellious son. Benvenuto, while musically talented, identified himself with the artisan side of his father, and only by the most monumental adolescent struggle was he able to prevail in becoming a goldsmith. Years later, in Rome, he still dreamed of the danger of a father's curse if he abandoned his music.

The other major conflict with the father is represented, I believe, in the *latent* content of the second memory. The father playing the viol alone by the fire in the basement of the house might very well represent the primal scene, but, even more probably, the salamander sporting alive in the heart of the fire is a disguised memory of the mother's pregnancy followed by the birth of a sibling. The summoning of Benvenuto and his sister to witness the miracle has the ring of the children being called to see the wonderful new baby. In this sense the great box on the ear would symbolize the agonizing traumatic effect the sudden disclosure of a new rival had for this *Wunderkind* who thought he alone was Benvenuto.

Actually, Cellini's brother Cecchino (Giovan Francesco) was born when Benvenuto was two, not five, though he is not mentioned until adolescence. A younger sister Liperata followed, whose birth date is not recorded in the literature. However, the mother was already 38 years old when Cecchino was born, and not too many years could have elapsed before the birth of Liperata. Thus it is quite possible that she was the child born when Cellini was five, and that the memory telescopes the emotional reaction to the birth of both siblings. (Describing the brother's tragic death in 1529, Cellini makes a curious slip, attributing to him the age of 25 which would make him four years younger, rather than two.) The main thrust of Cellini's sibling rivalry was directed toward this brother. Cecchino, well built, highly gifted in physical prowess and the use of arms, chose a soldierly career. He was brave, hotheaded, impetuous, quarrelsome, and fond of dissipation; in short, he fulfilled more accurately the description generally applied to Benvenuto, who, for the most part, was a serious worker and responsible artisan. Cellini first mentions this brother when he tells how, at sixteen, he saved Cecchino's life by fighting off a large group of adversaries who were bent on killing the boy. In the same year the wayward Cecchino, who was entering the service of the Medici, needed some respectable clothes. The two sisters gave him Benvenuto's fine new cloak and doublet, which he had bought with his own earnings as a budding goldsmith. When the injured Benvenuto sought redress from his father, he got a sanctimonious answer reminiscent of the parable of the prodigal son, and, infuriated, he ran off to Pisa for an entire year.

The final chapter in Benvenuto's relation with his brother was written in Rome in 1529. Benvenuto was now a famous artist, a favorite of Pope Clement VII, and Cecchino was stationed in Rome as a professional soldier. Cecchino got into a senseless brawl and was mortally wounded by a constable shooting an harquebus in self-defense. Cellini's description of Cecchino's subsequent death is the most poignant passage of his autobiography. His grief was uncontrollable, and he became so depressed that, for the only time in his life, he was unable to work. Nothing would cure his melancholy but the assassination of the guard who, he knew intellectually, was not at fault. "When I saw that the fever caused by always seeing him [the guard] about was depriving me of sleep and appetite, and was bringing me by degrees to sorry plight, I overcame my repugnance to so low and not quite praiseworthy an enterprise, and made my mind up one evening to rid myself of the torment" (p. 350). He then ambushed his man in the dark and slew him with a cutlass.

This depressive episode and its violent "cure" bespeak intense ambivalence, with repressed murderous feeling toward the brother, and the reactive need to save or revenge him. The aggressive reproach directed toward the self was externalized and discharged onto the unfortunate harquebusier.

Throughout his life, Cellini showed a recurrent neurotic pattern that in many respects repeated the episode of the sisters' giving his clothes away. He would attach himself to an idealized prince. Then some woman he antagonized would persuade the prince to overlook Cellini as a devoted son and transfer favor to a rival sibling-figure. Whereupon Cellini would act out or take flight. A classic example is his relation to Francis I. As we have already seen, the two were delighted with one another. This caused the jealousy of the king's arrogant manipulative mistress, Madame d'Etampes, who was also offended by Cellini's clumsy tactlessness. Among other vindictive acts, she tried to have his colossal Mars project, together with all his designs, turned over to another Italian artist (Primaticcio). When this was circumvented (partly by Cellini's threat to kill Primaticcio), she prevailed upon the king to rebuke Cellini—to put him in his place, so to speak—and the badgered Francis finally did so on the flimsy ground that Cellini was more interested in his own projects than in those of the king. This rebuke was administered publicly with some degree of harshness (probably because Francis really didn't have his heart in it). Benvenuto immediately replied with an impassioned defense, concluding as follows:

In all that I have done, I meant to act for the best, and at no point to swerve from your Majesty's expressed wishes. It is indeed true that I set up that huge Colossus to satisfy my own desire, *paying for it from my own purse.* . . . because I thought that, you being the great King you are, and I the trifling artist that I am, it was my duty to erect for your glory and my own a statue, the like of which the ancients never saw. Now, at the last, having been taught that God is not inclined to make me worthy of so glorious a service, I beseech your Majesty, instead of the noble recompense you had in mind to give me for my labors, bestow upon me only one small trifle of your favor, and therewith the leave to quit your kingdom. At this instant, if you condescend to my request, I shall return to Italy, always thanking God and your Majesty for the happy hours which I have passed in serving you [p. 385; my italics].

The sensitive Francis instantly responded with fulsome praise, gentleness, and reassurance of friendship, again calling Cellini "Mon Ami" — but it was too late. Cellini made off for Italy at the first opportunity. Now, the king had been the noblest patron Cellini ever had. He had been greatly instrumental in obtaining Cellini's release from the miserable dungeon of Castel St. Angelo, where Pope Paul had wrongly imprisoned him and where he had nearly died. In addition, he had been most generous both in praise and material support, giving Cellini a small chateau in which to live and work, and, though short of money himself because of the wars, supplying workmen, materials, and funds in a manner completely unlike the penny-pinching popes who preceded him or the conniving Medici duke who followed him. In spite of certain nuisances, which he handled adequately, Cellini had every reason to count his blessings in France, yet this kind of narcissistic humiliation from an idealized father from whom he expected complete love and appreciation was too much to endure. The affront to his grandiosity far outweighed his mature ego interests.

Although he sent word to the king that he was only visiting Florence to settle some family affairs and would return, Cellini must have known he would never come back. All through the journey he was obsessed about his decision: ". . . nor could I through the whole journey refrain from sighing and weeping. Sometimes, however, I consoled myself with God by saying: 'Lord God . . . Thou knowest that my object in this journey is only to carry alms to six poor miserable virgins and their mother, my own sister [Liperata]. They have indeed their father, but he is very old, and gains nothing by his trade; I fear therefore, lest they might too easily take to a bad course of life. Since, then, I am performing a true act of piety, I look to Thy Majesty for aid and counsel' " (p. 391).

Most historians go along with this rationalization, but it seems quite plain that Cellini had been narcissistically mortified and was too proud to go back. During the remainder of his life in Florence he had a multitude of opportunities to regret this flight, but although Francis sent the kindest messages urging him to return, he never did.

415

The nature of the narcissistic mortification resided in a defusion of a grandiose merger-fantasy. Cellini considered himself a prince among artists, on a par with an idealized, monarch like Francis. The Colossal Mars was the portrait of this idealized, omnipotent self-object.[3] When the king in his rebuke seemed to disavow *his* share in this merger, Cellini was filled with narcissistic rage that he could express only by flight. On the journey home, the rage gave way to grief and mourning, and a feeble attempt to justify his behavior as a pietistic act of family obligation.

My awareness of the deep and sudden narcissistic anguish that Cellini experienced in this episode reminded me painfully of an empathic lapse with a middle-aged woman patient who also suffered intense narcissistic vulnerability in relation to the birth of a younger brother. After a holiday break, she had brought to the analysis for the first time, walled-off recollections of her deep shock when the brother was born, followed by loneliness and sadness — somewhat later in the hour she associated to a time when she had sat up all night with her little dog which had been hit by a car and was dying. This latter incident was understood both as a reaction formation to aggressive feelings toward the brother and identification with the hurt little animal. In the days following, she developed a mood of snug contentment and said, "My relation with you is so different from my parents. It's not transference at all — it's *real*. My parents and I didn't choose each other, but I did choose you and you chose me, and I know I have an intense investment in you and you have an equal investment in me. And we are both nearly the same age, so it's not what I experienced at all with my parents, but something real." In response, I told her I could understand how she could feel that way, but she must once have had feelings like this with her parents too. At which, the patient suddenly felt cold all over, went to get her coat, and curled up under it, obviously depressed and deflated. She seemed literally to blanch and shrivel up.

My interpretation was essentially correct, but premature. The damage was eventually repaired, and we were able to get back on the track, even with some fruitful working through, but for a time the favorable development of a mirror transference, convincingly described by Kohut (1971), was seriously threatened. The blissful patient, glowing in expectation of the warm gaze of the analyst-parent, feels suddenly rebuffed and literally starts to freeze. This type of narcissistic vulnerability is certainly not rare, but it is especially prevalent in many artists and can often be observed both in the vicissitudes of the transference and in their

---

[3] Probably a common mechanism in the relationship of artist-patron and artist-collector.

extra-analytic object relations. In another connection (1953), I have described a similar catastrophic development in Melville, when he considered himself abandoned by Hawthorne, with whom he felt merged after writing *Moby Dick*. Under such conditions, some artists, like Melville, regress to disturbed noncreative states. Others, like Cellini, with more resilient ego strengths, better-established "collective alternates" (see Greenacre, 1957), and a talent for turning passivity to activity, use the setback as a spur to even greater creativity.

Though often considered a vain, proud, boastful man who overrated his own talents, Cellini, who despised bunglers and deeply revered certain idealized artists like Donatello, the ancients, and especially Michelangelo, was really quite diffident in measuring himself against the latter. Through most of his early maturity he established himself as the greatest goldsmith of his time, perhaps of all time, but he did not aspire to projects larger than decorative medallions, vases, or works like the exquisite golden salt-cellar (now in Vienna), in which he reached the peak of perfection in artisanship. In France, having grown proficient in bronze casting, he sought to become a great sculptor in bronze. When he returned to Florence in 1545, his first assignment under Duke Cosimo was the famous Perseus of the Loggia dei Lanzi, the creation of which is so dramatically depicted in the autobiography. This work took Cellini nine years to complete under difficult conditions marked by much vexation with both the duke and the duchess. But, in spite of the duke's cunning niggardliness, the work was a great artistic triumph, praised by the multitude in a manner intoxicating to Benvenuto.

In the meantime, he felt increasingly impelled to compete with Michelangelo himself in the noble medium of marble. He yearned desperately to stand with Leonardo, Raphael, and Michelangelo as one of the greatest artists of Florence. For a man in his fifties who had worked all his life in metal and gems, the venture into this difficult new art was a challenging one. Yet the few pieces he executed, notably the crucifix in black and white marble that now hangs in the Escorial, while lacking the sublimity of Michelangelo, still preserve the graceful nobility of the great Florentine tradition as it evolved in the Manneristic style, and are clearly superior to the works of Bandinelli and Ammanati, who were the established sculptors in Florence. Despite these achievements, Cellini struggled against the most intense frustration in his attempts to obtain marble and to be recognized by his prince as a legitimate worker in this medium. Once again we see the familiar and fateful pattern.

A huge block of marble had been quarried and brought with much

417

difficulty to Florence. Knowing that the duchess had intended this marble for Bandinelli, Cellini made frenzied efforts to secure it for himself, proposing to the duke that he follow the time-honored custom of setting up a contest and awarding the commission for the best model submitted. But he managed to antagonize the duchess to such a degree that, when Bandinelli suddenly died, the duchess, moved by both grief and spite, awarded the marble to Ammanati, who created the monstrous fountain of Neptune now standing in the Piazza in front of the Palazzo Vecchio. The Florentines have a song: "Oh Ammanati—how much marble did you ruin in this statue!" Cellini's sadness over losing the commission approached depressive proportions. He speaks of the marble as if it were a person, expressing sorrow and pity for its unhappy fate. In the same way that the unfinished Colossus at Fontainebleau would have represented a grandiose self-object, insuring his immortality, the marble was intended, even more than Perseus, as his monument, standing in the Piazza of Florence alongside those of Michelangelo and Donatello.

From that point on until his death eleven years later in 1571, Cellini's creative production was meager. He continued to work on various minor commissions, executing them in his customary masterly fashion, but he seems to have given up hope of creating the masterpiece that would rank him among the most illustrious sons of Florence.

The previous episodes illustrate that Cellini, in his failure to bring to fruition the two most ambitious projects of his career, was largely frustrated by the malice of two important ladies who, by virtue of their special relation to his great patrons, could be considered mother-surrogates. In each case they tried to transfer the project to another artist, a sibling figure, and in neither case was he adequately supported by his prince. These events bear a striking psychological similarity to the traumatic episode at sixteen, when his sisters gave his beautiful clothes to Cecchino, and probably the earlier trauma of betrayal by his mother when Cecchino was born.

There is no evidence that Cellini ever had a serious emotional involvement with any woman. He had many sexual encounters, which he describes in his memoirs in racy detail, but most of these were with prostitutes or depreciated wenches. The nearest thing to a romance was an intense passion for a beautiful Sicilian courtesan Angelica, but as soon as his burning longings were satisfied, he left her with a light heart when she and her mother displayed greediness. Cellini ultimately married at 64, apparently to legitimize the children of a liaison of his old age.

The lack of understanding, empathy, or meaningful experience in his relations with women, of course, raises the fundamental question of Cellini's relation with his mother. On this there is virtually no information. After the brief reference in the first pages of his autobiography, he does not mention her again. It would be intriguing to speculate that she died in his infancy following the birth of one of the younger siblings. Possibly the traumatic box on the ear is a reference to such an event. But in any case, it seems quite likely that Cellini's mother died early, since his sisters, not the mother, gave his clothes away, and she is the only member of the family never mentioned. Neither the definitive Bacci edition of his *Life* nor the unpublished Cellini documents printed by Calamandrei throw light on this question.[4] The answer must await further research in the archives in Florence.

In 1559, in the midst of his anguish and disappointment about the marble, Cellini claimed he was poisoned by a woman. He had become involved in a bizarre, complex legal entanglement with the Sbietta family, who had leased him a farm for the remainder of his life. During a visit to this family, the wife served him a meal following which he became violently ill with a colic that developed into bloody diarrhea. He was ill for about a year and then made a fair recovery. Cellini's allegation of poisoning, as well as many other accusations of scurrility toward the family, take on a somewhat paranoid tone, and much of his discourse at this point seems loose and incoherent, in contrast to the usual pungent sharpness of his style. Yet he continued his business relationship with the Sbiettas, and when the duke, on hearing the story, offered to take vengeance, Cellini restrained him, saying they had really done him a favor by "cleansing a mortal viscosity in his stomach and intestines and thus bettering his constitution."

The whole story has a peculiar flavor. While poisoning was certainly one of the favored varieties of infamy in the High Renaissance, I cannot refrain from offering an unprovable speculation that Cellini suffered a psychogenic attack of ulcerative colitis. Several years ago, at the Chicago Institute for Psychoanalysis, we studied this disease extensively, along with several other syndromes generally regarded as "psychosomatic" (Alexander et al., 1968). One of our strongest impressions, particularly in initial outbreaks of colitis in older people, was that the disease occurred when the patient inwardly gave up hope of attaining some dearly cherished ambition or narcissistic goal. Externally, the patient might continue the struggle, sometimes in a very productive way, but inwardly he felt defeated. As a result of the damage done to the sense

[4] I am indebted to Mr. John Pope-Hennessey, Director of the Victoria and Albert Museum and a leading expert in this area, for this information.

of self-esteem and self-cohesion, there ensued severe regression, often with partial fragmentation, paranoid ideation, and a retreat to somatization. In Cellini's case, the loss of the great block of marble represented a final defeat that the tired, aging artist could not master in his usual resilient fashion. He could no longer rely on his previous alloplastic solutions of flight or acting out. He must have experienced a profound inner change in his self-image of magical invincibility, and the year of illness seems quite compatible with the clinical and psychological picture of an episode of colitis.

But though he gave up in his own chosen field, Cellini was still able to turn to other avenues to insure his immortality both with God and posterity. He made some efforts to enter the Church and took the tonsure, but soon dropped out. It is hard to imagine even the aging Cellini as a monk. When, at 64, he married an obscure woman, it was presumably to legitimize their children, for the establishment of continuity of line is still another means of securing immortality and preserving one's narcissism in perpetuity. But, most important, he wrote his autobiography. He had already begun this work at 58, when it was becoming clear to him that the duke would never give him proper support for his great projects. Like any Florentine, Benvenuto had previously written some sonnets and other poems. These are rather tepid and flowery and show little gift. But the *Life* is a masterpiece. Since Cellini really disliked writing, he fortunately dictated most of it to an amanuensis, and its colloquial Tuscan vernacular springs forth with a vigor, wit, and poignant, human documentation that make far more fascinating reading than any of the polished works of his famous literary contemporaries. It is the most important and authentic picture ever drawn of the life of the late Renaissance. In addition, it ranks with the three or four finest autobiographies ever written. We are thus presented with one of history's great ironies: that this extraordinarily talented artist, who failed in his ambition to create a sculptural masterwork that would lift him to the highest rank in his art, left us, as a consolation prize, a work in a completely different and almost unfamiliar medium that ranks second to none.

REFERENCES

Alexander, F., French, T. W., & Pollock, G. H., eds. (1968), *Psychosomatic Specificity*. Chicago: University of Chicago Press.
Cellini, B. (1730), *The Life of Benvenuto Cellini by Himself*. New York: Liveright, 1942.

Greenacre, P. (1957), Childhood of the artist. In: *Emotional Growth*. New York: International Universities Press, 1971, pp. 479-504.

Kligerman, C. (1953), The psychology of Herman Melville. *Psychoanal. Rev.*, 40:125-143.

Kohut, H. (1971), *The Analysis of the Self*. New York: International Universities Press.

Symonds, J. A. (1887), Introduction to *The Life of Benvenuto Cellini*. New York: Liveright, 1942.

February, 1974

Mourning and Memorialization Through Music

GEORGE H. POLLOCK, M.D., PH.D. (*Chicago*)

Mourning, a natural process of adaptation to loss, can be expressed in many ways. Characteristically, we are most familiar with the deeply personal components of this process that Freud (1917) first described in his classic paper on "Mourning and Melancholia." I have earlier (1961) attempted to describe the various sequential phases of mourning in the normal adult and have further suggested that this adaptational process has evolved from the more primitive reactions to loss seen in higher mammals. We know that the mourning process is not limited to external loss through death, although it is most characteristically seen following such a separation. Anniversary reactions, as I have previously noted (cf. Pollock, 1970, 1972), are also manifestations of unresolved or abnormal mourning processes. Further expressions of mourning and memorialization may be found through creative acts—i.e., in works of art, literature, poetry, and music.

This essay will focus on musical expressions of the mourning process following object death and will specifically concern itself with compositions that range from the Requiem Mass, funeral music, memorial music, and laments to modern elegiac works. Particular musical compositions and what they may have meant to their composers will be used as illustrations of the thesis that mourning can occur through musical creations.

This present work is one of several papers that investigate certain

Director, Chicago Institute for Psychoanalysis; Fellow, Center for Psychosocial Studies, Chicago; Professor, Department of Psychiatry, Northwestern University.

This research was supported by the Anne Pollock Lederer Research Fund and the Fred M. Hellman Research Fund of the Chicago Institute for Psychoanalysis.

themes that relate psychoanalysis to music, but it is the logical precursor to my next work in this area, which deals in depth with the relation of childhood and adult losses through death to the musical life of Gustav Mahler (Pollock, 1974).

For many years I had intended to compile a list of musical compositions that dealt with death. This formidable task is no longer necessary, for the well-known British musicologist, Alec Robertson (1968), has written a monumental book on the music of mourning and consolation. Although Robertson does not discuss the intrapsychic aspects of mourning music and its meaning for both creators and listeners, his is the first approach to the topic, and I am deeply grateful to him for his systematic and comprehensive study. I have liberally used his material in this paper without constantly quoting or giving him the great amount of credit his work deserves. In a few instances I have used data from other sources as well.

The self and its component parts is perceived by the ego as an external object with its own intrapsychic representations. The body self and the psychic self can be aspects of these self-component parts. If there are changes, losses, or transitions in these self-as-object component representations, the ego can perceive and react to them with the adaptive mourning process. Ego, the major adaptive organization in this mourning process, deals with the self as external to it, as it does with objects and their representations. Hence, whatever applies to external object relations can also apply to the self relations. This adds an additional dimension to the ego's adaptive tasks—i.e., id, superego, external reality, and self. The creative resolution of the mourning for self or its components can be a self-creation. In the gifted composer this may be the Requiem.

My thesis is not that musical creativity depends upon object loss, but that, given such losses, the direction of musical creativity and creativity in general will be influenced by intrapsychic processes of mourning and memorialization. It may be of significance that Robertson's book, which was first published in England in 1968, bears the dedication "In loving memory of my brother, Mac Robertson, killed in action in France on 22 May 1915."

I

The Latin Requiem Mass had its origins in the prayers found in the catacombs, the underground cemeteries of the early Christians in Rome.

In all probability, man has always had rituals dealing with death, the dead, burials, and a concept of the afterlife (cf. Pollock, 1972, 1974b, 1975). In the catacombs, the Christians addressed their dead with such phrases as "Vivas in Deo" (Live in God), or "In Pace Christi" (In the Peace of Christ). Many prayers for the dead person begged forgiveness and salvation for the departed one's sins, but even more asked the dead person, who presumably was in afterlife, to intercede for his dear ones still on earth. Robertson (1968, p. 5) cites the following examples:

> Pray for your parents.
> Pray for your children.
> May he pray for us.
> Pray for us. Pray that we may be saved.
> Pray for the child you have left behind you.
> Live in Christ and pray for us.
>
> Anatolius, our first-born, ours for a
> little while, pray for us.

For these early Christians, death had no finality but led to immortality. Thus "Alexander is not dead, but lives above the stars, and his body rests in this tomb, a rest that will end with a resurrection" (Robertson, 1968, p. 6).

Requiem, rest, was to become the leading theme of the Mass for the Dead and subsequently became the Requiem Mass. However, rest, sleep, and peace, the main subjects of the music sung at burial or memorial rites, directly suggested immortality and eventual resurrection.

It was not until the close of the tenth century that one could speak of a specific Requiem Mass. Before that time, Masses for the Dead were not usually distinguished from other Masses. Whereas France and Spain had a dozen or more different formulas for the Mass, depending on the status of the dead they celebrated, Rome had a single one for all—king, pope, peasant, or pauper.

The earliest mention of a polyphonic Requiem Mass was in 1474, when the Burgundian composer Guillaume Dufay directed in his will that a work composed by him be performed at his own funeral. The score of this Requiem has been lost. Dufay wished his obsequies to be celebrated in Cambrai Cathedral (of which he was a canon, as well as Master of the Music), with bells, bright lights, and four candles burning before the statue of St. Anthony of Padua. On the same day, Masses were to be said for the repose of his soul. He further asked that those who took part in the service receive a due reward from his estate and that bread and money be provided to the poor. For the day after these rites, he prescribed that a

Requiem Mass be sung in the Chapel of St. Etienne by a dozen of the best singers chosen from among the vicars choral of high and low rank. After the Mass had ended, after the Requiescant in Pace a sequential prayer chosen by them was to be performed, followed by the De Profundis. The Requiem Mass to be performed was "Missam Meam de Requiem"—a mass of his own composition—*Missa de Requiem compilata per M. G. da Fay, copiée par Simon Mellet en 1470* (Robertson, 1968, pp. 26-27).

Dufay's request to have four candles burning before the statue of St. Anthony of Padua indicated his special veneration for this saint, an affection that is further borne out by the frequent mention in his will of a Mass and two motets dedicated to him. One might speculate that Dufay may have been thus beseeching his idealized saint to assure the immortality of his soul and ease his transition from life to death to afterlife.

The Requiem Mass of the Flemish composer, Johannes Ockeghem (c. 1420-1495), is the first known in the history of the church music of the early Renaissance. There is some evidence that Ockeghem studied with Dufay and probably was influenced by him.

Although the early Requiem Masses were sung, instruments were also used. An account of the Mass sung on the death of Philip of Castille in 1507 mentions that organs, trumpets, trombones, fiddles, and other string instruments were played. Brumel (c. 1460-1520), a student of Ockeghem, composed a Requiem that was printed in 1493, and de la Rue, also a follower of Ockeghem, wrote his Requiem in 1492.

Palestrina's Requiem is dated 1554. Thomas Luis de Victoria (c. 1548-1611) composed two Requiem Masses, one in 1585 and the other in 1603. The latter was in memory of Empress Maria, widow of Emperor Maximilian II, daughter of Emperor Charles V, and mother of two emperors. Empress Maria died on February 26, 1603, and was buried on March 1, and Victoria's Requiem was presented on April 23. In his dedication he called the Mass a "swan song" for the empress. However, Victoria did not publish any more works until he died on August 27, 1611. It may well have been his own "swan song"—a phenomenon that has been observed in other Requiem composers, for it has been suggested that the Requiem is a manifestation of the ante-mortem mourning of the composer for his own death. We will discuss this observation in greater detail in connection with Mozart's *Requiem*.

In 1621 Monteverdi was commissioned to compose a Requiem for the late Duke of Tuscany. Alessandro Scarlatti (1660-1720) also composed a Requiem Mass. John Blow (1649-1708) composed an *Ode on the Death of Henry Purcell* when Purcell suddenly died at the age of 36.

Michael Haydn (1737-1806), younger brother of Joseph Haydn (1732-1809), wrote a Requiem Mass for the funeral of Sigismund von Schrattenbach, the Archbishop of Salzburg, in December 1771. It may be that Haydn's Requiem was written not only for the Archbishop but also to commemorate the death of his young daughter, who died earlier in 1771 and whose loss undoubtedly greatly grieved him. Franz Joseph Haydn's (1732-1809) *Mass in Time of War* was written in 1796 as a lament for the dead when the Imperial Armies in Italy were being routed by the French forces.

Mozart, the genius who was so prolific in his musical productivity, died at 35 while writing his beautiful Requiem. Mozart was not unfamiliar with death. He and his sister (who was five years older) were the only survivors of their parents' seven children. Mozart, born on January 27, 1756, was to have his mother die when he was 22, on July 3, 1778. On April 4, 1787, Mozart, hearing that his father was quite ill, wrote him a letter in which he expressed his thoughts about death.

As death, when we come to consider it closely, is the time goal of an existence, I have formed during the last few years such close relations with this best and truest friend of mankind, that his image is not only no longer terrifying to me, but is indeed very soothing and consoling! And I thank my God for graciously granting me the opportunity . . . of learning that death is the key which unlocks the door to our true happiness. I never lie down at night without reflecting that — young as I am [he was 31] — I may not live to see another day. Yet no one of all my acquaintances could say that in company I am morose or disgruntled. For this blessing I daily thank my Creator and wish with all my heart that each of my fellow creatures could enjoy it" (Robertson, 1968, p. 64).

The question of the authenticity of Mozart's Requiem has been the source of much controversy and confusion. The authenticity problem concerns the question of which parts of the work were written by Mozart himself, which were carried out by him more or less extensively and then completed by someone else, and which were composed on the basis of Mozart's outlines and sketches (cf. Blume, 1963). Blume, in careful musical-historical detective work, concludes that the Requiem was indeed substantially composed by Mozart in 1791 and that it was completed after Mozart's death by Franz Süssmayer, with the aid of Mozartian sketches and instructions.

It was occasioned by the death of the wife of Count Franz von Walsegg, February 14, 1791. The widower conceived the idea of having a Requiem Mass performed on his country estate at Wiener Neustadt, and he passed the work off as his own. To preserve his secret, Walsegg used his estate manager, Leitgeb, as an intermediary, and Mozart never knew the commission came from Walsegg.

The history of the work is a dramatic one. In the last year of his life, Mozart allegedly wrote a letter in response to a request that he leave Vienna and seek employment in England. The letter, dated September, 1791, written in Italian without a named addressee and unsigned, states:

My dear Sir,

I wish I could follow your advice, but how could I do so? I feel stunned. I reason with difficulty and cannot get rid of the vision of this unknown man. I see him perpetually; he entreats me, presses me, and impatiently demands the work. I go on writing because composition tires me less than resting. Otherwise I have nothing here to fear. I know from what I suffer that the hour is come. I am at the point of death: I have come to an end before having had the enjoyment of my talent, life indeed was so beautiful, my career began under such fortunate auspices; but one cannot change one's own destiny. No one can measure his own days, one must resign oneself, it will be as providence wills, and so I finish my death-song. I must not leave it incomplete [Robertson, 1968, p. 65].

The unknown man, Count Walsegg's emissary, was a tall, thin, grave-looking man, dressed in gray from head to foot, who in July of 1791, had presented Mozart with an unsigned letter asking him to name his price for composing a Requiem. Mozart agreed and asked as the entire price of the work 50 ducats, without, however, fixing the time when the work would be delivered. The messenger came once more, paid the money and promised an additional sum, stipulated that the composer was to write precisely as he wished, and only when he felt like writing, but to make no effort to discover the person who gave the commission. The mystery surrounding the commission presumably seized Mozart's mind and it is said that he looked upon it as an omen. At the same time, he was busy with *The Magic Flute* and an opera for Leopold's coronation in Prague. The mysterious messenger again approached him in August, and Mozart assured him that the Requiem would be his first task. Again it is alleged that Mozart took this as a new warning not to postpone what he himself believed would be his last work. In October he worked uninterruptedly on the Requiem, frequently writing until two o'clock in the morning. Although physically exhausted, he continued to drive himself on what was in essence his dying song. Constance, his wife, noticed Mozart's growing infirmity and melancholy with increasing alarm. She tried to divert him, but in November he began to speak of death, saying with tears in his eyes: "I know very well I am writing the Requiem for myself. I am too conscious of myself." Constance, exceedingly alarmed, took the score of the Requiem from him, relieved now to have Mozart resting. Soon, however, he demanded the Requiem back and again became weak

428

and melancholy. Before long, he took to bed, never to leave it, though never losing consciousness. During the afternoon that preceded his last night of life, Mozart had the score of the Requiem brought to him, and several of his friends and relatives sang until they reached the Lacrimosa, when Mozart burst into tears and put the score aside. His sister-in-law Sophie came in the evening, and he said to her, "My dear, good Sophie, how glad I am you are here. You must stay to-night and see me die. I have the death taste on my tongue. I have the odor of death in my nostrils." Constance asked her sister to go for a clergyman. When she returned, she found Süssmayer at his bedside. Mozart was explaining to him how to finish the Requiem, remarking as he did so: "Did I not say that I was writing it for myself?" In the evening, the crisis came and Mozart died at one o'clock in the morning on December 5, 1791. Thirty-five years after his death, his sister-in-law Sophie wrote: "The last thing he did was to endeavor to imitate the kettle drums in the Requiem." Three medical opinions assigned three different causes for Mozart's premature death — inflammation of the brain, fever, and dropsy. Since there was little money, Mozart was buried in a common unmarked grave. Of his six children — four boys and two girls — only two boys survived infancy (Holmes, n.d.; Nohl, 1880; Turner, 1955).

Thus, we see how Mozart's Requiem did actually become his own Requiem, even though it was not sung at his pauper's funeral. Could one say that Mozart was mourning for himself? We will never know, but we do know that Mozart died while working on his Requiem, and we can conjecture that he knew he was about to die.

I have indicated that not infrequently after a composer wrote a Requiem composition, either he himself shortly died or he "died creatively," i.e., he no longer created music. I have suggested that this phenomenon might be explained as the composer's mourning for himself. The mourning process is related to change and transition. As such, it is a universal process. Grief, the specific reaction to the death of a significant other, is a subclass of the broader mourning process, the phases of which process I described in 1961. The loss of a particular state of oneself and the awareness of the disintegration of one's body and ego is well known to analysts from their clinical observations. I am suggesting that in Mozart's situation, as well as in that of the other composers whose mourning music was their last work, this music represented the creator's own mourning for himself and the already attempted beginning resolution of his mourning work, the emergence of a creative product that would remain, that had its own vitality. I have observed in writers, poets, painters, scientists, sculptors, and political leaders, as well as in com-

429

posers of music, the use of creative works for purposes of mourning the internal loss of self- or object representations, and at the same time as the focus of redirected creative "energies." In every mourning process there is a loss to the self organization. The precipitant of the process may be an external loss, or a perception of the loss of one's body or mind. However, the mourning process, which includes attempts at resolution that may or may not succeed, may go on almost from the initiation of the process. We observe the creative product when it attains greatness, as did Mozart's Requiem.

The next two major composers to write Requiem Masses were Cherubini and Berlioz. Cherubini's Requiem Mass in C Minor was commissioned in 1815 for the commemoration, in the following year, of the execution of Louis XVI. Early in 1836, Cherubini, in his 76th year, began work on a second Requiem Mass, this time in D Minor. He intended the work to be performed at his own funeral—which it was. Here again we may suggest that the musical composition reflects the mourning for the self before death has occurred, as well as the memorialization of the composer through his work.

Six months after Cherubini completed his D Minor Requiem Mass, Berlioz was commissioned by the French government to prepare a Requiem to be performed on the day of the annual service celebrated for the victims of the 1830 Revolution. One might call Berlioz's Requiem an anniversary mass.

Verdi's Requiem, intended to be performed in the concert hall and not in the church, had deep personal meaning for the composer. Alessandro Manzoni, political figure and Italian poet, was greatly admired by Verdi. Manzoni died in Milan on May 22, 1873. His death so deeply affected Verdi that he could not attend the funeral. Verdi had read Manzoni's novel *I Promessi Sposi* when he was sixteen and summed up the deep impression it made on him when he wrote, "It's that this is a true book; as true as the truth" (Robertson, 1968, p. 100). Manzoni's book became a primer and dictionary of the emerging Italian language. Verdi saw Manzoni as a saintly ideal. He wrote, "What can I say? How to describe the extraordinary, indefinable sensation the presence of the saint . . . produced in me. I would have gone down on my knees before him if we allowed to worship men. They say it is wrong to do so and it may be: although we raise up on altars many that have neither the talent nor the virtue of Manzoni" (Robertson, 1968, p. 100). All that Verdi felt, all his reverence for the "saintly man" is expressed in the Requiem—a composition that allowed Verdi not only to express his grief over the death of this idealized figure but also to honor his memory and thus immortalize the man as well as the composer. Verdi offered the Requiem for performance on May 22, 1874, the first anniversary of Manzoni's death. The work, which has also come to be known as the Manzoni Requiem, was a great artistic and financial success.

One movement of the Requiem had been written five years earlier as part of a plan to commemorate the composer Rossini on the first anniversary of his death. Verdi had announced a plan for each of thirteen Italian composers to contribute a movement for a composite mass to be performed only on succeeding anniversaries of Rossini's death. Neither composers nor performers were to receive any remuneration for their work. However, the concerts never took place, although the movements that the composers prepared are still in a library in Milan.

Musical memorial tributes were a common nineteenth-century tradition. Anton Bruckner (1824-1896) designated his Seventh Symphony "In Memoriam" for Richard Wagner. In 1876-1877, Antonin Dvořák (1841-1904) composed his deeply moving *Stabat Mater* in memory of his eldest daughter, who had just died. Modest Moussorgsky (1835-1881) memorialized his close friend, the painter Victor Hartmann, in one of his best-known works, *Pictures at an Exhibition*. After attending a memorial exhibition of Hartmann's paintings after his death in 1873 at the age of 39, Moussorgsky set ten of the artist's pictures to music as a memorial tribute to his dead friend. These piano compositions are highly descriptive and are considered masterpieces of musical characterization.

Dvořák's Requiem Mass, first performed in 1891, is not a mass in the customary fashion, but a full-length oratorio, and was almost contemporaneous with the Requiem Mass of Gabriel Fauré. Fauré composed his Requiem in memory of his father, who died in 1885, but by the time it was finished, his mother had also died, and so it commemorates both of his parents. Maurice Duruflé, a French organist and composer, born in 1902, composed his Requiem in 1947 and dedicated it to the memory of his father.

The personal Latin Requiem Mass had its origin in original prayers for and to the dead but became a vehicle for the expression of a composer's feelings following the loss of a parent, a child, or an idealized figure; as such, it can be considered an expressive, sublimated aspect of the mourning process. However, in addition, it has also been a means of publicly memorializing the dead as well as immortalizing the creator, whose musical work "lives" on after he is no longer present.

II

I turn now to other forms of music which, like the Latin Requiem Mass, are related to the mourning and memorialization process.

The *Stabat Mater*, a poem that vividly and poignantly pictures the Mother of Christ sorrowing at the foot of the cross as her son is dying, was frequently used as a musical text: Josquin des Prés, Palestrina, Pergolesi (who died at 26, like Mozart in such poverty that he was cast into the common burial pit of the poor), Alessandro Scarlatti, Caldara, Rossini, Dvořák (whose *Stabat Mater* was born of grief at the death of one of his children), Verdi, Gounod, Berkeley, Szymanowski, and Poulenc all composed music devoted to this theme. In 1936, moved by the tragic death of a friend in a car accident, Francois Poulenc made a pilgrimage to the shrine of Our Lady of Rocamadour, a pilgrimage that inspired his first religious work, *Litanies à la Vierge Noir,* and led to further religious pieces, culminating in 1949 with the *Stabat Mater.* In the dedication of this work, Poulenc commends the soul of his friend, Christian Berard, to Our Lady of Rocamadour. Poulenc had considered composing a Requiem Mass when his friend was killed, but felt unequal to dealing with the Day of Judgment. The *Stabat Mater*, the lamentations of the Holy Week Office of Tenebrae (which symbolizes the darkness that covered the earth from the sixth to the ninth hour after Christ died and were composed by Palestrina, Victoria, Lassus, Tallis, and Byrd), and Liszt's *Via Crucis* (Stations of the Cross), which also depicts the last hours of Christ's life, all deal with the grief and acute mourning for the dying and dead Christ.

Prayers asking that the dead may rest in peace are absent from both the official Lutheran and Anglican Services. The Lutheran reformers taught that souls freed from sin by faith in Christ alone and without any deeds, were saved and went directly to heaven. Luther and his followers rejected Purgatory, masses for the dead, and many other Roman Catholic practices. The concept of "rest" was retained, but was referred to as "rest in the Lord." At a funeral service in the church, a concluding Traüerlied (funeral cantata) was performed. Heinrich Schütz wrote such a piece, which was published in 1636, for the concluding funeral service for his good friend and patron, Prince Heinrich. These funeral cantatas were called German Requiems.

Henry Purcell wrote music for the funeral of Queen Mary (wife of William of Orange), who died of smallpox on December 28, 1694. Eight months after the funeral of Queen Mary, Purcell, himself, died at the age of 36.

Johann Sebastian Bach's mother and father both died within nine months of each other when he was nine to ten years old. He also had to bear the sorrow of the loss of seven of his thirteen children, and of his first wife when he was 35 years of age. Bach deals directly with death in many of his cantatas. In fact, Schweitzer, cited by Robertson (1968, p. 201), indicates that the totality of Bach's thought was transfigured by a serene longing for death. Whenever the text afforded the least pretext for it, Bach voiced this longing in his music, and nowhere is his musical speech so moving as in the cantatas in which he focuses on the release of the body from death, an experience with which he had early and frequent contact.

Brahms presumably called his greatest choral work *A German Requiem* to disassociate it from the Latin Requiem Mass and to make it clear that the text came from the Lutheran Bible, although Christ's name is never mentioned in the text. Brahms' Requiem, completed in 1866, was inspired by the deaths of Robert Schumann in 1856, and of his own mother in 1865. The work ends with a solo, "Now hath man sorrow but yet I shall again behold you and fill your heart with rejoicing," to which the chorus responds with "Oh Yea, I will give you comfort as one whom his mother comforts"—a reference that may refer to Brahms' grief over his mother's death and his hope to once again be with her. The catalogue of Brahms' works shows ample evidence of his intense preoccupation with death. In 1858, when he was 25 years old, he composed a Funeral Hymn. The majority of the Eleven Chorale Preludes, completed in the year before his own life ended, are also concerned with death. The final one is a most moving setting of words to melody. It states, "O Welt ich muss dich Lassen" ("Oh World, I must now leave you"). The Brahms Requiem is not an oratorio but a choral symphony. In it, Brahms quotes Christ when he says, "Blessed are they that mourn: for they shall be comforted" (Matthew 5:4). Brahms knew well the value of mourning through music.

III

A custom arose in the fifteenth century of writing laments for recently dead musicians in which they were named and in which the Requiem Mass was briefly quoted. These laments and memorial music were not limited to dead composers, although this may have been orginally true. I shall now cite several examples of this nonreligious music, which had its origins 500 years ago but which still continues to the present: Ockeghem's lament on the death of Gilles Binchois; Josquin des Prés's *La Déploration de Jehan Ockeghem;* Jacob Arcadelt's (c. 1510-1597) lament for Alessandro dei Medici, who was brutally murdered by his cousin Lorenzino in 1537; Morley's and Weelkes's elegies on the death of Henry Noel, an amateur musician and a favorite at the Court of Queen Elizabeth I; William Byrd's two funeral songs for Sir Philip Sydney, Knight; Jeremiah Clarke's music on Henry Purcell's death; Igor Stravinsky's *In Memoriam Dylan Thomas: Dirge-Canons and Song*, composed in 1959, after Dylan Thomas' death; Stravinsky's expression of grief, through his Funeral Song, at the loss of Rimsky-Korsakoff, his pupil and close friend, in 1908; Benjamin Britten's *Canticle in Memory of Noel Mewton-Wood*, a young Australian pianist, who killed himself at age 31 in December, 1953; Hugo Wolf's dedication of a group of his songs to the memory of his father, when Wolf was 23; Leonard Bernstein's *Mass* for John F. Kennedy.

Richard Strauss's *Vier Letze Lieder* (Four Last Songs) were composed a year before Strauss's death in 1949 and could be considered as self-laments of his own approaching death.

The great laments of David for Saul and Jonathan, and for his son Absalom have inspired musicians such as Josquin, Weelkes, Schutz, and Tomkins (1572-1656). Especially to be noted is Handel's oratorio *Saul,* in which passionate grief is transformed into sound, particularly when the bodies of the king and his son are borne to their graves in one of the greatest of funeral marches.

Modern elegiac works, though still composed, seemingly are not as common as was true in earlier times. Mention has already been made of Bernstein's *Mass* for John F. Kennedy. Another such work is Hindemith's *When Lilacs Last in the Door-Yard Bloom'd,* subtitled "A Requiem for Those We Love." This work, commemorating the recently deceased President Franklin D. Roosevelt, and those who had fallen in World War II, takes its title and text from a poem of Walt Whitman which was published in 1865 after Lincoln's assassination on Good Friday, 1865. Whitman memorialized Lincoln in his poetry, and Hindemith memorialized Franklin Roosevelt with his music.

The end of World War I also inspired requiems and memorial musical compositions. J. C. Fould composed *A World Requiem* in 1923 to commemorate those who died in this war. Elgar's *For the Fallen* was also dedicated to the memory of men who were lost in the war. Arthur Bliss's *Morning Heroes,* a symphony for orator, chorus, and orchestra, was composed in 1930 and dedicated "To the memory of Francis Kennard Bliss, my brother, and all other comrades killed in battle."

Frederick Delius' *Requiem,* composed between 1914-1916, is dedicated to "the memory of all young artists fallen in the war." In 1940, Benjamin Britten composed his *Sinfonia da Requiem,* the score of which bears the inscription, "In memory of my parents." After World War II, Britten was commissioned to prepare his War Requiem to celebrate the consecration of the new St. Michael's Cathedral in Coventry. Britten dedicated the War Requiem "in loving memory" to four of his friends who lost their lives in World War II.

On November 26, 1973, Joseph La Croix (DeDe) Pierce, one of the outstanding jazz trumpeters and singers of Creole songs, died and had a "Jazz Funeral." DeDe Pierce was buried in front of three brass bands, composed of musicians who had been his friends. The three bands escorted the coffin and the mourning family to the church, where a fourth band waited inside to play a jazz mass, and then finally to the cemetery, playing dirges. Playing jazz at a funeral was a New Orleans innovation that began during the nineteenth century.

Music, the expressive form closest to the human voice, has probably been used to express grief and mourning from the time of man's beginnings. Initially an expression of affect, it became linked to prayer and a concept of the afterlife. For the listener such music may not have the same significance as for the creator, who may express his mourning through a creative and sublimated process, that memorializes himself as well as the departed, for as long as his music exists he thereby achieves immortality.

The mourning process is a universal adaptational process to loss, change, and transition. It is an intrapsychic process having distinct stages and phases. Bereavement, one class of this process, has as its precipitant the loss of a meaningful external object. Mourning can also be initiated by other losses as well, such as changes and transitions reflecting bodily and psychic alterations. Mourning for the loss of self-organization may follow the same path as that seen and experienced following the external loss of the meaningful other. However, the mourning process is intrapsychic and includes the resolutional concluding phase, which may yield a creative product. In this essay I have suggested that the creation of a musical composition is the mourning for the loss and transition of the composer's self as well as the creative end-product of the mourning process, and has a new vitality of its own. This mourning creation may take the form of a new object tie, a new self-organization, a poem, a novel, an artistic production—such as a painting, a scientific advance, a political fulfillment, or some other form which will be determined by the premourning personality organization. In future presentations I hope to elaborate the internal changes accompanying the mourning process, their relationship to creativity and the aging process.

REFERENCES

Blume, F. (1963), Requiem but no peace. In: *The Creative World of Mozart,* ed. P. H. Lang. New York: W. W. Norton, pp. 103-126.
Freud, S. (1917), Mourning and melancholia. *Standard Edition,* 14:237-258. London: Hogarth Press, 1957.
Holmes, E. (n.d.), *The Life of Mozart.* London: J. M. Dent.
Nohl, L. (1880), *Life of Mozart.* Chicago: Jansen, McClurg.
Pollock, G. H. (1961), Mourning and adaptation. *Internat. J. Psycho-Anal.,* 42:341-361.
_____ (1970), Anniversary reactions, trauma and mourning. *Psychiat. Quart.,* 39:347-371.
_____ (1972), On mourning and anniversaries: The relationship of culturally constituted defensive systems to intrapsychic adaptive processes. *Israel Annals of Psychiat.,* 10:9-40.
_____ (1974a), Mourning through Music: Gustav Mahler. Presented to the Regional Conference of the Chicago Psychoanalytic Society, March 30, 1974, unpublished.
_____ (1974b), On anniversary suicide and mourning. In: *Depression and the Human Existence,* ed. T. Benedek & E. J. Anthony. Boston: Little, Brown (in press).
_____ (1975), On mourning, immortality and utopia. *J. Amer. Psychoanal. Assn.,* 23:334-362.
Robertson, A. (1968), *Requiem: Music of Mourning and Consolation.* New York: F. A. Praeger.
Turner, W. J. (1955), *Mozart: The Man and His Works.* Garden City, N. Y.: Doubleday.

April, 1974

Index

Compiled by Glenn Miller.

440

441